Southern Illinois University, Carbondale

FITZGERALD'S *The Great Gatsby:*
The Novel, The Critics, The Background

SCRIBNER
RESEARCH
ANTHOLOGIES

CHARLES SCRIBNER'S SONS   New York

PRINTING   20 21 YEAR   2 3 4 5

Printed in the United States of America
ISBN 0-02-395710-7
Library of Congress Catalog Card Number 77-108357

FITZGERALD'S *THE GREAT GATSBY*:
The Novel, The Critics, The Background

 **SCRIBNER**
RESEARCH
ANTHOLOGIES

Martin Steinmann, Jr., GENERAL EDITOR

3 copy!

Chapter III

About half way between West Egg and New York the motor-road joins the railroad and runs beside it for a quarter of a mile so as to skirt a desolate area of land — a valley of ashes — a fantastic farm where ashes grow like wheat into ridges and hills and grotesque gardens, where ashes take the forms of houses and chimneys and rising smoke and finally, with a transcendent effort, of ash-gray men who move dimly and already crumbling through the powdery air. Occasionally a line of grey cars crawls along an invisible track, gives out a ghastly creak and comes to rest, and immediately grey men swarm up with leaden spades and stir up an impenetrable cloud which screens their obscure purposes from profane regard.

But above the grey land and above the spasms of bleak dust which drift endlessly over it, you perceive, after a moment, the eyes of Dr. T. J. Eckleburg. The eyes of Dr. T. J. Eckleburg are blue and gigantic — their retinas are one yard high. They look out of no face but, instead from a pair of enormous yellow spectacles which pass over a non-existent nose. Evidently some wild wag of an oculist set them there to fatten his practice in the borough of Flushing and then sank down himself into eternal blindness, perhaps, or forgot them and moved away. But his eyes, brood on, dimmed a little by many paintless days under sun and rain, but watchful and aware in a spot of death

To the Memory of
MAXWELL E. PERKINS (1884-1947)

I am grateful to the many authors who have given me permission to reprint their work in this volume; to my colleague, John M. Howell; to Alan M. Cohn, chief of the Humanities Division, Morris Library, Southern Illinois University, Carbondale, and his staff; to the Office of Research and Projects, Graduate School, Southern Illinois University; to my colleagues at Charles Scribner's Sons, and the general editor of this series, Martin Steinmann, Jr.; and especially to my graduate research assistant, Cheryl LaFlam Breidenbach.

Preface

Each Scribner Research Anthology is a collection of written sources upon a single historical, political, literary, or scientific topic or problem—the Hungarian Revolt, Shakespeare's *Julius Cæsar,* or extrasensory perception, for example. In addition to these sources, it contains (1) "Guide to Research," an account of the rationale and the methods of research and of research-paper writing, (2) an introduction to the topic of the anthology, (3) suggested topics for controlled research, and (4) suggested sources and topics for library research.

Each anthology is designed to serve two purposes. First, each gives the student access to important sources—texts, documents, letters, diaries, essays, articles, reports, transcripts of hearings, for instance—on a given topic. Some of these sources are otherwise available in only a few libraries, some (manuscripts and historical and government documents) in only one. In any case, the collection as a whole is not otherwise available in one volume. Second, each anthology gives the student either all his sources for a controlled-research paper or some of them for a library-research paper. Each anthology can be valuable either for readings in courses in history, literature, science, or humanities or as the basis for a research paper in these or in other courses.

A controlled-research paper—a paper in which the student's search for sources is limited to, and in certain ways controlled by, those sources contained in one anthology—is not so noble an undertaking as a library-research paper. But it is often more successful—more rewarding for the student and easier for his instructor to teach effectively and judge fairly. Its advantages for both student and instructor are often considerable.

For the student, it sometimes provides sources unavailable in his school library. And it enables him to learn a good deal about research (selection, interpretation, and evaluation of sources; quotation and paraphrase; and documentation) without prior instruction in use of the library (and, incidentally, without overtaxing the facilities and the resources of his library and without loss of, or damage to, sources either irreplaceable or difficult and expensive to replace).

For the instructor, it permits focus of class discussion upon a limited set of topics. It enables him to track down the student's sources conveniently. And—perhaps the greatest advantage of all—it enables him to judge both conveniently and exactly how well the student has selected, interpreted, and evaluated his sources and how well he has quoted and paraphrased them.

In many schools, a controlled-research paper is either a preliminary to or a part of a library-research paper. A library-research paper is probably the most difficult paper that the student can be assigned to write. The problems that confront him are not simply those common to any paper—organization, paragraphing, and transitions, for instance—and those (already mentioned) common to all research papers. He has, in addition, the problem of using the library well—of, for example, using the card catalogue, periodical indexes, and other reference works. But, if the instructor assigns a controlled-research paper as a preliminary to or, as it were, an early part of a library-research paper, the student need not come to grips with all these problems at once.

Each Scribner Research Anthology is compiled according to the following editorial principles. Each source that is not anonymous is prefaced by a biographical note on its author. At the foot of the same page is a bibliographical note. Each source is reprinted exactly as it appears in the original except for (1) some typographical peculiarities, (2) explanatory notes, given in brackets, and (3) omissions, indicated by ellipses (". . ."). And, finally, for each source that has pagination in the original, page numbers are given in brackets within the source itself—thus: "[**320/321**]," where everything before the slash (and after the preceding slash, if any) is from page 320, and everything after the slash (and before the next slash, if any) is from page 321. For a source hitherto unpublished, no page numbers are given; and the student who uses it should cite the page numbers of the Scribner Research Anthology. Footnotes to a source are given as in the original. Where the original pagination of a footnote is not evident, its page number precedes it in brackets.

MARTIN STEINMANN, JR.

Bingham Bay
Lake Gogebic
August, 1960

Contents

Introduction

Shortly before his death, in 1940, F. Scott Fitzgerald had the humiliating experience of walking into a large city bookstore and finding that none of his books were carried in stock and his name had been forgotten. But since then things have changed. The emergence of *The Great Gatsby* from a position of comparative obscurity a generation ago to its present position as a modern classic is one of the most remarkable events in recent American literary history. According to a recent New York *Times* report on paperback sales, more people are buying *The Great Gatsby* today than any novel by any writer of Fitzgerald's generation, including Faulkner and Hemingway.

The essays and other background material in this volume have been selected to foster an understanding of why *The Great Gatsby* has gradually become, over the past forty-five years, the twentieth-century American novel that speaks more directly to the condition of man today than, perhaps, any other.

Fitzgerald's own personal experience was so important a source for his imaginative fiction that the readings in Part Two ("Intention and Genesis: The Author's View") are focussed around his life, insofar as it was concerned with the writing of *The Great Gatsby*. Included is the short story "Absolution," which served at one stage as the first chapter of a discarded early version of the novel. Fitzgerald's efforts to give objective form to a moral dilemma that had haunted him from childhood are illustrated by his correspondence with his editor, and by the introduction to *The Great Gatsby* he later wrote for the Modern Library edition. This biographical section ends with Kenneth Eble's brilliant account of the way Fitzgerald worked at revising the novel, based on the evidence of the manuscript now preserved in the library at Princeton University.

In Part Three ("Achievement: The Critics' Views") the literary reputation of *The Great Gatsby* across the years is illustrated by representative reviews and essays arranged in chronological order. They begin with some typically obtuse and superficial book reviews of *The Great Gatsby* from the year 1925 (with the exception of Gilbert Seldes' notice in the *Criterion*) and, skipping across the empty decade of the 1930's when *Gatsby* was overlooked by most of the critics and scholars, conclude with examples from the flood of essays and appreciations that the novel continues to inspire—with no let-up yet in sight. Included are not only the best of these essays but also a wide variety of points of view and examples of different critical approaches: general appreciations of the novel as well as more specialized studies of specific problems of form and content.

Few writers of his generation possessed a more passionate sense of time and place than Fitzgerald. Therefore, in Part Four ("The Jazz Age and *The Great Gatsby*") readings have been selected which emphasize the historical and social setting of the 1920's. *The Great Gatsby* is not an historical novel. Fitzgerald was writing about the contemporary world of the early Twenties through which he had just lived. But because of the moral understanding he brought to his interpretation of that world, because of the concreteness of his description, we are brought closer to that world in the pages of his novel than in the more factual accounts of many orthodox historians. Fitzgerald's rendering of that world of almost fifty years ago is still relevant—to our understanding of the past, and to our understanding of the world today.

These historical readings are divided into two parts. The first, "Crime and Corruption," is designed to illustrate the widespread moral corruption of the Twenties that Fitzgerald drew on for the background of his novel. This contemporary source material, together with the accompanying critical commentaries, documents not only the accuracy of Fitzgerald's description of the national scene but also his prophetic sense of the violent and disastrous end toward which it was heading—and finally reached in October, 1929, with the economic collapse that brought the so-called Boom years to their tragic close. The second part of the historical readings, "The American Dream," illustrates Fitzgerald's use of mythical and other thematic materials from the American past to give wider and deeper historical significance to his novel. Inevitably, these readings pose fundamental questions about the continuing vitality of such themes in American society today. Is the "American dream" adequately represented by the story of Gatsby's pursuit of the green light? Does it still reflect that shabby meretriciousness that so troubled Nick Carraway? Whatever our views, the fact remains that *The Great Gatsby* has become, over the years, one of the touchstones by which we now measure the quality of life in present-day America.

HENRY DAN PIPER

Southern Illinois University
Carbondale

PART ONE

THE NOVEL

Then wear the gold hat, if that will move her;
  If you can bounce high, bounce for her too,
Till she cry "Lover, gold-hatted, high-bouncing lover,
  I must have you!"

—THOMAS PARKE D'INVILLIERS

ONCE AGAIN

TO

ZELDA

The Great Gatsby *

F . S C O T T   F I T Z G E R A L D (1896–1940) began writing *The Great Gatsby*, his third novel, in St. Paul, Minnesota, in 1922. He worked at it off and on after he moved to Great Neck, Long Island, in 1923, but his progress was delayed by other writing commitments. In April, 1924, he scrapped most of what he had written thus far, replanned it and finished the final version during the summer of 1924 in the South of France. It was published on April 10, 1925.

CHAPTER I

In my younger and more vulnerable years my father gave me some advice that I've been turning over in my mind ever since.

"Whenever you feel like criticizing any one," he told me, "just remember that all the people in this world haven't had the advantages that you've had."

He didn't say any more, but we've always been unusually communicative in a reserved way, and I understood that he meant a great deal more than that. In consequence, I'm inclined to reserve all judgments, a habit that has opened up many curious natures to me and also made me the victim of not a few veteran bores. The abnormal mind is quick to detect and attach itself to this quality when it appears in a normal person, and so it came about that in college I was unjustly accused of being a politician, because I was privy to the secret griefs of wild, unknown men. Most of the confidences were unsought—frequently I have feigned sleep, preoccupation, or a hostile levity when I realized by some unmistakable sign that an intimate revelation was quivering on the horizon; for the intimate revelations of young men, or at least the terms in which they express them, are usually pla-giaristic and marred by obvious suppressions. Reserving judgments is a matter of infinite hope. I am still a little afraid of missing something if I forget that, as my father snobbishly suggested, and I snobbishly repeat, a sense of the fundamental decencies is parcelled out unequally at birth. [1/2]

And, after boasting this way of my tolerance, I come to the admission that it has a limit. Conduct may be founded on the hard rock or the wet marshes, but after a certain point I don't care what it's founded on. When I came back from the East last autumn I felt that I wanted the world to be in uniform and at a sort of moral attention forever; I wanted no more riotous excursions with privileged glimpses into the human heart. Only Gatsby, the man who gives his name to this book, was exempt from my reaction —Gatsby, who represented everything for which I have an unaffected scorn. If personality is an unbroken series of successful gestures, then there was something gorgeous about him, some heightened sensitivity to the promises of life, as if he were related to one of those intricate machines that register earthquakes ten thousand miles away. This responsiveness had nothing to do with that flabby impressionability which is dignified under the name of the "creative temperament"—it was an extraordinary gift for hope, a romantic readiness such as I have never found in any other person and which it is not likely I shall ever find again. No—Gatsby turned out all right at the end; it is what preyed on Gatsby, what foul dust floated in the wake of his dreams that temporarily closed out my interest in the abortive sorrows and short-winded elations of men.

My family have been prominent, well-to-do people in this Middle Western city for three generations. The Carraways are something of a clan, and we have a tradition that we're descended from the Dukes of Buccleuch, but the actual founder of my line was my grandfather's brother, who came here in fifty-one, sent a substitute to [2/3] the Civil War, and started the wholesale hardware business that my father carries on to-day.

I never saw this great-uncle, but I'm supposed to look like him—with special reference to the rather hardboiled painting that hangs in father's office. I graduated from New Haven in 1915, just a quarter of a century after my father, and a little later I participated in that delayed Teutonic migration known as the Great War. I enjoyed the counter-raid so thoroughly that I came back restless. Instead of being the warm center of the world, the Middle West now seemed like the ragged edge of the universe—so I decided to go East and learn the bond business. Everybody I knew was in the bond business, so I supposed it could support one more single man. All my aunts and uncles talked it over as if they were choosing a prep school for me, and finally said "Why—ye-es," with very grave, hesitant faces. Father agreed to finance me for a year, and after various delays I came East, permanently, I thought, in the spring of twenty-two.

The practical thing was to find rooms in the city, but it was a warm season, and I had just left a country of wide lawns and friendly trees, so when a young man at the office suggested that we take a house together in a commuting town, it sounded like a great idea. He found the house, a weatherbeaten cardboard bungalow at eighty a month, but at the last minute the firm ordered him to Washington, and I went out to the country alone. I had a dog—at least I had him for a few days until he ran away—and an old Dodge and a Finnish woman, who made my bed and cooked breakfast and muttered Finnish wisdom to herself over the electric stove.

It was lonely for a day or so until one morning some [3/4] man, more recently arrived than I, stopped me on the road.

"How do you get to West Egg village?" he asked helplessly.

I told him. And as I walked on I was lonely no longer. I was a guide, a pathfinder, an original settler. He had casually conferred on me the freedom of the neighborhood.

And so with the sunshine and the great bursts of leaves growing on the trees, just as things grow in fast movies, I had that familiar conviction that life was beginning over again with the summer.

There was so much to read, for one thing, and so much fine health to be pulled down out of the young breath-giving air. I bought a dozen volumes on banking and credit and investment securities, and they stood on my shelf in red and gold like new money from the mint, promising to unfold the shining secrets that only Midas and Morgan and Mæcenas knew. And I had the high intention of reading many other books besides. I was rather literary in college—one year I wrote a series of very solemn and obvious editorials for the *Yale News*—and now I was going to bring back all such things into my life and become again that most limited of all specialists, the "well-rounded man." This isn't just an epigram—life is much more successfully looked at from a single window, after all.

It was a matter of chance that I should have rented a house in one of the strangest communities in North America. It was on that slender riotous island which extends itself due east of New York—and where there are, among other natural curiosities, two unusual formations of land. Twenty miles from the city a pair of enor- [4/5] mous eggs, identical in contour and separated only by a courtesy bay, jut out into the most domesticated body of salt water in the Western hemisphere, the great wet barnyard of Long Island Sound. They are not perfect ovals—like the egg in the Columbus story, they are both crushed flat at the contact end—but their physical resemblance must be a source of perpetual confusion to the gulls that fly overhead. To the wingless a more arresting phenomenon is their dissimilarity in every particular except shape and size.

I lived at West Egg, the—well, the less fashionable of the two, though this is a most superficial tag to express the bizarre and not a little sinister contrast between them. My house was at the very tip of the egg, only fifty yards from the Sound, and squeezed between two huge places that rented for twelve or fifteen thousand a season. The one on my right was a colossal affair by any standard—it was a factual imitation of some Hôtel de Ville in Normandy, with a tower on one side, spanking new under a thin beard of raw ivy, and a marble swimming pool, and more than forty acres of lawn and garden. It was Gatsby's mansion. Or, rather, as I didn't know Mr. Gatsby, it was a mansion, inhabited by a gentleman of that name. My own house was an eyesore, but it was a small eyesore, and it had been overlooked, so I had a view of the water, a partial view of my neighbor's lawn, and the consoling proximity of millionaires—all for eighty dollars a month.

Across the courtesy bay the white palaces of fashionable East Egg glittered along the water, and the history of the summer really begins on the evening I drove over there to have dinner with the Tom Buchanans. Daisy was my second cousin once removed, and I'd [5/6] known Tom in college. And just after the war I spent two days with them in Chicago.

Her husband, among various physical accomplishments, had been one of the most powerful ends that ever played football at New Haven—a national figure in a way, one of those men who reach such an acute limited excellence at twenty-one that everything afterward savors of anticlimax. His family were enormously wealthy—even in college his freedom with money was a matter for reproach—but now he'd left Chicago and come East in a fashion that rather took your breath away; for instance, he'd brought down a string of polo ponies from Lake Forest. It was hard to realize that a man in my own generation was wealthy enough to do that.

Why they came East I don't know. They had spent a year in France for no particular reason, and then drifted here and there unrestfully wherever people played polo and were rich together. This was a permanent move, said Daisy over the telephone, but I didn't believe it—I had no sight into Daisy's heart, but I felt that Tom would drift on forever seeking, a little wistfully, for the dramatic turbulence of some irrecoverable football game.

And so it happened that on a warm windy evening I drove over to East Egg to see two old friends whom I scarcely knew at all. Their house was even more elaborate than I expected, a cheerful red-and-white Georgian Colonial mansion, overlooking the bay. The lawn started at the beach and ran toward the front door for a quarter of a mile, jumping over sun-dials and brick walks and burning gardens—finally when it reached the house drifting up the side in bright vines as though from [6/7] the momentum of its run. The front was broken by a line of French windows, glowing now with reflected gold and wide open to the warm windy afternoon, and Tom Buchanan in riding clothes was standing with his legs apart on the front porch.

He had changed since his New Haven years. Now he was a sturdy straw-haired man of thirty with a rather hard mouth and a supercilious manner. Two shining arrogant eyes had established dominance over his face and gave him the appearance of always leaning aggressively forward. Not even the effeminate swank of his riding clothes could hide the enormous power of that body—he seemed to fill those glistening boots until he strained the top lacing, and you could see a great pack of muscle shifting when his shoulder moved under his thin coat. It was a body capable of enormous leverage—a cruel body.

His speaking voice, a gruff husky tenor, added to the impression of fractiousness he conveyed. There was a touch of paternal contempt in it, even toward people he liked—and there were men at New Haven who had hated his guts.

"Now, don't think my opinion on these matters is final," he seemed to say, "just because I'm stronger and more of a man than you are." We were in the same senior society, and while we were never intimate I always had the impression that he approved of me and wanted me to like him with some harsh, defiant wistfulness of his own.

We talked for a few minutes on the sunny porch.

"I've got a nice place here," he said, his eyes flashing about restlessly.

Turning me around by one arm, he moved a broad [7/8] flat hand along the front vista, including in its sweep a sunken Italian garden, a half acre of deep, pungent roses, and a snub-nosed motor-boat that bumped the tide offshore.

"It belonged to Demaine, the oil man." He turned me around again, politely and abruptly. "We'll go inside."

We walked through a high hallway into a bright rosy-colored space, fragilely bound into the house by French windows at either end. The windows were ajar and gleaming white against the fresh grass outside that seemed to grow a little way into the house. A breeze blew through the room, blew curtains in at one end and out the other like pale flags, twisting them up toward the frosted wedding-cake of the ceiling, and then rippled over the wine-colored rug, making a shadow on it as wind does on the sea.

The only completely stationary object in the room was an enormous couch on which two young women were buoyed up as though upon an anchored balloon. They were both in white, and their dresses were rippling and fluttering as if they had just been blown back in after a short flight around the house. I must have stood for a few moments listening to the whip and snap of the curtains and the groan of a picture on the wall. Then there was a boom as Tom Buchanan shut the rear windows and the caught wind died out about the room, and the curtains and the rugs and the two young women ballooned slowly to the floor.

The younger of the two was a stranger to me. She was extended full length at her end of the divan, completely motionless, and with her chin raised a little, as if she were balancing something on it which was quite likely to fall. If she saw me out of the corner of her eyes she [8/9] gave no hint of it—indeed, I was almost surprised into murmuring an apology for having disturbed her by coming in.

The other girl, Daisy, made an attempt to rise—she leaned slightly forward with a conscientious expression—then she laughed, an absurd, charming little laugh, and I laughed too and came forward into the room.

"I'm p-paralyzed with happiness."

She laughed again, as if she said something very witty, and held my hand for a moment, looking up into my face, promising that there was no one in the world she so much wanted to see. That was a way she had. She hinted in a murmur that the surname of the balancing girl was Baker. (I've heard it said that Daisy's murmur was only to make people lean toward her; an irrelevant criticism that made it no less charming.)

At any rate, Miss Baker's lips fluttered, she nodded at me almost imperceptibly, and then quickly tipped her head back again—the object she was balancing had obviously tottered a little and given her something of a fright. Again a sort of apology arose to my lips. Almost any exhibition of complete self-sufficiency draws a stunned tribute from me.

I looked back at my cousin, who began to ask me questions in her low, thrilling voice. It was the kind of voice that the ear follows up and down, as if each speech is an arrangement of notes that will never be played again. Her face was sad and lovely with bright things in it, bright eyes and a bright passionate mouth, but there was an excitement in her voice that men who had cared for her found difficult to forget: a singing compulsion, a whispered "Listen," a promise that she had done gay, exciting things just a while since and [9/10] that there were gay, exciting things hovering in the next hour.

I told her how I had stopped off in Chicago for a day on my way East, and how a dozen people had sent their love through me.

"Do they miss me?" she cried ecstatically.

"The whole town is desolate. All the cars have the left rear wheel painted black as a mourning wreath, and there's a persistent wail all night along the north shore."

"How gorgeous! Let's go back, Tom. To-morrow!" Then she added irrelevantly: "You ought to see the baby."

"I'd like to."

"She's asleep. She's three years old. Haven't you ever seen her?"

"Never."

"Well, you ought to see her. She's——"

Tom Buchanan, who had been hovering restlessly about the room, stopped and rested his hand on my shoulder.

"What you doing, Nick?"

"I'm a bond man."

"Who with?"

I told him.

"Never heard of them," he remarked decisively.

This annoyed me.

"You will," I answered shortly. "You will if you stay in the East."

"Oh, I'll stay in the East, don't you worry," he said, glancing at Daisy and then back at me, as if he were alert for something more. "I'd be a God damned fool to live anywhere else." [10/11]

At this point Miss Baker said: "Absolutely!" with such suddenness that I started—it was the first word she had uttered since I came into the room. Evidently it surprised her as much as it did me, for she yawned and with a series of rapid, deft movements stood up into the room.

"I'm stiff," she complained, "I've been lying on that sofa for as long as I can remember."

"Don't look at me," Daisy retorted, "I've been trying to get you to New York all afternoon."

"No, thanks," said Miss Baker to the four cocktails just in from the pantry, "I'm absolutely in training."

Her host looked at her incredulously.

"You are!" He took down his drink as if it were a drop in the bottom of a glass. "How you ever get anything done is beyond me."

I looked at Miss Baker, wondering what it was she "got done." I enjoyed looking at her. She was a slender, small-breasted girl, with an erect carriage, which she accentuated by throwing her body backward at the shoulders like a young cadet. Her gray sun-strained eyes looked back at me with polite reciprocal curiosity out of a wan, charming, discontented face. It occurred to me now that I had seen her, or a picture of her, somewhere before.

"You live in West Egg," she remarked contemptuously. "I know somebody there."

"I don't know a single——"

"You must know Gatsby."

"Gatsby?" demanded Daisy. "What Gatsby?"

Before I could reply that he was my neighbor dinner was announced; wedging his tense arm imperatively [11/12] under mine, Tom Buchanan compelled me from the room as though he were moving a checker to another square.

Slenderly, languidly, their hands set lightly on their hips, the two young women preceded us out onto a rosy-colored porch, open toward the sunset, where four candles flickered on the table in the diminished wind.

"Why *candles?*" objected Daisy, frowning. She snapped them out with her fingers. "In two weeks it'll be the longest day in the year." She looked at us all radiantly. "Do you always watch for the longest day of the year and then miss it? I always watch for the longest day in the year and then miss it."

"We ought to plan something," yawned Miss Baker, sitting down at the table as if she were getting into bed.

"All right," said Daisy. "What'll we plan?" She turned to me helplessly: "What do people plan?"

Before I could answer her eyes fastened with an awed expression on her little finger.

"Look!" she complained; "I hurt it."

We all looked—the knuckle was black and blue.

"You did it, Tom," she said accusingly. "I know you didn't mean to, but you *did* do it. That's what I get for marrying a brute of a man, a great, big, hulking physical specimen of a——"

"I hate that word hulking," objected Tom crossly, "even in kidding."

"Hulking," insisted Daisy.

Sometimes she and Miss Baker talked at once, unobtrusively and with a bantering inconsequence that was never quite chatter, that was as cool as their white dresses and their impersonal eyes in the absence of all desire. They were here, and they accepted Tom and me, [12/13] making only a polite pleasant effort to entertain or to be entertained. They knew that presently dinner would be over and a little later the evening, too, would be over and casually put away. It was sharply different from the West, where an evening was hurried from phase to phase toward its close, in a continually disappointed anticipation or else in sheer nervous dread of the moment itself.

"You make me feel uncivilized, Daisy," I confessed on my second glass of corky but rather impressive claret. "Can't you talk about crops or something?"

I meant nothing in particular by this remark, but it was taken up in an unexpected way.

"Civilization's going to pieces," broke out Tom violently. "I've gotten to be a terrible pessimist about things. Have you read 'The Rise of the Colored Empires' by this man Goddard?"

"Why, no," I answered, rather surprised by his tone.

"Well, it's a fine book, and everybody ought to read it. The idea is if we don't look out the white race will be—will be utterly submerged. It's all scientific stuff; it's been proved."

"Tom's getting very profound," said Daisy, with an expression of unthoughtful sadness. "He reads deep books with long words in them. What was that word we——"

"Well, these books are all scientific," insisted Tom, glancing at her impatiently. "This fellow has worked out the whole thing. It's up to us, who are the dominant race, to watch out or these other races will have control of things."

"We've got to beat them down," whispered Daisy, winking ferociously toward the fervent sun. [13/14]

"You ought to live in California—" began Miss Baker, but Tom interrupted her by shifting heavily in his chair.

"This idea is that we're Nordics. I am, and you are, and you are, and—" After an infinitesimal hesitation he included Daisy with a slight nod, and she winked at me again. "—And we've produced all the things that go to make civilization—oh, science and art, and all that. Do you see?"

There was something pathetic in his concentration, as if his complacency, more acute than of old, was not enough to him any more. When, almost immediately, the telephone rang inside and the butler left the porch Daisy seized upon the momentary interruption and leaned toward me.

"I'll tell you a family secret," she whispered enthusiastically. "It's about the butler's nose. Do you want to hear about the butler's nose?"

"That's why I came over to-night."

"Well, he wasn't always a butler; he used to be the silver polisher for some people in New York that had a silver service for two hundred people. He had to polish it from morning till night, until finally it began to affect his nose——"

"Things went from bad to worse," suggested Miss Baker.

"Yes. Things went from bad to worse, until finally he had to give up his position."

For a moment the last sunshine fell with romantic affection upon her glowing face; her voice compelled me forward breathlessly as I listened—then the glow faded, each light deserting her with lingering regret, like children leaving a pleasant street at dusk.

The butler came back and murmured something close [14/15] to Tom's ear, whereupon Tom frowned, pushed back his chair, and without a word went inside. As if his absence quickened something within her, Daisy leaned forward again, her voice glowing and singing.

"I love to see you at my table, Nick. You remind me of a—of a rose, an absolute rose. Doesn't he?" She turned to Miss Baker for confirmation: "An absolute rose?"

This was untrue. I am not even faintly like a rose. She was only extemporizing, but a stirring warmth flowed from her, as if her heart was trying to come out to you concealed in one of those breathless, thrilling words. Then suddenly she threw her napkin on the table and excused herself and went into the house.

Miss Baker and I exchanged a short glance consciously devoid of meaning. I was about to speak when she sat up alertly and said "Sh!" in a warning voice. A subdued impassioned murmur was audible in the room beyond, and Miss Baker leaned forward unashamed, trying to hear. The murmur trembled on the verge of coherence, sank down, mounted excitedly, and then ceased altogether.

"This Mr. Gatsby you spoke of is my neighbor—" I said.

"Don't talk. I want to hear what happens."

"Is something happening?" I inquired innocently.

"You mean to say you don't know?" said Miss Baker, honestly surprised. "I thought everybody knew."

"I don't."

"Why—" she said hesitantly, "Tom's got some woman in New York."

"Got some woman?" I repeated blankly. Miss Baker nodded. [15/16]

"She might have the decency not to telephone him at dinner time. Don't you think?"

Almost before I had grasped her meaning there was the flutter of a dress and the crunch of leather boots, and Tom and Daisy were back at the table.

"It couldn't be helped!" cried Daisy with tense gayety.

She sat down, glanced searchingly at Miss Baker and then at me, and continued: "I looked outdoors for a minute, and it's very romantic outdoors. There's a bird on the lawn that I think must be a nightingale come over on the Cunard or White Star Line. He's singing away—" Her voice sang: "It's romantic, isn't it, Tom?"

"Very romantic," he said, and then miserably to me: "If it's light enough after dinner, I want to take you down to the stables."

The telephone rang inside, startlingly, and as Daisy shook her head decisively at Tom the subject of the stables, in fact all subjects, vanished into air. Among the broken fragments of the last five minutes at table I remember the candles being lit again, pointlessly, and I was conscious of wanting to look squarely at every one, and yet to avoid all eyes. I couldn't guess what Daisy and Tom were thinking, but I doubt if even Miss Baker, who seemed to have mastered a certain hardy scepticism, was able utterly to put this fifth guest's shrill metallic urgency out of mind. To a certain temperament the situation might have seemed intriguing—my own instinct was to telephone immediately for the police.

The horses, needless to say, were not mentioned again. Tom and Miss Baker, with several feet of twilight between them, strolled back into the library, as if to a vigil beside a perfectly tangible body, while, trying [16/17] to look pleasantly interested and a little deaf, I followed Daisy around a chain of connecting verandas to the porch in front. In its deep gloom we sat down side by side on a wicker settee.

Daisy took her face in her hands as if feeling its lovely shape, and her eyes moved gradually out into the velvet dusk. I saw that turbulent emotions possessed her, so I asked what I thought would be some sedative questions about her little girl.

"We don't know each other very well, Nick," she said suddenly. "Even if we are cousins. You didn't come to my wedding."

"I wasn't back from the war."

"That's true." She hesitated. "Well, I've had a very bad time, Nick, and I'm pretty cynical about everything."

Evidently she had reason to be. I waited but she didn't say any more, and after a moment I returned rather feebly to the subject of her daughter.

"I suppose she talks, and—eats, and everything."

"Oh, yes." She looked at me absently. "Listen, Nick; let me tell you what I said when she was born. Would you like to hear?"

"Very much."

"It'll show you how I've gotten to feel about—things. Well, she was less than an hour old and Tom was God knows where. I woke up out of the ether with an utterly abandoned feeling, and asked the nurse right away if it was a boy or a girl. She told me it was a girl, and so I turned my head away and wept. 'All right,' I said, 'I'm glad it's a girl. And I hope she'll

be a fool—that's the best thing a girl can be in this world, a beautiful little fool.' [17/18]

"You see I think everything's terrible anyhow," she went on in a convinced way. "Everybody thinks so—the most advanced people. And I *know*. I've been everywhere and seen everything and done everything." Her eyes flashed around her in a defiant way, rather like Tom's, and she laughed with thrilling scorn. "Sophisticated—God, I'm sophisticated!"

The instant her voice broke off, ceasing to compel my attention, my belief, I felt the basic insincerity of what she had said. It made me uneasy, as though the whole evening had been a trick of some sort to exact a contributory emotion from me. I waited, and sure enough, in a moment she looked at me with an absolute smirk on her lovely face, as if she had asserted her membership in a rather distinguished secret society to which she and Tom belonged.

Inside, the crimson room bloomed with light. Tom and Miss Baker sat at either end of the long couch and she read aloud to him from The Saturday Evening Post— the words, murmurous and uninflected, running together in a soothing tune. The lamp-light, bright on his boots and dull on the autumn-leaf yellow of her hair, glinted along the paper as she turned a page with a flutter of slender muscles in her arms.

When we came in she held us silent for a moment with a lifted hand.

"To be continued," she said, tossing the magazine on the table, "in our very next issue."

Her body asserted itself with a restless movement of her knee, and she stood up.

"Ten o'clock," she remarked, apparently finding the [18/19] time on the ceiling. "Time for this good girl to go to bed."

"Jordan's going to play in the tournament to-morrow," explained Daisy, "over at Westchester."

"Oh—you're *Jor*dan Baker."

I knew now why her face was familiar—its pleasing contemptuous expression had looked out at me from many rotogravure pictures of the sporting life at Asheville and Hot Springs and Palm Beach. I had heard some story of her too, a critical, unpleasant story, but what it was I had forgotten long ago.

"Good night," she said softly. "Wake me at eight, won't you?"

"If you'll get up."

"I will. Good night, Mr. Carraway. See you anon."

"Of course you will," confirmed Daisy. "In fact, I think I'll arrange a marriage. Come over often, Nick, and I'll sort of—oh—fling you together. You know—lock you up accidentally in linen closets and push you out to sea in a boat, and all that sort of thing——"

"Good night," called Miss Baker from the stairs. "I haven't heard a word."

"She's a nice girl," said Tom after a moment. "They oughtn't to let her run around the country this way."

"Who oughtn't to?" inquired Daisy coldly.

"Her family."

"Her family is one aunt about a thousand years old. Besides, Nick's going to look after her, aren't you, Nick? She's going to spend lots of week-ends out here this summer. I think the home influence will be very good for her."

Daisy and Tom looked at each other for a moment in silence. [19/20]

"Is she from New York?" I asked quickly.

"From Louisville. Our white girlhood was passed together there. Our beautiful white——"

"Did you give Nick a little heart-to-heart talk on the veranda?" demanded Tom suddenly.

"Did I?" She looked at me. "I can't seem to remember, but I think we talked about the Nordic race. Yes, I'm sure we did. It sort of crept up on us and first thing you know——"

"Don't believe everything you hear, Nick," he advised me.

I said lightly that I had heard nothing at all, and a few minutes later I got up to go home. They came to the door with me and stood side by side in a cheerful square of light. As I started my motor Daisy peremptorily called: "Wait!

"I forgot to ask you something, and it's important. We heard you were engaged to a girl out West."

"That's right," corroborated Tom kindly. "We heard that you were engaged."

"It's a libel. I'm too poor."

"But we heard it," insisted Daisy, surprising me by opening up again in a flower-like way. "We heard it from three people, so it must be true."

Of course I knew what they were referring to, but I wasn't even vaguely engaged. The fact that gossip had published the banns was one of the reasons I had come East. You can't stop going with an old friend on account of rumors, and on the other hand I had no intention of being rumored into marriage.

Their interest rather touched me and made them less remotely rich—nevertheless, I was confused and a little disgusted as I drove away. It seemed to me that the [20/21] thing for Daisy to do was to rush out of the house, child in arms—but apparently there were no such intentions in her head. As for Tom, the fact that he "had some woman in New York" was really less surprising than that he had been depressed by a book. Something was making him nibble at the edge of stale ideas as if his sturdy physical egotism no longer nourished his peremptory heart.

Already it was deep summer on roadhouse roofs and in front of wayside garages, where new red gas-pumps sat out in pools of light, and when I reached my estate at West Egg I ran the car under its shed and sat for a while on an abandoned grass roller in the yard. The wind had blown off, leaving a loud, bright night, with wings beating in the trees and a persistent organ sound as the full bellows of the earth blew the frogs full of life. The silhouette of a moving cat wavered across the moonlight, and turning my head to watch it, I saw that I was not alone—fifty feet away a figure had emerged from the shadow of my neighbor's mansion and was standing with his hands in his pockets regarding the silver pepper of the stars. Something in his leisurely movements and the secure position of his feet upon the lawn suggested that it was Mr. Gatsby himself, come out to determine what share was his of our local heavens.

I decided to call to him. Miss Baker had mentioned him at dinner, and that would do for an introduction. But I didn't call to him, for he gave a sudden intimation that he was content to be alone—he stretched out his arms toward the dark water in a curious way, and, far as I was from him, I could have sworn he was trembling. Involuntarily I glanced seaward—and distin- [21/22] guished nothing except a single green light, minute and far way, that might have been the end of a dock. When I looked once more for Gatsby he had vanished, and I was alone again in the unquiet darkness. [22/23]

CHAPTER II

About half way between West Egg and New York the motor road hastily joins the railroad and runs beside it for a quarter of a mile, so as to shrink away from a certain desolate area of land. This is a valley of ashes—a fantastic farm where ashes grow like wheat into ridges and hills and grotesque gardens; where ashes take the forms of houses and chimneys and rising smoke and, finally, with a transcendent effort, of ash-gray men who move dimly and already crumbling through the powdery air. Occasionally a line of gray cars crawls along an invisible track, gives out a ghastly creak, and comes to rest, and immediately the ash-gray men swarm up with leaden spades and stir up an impenetrable cloud, which screens their obscure operations from your sight.

But above the gray land and the spasms of bleak dust which drift endlessly over it, you perceive, after a moment, the eyes of Doctor T. J. Eckleburg. The eyes of Doctor T. J. Eckleburg are blue and gigantic—their retinas are one yard high. They look out of no face, but, instead, from a pair of enormous yellow spectacles which pass over a non-existent nose. Evidently some wild wag of an oculist set them there to fatten his practice in the borough of Queens, and then sank down himself into eternal blindness, or forgot them and moved away. But his eyes, dimmed a little by many paintless days under sun and rain, brood on over the solemn dumping ground.

The valley of ashes is bounded on one side by a [23/24] small foul river, and, when the drawbridge is up to let barges through, the passengers on waiting trains can stare at the dismal scene for as long as half an hour. There is always a halt there of at least a minute, and it was because of this that I first met Tom Buchanan's mistress.

The fact that he had one was insisted upon wherever he was known. His acquaintances resented the fact that he turned up in popular restaurants with her and, leaving her at a table, sauntered about, chatting with whomsoever he knew. Though I was curious to see her, I had no desire to meet her—but I did. I went up to New York with Tom on the train one afternoon, and when we stopped by the ashheaps he jumped to his feet and, taking hold of my elbow, literally forced me from the car.

"We're getting off," he insisted. "I want you to meet my girl."

I think he'd tanked up a good deal at luncheon, and his determination to have my company bordered on violence. The supercilious assumption was that on Sunday afternoon I had nothing better to do.

I followed him over a low whitewashed railroad fence, and we walked back a hundred yards along the road under Doctor Eckleburg's persistent stare. The only building in sight was a small block of yellow brick sitting on the edge of the waste land, a sort of compact Main Street ministering to it, and contiguous to absolutely nothing. One of the three shops it contained was for rent and another was an all-night restaurant, approached by a trail of ashes; the third was a garage— *Repairs*. GEORGE B. WILSON. *Cars bought and sold.*—and I followed Tom inside. [24/25]

The interior was unprosperous and bare; the only car visible was the dust-covered wreck of a Ford which crouched in a dim corner. It had occurred to me that this shadow of a garage must be a blind, and that sumptuous and romantic apartments were concealed overhead, when the proprietor himself appeared in the door of an office, wiping his hands on a piece of waste. He was a blond, spiritless man, anæmic, and faintly handsome. When he saw us a damp gleam of hope sprang into his light blue eyes.

"Hello, Wilson, old man," said Tom, slapping him jovially on the shoulder. "How's business?"

"I can't complain," answered Wilson unconvincingly. "When are you going to sell me that car?"

"Next week; I've got my man working on it now."

"Works pretty slow, don't he?"

"No, he doesn't," said Tom coldly. "And if you feel that way about it, maybe I'd better sell it somewhere else after all."

"I don't mean that," explained Wilson quickly. "I just meant——"

His voice faded off and Tom glanced impatiently around the garage. Then I heard footsteps on a stairs, and in a moment the thickish figure of a woman blocked out the light from the office door. She was in the middle thirties, and faintly stout, but she carried her surplus flesh sensuously as some women can. Her face, above a spotted dress of dark blue crêpe-de-chine, contained no facet or gleam of beauty, but there was an immediately perceptible vitality about her as if the nerves of her body were continually smouldering.

She smiled slowly and, walking through her husband as if he were a ghost, shook hands with Tom, looking him flush in the eye. [25/26] Then she wet her lips, and without turning around spoke to her husband in a soft, coarse voice:

"Get some chairs, why don't you, so somebody can sit down."

"Oh, sure," agreed Wilson hurriedly, and went toward the little office, mingling immediately with the cement color of the walls. A white ashen dust veiled his dark suit and his pale hair as it veiled everything in the vicinity—except his wife, who moved close to Tom.

"I want to see you," said Tom intently. "Get on the next train."

"All right."

"I'll meet you by the news-stand on the lower level."

She nodded and moved away from him just as George Wilson emerged with two chairs from his office door.

We waited for her down the road and out of sight. It was a few days before the Fourth of July, and a gray, scrawny Italian child was setting torpedoes in a row along the railroad track.

"Terrible place, isn't it," said Tom exchanging a frown with Doctor Eckleburg.

"Awful."

"It does her good to get away."

"Doesn't her husband object?"

"Wilson? He thinks she goes to see her sister in New York. He's so dumb he doesn't know he's alive."

So Tom Buchanan and his girl and I went up together to New York—or not quite together, for Mrs. Wilson sat discreetly in another car. Tom deferred that much to the sensibilities of those East Eggers who might be on the train.

She had changed her dress to a brown figured muslin, which stretched tight over her rather wide hips as Tom [26/27] helped her to the platform in New York. At the news-stand she bought a copy of *Town Tattle* and a moving-picture magazine, and in the station drug-store some cold cream and a small flask of perfume.

Up-stairs, in the solemn echoing drive she let four taxicabs drive away before she selected a new one, lavender-colored with gray upholstery, and in this we slid out from the mass of the station into the glowing sunshine. But immediately she turned sharply from the window and, leaning forward, tapped on the front glass.

"I want to get one of those dogs," she said earnestly. "I want to get one for the apartment. They're nice to have—a dog."

We backed up to a gray old man who bore an absurd resemblance to John D. Rockefeller. In a basket swung from his neck cowered a dozen very recent puppies of an indeterminate breed.

"What kind are they?" asked Mrs. Wilson eagerly, as he came to the taxi-window.

"All kinds. What kind do you want, lady?"

"I'd like to get one of those police dogs; I don't suppose you got that kind?"

The man peered doubtfully into the basket, plunged in his hand and drew one up, wriggling, by the back of the neck.

"That's no police dog," said Tom.

"No, it's not exactly a *police* dog," said the man with disappointment in his voice. "It's more of an Airedale." He passed his hand over the brown washrag of a back. "Look at that coat. Some coat. That's a dog that'll never bother you with catching cold."

"I think it's cute," said Mrs. Wilson enthusiastically. "How much is it?" [**27/ 28**]

"That dog?" He looked at it admiringly. "That dog will cost you ten dollars."

The Airedale—undoubtedly there was an airedale concerned in it somewhere, though its feet were startling white—changed hands and settled down into Mrs. Wilson's lap, where she fondled the weatherproof coat with rapture.

"Is it a boy or a girl?" she asked delicately.

"That dog? That dog's a boy."

"It's a bitch," said Tom decisively. "Here's your money. Go and buy ten more dogs with it."

We drove over to Fifth Avenue, so warm and soft, almost pastoral, on the summer Sunday afternoon that I wouldn't have been surprised to see a great flock of white sheep turn the corner.

"Hold on," I said, "I have to leave you here."

"No, you don't," interposed Tom quickly. "Myrtle'll be hurt if you don't come up to the apartment. Won't you, Myrtle?"

"Come on," she urged. "I'll telephone my sister Catherine. She's said to be very beautiful by people who ought to know."

"Well, I'd like to, but——"

We went on, cutting back again over the Park toward the West Hundreds. At 158th Street the cab stopped at one slice in a long white cake of apartment-houses. Throwing a regal homecoming glance around the neighborhood, Mrs. Wilson gathered up her dog and her other purchases, and went haughtily in.

"I'm going to have the McKees come up," she announced as we rose in the elevator. "And, of course, I got to call up my sister, too." [**28/29**]

The apartment was on the top floor— a small living-room, a small dining-room, a small bedroom, and a bath. The living-room was crowded to the doors with a set of tapestried furniture entirely too large for it, so that to move about was to stumble continually over scenes of ladies swinging in the gardens of Versailles. The only picture was an over-enlarged photograph, apparently a hen sitting on a blurred rock. Looked at from a distance, however, the hen resolved itself into a bonnet, and the countenance of a stout old lady beamed down into the room. Several old copies of *Town Tattle* lay on the table together with a copy of *Simon Called Peter*, and some of the small scandal magazines of Broadway. Mrs. Wilson was first concerned with the dog. A reluctant elevator-boy went for a box full of straw and some milk, to which he added on his own initiative a tin of large, hard dog-biscuits—one of which decomposed apathetically in the saucer of milk all afternoon. Meanwhile Tom brought out a bottle of whiskey from a locked bureau door.

I have been drunk just twice in my life, and the second time was that afternoon; so everything that happened has a dim, hazy cast over it, although until after eight o'clock the apartment was full of cheerful sun. Sitting on Tom's lap Mrs. Wilson called up several people on the telephone; then there were no cigarettes, and I went out to buy some at the drug-store on the corner. When I came back they had disappeared, so I sat down discreetly in the living-room and read a chapter of *Simon Called Peter*—either it was terrible stuff or the whiskey distorted things, because it didn't make any sense to me.

Just as Tom and Myrtle (after the first drink Mrs. [29/30] Wilson and I called each other by our first names) reappeared, company commenced to arrive at the apartment-door.

The sister, Catherine, was a slender, worldly girl of about thirty, with a solid, sticky bob of red hair, and a complexion powdered milky white. Her eyebrows had been plucked and then drawn on again at a more rakish angle, but the efforts of nature toward the restoration of the old alignment gave a blurred air to her face. When she moved about there was an incessant clicking as innumerable pottery bracelets jingled up and down upon her arms. She came in with such a proprietary haste, and looked around so possessively at the furniture that I wondered if she lived here. But when I asked her she laughed immoderately, repeated my question aloud, and told me she lived with a girl friend at a hotel.

Mr. McKee was a pale, feminine man from the flat below. He had just shaved, for there was a white spot of lather on his cheekbone, and he was most respectful in his greeting to every one in the room. He informed me that he was in the "artistic game," and I gathered later that he was a photographer and had made the dim enlargement of Mrs. Wilson's mother which hovered like an ectoplasm on the wall. His wife was shrill, languid, handsome, and horrible. She told me with pride that her husband had photographed her a hundred and twenty-seven times since they had been married.

Mrs. Wilson had changed her costume some time before, and was now attired in an elaborate afternoon dress of cream-colored chiffon, which gave out a continual rustle as she swept about the room. With the influence of the dress her personality had also undergone a change. The intense vitality that had been so [30/31] remarkable in the garage was converted into impressive hauteur. Her laughter, her gestures, her assertions became more violently affected moment by moment, and as she expanded the room grew smaller around her, until she seemed to be revolving on a noisy, creaking pivot through the smoky air.

"My dear," she told her sister in a high, mincing shout, "most of these fellas will cheat you every time. All they think of is money. I had a woman up here last week to look at my feet, and when she gave me the bill you'd of thought she had my appendicitis out."

"What was the name of the woman?" asked Mrs. McKee.

"Mrs. Eberhardt. She goes around looking at people's feet in their own homes."

"I like your dress," remarked Mrs. McKee, "I think it's adorable."

Mrs. Wilson rejected the compliment by raising her eyebrow in disdain.

"It's just a crazy old thing," she said. "I just slip it on sometimes when I don't care what I look like."

"But it looks wonderful on you, if you know what I mean," pursued Mrs. McKee. "If Chester could only get you in that pose I think he could make something of it."

We all looked in silence at Mrs. Wilson, who removed a strand of hair from over her eyes and looked back at us with a brilliant smile. Mr. McKee regarded her intently with his head on one side, and then moved his hand back and forth slowly in front of his face.

"I should change the light," he said after a moment. "I'd like to bring out the modelling of the features. And I'd try to get hold of all the back hair." **[31/32]**

"I wouldn't think of changing the light," cried Mrs. McKee. "I think it's——"

Her husband said *"Sh!"* and we all looked at the subject again, whereupon Tom Buchanan yawned audibly and got to his feet.

"You McKees have something to drink," he said. "Get some more ice and mineral water, Myrtle, before everybody goes to sleep."

"I told that boy about the ice." Myrtle raised her eyebrows in despair at the shiftlessness of the lower orders. "These people! You have to keep after them all the time."

She looked at me and laughed pointlessly. Then she flounced over to the dog, kissed it with ecstasy, and swept into the kitchen, implying that a dozen chefs awaited her orders there.

"I've done some nice things out on Long Island," asserted Mr. McKee.

Tom looked at him blankly.

"Two of them we have framed downstairs."

"Two what?" demanded Tom.

"Two studies. One of them I call *Montauk Point—The Gulls,* and the other I call *Montauk Point—The Sea.*"

The sister Catherine sat down beside me on the couch.

"Do you live down on Long Island, too?" she inquired.

"I live at West Egg."

"Really? I was down there at a party about a month ago. At a man named Gatsby's. Do you know him?"

"I live next door to him." **[32/33]**

"Well, they say he's a nephew or a cousin of Kaiser Wilhelm's. That's where all his money comes from."

"Really?"

She nodded.

"I'm scared of him. I'd hate to have him get anything on me."

This absorbing information about my neighbor was interrupted by Mrs. McKee's pointing suddenly at Catherine:

"Chester, I think you could do something with *her,*" she broke out, but Mr. McKee only nodded in a bored way, and turned his attention to Tom.

"I'd like to do more work on Long Island, if I could get the entry. All I ask is that they should give me a start."

"Ask Myrtle," said Tom, breaking into a short shout of laughter as Mrs. Wilson entered with a tray. "She'll give you a letter of introduction, won't you, Myrtle?"

"Do what?" she asked, startled.

"You'll give McKee a letter of introduction to your husband, so he can do some studies of him." His lips moved silently for a moment as he invented. *"George B. Wilson at the Gasoline Pump,* or something like that."

Catherine leaned close to me and whispered in my ear:

"Neither of them can stand the person they're married to."

"Can't they?"

"Can't *stand* them." She looked at Myrtle and then at Tom. "What I say is, why go on living with them if they can't stand them? If I was them I'd get a divorce and get married to each other right away." **[33/34]**

"Doesn't she like Wilson either?"

The answer to this was unexpected. It came from Myrtle, who had overheard the question, and it was violent and obscene.

"You see," cried Catherine triumphantly. She lowered her voice again. "It's really his wife that's keeping them apart. She's a Catholic, and they don't believe in divorce."

Daisy was not a Catholic, and I was a little shocked at the elaborateness of the lie.

"When they do get married," continued Catherine, "they're going West to live for a while until it blows over."

"It'd be more discreet to go to Europe."

"Oh, do you like Europe?" she exclaimed surprisingly. "I just got back from Monte Carlo."

"Really."

"Just last year. I went over there with another girl."

"Stay long?"

"No, we just went to Monte Carlo and back. We went by way of Marseilles. We had over twelve hundred dollars when we started, but we got gypped out of it all in two days in the private rooms. We had an awful time getting back, I can tell you. God, how I hated that town!"

The late afternoon sky bloomed in the window for a moment like the blue honey of the Mediterranean—then the shrill voice of Mrs. McKee called me back into the room.

"I almost made a mistake, too," she declared vigorously. "I almost married a little kike who'd been after me for years. I knew he was below me. Everybody kept [34/35] saying to me: 'Lucille, that man's 'way below you!' But if I hadn't met Chester, he'd of got me sure."

"Yes, but listen," said Myrtle Wilson, nodding her head up and down, "at least you didn't marry him."

"I know I didn't."

"Well, I married him," said Myrtle, ambiguously. "And that's the difference between your case and mine."

"Why did you, Myrtle?" demanded Catherine. "Nobody forced you to."

Myrtle considered.

"I married him because I thought he was a gentleman," she said finally. "I thought he knew something about breeding, but he wasn't fit to lick my shoe."

"You were crazy about him for a while," said Catherine.

"Crazy about him!" cried Myrtle incredulously. "Who said I was crazy about him? I never was any more crazy about him than I was about that man there."

She pointed suddenly at me, and every one looked at me accusingly. I tried to show by my expression that I had played no part in her past.

"The only *crazy* I was was when I married him. I knew right away I made a mistake. He borrowed somebody's best suit to get married in, and never even told me about it, and the man came after it one day when he was out." She looked around to see who was listening. " 'Oh, is that your suit?' I said. 'This is the first I ever heard about it.' But I gave it to him and then I lay down and cried to beat the band all afternoon."

"She really ought to get away from him," resumed Catherine to me. "They've been living over that garage for eleven years. And Tom's the first sweetie she ever had." [35/36]

The bottle of whiskey—a second one—was now in constant demand by all present, excepting Catherine, who "felt just as good on nothing at all." Tom rang for the janitor and sent him for some celebrated sandwiches, which were a complete supper in themselves. I wanted to get out and walk eastward toward the park through the soft twilight, but each time I tried to go I became entangled in some wild, strident argument which pulled me back, as if with ropes, into my chair. Yet high over the city our line of yellow windows must have contributed their share of human secrecy to the casual watcher in the darkening streets, and I was him too, looking up and wondering. I was within and without, simultaneously enchanted and repelled by the inexhaustible variety of life.

Myrtle pulled her chair close to mine, and suddenly her warm breath poured over me the story of her first meeting with Tom.

"It was on the two little seats facing each other that are always the last ones left on the train. I was going up to New York to see my sister and spend the night. He had on a dress suit and patent leather shoes, and I couldn't keep my eyes off him, but every time he looked at me I had to pretend to be looking at the advertisement over his head. When we came into the station he was next to me, and his white shirt-front pressed against my arm, and so I told him I'd have to call policeman, but he knew I lied. I was so excited that when I got into a taxi with him I didn't hardly know I wasn't getting into a subway train. All I kept thinking about, over and over, was 'You can't live forever; you can't live forever.' " [36/37]

She turned to Mrs. McKee and the room rang full of her artificial laughter.

"My dear," she cried, "I'm going to give you this dress as soon as I'm through with it. I've got to get another one tomorrow. I'm going to make a list of all the things I've got to get. A massage and a wave, and a collar for the dog, and one of those cute little ash-trays where you touch a spring, and a wreath with a black silk bow for mother's grave that'll last all summer. I got to write down a list so I won't forget all the things I got to do."

It was nine o'clock—almost immediately afterward I looked at my watch and found it was ten. Mr. McKee was asleep on a chair with his fists clenched in his lap, like a photograph of a man of action. Taking out my handkerchief I wiped from his cheek the remains of the spot of dried lather that had worried me all the afternoon.

The little dog was sitting on the table looking with blind eyes through the smoke, and from time to time groaning faintly. People disappeared, reappeared, made plans to go somewhere, and then lost each other, searched for each other, found each other a few feet away. Some time toward midnight Tom Buchanan and Mrs. Wilson stood face to face, discussing in impassioned voices whether Mrs. Wilson had any right to mention Daisy's name.

"Daisy! Daisy! Daisy!" shouted Mrs. Wilson. "I'll say it whenever I want to! Daisy! Dai——"

Making a short deft movement, Tom Buchanan broke her nose with his open hand.

Then there were bloody towels upon the bathroom [37/38] floor, and women's voices scolding, and high over the confusion a long broken wail of pain. Mr. McKee awoke from his doze and started in a daze toward the door. When he had gone halfway he turned around and stared at the scene—his wife and Catherine scolding and consoling as they stumbled here and there among the crowded furniture with articles of aid, and the despairing figure on the couch, bleeding fluently, and trying to spread a copy of *Town Tattle* over the tapestry scenes of Versailles. Then Mr. McKee turned and continued on out the door. Taking my hat from the chandelier, I followed.

"Come to lunch some day," he suggested, as we groaned down in the elevator.

"Where?"

"Anywhere."

"Keep your hands off the lever," snapped the elevator boy.

"I beg your pardon," said Mr. McKee with dignity, "I didn't know I was touching it."

"All right," I agreed, "I'll be glad to."

. . . I was standing beside his bed and he was sitting up between the sheets, clad in his underwear, with a great portfolio in his hands.

"Beauty and the Beast . . . Loneliness . . . Old Grocery Horse . . . Brook'n Bridge. . . ."

Then I was lying half asleep in the cold lower level of the Pennsylvania Station, staring at the morning *Tribune*, and waiting for the four o'clock train. [38/39]

CHAPTER III

There was music from my neighbor's house through the summer nights. In his blue gardens men and girls came and went like moths among the whisperings and the champagne and the stars. At high tide in the afternoon I watched his guests diving from the tower of his raft, or taking the sun on the hot sand of his beach while his two motor-boats slit the waters of the Sound, drawing aquaplanes over cataracts of foam. On week-ends his Rolls-Royce became an omnibus, bearing parties to and from the city between nine in the morning and long past midnight, while his station wagon scampered like a brisk yellow bug to meet all trains. And on Mondays eight servants, including an extra gardener, toiled all day with mops and scrubbing-brushes and hammers and garden-shears, repairing the ravages of the night before.

Every Friday five crates of oranges and lemons arrived from a fruiterer in New York—every Monday these same oranges and lemons left his back door in a pyramid of pulpless halves. There was a machine in the kitchen which could extract the juice of two hundred oranges in half an hour if a little button was pressed two hundred times by a butler's thumb.

At least once a fortnight a corps of caterers came down with several hundred feet of canvas and enough colored lights to make a Christmas tree of Gatsby's enormous garden. On buffet tables, garnished with glistening hors-d'oeuvre, spiced baked hams crowded against salads of [39/40] harlequin designs and pastry pigs and turkeys bewitched to a dark gold. In the main hall a bar with a real brass rail was set up, and stocked with gins and liquors and with cordials so long forgotten that most of his female guests were too young to know one from another.

By seven o'clock the orchestra has arrived, no thin five-piece affair, but a whole pitful of oboes and trombones and saxophones and viols and cornets and piccolos, and low and high drums. The last swimmers have come in from the beach now and are dressing up-stairs; the cars from New York are parked five deep in the drive, and already the halls and salons and verandas are gaudy with primary colors, and hair shorn in strange new ways, and shawls beyond the dreams of Castile. The bar is in full swing, and floating rounds of cocktails permeate the garden outside, until the air is alive with chatter and laughter, and casual innuendo and introductions forgotten on the spot, and enthusiastic meetings between women who never knew each other's names.

The lights grow brighter as the earth lurches away from the sun, and now the orchestra is playing yellow cocktail music, and the opera of voices pitches a key higher. Laughter is easier minute by minute, spilled with prodigality, tipped out

at a cheerful word. The groups change more swiftly, swell with new arrivals, dissolve and form in the same breath; already there are wanderers, confident girls who weave here and there among the stouter and more stable, become for a sharp, joyous moment the center of a group, and then, excited with triumph, glide on through the sea-change of faces and voices and color under the constantly changing light. [40/41]

Suddenly one of these gypsies, in trembling opal, seizes a cocktail out of the air, dumps it down for courage and, moving her hands like Frisco, dances out alone on the canvas platform. A momentary hush; the orchestra leader varies his rhythm obligingly for her, and there is a burst of chatter as the erroneous news goes around that she is Gilda Gray's understudy from the *Follies*. The party has begun.

I believe that on the first night I went to Gatsby's house I was one of the few guests who had actually been invited. People were not invited—they went there. They got into automobiles which bore them out to Long Island, and somehow they ended up at Gatsby's door. Once there they were introduced by somebody who knew Gatsby, and after that they conducted themselves according to the rules of behavior associated with amusement parks. Sometimes they came and went without having met Gatsby at all, came for the party with a simplicity of heart that was its own ticket of admission.

I had been actually invited. A chauffeur in a uniform of robin's-egg blue crossed my lawn early that Saturday morning with a surprisingly formal note from his employer: the honor would be entirely Gatsby's, it said, if I would attend his "little party" that night. He had seen me several times, and had intended to call on me long before, but a peculiar combination of circumstances had prevented it—signed Jay Gatsby, in a majestic hand.

Dressed up in white flannels I went over to his lawn a little after seven, and wandered around rather ill at ease among swirls and eddies of people I didn't know—though here and there was a face I had noticed on the commuting train. I was immediately struck by the number of young Englishmen dotted about; all well dressed, [41/42] all looking a little hungry, and all talking in low, earnest voices to solid and prosperous Americans. I was sure that they were selling something: bonds or insurance or automobiles. They were at least agonizingly aware of the easy money in the vicinity and convinced that it was theirs for a few words in the right key.

As soon as I arrived I made an attempt to find my host, but the two or three people of whom I asked his whereabouts stared at me in such an amazed way, and denied so vehemently any knowledge of his movements, that I slunk off in the direction of the cocktail table—the only place in the garden where a single man could linger without looking purposeless and alone.

I was on my way to get roaring drunk from sheer embarrassment when Jordan Baker came out of the house and stood at the head of the marble steps, leaning a little backward and looking with contemptuous interest down into the garden.

Welcome or not, I found it necessary to attach myself to some one before I should begin to address cordial remarks to the passers-by.

"Hello!" I roared, advancing toward her. My voice seemed unnaturally loud across the garden.

"I thought you might be here," she responded absently as I came up. "I remembered you lived next door to——"

She held my hand impersonally, as a promise that she'd take care of me in a minute, and gave ear to two girls in twin yellow dresses, who stopped at the foot of the steps.

"Hello!" they cried together. "Sorry you didn't win."

That was for the golf tournament. She had lost in the finals the week before. [42/43]

"You don't know who we are," said one of the girls in yellow, "but we met you here about a month ago."

"You've dyed your hair since then," remarked Jordan, and I started, but the girls had moved casually on and her remark was addressed to the premature moon, produced like the supper, no doubt, out of a caterer's basket. With Jordan's slender golden arm resting in mine, we descended the steps and sauntered about the garden. A tray of cocktails floated at us through the twilight, and we sat down at a table with the two girls in yellow and three men, each one introduced to us as Mr. Mumble.

"Do you come to these parties often?" inquired Jordan of the girl beside her.

"The last one was the one I met you at," answered the girl, in an alert confident voice. She turned to her companion: "Wasn't it for you, Lucille?"

It was for Lucille, too.

"I like to come," Lucille said. "I never care what I do, so I always have a good time. When I was here last I tore my gown on a chair, and he asked me my name and address—inside of a week I got a package from Croirier's with a new evening gown in it."

"Did you keep it?" asked Jordan.

"Sure I did. I was going to wear it tonight, but it was too big in the bust and had to be altered. It was gas blue with lavender beads. Two hundred and sixty-five dollars."

"There's something funny about a fellow that'll do a thing like that," said the other girl eagerly. "He doesn't want any trouble with anybody."

"Who doesn't?" I inquired.

"Gatsby. Somebody told me——" [43/44]

The two girls and Jordan leaned together confidentially.

"Somebody told me they thought he killed a man once."

A thrill passed over all of us. The three Mr. Mumbles bent forward and listened eagerly.

"I don't think it's so much that," argued Lucille sceptically; "it's more that he was a German spy during the war."

One of the men nodded in confirmation.

"I heard that from a man who knew all about him, grew up with him in Germany," he assured us positively.

"Oh, no," said the first girl, "it couldn't be that, because he was in the American army during the war." As our credulity switched back to her she leaned forward with enthusiasm. "You look at him sometimes when he thinks nobody's looking at him. I'll bet he killed a man."

She narrowed her eyes and shivered. Lucille shivered. We all turned and looked around for Gatsby. It was testimony to the romantic speculation he inspired that there were whispers about him from those who had found little that it was necessary to whisper about in this world.

The first supper—there would be another one after midnight—was now being served, and Jordan invited me to join her own party, who were spread around a table on the other side of the garden. There were three married couples and Jordan's escort, a persistent undergraduate given to violent innuendo, and obviously under the impression that sooner or later Jordan was going to yield him up her person to a greater or lesser degree. [**44/45**] Instead of rambling, this party had preserved a dignified homogeneity, and assumed to itself the function of representing the staid nobility of the countryside—East Egg condescending to West Egg, and carefully on guard against its spectroscopic gayety.

"Let's get out," whispered Jordan, after a somehow wasteful and inappropriate half-hour; "this is much too polite for me."

We got up, and she explained that we were going to find the host: I had never met him, she said, and it was making me uneasy. The undergraduate nodded in a cynical, melancholy way.

The bar, where we glanced first, was crowded, but Gatsby was not there. She couldn't find him from the top of the steps, and he wasn't on the veranda. On a chance we tried an important-looking door, and walked into a high Gothic library, panelled with carved English oak, and probably transported complete from some ruin overseas.

A stout, middle-aged man, with enormous owl-eyed spectacles, was sitting somewhat drunk on the edge of a great table, starring with unsteady concentration at the shelves of books. As we entered he wheeled excitedly around and examined Jordan from head to foot.

"What do you think?" he demanded impetuously.

"About what?"

He waved his hand toward the bookshelves.

"About that. As a matter of fact you needn't bother to ascertain. I ascertained. They're real."

"The books?"

He nodded.

"Absolutely real—have pages and everything. I thought they'd be a nice durable cardboard. Matter of [**45/46**] fact, they're absolutely real. Pages and—Here! Lemme show you."

Taking our scepticism for granted, he rushed to the bookcases and returned with Volume One of the "Stoddard Lectures."

"See!" he cried triumphantly. "It's a bona-fide piece of printed matter. It fooled me. This fella's a regular Belasco. It's a triumph. What thoroughness! What realism! Knew when to stop, too—didn't cut the pages. But what do you want? What do you expect?"

He snatched the book from me and replaced it hastily on its shelf, muttering that if one brick was removed the whole library was liable to collapse.

"Who brought you?" he demanded. "Or did you just come? I was brought. Most people were brought."

Jordan looked at him alertly, cheerfully, without answering.

"I was brought by a woman named Roosevelt," he continued. "Mrs. Claud Roosevelt. Do you know her? I met her somewhere last night. I've been drunk for about a week now, and I thought it might sober me up to sit in a library."

"Has it?"

"A little bit, I think. I can't tell yet. I've only been here an hour. Did I tell you about the books? They're real. They're——"

"You told us."

We shook hands with him gravely and went back outdoors.

There was dancing now on the canvas in the garden; old men pushing young girls backward in eternal graceless circles, superior couples holding each other tortuously, fashionably, and keeping in the corners—and a [46/47] great number of single girls dancing individualistically or relieving the orchestra for a moment of the burden of the banjo or the traps. By midnight the hilarity had increased. A celebrated tenor had sung in Italian, and a notorious contralto had sung in jazz, and between the numbers people were doing "stunts" all over the garden, while happy, vacuous bursts of laughter rose toward the summer sky. A pair of stage twins, who turned out to be the girls in yellow, did a baby act in costume, and champagne was served in glasses bigger than finger-bowls. The moon had risen higher, and floating in the Sound was a triangle of silver scales, trembling a little to the stiff, tinny drip of the banjoes on the lawn.

I was still with Jordan Baker. We were sitting at a table with a man of about my age and a rowdy little girl, who gave way upon the slightest provocation to uncontrollable laughter. I was enjoying myself now. I had taken two finger-bowls of champagne, and the scene had changed before my eyes into something significant, elemental, and profound.

At a lull in the entertainment the man looked at me and smiled.

"Your face is familiar," he said, politely. "Weren't you in the Third Division during the war?"

"Why, yes. I was in the ninth machine-gun battalion."

"I was in the Seventh Infantry until June nineteen-eighteen. I knew I'd seen you somewhere before."

We talked for a moment about some wet, gray little villages in France. Evidently he lived in this vicinity, for he told me that he had just bought a hydroplane, and was going to try it out in the morning.

"Want to go with me, old sport? Just near the shore along the Sound." [47/48]

"What time?"

"Any time that suits you best."

It was on the tip of my tongue to ask his name when Jordan looked around and smiled.

"Having a gay time now?" she inquired.

"Much better." I turned again to my new acquaintance. "This is an unusual party for me. I haven't even seen the host. I live over there—" I waved my hand at the invisible hedge in the distance, "and this man Gatsby sent over his chauffeur with an invitation."

For a moment he looked at me as if he failed to understand.

"I'm Gatsby," he said suddenly.

"What!" I exclaimed. "Oh, I beg your pardon."

"I thought you knew, old sport. I'm afraid I'm not a very good host."

He smiled understandingly—much more than understandingly. It was one of those rare smiles with a quality of eternal reassurance in it, that you may come across four or five times in life. It faced—or seemed to face—the whole external world for an instant, and then concentrated on *you* with an irresistible prejudice in your favor. It understood you just as far as you wanted to be understood, believed in you as you would like to believe in yourself, and assured you that it had precisely the impression of you that, at your best, you hoped to convey. Precisely at that point it vanished—and I was looking at an elegant young roughneck, a year or two over thirty, whose elaborate formality of speech just missed being absurd. Some time before he introduced himself I'd got a strong impression that he was picking his words with care.

Almost at the moment when Mr. Gatsby

identified [48/49] himself, a butler hurried toward him with the information that Chicago was calling him on the wire. He excused himself with a small bow that included each of us in turn.

"If you want anything just ask for it, old sport," he urged me. "Excuse me. I will rejoin you later."

When he was gone I turned immediately to Jordan—constrained to assure her of my surprise. I had expected that Mr. Gatsby would be a florid and corpulent person in his middle years.

"Who is he?" I demanded. "Do you know?"

"He's just a man named Gatsby."

"Where is he from, I mean? And what does he do?"

"Now *you're* started on the subject," she answered with a wan smile. "Well, he told me once he was an Oxford man."

A dim background started to take shape behind him, but at her next remark it faded away.

"However, I don't believe it."

"Why not?"

"I don't know," she insisted, "I just don't think he went there."

Something in her tone reminded me of the other girl's "I think he killed a man," and had the effect of stimulating my curiosity. I would have accepted without question the information that Gatsby sprang from the swamps of Louisiana or from the lower East Side of New York. That was comprehensible. But young men didn't—at least in my provincial inexperience I believed they didn't—drift coolly out of nowhere and buy a palace on Long Island Sound.

"Anyhow, he gives large parties," said Jordan, changing the subject with an urban distaste for the concrete. [49/50] "And I like large parties. They're so intimate. At small parties there isn't any privacy."

There was the boom of a bass drum, and the voice of the orchestra leader rang out suddenly above the echolalia of the garden.

"Ladies and gentlemen," he cried. "At the request of Mr. Gatsby we are going to play for you Mr. Vladimir Tostoff's latest work, which attracted so much attention at Carnegie Hall last May. If you read the papers you know there was a big sensation." He smiled with jovial condescension, and added: "Some sensation!" Whereupon everybody laughed.

"The piece is known," he concluded lustily, "as Vladimir Tostoff's *Jazz History of the World*."

The nature of Mr. Tostoff's composition eluded me, because just as it began my eyes fell on Gatsby, standing alone on the marble steps and looking from one group to another with approving eyes. His tanned skin was drawn attractively tight on his face and his short hair looked as though it were trimmed every day. I could see nothing sinister about him. I wondered if the fact that he was not drinking helped to set him off from his guests, for it seemed to me that he grew more correct as the fraternal hilarity increased. When the *Jazz History of the World* was over, girls were putting their heads on men's shoulders in a puppyish, convivial way, girls were swooning backward playfully into men's arms, even into groups, knowing that some one would arrest their falls—but no one swooned backward on Gatsby, and no French bob touched Gatsby's shoulder, and no singing quartets were formed with Gatsby's head for one link.

"I beg your pardon." [50/51]

Gatsby's butler was suddenly standing beside us.

"Miss Baker?" he inquired. "I beg your pardon, but Mr. Gatsby would like to speak to you alone."

"With me?" she exclaimed in surprise.

"Yes, madame."

She got up slowly, raising her eyebrows at me in astonishment, and followed the butler toward the house. I noticed that she wore her evening-dress, all her dresses, like sports clothes—there was a jauntiness about her movements as if she had first learned to walk upon golf courses on clean, crisp mornings.

I was alone and it was almost two. For some time confused and intriguing sounds had issued from a long, many-windowed room which overhung the terrace. Eluding Jordan's undergraduate, who was now engaged in an obstetrical conversation with two chorus girls, and who implored me to join him, I went inside.

The large room was full of people. One of the girls in yellow was playing the piano, and beside her stood a tall, red-haired young lady from a famous chorus, engaged in song. She had drunk a quantity of champagne, and during the course of her song she had decided, ineptly, that everything was very, very sad—she was not only singing, she was weeping too. Whenever there was a pause in the song she filled it with gasping, broken sobs, and then took up the lyric again in a quavering soprano. The tears coursed down her cheeks—not freely, however, for when they came into contact with her heavily beaded eyelashes they assumed an inky color, and pursued the rest of their way in slow black rivulets. A humorous suggestion was made that she sing the notes on her face, whereupon she threw up her hands, sank into a chair, and went off into a deep vinous sleep. [51/52]

"She had a fight with a man who says he's her husband," explained a girl at my elbow.

I looked around. Most of the remaining women were now having fights with men said to be their husbands. Even Jordan's party, the quartet from East Egg, were rent asunder by dissension. One of the men was talking with curious intensity to a young actress, and his wife, after attempting to laugh at the situation in a dignified and indifferent way, broke down entirely and resorted to flank attacks—at intervals she appeared suddenly at his side like an angry diamond, and hissed: "You promised!" into his ear.

The reluctance to go home was not confined to wayward men. The hall was at present occupied by two deplorably sober men and their highly indignant wives.

The wives were sympathizing with each other in slightly raised voices.

"Whenever he sees I'm having a good time he wants to go home."

"Never heard anything so selfish in my life."

"We're always the first ones to leave."

"So are we."

"Well, we're almost the last tonight," said one of the men sheepishly. "The orchestra left half an hour ago."

In spite of this wives' agreement that such malevolence was beyond credibility, the dispute ended in a short struggle, and both wives were lifted, kicking, into the night.

As I waited for my hat in the hall the door of the library opened and Jordan Baker and Gatsby came out together. He was saying some last word to her, but the eagerness in his manner tightened abruptly into formal- [52/53] ity as several people approached him to say good-by.

Jordan's party were calling impatiently to her from the porch, but she lingered for a moment to shake hands.

"I've just heard the most amazing thing," she whispered. "How long were we in there?"

"Why, about an hour."

"It was . . . simply amazing," she repeated abstractedly. "But I swore I wouldn't tell it and here I am tantalizing you." She yawned gracefully in my face. "Please come and see me. . . . Phone book. . . . Under the name of Mrs. Sigourney Howard. . . . My aunt. . . ." She was hurrying off as she talked—her brown hand waved a jaunty salute as she melted into her party at the door.

Rather ashamed that on my first appearance I had stayed so late, I joined the last of Gatsby's guests, who were clustered around him. I wanted to explain that I'd hunted for him early in the evening and to apologize for not having known him in the garden.

"Don't mention it," he enjoined me eagerly. "Don't give it another thought, old sport." The familiar expression held no more familiarity than the hand which reassuringly brushed my shoulder. "And don't forget we're going up in the hydroplane tomorrow morning, at nine o'clock."

Then the butler, behind his shoulder:

"Philadelphia wants you on the 'phone, sir."

"All right, in a minute. Tell them I'll be right there. . . . Good night."

"Good night."

"Good night." He smiled—and suddenly there [53/54] seemed to be a pleasant significance in having been among the last to go, as if he had desired it all the time. "Good night, old sport. . . . Good night."

But as I walked down the steps I saw that the evening was not quite over. Fifty feet from the door a dozen headlights illuminated a bizarre and tumultuous scene. In the ditch beside the road, right side up, but violently shorn of one wheel, rested a new coupé which had left Gatsby's drive not two minutes before. The sharp jut of a wall accounted for the detachment of the wheel, which was now getting considerable attention from half a dozen curious chauffeurs. However, as they had left their cars blocking the road, a harsh, discordant din from those in the rear had been audible for some time, and added to the already violent confusion of the scene.

A man in a long duster had dismounted from the wreck and now stood in the middle of the road, looking from the car to the tire and from the tire to the observers in a pleasant, puzzled way.

"See!" he explained. "It went in the ditch."

The fact was infinitely astonishing to him, and I recognized first the unusual quality of wonder, and then the man—it was the late patron of Gatsby's library.

"How'd it happen?"

He shrugged his shoulders.

"I know nothing whatever about mechanics," he said decisively.

"But how did it happen? Did you run into the wall?"

"Don't ask me," said Owl Eyes, washing his hands of the whole matter. "I know very little about driving—next to nothing. It happened, and that's all I know." [54/55]

"Well, if you're a poor driver you oughtn't to try driving at night."

"But I wasn't even trying," he explained indignantly, "I wasn't even trying."

An awed hush fell upon the bystanders.

"Do you want to commit suicide?"

"You're lucky it was just a wheel! A bad driver and not even *try*ing!"

"You don't understand," explained the criminal. "I wasn't driving. There's another man in the car."

The shock that followed this declaration found voice in a sustained "Ah-h-h!" as the door of the coupé swung slowly open. The crowd—it was now a crowd—stepped back involuntarily, and when the door had opened wide there was a ghostly pause. Then, very gradually, part by part, a pale, dangling individual stepped out of the wreck, pawing tentatively at the ground with a large uncertain dancing shoe.

Blinded by the glare of the headlights and confused by the incessant groaning of the horns, the apparition stood swaying for a moment before he perceived the man in the duster.

"Wha's matter?" he inquired calmly. "Did we run outa gas?"

"Look!"

Half a dozen fingers pointed at the amputated wheel—he stared at it for a moment, and then looked upward as though he suspected that it had dropped from the sky.

"It came off," some one explained.

He nodded.

"At first I din' notice we'd stopped." [55/56]

A pause. Then, taking a long breath and straightening his shoulders, he remarked in a determined voice:

"Wonder'ff tell me where there's a gas'line station?"

At least a dozen men, some of them a

little better off than he was, explained to him that wheel and car were no longer joined by any physical bond.

"Back out," he suggested after a moment. "Put her in reverse."

"But the *wheel's* off!"

He hesitated.

"No harm in trying," he said.

The caterwauling horns had reached a crescendo and I turned away and cut across the lawn toward home. I glanced back once. A wafer of a moon was shining over Gatsby's house, making the night fine as before, and surviving the laughter and the sound of his still glowing garden. A sudden emptiness seemed to flow now from the windows and the great doors, endowing with complete isolation the figure of the host, who stood on the porch, his hand up in a formal gesture of farewell.

Reading over what I have written so far, I see I have given the impression that the events of three nights several weeks apart were all that absorbed me. On the contrary, they were merely casual events in a crowded summer, and, until much later, they absorbed me infinitely less than my personal affairs.

Most of the time I worked. In the early morning the sun threw my shadow westward as I hurried down the white chasms of lower New York to the Probity Trust. I knew the other clerks and young bond-salesmen by their first names, and lunched with them in dark, [56/57] crowded restaurants on little pig sausages and mashed potatoes and coffee. I even had a short affair with a girl who lived in Jersey City and worked in the accounting department, but her brother began throwing mean looks in my direction, so when she went on her vacation in July I let it blow quietly away.

I took dinner usually at the Yale Club —for some reason it was the gloomiest event of my day—and then I went upstairs to the library and studied investments and securities for a conscientious hour. There were generally a few rioters around, but they never came into the library, so it was a good place to work. After that, if the night was mellow, I strolled down Madison Avenue past the old Murray Hill Hotel, and over 33d Street to the Pennsylvania Station.

I began to like New York, the racy, adventurous feel of it at night, and the satisfaction that the constant flicker of men and women and machines gives to the restless eye. I liked to walk up Fifth Avenue and pick out romantic women from the crowd and imagine that in a few minutes I was going to enter into their lives, and no one would ever know or disapprove. Sometimes, in my mind, I followed them to their apartments on the corners of hidden streets, and they turned and smiled back at me before they faded through a door into warm darkness. At the enchanted metropolitan twilight I felt a haunting loneliness sometimes, and felt it in others—poor young clerks who loitered in front of windows waiting until it was time for a solitary restaurant dinner—young clerks in the dusk, wasting the most poignant moments of night and life.

Again at eight o'clock, when the dark lanes of the Forties were lined five deep with throbbing taxicabs, [57/58] for the theater district, I felt a sinking in my heart. Forms leaned together in the taxis as they waited, and voices sang, and there was laughter from unheard jokes, and lighted cigarettes outlined unintelligible gestures inside. Imagining that I, too, was hurrying toward gayety and sharing their intimate excitement, I wished them well.

For a while I lost sight of Jordan Baker, and then in midsummer I found her again. At first I was flattered to go places with her, because she was a golf champion, and everyone knew her name. Then it was something more. I wasn't actually in love, but I felt a sort of tender curiosity. The bored haughty face that she turned to the world concealed something—most affectations conceal something eventually, even though they don't in the beginning—

and one day I found what it was. When we were on a house-party together up in Warwick, she left a borrowed car out in the rain with the top down, and then lied about it—and suddenly I remembered the story about her that had eluded me that night at Daisy's. At her first big golf tournament there was a row that nearly reached the newspapers—a suggestion that she had moved her ball from a bad lie in the semi-final round. The thing approached the proportions of a scandal—then died away. A caddy retracted his statement, and the only other witness admitted that he might have been mistaken. The incident and the name had remained together in my mind.

Jordan Baker instinctively avoided clever, shrewd men, and now I saw that this was because she felt safer on a plane where any divergence from a code would be thought impossible. She was incurably dishonest. She wasn't able to endure being at a disadvantage and, [58/59] given this unwillingness, I suppose she had begun dealing in subterfuges when she was very young in order to keep that cool, insolent smile turned to the world and yet satisfy the demands of her hard, jaunty body.

It made no difference to me. Dishonesty in a woman is a thing you never blame deeply—I was casually sorry, and then I forgot. It was on that same house-party that we had a curious conversation about driving a car. It started because she passed so close to some workman that our fender flicked a button on one man's coat.

"You're a rotten driver," I protested. "Either you ought to be more careful, or you oughtn't to drive at all."

"I am careful."

"No, you're not."

"Well, other people are," she said lightly.

"What's that got to do with it?"

"They'll keep out of my way," she insisted. "It takes two to make an accident."

"Suppose you met somebody just as careless as yourself."

"I hope I never will," she answered. "I hate careless people. That's why I like you."

Her gray, sun-strained eyes stared straight ahead, but she had deliberately shifted our relations, and for a moment I thought I loved her. But I am slow-thinking and full of interior rules that act as brakes on my desires, and I knew that first I had to get myself definitely out of that tangle back home. I'd been writing letters once a week and signing them: "Love, Nick," and all I could think of was how, when that certain girl played tennis, a faint mustache of perspiration appeared on her [59/60] upper lip. Nevertheless there was a vague understanding that had to be tactfully broken off before I was free.

Every one suspects himself of at least one of the cardinal virtues, and this is mine: I am one of the few honest people that I have ever known. [60/61]

CHAPTER IV

On Sunday morning while church bells rang in the villages alongshore, the world and its mistress returned to Gatsby's house and twinkled hilariously on his lawn.

"He's a bootlegger," said the young ladies, moving somewhere between his cocktails and his flowers. "One time he killed a man who had found out that he was nephew to Von Hindenburg and second cousin to the devil. Reach me a rose, honey, and pour me a last drop into that there crystal glass."

Once I wrote down on the empty spaces of a time-table the names of those who came to Gatsby's house that summer. It is an old timetable now, disintegrating at its folds, and headed "This schedule in effect July 5th, 1922." But I can still read the gray names, and they will give you a better impression than my generalities of those who accepted Gatsby's hospitality and paid him the subtle tribute of knowing nothing whatever about him.

From East Egg, then, came the Chester

Beckers and the Leeches, and a man named Bunsen, whom I knew at Yale, and Doctor Webster Civet, who was drowned last summer up in Maine. And the Hornbeams and the Willie Voltaires, and a whole clan named Blackbuck, who always gathered in a corner and flipped up their noses like goats at whosoever came near. And the Ismays and the Chrysties (or rather Hubert Auerbach and Mr. Chrystie's wife), and Edgar Beaver, whose [61/62] hair, they say, turned cotton-white one winter afternoon for no good reason at all.

Clarence Endive was from East Egg, as I remember. He came only once, in white knickerbockers, and had a fight with a bum named Etty in the garden. From farther out on the Island came the Cheadles and the O. R. P. Schraeders, and the Stonewall Jackson Abrams of Georgia, and the Fishguards and the Ripley Snells. Snell was there three days before he went to the penitentiary, so drunk out on the gravel drive that Mrs. Ulysses Swett's automobile ran over his right hand. The Dancies came, too, and S. B. Whitebait, who was well over sixty, and Maurice A. Flink, and the Hammerheads, and Beluga the tobacco importer, and Beluga's girls.

From West Egg came the Poles and the Mulreadys and Cecil Roebuck and Cecil Schoen and Gulick the State senator and Newton Orchid, who controlled Films Par Excellence, and Eckhaust and Clyde Cohen and Don S. Schwartze (the son) and Arthur McCarty, all connected with the movies in one way or another. And the Catlips and the Bembergs and G. Earl Muldoon, brother to that Muldoon who afterward strangled his wife. Da Fontano the promoter came there, and Ed Legros and James B. ("Rot-Gut") Ferret and the De Jongs and Ernest Lilly—they came to gamble, and when Ferret wandered into the garden it meant he was cleaned out and Associated Traction would have to fluctuate profitably next day.

A man named Klipspringer was there so often and so long that he became known as "the boarder"—I doubt if he

had any other home. Of theatrical people there were Gus Waize and Horace O'Donavan and Lester [62/63] Meyer and George Duckweed and Francis Bull. Also from New York were the Chromes and the Backhyssons and the Dennickers and Russel Betty and the Corrigans and the Kellehers and the Dewars and the Scullys and S. W. Belcher and the Smirkes and the young Quinns, divorced now, and Henry L. Palmetto, who killed himself by jumping in front of a subway train in Times Square.

Benny McClenahan arrived always with four girls. They were never quite the same ones in physical person, but they were so identical one with another that it inevitably seemed they had been there before. I have forgotten their names—Jacqueline, I think, or else Consuela, or Gloria or Judy or June, and their last names were either the melodious names of flowers and months or the sterner ones of the great American capitalists whose cousins, if pressed, they would confess themselves to be.

In addition to all these I can remember that Faustina O'Brien came there at least once and the Baedeker girls and young Brewer, who had his nose shot off in the war, and Mr. Albrucksburger and Miss Haag, his fiancée, and Ardita Fitz-Peters and Mr. P. Jewett, once head of the American Legion, and Miss Claudia Hip, with a man reputed to be her chauffeur, and a prince of something, whom we called Duke, and whose name, if I ever knew it, I have forgotten.

All these people came to Gatsby's house in the summer.

At nine o'clock, one morning late in July, Gatsby's gorgeous car lurched up the rocky drive to my door and gave out a burst of melody from its three-noted horn. [63/64] It was the first time he had called on me, though I had gone to two of his parties, mounted in his hydroplane, and, at his urgent invitation, made frequent use of his beach.

"Good morning, old sport. You're having lunch with me today and I thought we'd ride up together."

He was balancing himself on the running board of his car with that resourcefulness of movement that is so peculiarly American—that comes, I suppose, with the absence of lifting work or rigid sitting in youth and, even more, with the formless grace of our nervous, sporadic games. This quality was continually breaking through his punctilious manner in the shape of restlessness. He was never quite still; there was always a tapping foot somewhere or the impatient opening and closing of a hand.

He saw me looking with admiration at his car.

"It's pretty, isn't it, old sport!" He jumped off to give me a better view. "Haven't you ever seen it before?"

I'd seen it. Everybody had seen it. It was a rich cream color, bright with nickel, swollen here and there in its monstrous length with triumphant hat-boxes and supper-boxes and tool-boxes, and terraced with a labyrinth of wind-shields that mirrored a dozen suns. Sitting down behind many layers of glass in a sort of green leather conservatory, we started to town.

I had talked with him perhaps half a dozen times in the past month and found, to my disappointment, that he had little to say. So my first impression, that he was a person of some undefined consequence, had gradually faded and he had become simply the proprietor of an elaborate roadhouse next door. [64/65]

And then came that disconcerting ride. We hadn't reached West Egg Village before Gatsby began leaving his elegant sentences unfinished and slapping himself indecisively on the knee of his caramel-colored suit.

"Look here, old sport," he broke out surprisingly, "what's your opinion of me, anyhow?"

A little overwhelmed, I began the generalized evasions which that question deserves.

"Well, I'm going to tell you something about my life," he interrupted. "I don't want you to get a wrong idea of me from all these stories you hear."

So he was aware of the bizarre accusations that flavored conversation in his halls.

"I'll tell you God's truth." His right hand suddenly ordered divine retribution to stand by. "I am the son of some wealthy people in the Middle West—all dead now. I was brought up in America but educated at Oxford, because all my ancestors have been educated there for many years. It is a family tradition."

He looked at me sideways—and I knew why Jordan Baker had believed he was lying. He hurried the phrase "educated at Oxford," or swallowed it, or choked on it, as though it had bothered him before. And with this doubt, his whole statement fell to pieces, and I wondered if there wasn't something a little sinister about him, after all.

"What part of the Middle West?" I inquired casually.

"San Francisco."

"I see."

"My family all died and I came into a good deal of money."

His voice was solemn, as if the memory of that sud- [65/66] den extinction of a clan still haunted him. For a moment I suspected that he was pulling my leg, but a glance at him convinced me otherwise.

"After that I lived like a young rajah in all the capitals of Europe—Paris, Venice, Rome—collecting jewels, chiefly rubies, hunting big game, painting a little, things for myself only, and trying to forget something very sad that had happened to me long ago."

With an effort I managed to restrain my incredulous laughter. The very phrases were worn so threadbare that they evoked no image except that of a turbaned "character" leaking sawdust at every pore as he pursued a tiger through the Bois de Boulogne.

"Then came the war, old sport. It was a great relief, and I tried very hard to die, but I seemed to bear an enchanted life. I accepted a commission as first lieutenant when it began. In the Argonne Forest I took two machine-gun detachments so far forward that there was a half mile gap on either side of us where the infantry couldn't advance. We stayed there two days and two nights, a hundred and thirty men with sixteen Lewis guns, and when the infantry came up at last they found the insignia of three German divisions among the piles of dead. I was promoted to be a major, and every Allied government gave me a decoration—even Montenegro, little Montenegro down on the Adriatic Sea!"

Little Montenegro! He lifted up the words and nodded at them—with his smile. The smile comprehended Montenegro's troubled history and sympathized with the brave struggles of the Montenegrin people. It appreciated fully the chain of national circumstances which had elicited this tribute from Montenegro's warm [66/67] little heart. My incredulity was submerged in fascination now; it was like skimming hastily through a dozen magazines.

He reached in his pocket, and a piece of metal, slung on a ribbon, fell into my palm.

"That's the one from Montenegro."

To my astonishment, the thing had an authentic look. "Orderi di Danilo," ran the circular legend, "Montenegro, Nicolas Rex."

"Turn it."

"Major Jay Gatsby," I read, "For Valour Extraordinary."

"Here's another thing I always carry. A souvenir of Oxford days. It was taken in Trinity Quad—the man on my left is now the Earl of Doncaster."

It was a photograph of half a dozen young men in blazers loafing in an archway through which were visible a host of spires. There was Gatsby, looking a little, not much, younger—with a cricket bat in his hand.

Then it was all true. I saw the skins of tigers flaming in his palace on the Grand Canal; I saw him opening a chest of rubies to ease, with their crimson-lighted depths, the gnawings of his broken heart.

"I'm going to make a big request of you today," he said, pocketing his souvenirs with satisfaction, "so I thought you ought to know something about me. I didn't want you to think I was just nobody. You see, I usually find myself among strangers because I drift here and there trying to forget the sad thing that happened to me." He hesitated. "You'll hear about it this afternoon." [67/68]

"At lunch?"

"No, this afternoon. I happened to find out that you're taking Miss Baker to tea."

"Do you mean you're in love with Miss Baker?"

"No, old sport, I'm not. But Miss Baker has kindly consented to speak to you about this matter."

I hadn't the faintest idea what "this matter" was, but I was more annoyed than interested. I hadn't asked Jordan to tea in order to discuss Mr. Jay Gatsby. I was sure the request would be something utterly fantastic, and for a moment I was sorry I'd ever set foot upon his overpopulated lawn.

He wouldn't say another word. His correctness grew on him as we neared the city. We passed Port Roosevelt, where there was a glimpse of red-belted ocean-going ships, and sped along a cobbled slum lined with the dark, undeserted saloons of the faded-gilt nineteen-hundreds. Then the valley of ashes opened out on both sides of us, and I had a glimpse of Mrs. Wilson straining at the garage pump with panting vitality as we went by.

With fenders spread like wings we scattered light through half Astoria—only half, for as we twisted among the pillars of the elevated I heard the familiar "jug-jug-*spat!*" of a motorcycle, and a frantic policeman rode alongside.

"All right, old sport," called Gatsby. We slowed down. Taking a white card from his wallet, he waved it before the man's eyes.

"Right you are," agreed the policeman,

tipping his cap. "Know you next time, Mr. Gatsby. Excuse *me!"*

"What was that?" I inquired. "The picture of Oxford?" [68/69]

"I was able to do the commissioner a favor once, and he sends me a Christmas card every year."

Over the great bridge, with the sunlight through the girders making a constant flicker upon the moving cars, with the city rising up across the river in white heaps and sugar lumps all built with a wish out of non-olfactory money. The city seen from the Queensboro Bridge is always the city seen for the first time, in its first wild promise of all the mystery and the beauty in the world.

A dead man passed us in a hearse heaped with blooms, followed by two carriages with drawn blinds, and by more cheerful carriages for friends. The friends looked out at us with the tragic eyes and short upper lips of southeastern Europe, and I was glad that the sight of Gatsby's splendid car was included in their somber holiday. As we crossed Blackwell's Island a limousine passed us, driven by a white chauffeur, in which sat three modish negroes, two bucks and a girl. I laughed aloud as the yolks of their eyeballs rolled toward us in haughty rivalry.

"Anything can happen now that we've slid over this bridge," I thought; "anything at all. . . ."

Even Gatsby could happen, without any particular wonder.

Roaring noon. In a well-fanned Forty-second Street cellar I met Gatsby for lunch. Blinking away the brightness of the street outside, my eyes picked him out obscurely in the anteroom, talking to another man.

"Mr. Carraway, this is my friend Mr. Wolfsheim."

A small, flat-nosed Jew raised his large head and regarded me with two fine growths of hair which [69/70] luxuriated in either nostril. After a moment I discovered his tiny eyes in the half-darkness.

"—So I took one look at him," said Mr. Wolfsheim, shaking my hand earnestly, "and what do you think I did?"

"What?" I inquired politely.

But evidently he was not addressing me, for he dropped my hand and covered Gatsby with his expressive nose.

"I handed the money to Katspaugh and I sid: 'All right, Katspaugh, don't pay him a penny till he shuts his mouth.' He shut it then and there."

Gatsby took an arm of each of us and moved forward into the restaurant, whereupon Mr. Wolfsheim swallowed a new sentence he was starting and lapsed into a somnambulatory abstraction.

"Highballs?" asked the head waiter.

"This is a nice restaurant here," said Mr. Wolfsheim, looking at the Presbyterian nymphs on the ceiling. "But I like across the street better!"

"Yes, highballs," agreed Gatsby, and then to Mr. Wolfsheim: "It's too hot over there."

"Hot and small—yes," said Mr. Wolfsheim, "but full of memories."

"What place is that?" I asked.

"The old Metropole."

"The old Metropole," brooded Mr. Wolfsheim gloomily. "Filled with faces dead and gone. Filled with friends gone now forever. I can't forget so long as I live the night they shot Rosy Rosenthal there. It was six of us at the table, and Rosy had eat and drunk a lot all evening. When it was almost morning the waiter came up to him [70/71] with a funny look and says somebody wants to speak to him outside. 'All right,' says Rosy, and begins to get up, and I pulled him down in his chair.

"'Let the bastards come in here if they want you, Rosy, but don't you, so help me, move outside this room.'

"It was four o'clock in the morning then, and if we'd of raised the blinds we'd of seen daylight."

"Did he go?" I asked innocently.

"Sure he went." Mr. Wolfsheim's nose flashed at me indignantly. "He turned around in the door and says: 'Don't let that waiter take away my coffee!' Then he went out on the sidewalk, and they shot him three times in his full belly and drove away."

"Four of them were electrocuted," I said, remembering.

"Five, with Becker." His nostrils turned to me in an interested way. "I understand you're looking for a business gonnegtion."

The juxtaposition of these two remarks was startling. Gatsby answered for me:

"Oh, no," he exclaimed, "this isn't the man."

"No?" Mr. Wolfsheim seemed disappointed.

"This is just a friend. I told you we'd talk about that some other time."

"I beg your pardon," said Mr. Wolfsheim, "I had a wrong man."

A succulent hash arrived, and Mr. Wolfsheim, forgetting the more sentimental atmosphere of the old Metropole, began to eat with ferocious delicacy. His eyes, meanwhile, roved very slowly all around the room—he completed the arc by turning to inspect the people [71/72] directly behind. I think that, except for my presence, he would have taken one short glance beneath our own table.

"Look here, old sport," said Gatsby, leaning toward me, "I'm afraid I made you a little angry this morning in the car."

There was the smile again, but this time I held out against it.

"I don't like mysteries," I answered, "and I don't understand why you won't come out frankly and tell me what you want. Why has it all got to come through Miss Baker?"

"Oh, it's nothing underhand," he assured me. "Miss Baker's a great sportswoman, you know, and she'd never do anything that wasn't all right."

Suddenly he looked at his watch, jumped up, and hurried from the room, leaving me with Mr. Wolfsheim at the table.

"He has to telephone," said Mr. Wolfsheim, following him with his eyes. "Fine fellow, isn't he? Handsome to look at and a perfect gentleman."

"Yes."

"He's an Oggsford man."

"Oh!"

"He went to Oggsford College in England. You know Oggsford College?"

"I've heard of it."

"It's one of the most famous colleges in the world."

"Have you known Gatsby for a long time?" I inquired.

"Several years," he answered in a gratified way. "I made the pleasure of his acquaintance just after the war. But I knew I had discovered a man of fine breed-[72/73]ing after I talked with him an hour. I said to myself: 'There's the kind of man you'd like to take home and introduce to your mother and sister.'" He paused. "I see you're looking at my cuff buttons."

I hadn't been looking at them, but I did now. They were composed of oddly familiar pieces of ivory.

"Finest specimens of human molars," he informed me.

"Well!" I inspected them. "That's a very interesting idea."

"Yeah." He flipped his sleeves up under his coat. "Yeah, Gatsby's very careful about women. He would never so much as look at a friend's wife."

When the subject of this instinctive trust returned to the table and sat down Mr. Wolfsheim drank his coffee with a jerk and got to his feet.

"I have enjoyed my lunch," he said, "and I'm going to run off from you two young men before I outstay my welcome."

"Don't hurry, Meyer," said Gatsby, without enthusiasm. Mr. Wolfsheim raised his hand in a sort of benediction.

"You're very polite, but I belong to another generation," he announced solemnly. "You sit here and discuss your sports and your young ladies and your—" He supplied an imaginary noun with another wave of his hand. "As for me, I am fifty years old, and I won't impose myself on you any longer."

As he shook hands and turned away his tragic nose was trembling. I wondered if I had said anything to offend him.

"He becomes very sentimental sometimes," explained Gatsby. "This is one of his sentimental days. He's quite [73/74] a character around New York—a denizen of Broadway."

"Who is he, anyhow, an actor?"

"No."

"A dentist?"

"Meyer Wolfsheim? No, he's a gambler." Gatsby hesitated, then added coolly: "He's the man who fixed the World's Series back in 1919."

"Fixed the World's Series?" I repeated.

The idea staggered me. I remembered, of course, that the World's Series had been fixed in 1919, but if I had thought of it at all I would have thought of it as a thing that merely *happened,* the end of some inevitable chain. It never occurred to me that one man could start to play with the faith of fifty million people—with the single-mindedness of a burglar blowing a safe.

"How did he happen to do that?" I asked after a minute.

"He just saw the opportunity."

"Why isn't he in jail?"

"They can't get him, old sport. He's a smart man."

I insisted on paying the check. As the waiter brought my change I caught sight of Tom Buchanan across the crowded room.

"Come along with me for a minute," I said; "I've got to say hello to some one."

When he saw us Tom jumped up and took half a dozen steps in our direction.

"Where've you been?" he demanded eagerly. "Daisy's furious because you haven't called up."

"This is Mr. Gatsby, Mr. Buchanan." [74/75]

They shook hands briefly, and a strained, unfamiliar look of embarrassment came over Gatsby's face.

"How've you been, anyhow?" demanded Tom of me. "How'd you happen to come up this far to eat?"

"I've been having lunch with Mr. Gatsby."

I turned toward Mr. Gatsby, but he was no longer there.

One October day in nineteen-seventeen——

(said Jordan Baker that afternoon, sitting up very straight on a straight chair in the tea-garden at the Plaza Hotel)

—I was walking along from one place to another, half on the sidewalks and half on the lawns. I was happier on the lawns because I had on shoes from England with rubber nobs on the soles that bit into the soft ground. I had on a new plaid skirt also that blew a little in the wind, and whenever this happened the red, white, and blue banners in front of all the houses stretched out stiff and said *tut-tut-tut-tut,* in a disapproving way.

The largest of the banners and the largest of the lawns belonged to Daisy Fay's house. She was just eighteen, two years older than me, and by far the most popular of all the young girls in Louisville. She dressed in white, and had a little white roadster, and all day long the telephone rang in her house and excited young officers from Camp Taylor demanded the privilege of monopolizing her that night. "Anyways, for an hour!"

When I came opposite her house that morning her white roadster was beside the curb, and she was sitting [75/76] in it with a lieutenant I had never seen before. They were so engrossed in each other that she didn't see me until I was five feet away.

"Hello, Jordan," she called unexpectedly. "Please come here."

I was flattered that she wanted to speak to me, because of all the older girls I admired her most. She asked me if I was going to the Red Cross and make bandages. I was. Well, then, would I tell them that she couldn't come that day? The officer looked at Daisy while she was speaking, in a way that every young girl wants to be looked at some time, and because it seemed romantic to me I have remembered the incident ever since. His name was Jay Gatsby, and I didn't lay eyes on him again for over four years—even after I'd met him on Long Island I didn't realize it was the same man.

That was nineteen-seventeen. By the next year I had a few beaux myself, and I began to play in tournaments, so I didn't see Daisy very often. She went with a slightly older crowd—when she went with anyone at all. Wild rumors were circulating about her—how her mother had found her packing her bag one winter night to go to New York and say good-by to a soldier who was going overseas. She was effectually prevented, but she wasn't on speaking terms with her family for several weeks. After that she didn't play around with the soldiers any more, but only with a few flat-footed, short-sighted young men in town, who couldn't get into the army at all.

By the next autumn she was gay again, gay as ever. She had a début after the Armistice, and in February she was presumably engaged to a man from New [76/77] Orleans. In June she married Tom Buchanan of Chicago, with more pomp and circumstance than Louisville ever knew before. He came down with a hundred people in four private cars, and hired a whole floor of the Muhlbach Hotel, and the day before the wedding he gave her a string of pearls valued at three hundred and fifty thousand dollars.

I was a bridesmaid. I came into her room half an hour before the bridal dinner, and found her lying on her bed as lovely as the June night in her flowered dress—and as drunk as a monkey. She had a bottle of Sauterne in one hand and a letter in the other.

" 'Gratulate me," she muttered. "Never had a drink before, but oh how I do enjoy it."

"What's the matter, Daisy?"

I was scared, I can tell you; I'd never seen a girl like that before.

"Here, deares'." She groped around in a waste-basket she had with her on the bed and pulled out the string of pearls. "Take 'em down-stairs and give 'em back

to whoever they belong to. Tell 'em all Daisy's change' her mine. Say: 'Daisy's change' her mine!' "

She began to cry—she cried and cried. I rushed out and found her mother's maid, and we locked the door and got her into a cold bath. She wouldn't let go of the letter. She took it into the tub with her and squeezed it up into a wet ball, and only let me leave it in the soap-dish when she saw that it was coming to pieces like snow.

But she didn't say another word. We gave her spirits of ammonia and put ice on her forehead and hooked her back into her dress, and half an hour later, when we walked out of the room, the pearls were around [77/78] her neck and the incident was over. Next day at five o'clock she married Tom Buchanan without so much as a shiver, and started off on a three months' trip to the South Seas.

I saw them in Santa Barbara when they came back, and I thought I'd never seen a girl so mad about her husband. If he left the room for a minute she'd look around uneasily, and say: "Where's Tom gone?" and wear the most abstracted expression until she saw him coming in the door. She used to sit on the sand with his head in her lap by the hour, rubbing her fingers over his eyes and looking at him with unfathomable delight. It was touching to see them together—it made you laugh in a hushed, fascinated way. That was in August. A week after I left Santa Barbara Tom ran into a wagon on the Ventura road one night, and ripped a front wheel off his car. The girl who was with him got into the papers, too, because her arm was broken—she was one of the chambermaids in the Santa Barbara Hotel.

The next April Daisy had her little girl, and they went to France for a year. I saw them one spring in Cannes, and later in Deauville, and then they came back to Chicago to settle down. Daisy was popular in Chicago, as you know. They moved with a fast crowd, all of them young and rich and wild, but she came out with an absolutely perfect reputation. Perhaps because she doesn't drink. It's a great advantage not to drink among hard-drinking people. You can hold your tongue, and, moreover, you can time any little irregularity of your own so that everybody else is so blind that they don't see or care. Perhaps Daisy never [**78/79**] went in for amour at all—and yet there's something in that voice of hers. . . .

Well, about six weeks ago, she heard the name Gatsby for the first time in years. It was when I asked you—do you remember?—if you knew Gatsby in West Egg. After you had gone home she came into my room and woke me up, and said: "What Gatsby?" and when I described him—I was half asleep—she said in the strangest voice that it must be the man she used to know. It wasn't until then that I connected this Gatsby with the officer in her white car.

When Jordan Baker had finished telling all this we had left the Plaza for half an hour and were driving in a victoria through Central Park. The sun had gone down behind the tall apartments of the movie stars in the West Fifties, and the clear voices of little girls, already gathered like crickets on the grass, rose through the hot twilight:

> *"I'm the Sheik of Araby.*
> *Your love belongs to me.*
> *At night when you're asleep*
> *Into your tent I'll creep——"*

It was a strange coincidence," I said.
"But it wasn't a coincidence at all."
"Why not?"
"Gatsby bought that house so that Daisy would be just across the bay."

Then it had not been merely the stars which he had aspired on that June night. He came alive to me, delivered suddenly from the womb of his purposeless splendor. [**79/80**]

"He wants to know," continued Jordan, "if you'll invite Daisy to your house some afternoon and then let him come over."

The modesty of the demand shook me. He had waited five years and bought a mansion where he dispensed starlight to casual moths—so .that he could "come over" some afternoon to a stranger's garden.

"Did I have to know all this before he could ask such a little thing?"

"He's afraid, he's waited so long. He thought you might be offended. You see, he's a regular tough underneath it all."

Something worried me.

"Why didn't he ask you to arrange a meeting?"

"He wants her to see his house," she explained. "And your house is right next door."

"Oh!"

"I think he half expected her to wander into one of his parties, some night," went on Jordan, "but she never did. Then he began asking people casually if they knew her, and I was the first one he found. It was that night he sent for me at his dance, and you should have heard the elaborate way he worked up to it. Of course, I immediately suggested a luncheon in New York—and I thought he'd go mad:

" 'I don't want to do anything out of the way!' he kept saying. 'I want to see her right next door.'

"When I said you were a particular friend of Tom's, he started to abandon the whole idea. He doesn't know very much about Tom, though he says he's read a Chicago paper for years just on the chance of catching a glimpse of Daisy's name."

It was dark now, and as we dipped under a little [**80/81**]bridge I put my arm around Jordan's golden shoulder and drew her toward me and asked her to dinner. Suddenly I wasn't thinking of Daisy and Gatsby any more, but of this clean, hard, limited person, who dealt in universal skepticism, and who leaned back jauntily just within the circle of my arm. A phrase began to beat in my ears with a sort of heady excitement: "There are only the pursued, the pursuing, the busy, and the tired."

"And Daisy ought to have something in her life," murmured Jordan to me.

"Does she want to see Gatsby?"

"She's not to know about it. Gatsby doesn't want her to know. You're just supposed to invite her to tea."

We passed a barrier of dark trees, and then the façade of Fifty-ninth Street, a block of delicate pale light, beamed down into the park. Unlike Gatsby and Tom Buchanan, I had no girl whose disembodied face floated along the dark cornices and blinding signs, and so I drew up the girl beside me, tightening my arms. Her wan, scornful mouth smiled, and so I drew her up again closer, this time to my face. [81/82]

CHAPTER V

When I came home to West Egg that night I was afraid for a moment that my house was on fire. Two o'clock and the whole corner of the peninsula was blazing with light, which fell unreal on the shrubbery and made thin elongating glints upon the roadside wires. Turning a corner, I saw that it was Gatsby's house, lit from tower to cellar.

At first I thought it was another party, a wild rout that had resolved itself into "hide-and-go-seek" or "sardines-in-the-box" with all the house thrown open to the game. But there wasn't a sound. Only wind in the trees, which blew the wires and made the lights go off and on again as if the house had winked into the darkness. As my taxi groaned away I saw Gatsby walking toward me across his lawn.

"Your place looks like the World's Fair," I said.

"Does it?" He turned his eyes toward it absently. "I have been glancing into some of the rooms. Let's go to Coney Island, old sport. In my car."

"It's too late."

"Well, suppose we take a plunge in the swimming-pool? I haven't made use of it all summer."

"I've got to go to bed."

"All right."

He waited, looking at me with suppressed eagerness.

"I talked with Miss Baker," I said after a moment. "I'm going to call up Daisy tomorrow and invite her over here to tea." [82/83]

"Oh, that's all right," he said carelessly. "I don't want to put you to any trouble."

"What day would suit you?"

"What day would suit *you?*" he corrected me quickly. "I don't want to put you to any trouble, you see."

"How about the day after tomorrow?"

He considered for a moment. Then, with reluctance:

"I want to get the grass cut," he said.

We both looked at the grass—there was a sharp line where my ragged lawn ended and the darker, well-kept expanse of his began. I suspected that he meant my grass.

"There's another little thing," he said uncertainly, and hesitated.

"Would you rather put it off for a few days?" I asked.

"Oh, it isn't about that. At least—" He fumbled .with a series of beginnings "Why, I thought—why, look here, old sport, you don't make much money, do you?"

"Not very much."

This seemed to reassure him and he continued more confidently.

"I thought you didn't, if you'll pardon my—you see, I carry on a little business on the side, a sort of side line, you understand. And I thought that if you don't make very much—You're selling bonds, aren't you, old sport?"

"Trying to."

"Well, this would interest you. It wouldn't take up much of your time and you might pick up a nice bit of money.

It happens to be a rather confidential sort of thing."

I realize now that under different circumstances that conversation might have been one of the crises of my life. But, because the offer was obviously and tactlessly [83/84] for a service to be rendered, I had no choice except to cut him off there.

"I've got my hands full," I said. "I'm much obliged but I couldn't take on any more work."

"You wouldn't have to do any business with Wolfsheim." Evidently he thought that I was shying away from the "gonnegtion" mentioned at lunch, but I assured him he was wrong. He waited a moment longer, hoping I'd begin a conversation, but I was too absorbed to be responsive, so he went unwillingly home.

The evening had made me light-headed and happy; I think I walked into a deep sleep as I entered my front door. So I don't know whether or not Gatsby went to Coney Island, or for how many hours he "glanced into rooms" while his house blazed gaudily on. I called up Daisy from the office next morning, and invited her to come to tea.

"Don't bring Tom," I warned her.

"What?"

"Don't bring Tom."

"Who is 'Tom'?" she asked innocently.

The day agreed upon was pouring rain. At eleven o'clock a man in a raincoat, dragging a lawn-mower, tapped at my front door and said that Mr. Gatsby had sent him over to cut my grass. This reminded me that I had forgotten to tell my Finn to come back, so I drove into West Egg Village to search for her among soggy whitewashed alleys and to buy some cups and lemons and flowers.

The flowers were unnecessary, for at two o'clock a greenhouse arrived from Gatsby's, with innumerable receptacles to contain it. An hour later the front door opened nervously, and Gatsby, in a white flannel suit, [84/85] silver shirt, and gold-colored tie, hurried in. He was pale, and there were dark signs of sleeplessness beneath his eyes.

"Is everything all right?" he asked immediately.

"The grass looks fine, if that's what you mean."

"What grass?" he inquired blankly. "Oh, the grass in the yard." He looked out the window at it, but, judging from his expression, I don't believe he saw a thing.

"Looks very good," he remarked vaguely. "One of the papers said they thought the rain would stop about four. I think it was *The Journal.* Have you got everything you need in the shape of—of tea?"

I took him into the pantry, where he looked a little reproachfully at the Finn. Together we scrutinized the twelve lemon cakes from the delicatessen shop.

"Will they do?" I asked.

"Of course, of course! They're fine!" and he added hollowly, ". . . old sport."

The rain cooled about half-past three to a damp mist, through which occasional thin drops swam like dew. Gatsby looked with vacant eyes through a copy of Clay's *Economics,* starting at the Finnish tread that shook the kitchen floor, and peering toward the bleared windows from time to time as if a series of invisible but alarming happenings were taking place outside. Finally he got up and informed me, in an uncertain voice, that he was going home.

"Why's that?"

"Nobody's coming to tea. It's too late!" He looked at his watch as if there was some pressing demand on his time elsewhere. "I can't wait all day."

"Don't be silly; it's just two minutes to four." [85/86]

He sat down miserably, as if I had pushed him, and simultaneously there was the sound of a motor turning into my lane. We both jumped up, and, a little harrowed myself, I went out into the yard.

Under the dripping bare lilac-trees a large open car was coming up the drive.

It stopped. Daisy's face, tipped sideways beneath a three-cornered lavender hat, looked out at me with a bright ecstatic smile.

"Is this absolutely where you live, my dearest one?"

The exhilarating ripple of her voice was a wild tonic in the rain. I had to follow the sound of it for a moment, up and down, with my ear alone, before any words came through. A damp streak of hair lay like a dash of blue paint across her cheek, and her hand was wet with glistening drops as I took it to help her from the car.

"Are you in love with me," she said low in my ear, "or why did I have to come alone?"

"That's the secret of Castle Rackrent. Tell your chauffeur to go far away and spend an hour."

"Come back in an hour, Ferdie." Then in a grave murmur: "His name is Ferdie."

"Does the gasoline affect his nose?"

"I don't think so," she innocently. "Why?"

We went in. To my overwhelming surprise the living-room was deserted.

"Well, that's funny," I exclaimed.

"What's funny?"

She turned her head as there was a light dignified knocking at the front door. I went out and opened it. Gatsby, pale as death, with his hands plunged like weights in his coat pockets, was standing in a puddle of water glaring tragically into my eyes. [86/87]

With his hands still in his coat pockets he stalked by me into the hall, turned sharply as if he were on a wire, and disappeared into the living-room. It wasn't a bit funny. Aware of the loud beating of my own heart I pulled the door to against the increasing rain.

For half a minute there wasn't a sound. Then from the living-room I heard a sort of choking murmur and part of a laugh, followed by Daisy's voice on a clear artificial note:

"I certainly am awfully glad to see you again."

A pause; it endured horribly. I had nothing to do in the hall, so I went into the room.

Gatsby, his hands still in his pockets, was reclining against the mantelpiece in a strained counterfeit of perfect ease, even of boredom. His head leaned back so far that it rested against the face of a defunct mantelpiece clock, and from this position his distraught eyes stared down at Daisy, who was sitting, frightened but graceful, on the edge of a stiff chair.

"We've met before," muttered Gatsby. His eyes glanced momentarily at me, and his lips parted with an abortive attempt at a laugh. Luckily the clock took this moment to tilt dangerously at the pressure of his head, whereupon he turned and caught it with trembling fingers and set it back in place. Then he sat down, rigidly, his elbow on the arm of the sofa and his chin in his hand.

"I'm sorry about the clock," he said.

My own face had now assumed a deep tropical burn. I couldn't muster up a single commonplace out of the thousand in my head.

"It's an old clock," I told them idiotically. [87/88]

I think we all believed for a moment that it had smashed in pieces on the floor.

"We haven't met for many years," said Daisy, her voice as matter-of-fact as it could ever be.

"Five years next November."

The automatic quality of Gatsby's answer set us all back at least another minute. I had them both on their feet with the desperate suggestion that they help me make tea in the kitchen when the demoniac Finn brought it in on a tray.

Amid the welcome confusion of cups and cakes a certain physical decency established itself. Gatsby got himself into a shadow and, while Daisy and I talked, looked conscientiously from one to the other of us with tense, unhappy eyes.

However, as calmness wasn't an end in itself, I made an excuse at the first possible moment, and got to my feet.

"Where are you going?" demanded Gatsby in immediate alarm.

"I'll be back."

"I've got to speak to you about something before you go."

He followed me wildly into the kitchen, closed the door, and whispered: "Oh, God!" in a miserable way.

"What's the matter?"

"This is a terrible mistake," he said, shaking his head from side to side, "a terrible, terrible mistake."

"You're just embarrassed, that's all," and luckily I added: "Daisy's embarrassed too."

"She's embarrassed?" he repeated incredulously.

"Just as much as you are."

"Don't talk so loud."

"You're acting like a little boy," I broke out im- [88/89] patiently. "Not only that, but you're rude. Daisy's sitting in there all alone."

He raised his hand to stop my words, looked at me with unforgettable reproach, and, opening the door cautiously, went back into the other room.

I walked out the back way—just as Gatsby had when he had made his nervous circuit of the house half an hour before—and ran for a huge black knotted tree, whose massed leaves made a fabric against the rain. Once more it was pouring, and my irregular lawn, well-shaved by Gatsby's gardener, abounded in small muddy swamps and prehistoric marshes. There was nothing to look at from under the tree except Gatsby's enormous house, so I stared at it, like Kant at his church steeple, for half an hour. A brewer had built it early in the "period" craze, a decade before, and there was a story that he'd agreed to pay five years' taxes on all the neighboring cottages if the owners would have their roofs thatched with straw. Perhaps their refusal took the heart

out of his plan to Found a Family—he went into an immediate decline. His children sold his house with the black wreath still on the door. Americans, while occasionally willing to be serfs, have always been obstinate about being peasantry.

After half an hour, the sun shone again, and the grocer's automobile rounded Gatsby's drive with the raw material for his servants' dinner—I felt sure he wouldn't eat a spoonful. A maid began opening the upper windows of his house, appeared momentarily in each, and, leaning from a large central bay, spat meditatively into the garden. It was time I went back. While the rain continued it had seemed like the mur- [89/90] mur of their voices, rising and swelling a little now and then with gusts of emotion. But in the new silence I felt that silence had fallen within the house too.

I went in—after making every possible noise in the kitchen, short of pushing over the stove—but I don't believe they heard a sound. They were sitting at either end of the couch, looking at each other as if some question had been asked, or was in the air, and every vestige of embarrassment was gone. Daisy's face was smeared with tears, and when I came in she jumped up and began wiping at it with her handkerchief before a mirror. But there was a change in Gatsby that was simply confounding. He literally glowed; without a word or a gesture of exultation a new well-being radiated from him and filled the little room.

"Oh, hello, old sport," he said, as if he hadn't seen me for years. I thought for a moment he was going to shake hands.

"It's stopped raining."

"Has it?" When he realized what I was talking about, that there were twinkle-bells of sunshine in the room, he smiled like a weather man, like an ecstatic patron of recurrent light, and repeated the news to Daisy. "What do you think of that? It's stopped raining."

"I'm glad, Jay." Her throat, full of ach-

ing, grieving beauty, told only of her unexpected joy.

"I want you and Daisy to come over to
my house," he said, "I'd like to show her
around."

"You're sure you want me to come?"

"Absolutely, old sport."

Daisy went up-stairs to wash her face—
too late I [**90/91**] thought with humilia-
tion of my towels—while Gatsby and I
waited on the lawn.

"My house looks well, doesn't it?" he
demanded. "See how the whole front of
it catches the light."

I agreed that it was splendid.

"Yes." His eyes went over it, every
arched door and square tower. "It took
me just three years to earn the money that
bought it."

"I thought you inherited your money."

"I did, old sport," he said automatically,
"but I lost most of it in the big panic—
the panic of the war."

I think he hardly knew what he was
saying, for when I asked him what business he was in he answered: "That's my
affair," before he realized that it wasn't
an appropriate reply.

"Oh, I've been in several things," he
corrected himself. "I was in the drug business and then I was in the oil business.
But I'm not in either one now." He looked
at me with more attention. "Do you mean
you've been thinking over what I proposed
the other night?"

Before I could answer, Daisy came out
of the house and two rows of brass buttons
on her dress gleamed in the sunlight.

"That huge place *there*?" she cried
pointing.

"Do you like it?"

"I love it, but I don't see how you live
there all alone."

"I keep it always full of interesting people, night and day. People who do interesting things. Celebrated people."

Instead of taking the short cut along the
Sound we went down to the road and entered by the big postern. [**91/92**] With

enchanting murmurs Daisy admired this
aspect or that of the feudal silhouette
against the sky, admired the gardens, the
sparkling odor of jonquils and the frothy
odor of hawthorn and plum blossoms and
the pale gold odor of kiss-me-at-the-gate.
It was strange to reach the marble steps
and find no stir of bright dresses in and
out of the door, and hear no sound but
bird voices in the trees.

And inside, as we wandered through
Marie Antoinette music-rooms and Restoration salons, I felt that there were guests
concealed behind every couch and table,
under orders to be breathlessly silent until
we had passed through. As Gatsby closed
the door of "the Merton College Library"
I could have sworn I heard the owl-eyed
man break into ghostly laughter.

We went upstairs, through period bedrooms swathed in rose and lavender silk
and vivid with new flowers, through dress-
ing-rooms and poolrooms, and bathrooms,
with sunken baths—intruding into one
chamber where a dishevelled man in pajamas was doing liver exercises on the floor.
It was Mr. Klipspringer, the "boarder." I
had seen him wandering hungrily about
the beach that morning. Finally we came
to Gatsby's own apartment, a bedroom
and a bath, and an Adam study, where we
sat down and drank a glass of some Char-
treuse he took from a cupboard in the wall.

He hadn't once ceased looking at Daisy,
and I think he revalued everything in his
house according to the measure of response
it drew from her well-loved eyes. Sometimes, too, he stared around at his possessions in a dazed way, as though in her
actual and astounding presence none of it
was any longer real. Once he nearly
toppled down a flight of stairs. [**92/93**]

His bedroom was the simplest room of
all—except where the dresser was garnished with a toilet set of pure dull gold.
Daisy took the brush with delight, and
smoothed her hair, whereupon Gatsby sat
down and shaded his eyes and began to
laugh.

"It's the funniest thing, old sport," he said hilariously. "I can't—when I try to——"

He had passed visibly through two states and was entering upon a third. After his embarrassment and his unreasoning joy he was consumed with wonder at her presence. He had been full of the idea so long, dreamed it right through to the end, waited with his teeth set, so to speak, at an inconceivable pitch of intensity. Now, in the reaction, he was running down like an over-wound clock.

Recovering himself in a minute he opened for us two hulking patent cabinets which held his massed suits and dressing-gowns and ties, and his shirts, piled like bricks in stacks a dozen high.

"I've got a man in England who buys me clothes. He sends over a selection of things at the beginning of each season, spring and fall."

He took out a pile of shirts and began throwing them, one by one, before us, shirts of sheer linen and thick silk and fine flannel, which lost their folds as they fell and covered the table in many-colored disarray. While we admired he brought more and the soft rich heap mounted higher—shirts with stripes and scrolls and plaids in coral and apple-green and lavender and faint orange, with monograms of Indian blue. Suddenly, with a strained sound, Daisy bent her head into the shirts and began to cry stormily.

"They're such beautiful shirts," she sobbed, her voice [**93/94**] muffled in the thick folds. "It makes me sad because I've never seen such—such beautiful shirts before."

After the house, we were to see the grounds and the swimming-pool, and the hydroplane and the mid-summer flowers—but outside Gatsby's window it began to rain again, so we stood in a row looking at the corrugated surface of the Sound.

"If it wasn't for the mist we could see your home across the bay," said Gatsby.

"You always have a green light that burns all night at the end of your dock."

Daisy put her arm through his abruptly, but he seemed absorbed in what he had just said. Possibly it had occurred to him that the colossal significance of that light had now vanished forever. Compared to the great distance that had separated him from Daisy it had seemed very near to her, almost touching her. It had seemed as close as a star to the moon. Now it was again a green light on a dock. His count of enchanted objects had diminished by one.

I began to walk about the room, examining various indefinite objects in the half darkness. A large photograph of an elderly man in yachting costume attracted me, hung on the wall over his desk.

"Who's this?"

"That? That's Mr. Dan Cody, old sport."

The name sounded faintly familiar.

"He's dead now. He used to be my best friend years ago."

There was a small picture of Gatsby, also in yachting costume, on the bureau—Gatsby with his head thrown back defiantly—taken apparently when he was about eighteen. [**94/95**]

"I adore it," exclaimed Daisy. "The pompadour! You never told me you had a pompadour—or a yacht."

"Look at this," said Gatsby quickly. "Here's a lot of clippings—about you."

They stood side by side examining it. I was going to ask to see the rubies when the phone rang, and Gatsby took up the receiver.

"Yes. . . . Well, I can't talk now. . . . I can't talk now, old sport. . . . I said a *small* town. . . . He must know what a small town is. . . . Well, he's no use to us if Detroit is his idea of a small town. . . ."

He rang off.

"Come here *quick!*" cried Daisy at the window.

The rain was still falling, but the darkness had parted in the west, and there was a pink and golden billow of foamy clouds above the sea.

"Look at that," she whispered, and then after a moment: "I'd like to just get one of those pink clouds and put you in it and push you around."

I tried to go then, but they wouldn't hear of it; perhaps my presence made them feel more satisfactorily alone.

"I know what we'll do," said Gatsby, "we'll have Klipspringer play the piano."

He went out of the room calling "Ewing!" and returned in a few minutes accompanied by an embarrassed, slightly worn young man, with shell-rimmed glasses and scanty blond hair. He was now decently clothed in a sport shirt, open at the neck, sneakers, and duck trousers of a nebulous hue.

"Did we interrupt your exercises?" inquired Daisy politely.

"I was asleep," cried Mr. Klipspringer, in a spasm of [95/96] embarrassment. "That is, I'd *been* asleep. Then I got up. . . ."

"Klipspringer plays the piano," said Gatsby, cutting him off. "Don't you, Ewing, old sport?"

"I don't play well. I don't—I hardly play at all. I'm all out of prac——"

"We'll go downstairs," interrupted Gatsby. He flipped a switch. The gray windows disappeared as the house glowed full of light.

In the music-room Gatsby turned on a solitary lamp beside the piano. He lit Daisy's cigarette from a trembling match, and sat down with her on a couch far across the room, where there was no light save what the gleaming floor bounced in from the hall.

When Klipspringer had played *The Love Nest* he turned around on the bench and searched unhappily for Gatsby in the gloom.

"I'm all out of practice, you see. I told you I couldn't play. I'm all out of prac——"

"Don't talk so much, old sport," commanded Gatsby. "Play!"

"In the morning,
In the evening,
Ain't we got fun——"

Outside the wind was loud and there was a faint flow of thunder along the Sound. All the lights were going on in West Egg now; the electric trains, men-carrying, were plunging home through the rain from New York. It was the hour of a profound human change, and excitement was generating on the air

"One thing's sure and nothing's surer
The rich get richer and the poor get—
children.   [96/97]

In the meantime,
In between time——"

As I went over to say good-by I saw that the expression of bewilderment had come back into Gatsby's face, as though a faint doubt had occurred to him as to the quality of his present happiness. Almost five years! There must have been moments even that afternoon when Daisy tumbled short of his dreams—not through her own fault, but because of the colossal vitality of his illusion. It had gone beyond her, beyond everything. He had thrown himself into it with a creative passion, adding to it all the time, decking it out with every bright feather that drifted his way. No amount of fire or freshness can challenge what a man will store up in his ghostly heart.

As I watched him he adjusted himself a little, visibly. His hand took hold of hers, and as she said something low in his ear he turned toward her with a rush of emotion. I think that voice held him most, with its fluctuating, feverish warmth, because it couldn't be over-dreamed—that voice was a deathless song.

They had forgotten me, but Daisy glanced up and held out her hand; Gatsby didn't know me now at all. I looked once more at them and they looked back at me, remotely, possessed by intense life. Then I went out of the room and down the marble steps into the rain, leaving them there together. [**97/98**]

CHAPTER VI

About this time an ambitious young reporter from New York arrived one morning at Gatsby's door and asked him if he had anything to say.

"Anything to say about what?" inquired Gatsby politely.

"Why—any statement to give out."

It transpired after a confused five minutes that the man had heard Gatsby's name around his office in a connection which he either wouldn't reveal or didn't fully understand. This was his day off and with laudable initiative he had hurried out "to see."

It was a random shot, and yet the reporter's instinct was right. Gatsby's notoriety, spread about by the hundreds who had accepted his hospitality and so become authorities upon his past, had increased all summer until he fell just short of being news. Contemporary legends such as the "underground pipe-line to Canada" attached themselves to him, and there was one persistent story that he didn't live in a house at all, but in a boat that looked like a house and was moved secretly up and down the Long Island shore. Just why these inventions were a source of satisfaction to James Gatz of North Dakota isn't easy to say.

James Gatz—that was really, or at least legally, his name. He had changed it at the age of seventeen and at the specific moment that witnessed the beginning of his career—when he saw Dan Cody's yacht drop anchor over the most insidious flat on Lake Superior. It was [**98/99**] James Gatz who had been loafing along the beach that afternoon in a torn green jersey and a pair of canvas pants, but it was already Jay Gatsby who borrowed a rowboat, pulled out to the *Tuolomee,* and informed Cody that a wind might catch

him and break him up in half an hour.

I suppose he'd had the name ready for a long time, even then. His parents were shiftless and unsuccessful farm people—his imagination had never really accepted them as his parents at all. The truth was that Jay Gatsby of West Egg, Long Island, sprang from his Platonic conception of himself. He was a son of God—a phrase which, if it means anything, means just that—and he must be about His Father's business, the service of a vast, vulgar, and meretricious beauty. So he invented just the sort of Jay Gatsby that a seventeen-year-old boy would be likely to invent, and to this conception he was faithful to the end.

For over a year he had been beating his way along the south shore of Lake Superior as a clam-digger and a salmon-fisher or in any other capacity that brought him food and bed. His brown, hardening body lived naturally through the half-fierce, half-lazy work of the bracing days. He knew women early, and since they spoiled him he became contemptuous of them, of young virgins because they were ignorant, of the others because they were hysterical about things which in his overwhelming self-absorption he took for granted.

But his heart was in a constant, turbulent riot. The most grotesque and fantastic conceits haunted him in his bed at night. A universe of ineffable gaudiness spun itself out in his brain while the clock ticked on the washstand and the moon soaked with wet light his tangled [**99/100**] clothes upon the floor. Each night he added to the pattern of his fancies until drowsiness closed down upon some vivid scene with an oblivious embrace. For a while these reveries provided an outlet for his imagination; they were a satisfactory hint of the unreality of reality, a promise that the rock of the world was founded securely on a fairy's wing.

An instinct toward his future glory had led him, some months before, to the small

Lutheran college of St. Olaf in southern Minnesota. He stayed there two weeks, dismayed at its ferocious indifference to the drums of his destiny, to destiny itself, and despising the janitor's work with which he was to pay his way through. Then he drifted back to Lake Superior, and he was still searching for something to do on the day that Dan Cody's yacht dropped anchor in the shallows alongshore.

Cody was fifty years old then, a product of the Nevada silver fields, of the Yukon, of every rush for metal since seventy-five. The transactions in Montana copper that made him many times a millionaire found him physically robust but on the verge of soft-mindedness, and, suspecting this, an infinite number of women tried to separate him from his money. The none too savory ramifications by which Ella Kaye, the newspaper woman, played Madame de Maintenon to his weakness and sent him to sea in a yacht, were common knowledge to the turgid sub-journalism of 1902. He had been coasting along all too hospitable shores for five years when he turned up as James Gatz's destiny in Little Girl Bay.

To young Gatz, resting on his oars and looking up at the railed deck, that yacht represented all the beauty [100/101] and glamour in the world. I suppose he smiled at Cody—he had probably discovered that people liked him when he smiled. At any rate Cody asked him a few questions (one of them elicited the brand new name) and found that he was quick and extravagantly ambitious. A few days later he took him to Duluth and bought him a blue coat, six pairs of white duck trousers, and a yachting cap. And when the *Tuolomee* left for the West Indies and the Barbary Coast Gatsby left too.

He was employed in a vague personal capacity—while he remained with Cody he was in turn steward, mate, skipper, secretary, and even jailor, for Dan Cody sober knew what lavish doings Dan Cody drunk might soon be about, and he provided for

such contingencies by reposing more and more trust in Gatsby. The arrangement lasted five years, during which the boat went three times around the Continent. It might have lasted indefinitely except for the fact that Ella Kaye came on board one night in Boston and a week later·Dan Cody inhospitably died.

I remember the portrait of him up in Gatsby's bedroom, a gray, florid man with a hard, empty face—the pioneer debauchee, who during one phase of American life brought back to the Eastern seaboard the savage violence of the frontier brothel and saloon. It was indirectly due to Cody that Gatsby drank so little. Sometimes in the course of gay parties women used to rub champagne into his hair; for himself he formed the habit of letting liquor alone.

And it was from Cody that he inherited money—a legacy of twenty-five thousand dollars. He didn't get it. He never understood the legal device that was used against him, but what remained of the millions went [101/102] intact to Ella Kaye. He was left with his singularly appropriate education; the vague contour of Jay Gatsby had filled out to the substantiality of a man.

He told me all this very much later, but I've put it down here with the idea of exploding those first wild rumors about his antecedents, which weren't even faintly true. Moreover he told it to me at a time of confusion, when I had reached the point of believing everything and nothing about him. So I take advantage of this short halt, while Gatsby, so to speak, caught his breath, to clear this set of misconceptions away.

It was a halt, too, in my association with his affairs. For several weeks I didn't see him or hear his voice on the phone—mostly I was in New York, trotting around with Jordan and trying to ingratiate myself with her senile aunt—but finally I went over to his house one Sunday afternoon. I hadn't been there two minutes when somebody brought Tom Buchanan in for a drink. I was startled, naturally, but the really surprising thing was that it hadn't happened before.

They were a party of three on horseback —Tom and a man named Sloane and a pretty woman in a brown riding-habit, who had been there previously.

"I'm delighted to see you," said Gatsby, standing on his porch. "I'm delighted that you dropped in."

As though they cared!

"Sit right down. Have a cigarette or a cigar." He walked around the room quickly, ringing bells. "I'll have something to drink for you in just a minute."

He was profoundly affected by the fact that Tom was there. But he would be uneasy anyhow until he had given them something, realizing in a vague way that that was all they came for. Mr. Sloane wanted nothing. [102/103] A lemonade? No, thanks. A little champagne? Nothing at all, thanks. . . . I'm sorry——

"Did you have a nice ride?"

"Very good roads around here."

"I suppose the automobiles——"

"Yeah."

Moved by an irresistible impulse, Gatsby turned to Tom, who had accepted the introduction as a stranger.

"I believe we've met somewhere before, Mr. Buchanan."

"Oh, yes," said Tom, gruffly polite, but obviously not remembering. "So we did. I remember very well."

"About two weeks ago."

"That's right. You were with Nick here."

"I know your wife," continued Gatsby, almost aggressively.

"That so?"

Tom turned to me.

"You live near here, Nick?"

"Next door."

"That so?"

Mr. Sloane didn't enter into the conversation, but lounged back haughtily in his chair; the woman said nothing either —until unexpectedly, after two highballs, she became cordial.

"We'll all come over to your next party, Mr. Gatsby," she suggested. "What do you say?"

"Certainly; I'd be delighted to have you."

"Be ver' nice," said Mr. Sloane, without gratitude. "Well—think ought to be starting home."

"Please don't hurry," Gatsby urged them. He had control of himself now, and he wanted to see more of Tom. "Why don't you—why don't you stay for supper? [103/104] I wouldn't be surprised if some other people dropped in from New York."

"You come to supper with *me*," said the lady enthusiastically. "Both of you."

This included me. Mr. Sloane got to his feet.

"Come along," he said—but to her only.

"I mean it," she insisted. "I'd love to have you. Lots of room."

Gatsby looked at me questioningly. He wanted to go, and he didn't see that Mr. Sloane had determined he shouldn't.

"I'm afraid I won't be able to," I said.

"Well, you come," she urged, concentrating on Gatsby.

Mr. Sloane murmured something close to her ear.

"We won't be late if we start now," she insisted aloud.

"I haven't got a horse," said Gatsby. "I used to ride in the army, but I've never bought a horse. I'll have to follow you in my car. Excuse me for just a minute."

The rest of us walked out on the porch, where Sloane and the lady began an impassioned conversation aside.

"My God, I believe the man's coming," said Tom. "Doesn't he know she doesn't want him?"

"She says she does want him."

"She has a big dinner party and he won't know a soul there." He frowned. "I wonder where in the devil he met Daisy. By God, I may be old-fashioned in my ideas, but women run around too much these days to suit me. They meet all kinds of crazy fish."

Suddenly Mr. Sloane and the lady walked down the steps and mounted their horses.

"Come on," said Mr. Sloane to Tom, "we're late. [104/105] We've got to go." And then to me: "Tell him we couldn't wait, will you?"

Tom and I shook hands, the rest of us exchanged a cool nod, and they trotted quickly down the drive, disappearing under the August foliage just as Gatsby, with hat and light overcoat in hand, came out the front door.

Tom was evidently perturbed at Daisy's running around alone, for on the following Saturday night he came with her to Gatsby's party. Perhaps his presence gave the evening its peculiar quality of oppressiveness—it stands out in my memory from Gatsby's other parties that summer. There were the same people, or at least the same sort of people, the same profusion of champagne, the same many-colored, many-keyed commotion, but I felt an unpleasantness in the air, a pervading harshness that hadn't been there before. Or perhaps I had merely grown used to it, grown to accept West Egg as a world complete in itself, with its own standards and its own great figures, second to nothing because it had no consciousness of being so, and now I was looking at it again, through Daisy's eyes. It is invariably saddening to look through new eyes at things upon which you have expended your own powers of adjustment.

They arrived at twilight, and, as we strolled out among the sparkling hundreds, Daisy's voice was playing murmurous tricks in her throat.

"These things excite me *so*," she whispered. "If you want to kiss me any time during the evening, Nick, just let me know and I'll be glad to arrange it for you. Just mention my name. Or present a green card. I'm giving out green——" [105/106]

"Look around," suggested Gatsby.

"I'm looking around. I'm having a marvellous——"

"You must see the faces of many people you've heard about."

Tom's arrogant eyes roamed the crowd. "We don't go around very much," he said; "in fact, I was just thinking I don't know a soul here."

"Perhaps you know that lady," Gatsby indicated a gorgeous, scarcely human orchid of a woman who sat in state under a white-plum tree. Tom and Daisy stared, with that peculiarly unreal feeling that accompanies the recognition of a hitherto ghostly celebrity of the movies.

"She's lovely," said Daisy.

"The man bending over her is her director."

He took them ceremoniously from group to group:

"Mrs. Buchanan . . . and Mr. Buchanan—" After an instant's hesitation he added: "the polo player."

"Oh, no," objected Tom quickly, "not me."

But evidently the sound of it pleased Gatsby, for Tom remained "the polo player" for the rest of the evening.

"I've never met so many celebrities," Daisy exclaimed. "I liked that man—what was his name?—with the sort of blue nose."

Gatsby identified him, adding that he was a small producer.

"Well, I liked him anyhow."

"I'd a little rather not be the polo player," said Tom pleasantly, "I'd rather look at all these famous people in—in oblivion."

Daisy and Gatsby danced. I remember being surprised by his graceful, conservative fox-trot—I had never seen [106/107] him dance before. Then they sauntered over to my house and sat on the steps for half an hour, while at her request I remained watchfully in the garden. "In case there's a fire or a flood," she explained, "or any act of God."

Tom appeared from his oblivion as we were sitting down to supper together. "Do you mind if I eat with some people over here?" he said. "A fellow's getting off some funny stuff."

"Go ahead," answered Daisy genially, "and if you want to take down any addresses here's my little gold pencil." . . . She looked around after a moment and told me the girl was "common but pretty," and I knew that except for the half-hour she'd been alone with Gatsby she wasn't having a good time.

We were at a particularly tipsy table. That was my fault—Gatsby had been called to the phone, and I'd enjoyed these same people only two weeks before. But what had amused me then turned septic on the air now.

"How do you feel, Miss Baedeker?"

The girl addressed was trying, unsuccessfully, to slump against my shoulder. At this inquiry she sat up and opened her eyes.

"Wha'?"

A massive and lethargic woman, who had been urging Daisy to play golf with her at the local club to-morrow, spoke in Miss Baedeker's defence:

"Oh, she's all right now. When she's had five or six cocktails she always starts screaming like that. I tell her she ought to leave it alone."

"I do leave it alone," affirmed the accused hollowly.

"We heard you yelling, so I said to Doc Civet here: 'There's somebody that needs your help, Doc.'" [107/108]

"She's much obliged, I'm sure," said another friend, without gratitude, "but you got her dress all wet when you stuck her head in the pool."

"Anything I hate is to get my head stuck in a pool," mumbled Miss Baedeker. "They almost drowned me once over in New Jersey."

"Then you ought to leave it alone," countered Doctor Civet.

"Speak for yourself!" cried Miss Baedeker violently. "Your hand shakes. I wouldn't let you operate on me!"

It was like that. Almost the last thing I remember was standing with Daisy and watching the moving-picture director and his Star. They were still under the white-plum tree and their faces were touching except for a pale, thin ray of moonlight between. It occurred to me that he had been very slowly bending toward her all evening to attain this proximity, and even while I watched I saw him stoop one ultimate degree and kiss at her cheek.

"I like her," said Daisy, "I think she's lovely."

But the rest offended her—and inarguably, because it wasn't a gesture but an emotion. She was appalled by West Egg, this unprecedented "place" that Broadway had begotten upon a Long Island fishing village—appalled by its raw vigor that chafed under the old euphemisms and by the too obtrusive fate that herded its inhabitants along a short-cut from nothing to nothing. She saw something awful in the very simplicity she failed to understand.

I sat on the front steps with them while they waited for their car. It was dark here in front; only the bright door sent ten square feet of light volleying out into the [108/109] soft black morning. Sometimes a shadow moved against a dressing-room blind above, gave way to another shadow, an indefinite procession of shadows, that rouged and powdered in an invisible glass.

"Who is this Gatsby anyhow?" demanded Tom suddenly. "Some big bootlegger?"

"Where'd you hear that?" I inquired.

"I didn't hear it. I imagined it. A lot of these newly rich people are just big bootleggers, you know."

"Not Gatsby," I said shortly.

He was silent for a moment. The pebbles of the drive crunched under his feet.

"Well, he certainly must have strained himself to get this menagerie together."

A breeze stirred the gray haze of Daisy's fur collar.

"At least they're more interesting than the people we know," she said with an effort.

"You didn't look so interested."

"Well, I was."

Tom laughed and turned to me.

"Did you notice Daisy's face when that girl asked her to put her under a cold shower?"

Daisy began to sing with the music in a husky, rhythmic whisper, bringing out a meaning in each word that it had never had before and would never have again. When the melody rose, her voice broke up sweetly, following it, in a way contralto voices have, and each change tipped out a little of her warm human magic upon the air.

"Lots of people come who haven't been invited," she said suddenly. "That girl hadn't been invited. They simply force their way in and he's too polite to object." [109/110]

"I'd like to know who he is and what he does," insisted Tom. "And I think I'll make a point of finding out."

"I can tell you right now," she answered. "He owned some drug-stores, a lot of drug-stores. He built them up himself."

The dilatory limousine came rolling up the drive.

"Good night, Nick," said Daisy.

Her glance left me and sought the lighted top of the steps, where *Three O'Clock in the Morning*, a neat, sad little waltz of that year, was drifting out the open door. After all, in the very casualness of Gatsby's party there were romantic possibilities totally absent from her world. What was it up there in the song that seemed to be calling her back inside? What would happen now in the dim, incalculable hours? Perhaps some unbelievable guest would arrive, a person infinitely rare and to be marvelled at, some authentically radiant young girl who with one fresh glance at Gatsby, one moment of magical encounter, would blot out those five years of unwavering devotion.

I stayed late that night, Gatsby asked me to wait until he was free, and I lingered in the garden until the inevitable swimming party had run up, chilled and exalted, from the black beach, until the lights were extinguished in the guestrooms overhead. When he came down the steps at last the tanned skin was drawn unusually tight on his face, and his eyes were bright and tired.

"She didn't like it," he said immediately.

"Of course she did."

"She didn't like it," he insisted. "She didn't have a good time." [110/111]

He was silent, and I guessed at his unutterable depression.

"I feel far away from her," he said. "It's hard to make her understand."

"You mean about the dance?"

"The dance?" He dismissed all the dances he had given with a snap of his fingers. "Old sport, the dance is unimportant."

He wanted nothing less of Daisy than that she should go to Tom and say: "I never loved you." After she had obliterated four years with that sentence they could decide upon the more practical measures to be taken. One of them was that, after she was free, they were to go back to Louisville and be married from her house—just as if it were five years ago.

"And she doesn't understand," he said. "She used to be able to understand. We'd sit for hours——"

He broke off and began to walk up and down a desolate path of fruit rinds and discarded favors and crushed flowers.

"I wouldn't ask too much of her," I ventured. "You can't repeat the past."

"Can't repeat the past?" he cried incredulously. "Why of course you can!"

He looked around him wildly, as if the past were lurking here in the shadow of his house, just out of reach of his hand.

"I'm going to fix everything just the way it was before," he said, nodding determinedly. "She'll see."

He talked a lot about the past, and I gathered that he wanted to recover something, some idea of himself perhaps, that had gone into loving Daisy. His life had been confused and disordered since then, but if he [111/113] could once return to a certain starting place and go over it all slowly, he could find out what that thing was. . . .

. . . One autumn night, five years before, they had been walking down the street when the leaves were falling, and they came to a place where there were no trees and the sidewalk was white with moonlight. They stopped here and turned toward each other. Now it was a cool night with that mysterious excitement in it which comes at the two changes of the year. The quiet lights in the houses were humming out into the darkness and there was a stir and bustle among the stars. Out of the corner of his eye Gatsby saw that the blocks of the sidewalks really formed a ladder and mounted to a secret place above the trees—he could climb to it, if he climbed alone, and once there he could suck on the pap of life, gulp down the incomparable milk of wonder.

His heart beat faster and faster as Daisy's white face came up to his own. He knew that when he kissed this girl, and forever wed his unutterable visions to her perishable breath, his mind would never romp again like the mind of God. So he waited, listening for a moment longer to the tuning-fork that had been struck upon a star. Then he kissed her. At his lips' touch she blossomed for him like a flower and the incarnation was complete.

Through all he said, even through his appalling sentimentality, I was reminded of something—an elusive rhythm, a fragment of lost words, that I had heard somewhere a long time ago. For a moment a phrase tried to take shape in my mouth and my lips parted like a dumb man's, as though there was more struggling upon them than a wisp of startled air. But they made no sound, and what I had almost remembered was uncommunicable forever. [112/113]

CHAPTER VII

It was when curiosity about Gatsby was at its highest that the lights in his house failed to go on one Saturday night—and, as obscurely as it had begun, his career as Trimalchio was over. Only gradually did I become aware that the automobiles which turned expectantly into his drive stayed for just a minute and then drove sulkily away. Wondering if he were sick I went over to find out—an unfamiliar butler with a villainous face squinted at me suspiciously from the door.

"Is Mr. Gatsby sick?"

"Nope." After a pause he added "sir" in a dilatory, grudging way.

"I hadn't seen him around, and I was rather worried. Tell him Mr. Carraway came over."

"Who?" he demanded rudely.

"Carraway."

"Carraway. All right, I'll tell him."

Abruptly he slammed the door.

My Finn informed me that Gatsby had dismissed every servant in his house a week ago and replaced them with half a dozen others, who never went into West Egg Village to be bribed by the tradesmen, but ordered moderate supplies over the telephone. The grocery boy reported that the kitchen looked like a pigsty, and the general opinion in the village was that the new people weren't servants at all.

Next day Gatsby called me on the phone.

"Going away?" I inquired. [113/114]

"No, old sport."

"I hear you fired all your servants."

"I wanted somebody who wouldn't gossip. Daisy comes over quite often—in the afternoons."

So the whole caravansary had fallen in like a card house at the disapproval in her eyes.

"They're some people Wolfsheim wanted to do something for. They're all
brothers and sisters. They used to run a
small hotel."

"I see."

He was calling up at Daisy's request—
would I come to lunch at her house to-
morrow? Miss Baker would be there. Half
an hour later Daisy herself telephoned
and seemed relieved to find that I was
coming. Something was up. And yet I
couldn't believe that they would choose
this occasion for a scene—especially for the
rather harrowing scene that Gatsby had
outlined in the garden.

The next day was broiling, almost the
last, certainly the warmest, of the summer. As my train emerged from the tunnel
into sunlight, only the hot whistles of the
National Biscuit Company broke the simmering hush at noon. The straw seats of
the car hovered on the edge of combustion; the woman next to me perspired
delicately for a while into her white shirtwaist, and then, as her newspaper dampened under her fingers, lapsed despairingly
into deep heat with a desolate cry. Her
pocket-book slapped to the floor.

"Oh, my!" she gasped.

I picked it up with a weary bend and
handed it back to her, holding it at arm's
length and by the extreme tip of the corners to indicate that I had no designs upon
[114/115] it—but every one near by, including the woman, suspected me just
the same.

"Hot!" said the conductor to familiar
faces. "Some weather! . . . Hot! . . . Hot!
. . . Hot! . . . Is it hot enough for you? Is
it hot? Is it . . .?"

My commutation ticket came back to
me with a dark stain from his hand. That
any one should care in this heat whose
flushed lips he kissed, whose head made
damp the pajama pocket over his heart!

. . . Through the hall of the Buchanans'
house blew a faint wind, carrying the
sound of the telephone bell out to Gatsby
and me as we waited at the door.

"The master's body!" roared the butler

into the mouthpiece. "I'm sorry, madame,
but we can't furnish it—it's far too hot to
touch this noon!"

What he really said was: "Yes . . . Yes
. . . I'll see."

He set down the receiver and came
toward us, glistening slightly, to take our
stiff straw hats.

"Madame expects you in the salon!" he
cried, needlessly indicating the direction.
In this heat every extra gesture was an
affront to the common store of life.

The room, shadowed well with awnings,
was dark and cool. Daisy and Jordan lay
upon an enormous couch, like silver idols
weighing down their own white dresses
against the singing breeze of the fans.

"We can't move," they said together.

Jordan's fingers, powdered white over
their tan, rested for a moment in mine.

"And Mr. Thomas Buchanan, the ath-
lete?" I inquired.

Simultaneously I heard his voice, gruff,
muffled, husky, at the hall telephone.

Gatsby stood in the centre of the crimson carpet and [115/116] gazed around
with fascinated eyes. Daisy watched him
and laughed, her sweet, exciting laugh; a
tiny gust of powder rose from her bosom
into the air.

"The rumor is," whispered Jordan,
"that that's Tom's girl on the telephone."

We were silent. The voice in the hall
rose high with annoyance: "Very well,
then, I won't sell you the car at all. . . .
I'm under no obligations to you at all . . .
and as for your bothering me about it at
lunch time, I won't stand that at all!"

"Holding down the receiver," said
Daisy cynically.

"No, he's not," I assured her. "It's a
bona-fide deal. I happen to know about
it."

Tom flung open the door, blocked out
its space for a moment with his thick body,
and hurried into the room.

"Mr. Gatsby!" He put out his broad,
flat hand with well-concealed dislike. "I'm
glad to see you, sir. . . . Nick. . . ."

"Make us a cold drink," cried Daisy.

As he left the room again she got up and went over to Gatsby and pulled his face down, kissing him on the mouth.

"You know I love you," she murmured.

"You forget there's a lady present," said Jordan.

Daisy looked around doubtfully.

"You kiss Nick too."

"What a low, vulgar girl!"

"I don't care!" cried Daisy, and began to clog on the brick fireplace. Then she remembered the heat and sat down guiltily on the couch just as a freshly laundered nurse leading a little girl came into the room.

"Bles-sed pre-cious," she crooned, holding out her arms. "Come to your own mother that loves you." [116/117]

The child, relinquished by the nurse, rushed across the room and rooted shyly into her mother's dress.

"The bles-sed pre-cious! Did mother get powder on your old yellowy hair? Stand up now, and say—How-de-do."

Gatsby and I in turn leaned down and took the small reluctant hand. Afterward he kept looking at the child with surprise. I don't think he had ever really believed in its existence before.

"I got dressed before luncheon," said the child, turning eagerly to Daisy.

"That's because your mother wanted to show you off." Her face bent into the single wrinkle of the small white neck. "You dream, you. You absolute little dream."

"Yes," admitted the child calmly. "Aunt Jordan's got on a white dress too."

"How do you like mother's friends?" Daisy turned her around so that she faced Gatsby. "Do you think they're pretty?"

"Where's Daddy?"

"She doesn't look like her father," explained Daisy. "She looks like me. She's got my hair and shape of the face."

Daisy sat back upon the couch. The nurse took a step forward and held out her hand.

"Come, Pammy."

"Good-by, sweetheart!"

With a reluctant backward glance the well-disciplined child held to her nurse's hand and was pulled out the door, just as Tom came back, preceding four gin rickeys that clicked full of ice.

Gatsby took up his drink. [117/118]

"They certainly look cool," he said, with visible tension.

We drank in long, greedy swallows.

"I read somewhere that the sun's getting hotter every year," said Tom genially. "It seems that pretty soon the earth's going to fall into the sun—or wait a minute—it's just the opposite—the sun's getting colder every year.

"Come outside," he suggested to Gatsby, "I'd like you to have a look at the place."

I went with them out to the veranda. On the green Sound, stagnant in the heat, one small sail crawled slowly toward the fresher sea. Gatsby's eyes followed it momentarily, he raised his hand and pointed across the bay.

"I'm right across from you."

"So you are."

Our eyes lifted over the rose-beds and the hot lawn and the weedy refuse of the dog-days alongshore. Slowly the white wings of the boat moved against the blue cool limit of the sky. Ahead lay the scalloped ocean and the abounding blessed isles.

"There's sport for you," said Tom, nodding. "I'd like to be out there with him for about an hour."

We had luncheon in the dining-room, darkened too against the heat, and drank down nervous gayety with the cold ale.

"What'll we do with ourselves this afternoon?" cried Daisy, "and the day after that, and the next thirty years?"

"Don't be morbid," Jordan said. "Life starts all over again when it gets crisp in the fall."

"But it's so hot," insisted Daisy, on the verge of tears, "and everything's so confused. Let's all go to town!" [118/119]

Her voice struggled on through the heat, beating against it, molding its senselessness into forms.

"I've heard of making a garage out of a stable," Tom was saying to Gatsby, "but I'm the first man who ever made a stable out of a garage."

"Who wants to go to town?" demanded Daisy insistently. Gatsby's eyes floated toward her. "Ah," she cried, "you look so cool."

Their eyes met, and they stared together at each other, alone in space. With an effort she glanced down at the table.

"You always look so cool," she repeated.

She had told him that she loved him, and Tom Buchanan saw. He was astounded. His mouth opened a little, and he looked at Gatsby, and then back at Daisy as if he had just recognized her as some one he knew a long time ago.

"You resemble the advertisement of the man," she went on innocently. "You know the advertisement of the man——"

"All right," broke in Tom quickly, "I'm perfectly willing to go to town. Come on—we're all going to town."

He got up, his eyes still flashing between Gatsby and his wife. No one moved.

"Come on!" His temper cracked a little. "What's the matter, anyhow? If we're going to town, let's start."

His hand, trembling with his effort at self-control, bore to his lips the last of his glass of ale. Daisy's voice got us to our feet and out on to the blazing gravel drive.

"Are we just going to go?" she objected. "Like this? Aren't we going to let any one smoke a cigarette first?"

"Everybody smoked all through lunch." [119/120]

"Oh, let's have fun," she begged him. "It's too hot to fuss."

He didn't answer.

"Have it your own way," she said. "Come on, Jordan."

They went upstairs to get ready while we three men stood there shuffling the hot pebbles with our feet. A silver curve of the moon hovered already in the western sky. Gatsby started to speak, changed his mind, but not before Tom wheeled and faced him expectantly.

"Have you got your stables here?" asked Gatsby with an effort.

"About a quarter of a mile down the road."

"Oh."

A pause.

"I don't see the idea of going to town," broke out Tom savagely. "Women get these notions in their heads——"

"Shall we take anything to drink?" called Daisy from an upper window.

"I'll get some whiskey," answered Tom. He went inside.

Gatsby turned to me rigidly:

"I can't say anything in his house, old sport."

"She's got an indiscreet voice," I remarked. "It's full of—" I hesitated.

"Her voice is full of money," he said suddenly.

That was it. I'd never understood before. It was full of money—that was the inexhaustible charm that rose and fell in it, the jingle of it, the cymbals' song of it. . . . High in a white palace the king's daughter, the golden girl. . . .

Tom came out of the house wrapping a quart bottle in a towel, followed by Daisy and Jordan wearing small [120/121] tight hats of metallic cloth and carrying light capes over their arms.

"Shall we all go in my car?" suggested Gatsby. He felt the hot, green leather of the seat. "I ought to have left it in the shade."

"Is it standard shift?" demanded Tom.

"Yes."

"Well, you take my coupé and let me drive your car to town."

The suggestion was distasteful to Gatsby.

"I don't think there's much gas," he objected.

"Plenty of gas," said Tom boisterously. He looked at the gauge. "And if it runs out I can stop at a drug-store. You can buy anything at a drug-store nowadays."

A pause followed this apparently pointless remark. Daisy looked at Tom frowning, and an indefinable expression, at once definitely unfamiliar and vaguely recognizable, as if I had only heard it described in words, passed over Gatsby's face.

"Come on, Daisy," said Tom, pressing her with his hand toward Gatsby's car. "I'll take you in this circus wagon."

He opened the door, but she moved out from the circle of his arm.

"You take Nick and Jordan. We'll follow you in the coupé."

She walked close to Gatsby, touching his coat with her hand. Jordan and Tom and I got into the front seat of Gatsby's car, Tom pushed the unfamiliar gears tentatively, and we shot off into the oppressive heat, leaving them out of sight behind.

"Did you see that?" demanded Tom.
[121/122]

"See what?"

He looked at me keenly, realizing that Jordan and I must have known all along.

"You think I'm pretty dumb, don't you?" he suggested. "Perhaps I am, but I have a—almost a second sight, sometimes, that tells me what to do. Maybe you don't believe that, but science——"

He paused. The immediate contingency overtook him, pulled him back from the edge of the theoretical abyss.

"I've made a small investigation of this fellow," he continued. "I could have gone deeper if I'd known——"

"Do you mean you've been to a medium?" inquired Jordan humorously.

"What?" Confused, he stared at us as we laughed. "A medium?"

"About Gatsby."

"About Gatsby! No, I haven't. I said I'd been making a small investigation of his past."

"And you found he was an Oxford man," said Jordan helpfully.

"An Oxford man!" He was incredulous. "Like hell he is! He wears a pink suit."

"Nevertheless he's an Oxford man."

"Oxford, New Mexico," snorted Tom contemptuously, "or something like that."

"Listen, Tom. If you're such a snob, why did you invite him to lunch?" demanded Jordan crossly.

"Daisy invited him; she knew him before we were married—God knows where!"

We were all irritable now with the fading ale, and aware of it we drove for a while in silence. Then as Doctor T. J. Eckleburg's faded eyes came into sight [122/123] down the road, I remembered Gatsby's caution about gasoline.

"We've got enough to get us to town," said Tom.

"But there's a garage right here," objected Jordan. "I don't want to get stalled in this baking heat."

Tom threw on both brakes impatiently, and we slid to an abrupt dusty stop under Wilson's sign. After a moment the proprietor emerged from the interior of his establishment and gazed hollow-eyed at the car.

"Let's have some gas!" cried Tom roughly. "What do you think we stopped for—to admire the view?"

"I'm sick," said Wilson without moving. "Been sick all day."

"What's the matter?"

"I'm all run down."

"Well, shall I help myself?" Tom demanded. "You sounded well enough on the phone."

With an effort Wilson left the shade and support of the doorway and, breathing hard, unscrewed the cap of the tank. In the sunlight his face was green.

"I didn't mean to interrupt your lunch," he said. "But I need money pretty bad, and I was wondering what you were going to do with your old car."

"How do you like this one?" inquired Tom. "I bought it last week."

"It's a nice yellow one," said Wilson, as he strained at the handle.

"Like to buy it?"

"Big chance," Wilson smiled faintly. "No, but I could make some money on the other."

"What do you want money for, all of a sudden?"

"I've been here too long. I want to get

away. My wife and I want to go West."
[123/124]

"Your wife does," exclaimed Tom, startled.

"She's been talking about it for ten years." He rested for a moment against the pump, shading his eyes. "And now she's going whether she wants to or not. I'm going to get her away."

The coupé flashed by us with a flurry of dust and the flash of a waving hand.

"What do I owe you?" demanded Tom harshly.

"I just got wised up to something funny the last two days," remarked Wilson. "That's why I want to get away. That's why I been bothering you about the car."

"What do I owe you?"

"Dollar twenty."

The relentless beating heat was beginning to confuse me and I had a bad moment there before I realized that so far his suspicions hadn't alighted on Tom. He had discovered that Myrtle had some sort of life apart from him in another world, and the shock had made him physically sick. I stared at him and then at Tom, who had made a parallel discovery less than an hour before—and it occurred to me that there was no difference between men, in intelligence or race, so profound as the difference between the sick and the well. Wilson was so sick that he looked guilty, unforgivably guilty—as if he just got some poor girl with child.

"I'll let you have that car," said Tom. "I'll send it over to-morrow afternoon."

That locality was always vaguely disquieting, even in the broad glare of afternoon, and now I turned my head as though I had been warned of something behind. Over the ashheaps the giant eyes of Doctor T. J. Eckleburg kept their vigil, but I perceived, after a mo- [124/125] ment, that the other eyes were regarding us with peculiar intensity from less than twenty feet away.

In one of the windows over the garage the curtains had been moved aside a little, and Myrtle Wilson was peering down at the car. So engrossed was she that she had no consciousness of being observed, and one emotion after another crept into her face like objects into a slowly developing picture. Her expression was curiously familiar—it was an expression I had often seen on women's faces, but on Myrtle Wilson's face it seemed purposeless and inexplicable until I realized that her eyes, wide with jealous terror, were fixed not on Tom, but on Jordan Baker, whom she took to be his wife.

There is no confusion like the confusion of a simple mind, and as we drove away Tom was feeling the hot whips of panic. His wife and his mistress, until an hour ago secure and inviolate, were slipping precipitately from his control. Instinct made him step on the accelerator with the double purpose of overtaking Daisy and leaving Wilson behind, and we sped along toward Astoria at fifty miles an hour, until, among the spidery girders of the elevated, we came in sight of the easy-going blue coupé.

"Those big movies around Fiftieth Street are cool," suggested Jordan. "I love New York on summer afternoons when every one's away. There's something very sensuous about it—overripe, as if all sorts of funny fruits were going to fall into your hands."

The word "sensuous" had the effect of further disquieting Tom, but before he could invent a protest the coupé came to a stop, and Daisy signalled us to draw up alongside. [125/126]

"Where are we going?" she cried.

"How about the movies?"

"It's so hot," she complained. "You go. We'll ride around and meet you after." With an effort her wit rose faintly, "We'll meet you on some corner. I'll be the man smoking two cigarettes."

"We can't argue about it here," Tom said impatiently, as a truck gave out a cursing whistle behind us. "You follow me to the south side of Central Park, in front of the Plaza."

Several times he turned his head and looked back for their car, and if the traffic delayed them he slowed up until they came into sight. I think he was afraid they would dart down a side street and out of his life forever.

But they didn't. And we all took the less explicable step of engaging the parlor of a suite in the Plaza Hotel.

The prolonged and tumultuous argument that ended by herding us into that room eludes me, though I have a sharp physical memory that, in the course of it, my underwear kept climbing like a damp snake around my legs and intermittent beads of sweat raced cool across my back. The notion originated with Daisy's suggestion that we hire five bathrooms and take cold baths, and then assumed more tangible form as "a place to have a mint julep." Each of us said over and over that it was a "crazy idea"—we all talked at once to a baffled clerk and thought, or pretended to think, that we were being very funny . . .

The room was large and stifling, and, though it was already four o'clock, opening the windows admitted only a gust of hot shrubbery from the Park. Daisy went [126/127] to the mirror and stood with her back to us, fixing her hair.

"It's a swell suite," whispered Jordan respectfully, and every one laughed.

"Open another window," commanded Daisy, without turning around.

"There aren't any more."

"Well, we'd better telephone for an axe——"

"The thing to do is to forget about the heat," said Tom impatiently. "You make it ten times worse by crabbing about it."

He unrolled the bottle of whiskey from the towel and put it on the table.

"Why not let her alone, old sport?" remarked Gatsby. "You're the one that wanted to come to town."

There was a moment of silence. The telephone book slipped from its nail and splashed to the floor, whereupon Jordan whispered, "Excuse me"—but this time no one laughed.

"I'll pick it up," I offered.

"I've got it." Gatsby examined the parted string, muttered "Hum!" in an interested way, and tossed the book on a chair.

"That's a great expression of yours, isn't it?" said Tom sharply.

"What is?"

"All this 'old sport' business. Where'd you pick that up?"

"Now see here, Tom," said Daisy, turning around from the mirror, "if you're going to make personal remarks I won't stay here a minute. Call up and order some ice for the mint julep." [127/128]

As Tom took up the receiver the compressed heat exploded into sound and we were listening to the portentous chords of Mendelssohn's Wedding March from the ballroom below.

"Imagine marrying anybody in this heat!" cried Jordan dismally.

"Still—I was married in the middle of June," Daisy remembered, "Louisville in June! Somebody fainted. Who was it fainted, Tom?"

"Biloxi," he answered shortly.

"A man named Biloxi. 'Blocks' Biloxi, and he made boxes—that's a fact—and he was from Biloxi, Tennessee."

"They carried him into my house," appended Jordan, "because we lived just two doors from the church. And he stayed three weeks, until Daddy told him he had to get out. The day after he left Daddy died." After a moment she added as if she might have sounded irreverent, "There wasn't any connection."

"I used to know a Bill Biloxi from Memphis," I remarked.

"That was his cousin. I knew his whole family history before he left. He gave me an aluminum putter that I use today."

The music had died down as the ceremony began and now a long cheer floated in at the window, followed by intermittent cries of "Yea—ea—ea!" and finally by a burst of jazz as the dancing began.

"We're getting old," said Daisy. "If we were young we'd rise and dance."

"Remember Biloxi," Jordan warned her. "Where'd you know him, Tom?" [128/129]

"Biloxi?" He concentrated with an effort. "I didn't know him. He was a friend of Daisy's."

"He was not," she denied. "I'd never seen him before. He came down in the private car."

"Well, he said he knew you. He said he was raised in Louisville. Asa Bird brought him around at the last minute and asked if we had room for him."

Jordan smiled.

"He was probably bumming his way home. He told me he was president of your class at Yale."

Tom and I looked at each other blankly.

"Biloxi?"

"First place, we didn't have any president——"

Gatsby's foot beat a short, restless tattoo and Tom eyed him suddenly.

"By the way, Mr. Gatsby, I understand you're an Oxford man."

"Not exactly."

"Oh, yes, I understand you went to Oxford."

"Yes—I went there."

A pause. Then Tom's voice, incredulous and insulting:

"You must have gone there about the time Biloxi went to New Haven."

Another pause. A waiter knocked and came in with crushed mint and ice, but the silence was unbroken by his "thank you" and the soft closing of the door. This tremendous detail was to be cleared up at last.

"I told you I went there," said Gatsby.

"I heard you, but I'd like to know when."

"It was in nineteen-nineteen. I only stayed five months. That's why I can't really call myself an Oxford man." [129/130]

Tom glanced around to see if we mirrored his unbelief. But we were all looking at Gatsby.

"It was an opportunity they gave to some of the officers after the Armistice," he continued. "We could go to any of the universities in England or France."

I wanted to get up and slap him on the back. I had one of those renewals of complete faith in him that I'd experienced before.

Daisy rose, smiling faintly, and went to the table.

"Open the whiskey, Tom," she ordered, "and I'll make you a mint julep. Then you won't seem so stupid to yourself. . . . Look at the mint!"

"Wait a minute," snapped Tom, "I want to ask Mr. Gatsby one more question."

"Go on," Gatsby said politely.

"What kind of a row are you trying to cause in my house anyhow?"

They were out in the open at last and Gatsby was content.

"He isn't causing a row," Daisy looked desperately from one to the other. "You're causing a row. Please have a little self-control."

"Self-control!" repeated Tom incredulously. "I suppose the latest thing is to sit back and let Mr. Nobody from Nowhere make love to your wife. Well, if that's the idea you can count me out. . . . Nowadays people begin by sneering at family life and family institutions, and next they'll throw everything overboard and have intermarriage between black and white."

Flushed with his impassioned gibberish, he saw himself standing alone on the last barrier of civilization.

"We're all white here," murmured Jordan.

"I know I'm not very popular. I don't give big parties. [130/131] I suppose you've got to make your house into a pigsty in order to have any friends—in the modern world."

Angry as I was, as we all were, I was tempted to laugh whenever he opened his mouth. The transition from libertine to prig was so complete.

"I've got something to tell *you*, old sport—" began Gatsby. But Daisy guessed at his intention.

"Please don't!" she interrupted helplessly. "Please let's all go home. Why don't we all go home?"

"That's a good idea." I got up. "Come on, Tom. Nobody wants a drink."

"I want to know what Mr. Gatsby has to tell me."

"Your wife doesn't love you," said Gatsby. "She's never loved you. She loves me."

"You must be crazy!" exclaimed Tom automatically.

Gatsby sprang to his feet, vivid with excitement.

"She never loved you, do you hear?" he cried. "She only married you because I was poor and she was tired of waiting for me. It was a terrible mistake, but in her heart she never loved any one except me!"

At this point Jordan and I tried to go, but Tom and Gatsby insisted with competitive firmness that we remain—as though neither of them had anything to conceal and it would be a privilege to partake vicariously of their emotions.

"Sit down, Daisy," Tom's voice groped unsuccessfully for the paternal note. "What's been going on? I want to hear all about it."

"I told you what's been going on," said Gatsby. "Going on for five years—and you didn't know."

Tom turned to Daisy sharply.

"You've been seeing this fellow for five years?"

"Not seeing," said Gatsby. "No, we couldn't meet. [131/132] But both of us loved each other all that time, old sport, and you didn't know. I used to laugh

sometimes"—but there was no laughter in his eyes—"to think that you didn't know."

"Oh—that's all." Tom tapped his thick fingers together like a clergyman and leaned back in his chair.

"You're crazy!" he exploded. "I can't speak about what happened five years ago, because I didn't know Daisy then—and I'll be damned if I see how you got within a mile of her unless you brought the groceries to the back door. But all the rest of that's a God damned lie. Daisy loved me when she married me and she loves me now."

"No," said Gatsby, shaking his head.

"She does, though. The trouble is that sometimes she gets foolish ideas in her head and doesn't know what she's doing." He nodded sagely. "And what's more, I love Daisy too. Once in a while I go off on a spree and make a fool of myself, but I always come back, and in my heart I love her all the time."

"You're revolting," said Daisy. She turned to me, and her voice, dropping an octave lower, filled the room with thrilling scorn: "Do you know why we left Chicago? I'm surprised that they didn't treat you to the story of that little spree."

Gatsby walked over and stood beside her.

"Daisy, that's all over now," he said earnestly. "It doesn't matter any more. Just tell him the truth—that you never loved him—and it's all wiped out forever."

She looked at him blindly. "Why—how could I love him—possibly?"

"You never loved him."

She hesitated. Her eyes fell on Jordan and me with a sort of appeal, as though she realized at last what she [132/133] was doing—and as though she had never, all along, intended doing anything at all. But it was done now. It was too late.

"I never loved him," she said, with perceptible reluctance.

"Not at Kapiolani?" demanded Tom suddenly.

"No."

From the ballroom beneath, muffled and suffocating chords were drifting up on hot waves of air.

"Not that day I carried you down from the Punch Bowl to keep your shoes dry?" There was a husky tenderness in his tone. . . . "Daisy?"

"Please don't." Her voice was cold, but the rancor was gone from it. She looked at Gatsby. "There, Jay," she said—but her hand as she tried to light a cigarette was trembling. Suddenly she threw the cigarette and the burning match on the carpet.

"Oh, you want too much!" she cried to Gatsby. "I love you now—isn't that enough? I can't help what's past." She began to sob helplessly. "I did love him once—but I loved you too."

Gatsby's eyes opened and closed.

"You loved me *too*?" he repeated.

"Even that's a lie," said Tom savagely. "She didn't know you were alive. Why—there're things between Daisy and me that you'll never know, things that neither of us can ever forget."

The words seemed to bite physically into Gatsby.

"I want to speak to Daisy alone," he insisted. "She's all excited now—"

"Even alone I can't say I never loved Tom," she admitted in a pitiful voice. "It wouldn't be true."

"Of course it wouldn't," agreed Tom.

She turned to her husband. [**133/134**]

"As if it mattered to you," she said.

"Of course it matters. I'm going to take better care of you from now on."

"You don't understand," said Gatsby, with a touch of panic. "You're not going to take care of her any more."

"I'm not?" Tom opened his eyes wide and laughed. He could afford to control himself now. "Why's that?"

"Daisy's leaving you."

"Nonsense."

"I am, though," she said with a visible effort.

"She's not leaving me!" Tom's words suddenly leaned down over Gatsby. "Certainly not for a common swindler who'd have to steal the ring he put on her finger."

"I won't stand this!" cried Daisy. "Oh, please let's get out."

"Who are you, anyhow?" broke out Tom. "You're one of that bunch that hangs around with Meyer Wolfsheim—that much I happen to know. I've made a little investigation into your affairs—and I'll carry it further to-morrow."

"You can suit yourself about that, old sport," said Gatsby steadily.

"I found out what your 'drug-stores' were." He turned to us and spoke rapidly. "He and this Wolfsheim bought up a lot of side-street drug-stores here and in Chicago and sold grain alcohol over the counter. That's one of his little stunts. I picked him for a bootlegger the first time I saw him, and I wasn't far wrong."

"What about it?" said Gatsby politely. "I guess your friend Walter Chase wasn't too proud to come in on it."

"And you left him in the lurch, didn't you? You let him go to jail for a month over in New Jersey. God! You ought to hear Walter on the subject of *you*." [**134/135**]

"He came to us dead broke. He was very glad to pick up some money, old sport."

"Don't you call me 'old sport'!" cried Tom. Gatsby said nothing. "Walter could have you up on the betting laws too, but Wolfsheim scared him into shutting his mouth."

That unfamiliar yet recognizable look was back again in Gatsby's face.

"That drug-store business was just small change," continued Tom slowly, "but you've got something on now that Walter's afraid to tell me about."

I glanced at Daisy, who was staring terrified between Gatsby and her husband, and at Jordan, who had begun to balance an invisible but absorbing object on the tip of her chin. Then I turned back to Gatsby—and was startled at his expression. He looked—and this is said in all contempt for the babbled slander of his garden—as if he had "killed a man." For a moment the set of his face could be described in just that fantastic way.

It passed, and he began to talk excitedly to Daisy, denying everything, defending his name against accusations that had not been made. But with every word she was drawing further and further into herself, so he gave that up, and only the dead dream fought on as the afternoon slipped away, trying to touch what was no longer tangible, struggling unhappily, undespairingly, toward that lost voice across the room.

The voice begged again to go.

"*Please*, Tom! I can't stand this any more."

Her frightened eyes told that whatever intentions, whatever courage she had had, were definitely gone.

"You two start on home, Daisy," said Tom. "In Mr. Gatsby's car." [135/136]

She looked at Tom, alarmed now, but he insisted with magnanimous scorn.

"Go on. He won't annoy you. I think he realizes that his presumptuous little flirtation is over."

They were gone, without a word, snapped out, made accidental, isolated, like ghosts, even from our pity.

After a moment Tom got up and began wrapping the unopened bottle of whiskey in the towel.

"Want any of this stuff? Jordan? . . . Nick?"

I didn't answer.

"Nick?" He asked again.

"What?"

"Want any?"

"No . . . I just remembered that today's my birthday."

I was thirty. Before me stretched the portentous, menacing road of a new decade.

It was seven o'clock when we got into the coupé with him and started for Long Island. Tom talked incessantly, exulting and laughing, but his voice was as remote from Jordan and me as the foreign clamor on the sidewalk or the tumult of the elevated overhead. Human sympathy has its

limits, and we were content to let all their tragic arguments fade with the city lights behind. Thirty—the promise of a decade of loneliness, a thinning list of single men to know, a thinning briefcase of enthusiasm, thinning hair. But there was Jordan beside me, who, unlike Daisy, was too wise ever to carry well-forgotten dreams from age to age. As we passed over the dark bridge her wan face fell lazily against my coat's shoulder and the formidable stroke of thirty died away with the reassuring pressure of her hand. [136/137]

So we drove on toward death through the cooling twilight.

The young Greek, Michaelis, who ran the coffee joint beside the ashheaps was the principal witness at the inquest. He had slept through the heat until after five, when he strolled over to the garage, and found George Wilson sick in his office —really sick, pale as his own pale hair and shaking all over. Michaelis advised him to go to bed, but Wilson refused, saying that he'd miss a lot of business if he did. While his neighbor was trying to persuade him a violent racket broke out overhead.

"I've got my wife locked in up there," explained Wilson calmly. "She's going to stay there till the day after to-morrow, and then we're going to move away."

Michaelis was astonished; they had been neighbors for four years, and Wilson had never seemed faintly capable of such a statement. Generally he was one of these worn-out men: when he wasn't working, he sat on a chair in the doorway and stared at the people and the cars that passed along the road. When any one spoke to him he invariably laughed in an agreeable, colorless way. He was his wife's man and not his own.

So naturally Michaelis tried to find out what had happened, but Wilson wouldn't say a word—instead he began to throw curious, suspicious glances at his visitor and ask him what he'd been doing at certain times on certain days. Just as the latter was getting uneasy, some workmen came past the door bound for his restaurant, and Michaelis took the opportunity to get away, intending to come back later. But he didn't. He supposed he forgot to, that's all. When he came outside again, a little after seven, he was reminded of the conversation [137/138] because he heard Mrs. Wilson's voice, loud and scolding, down-stairs in the garage.

"Beat me!" he heard her cry. "Throw me down and beat me, you dirty little coward!"

A moment later she rushed out into the dusk, waving her hands and shouting—before he could move from his door the business was over.

The "death car" as the newspapers called it, didn't stop; it came out of the gathering darkness, wavered tragically for a moment, and then disappeared around the next bend. Michaelis wasn't even sure of its color—he told the first policeman that it was light green. The other car, the one going toward New York, came to rest a hundred yards beyond, and its driver hurried back to where Myrtle Wilson, her life violently extinguished, knelt in the road and mingled her thick dark blood with the dust.

Michaelis and this man reached her first, but when they had torn open her shirtwaist, still damp with perspiration, they saw that her left breast was swinging loose like a flap, and there was no need to listen for the heart beneath. The mouth was wide open and ripped at the corners, as though she had choked a little in giving up the tremendous vitality she had stored so long.

We saw the three or four automobiles and the crowd when we were still some distance away.

"Wreck!" said Tom. "That's good. Wilson'll have a little business at last."

He slowed down, but still without any intention of stopping, until, as we came nearer, the hushed, intent [138/139] faces of the people at the garage door made him automatically put on the brakes.

"We'll take a look," he said doubtfully, "just a look."

I became aware now of a hollow, wailing sound which issued incessantly from the garage, a sound which as we got out of the coupé and walked toward the door resolved itself into the words "Oh, my God!" uttered over and over in a gasping moan.

"There's some bad trouble here," said Tom excitedly.

He reached up on tiptoes and peered over a circle of heads into the garage, which was lit only by a yellow light in a swinging wire basket overhead. Then he made a harsh sound in his throat, and with a violent thrusting movement of his powerful arms pushed his way through.

The circle closed up again with a running murmur of expostulation; it was a minute before I could see anything at all. Then new arrivals deranged the line, and Jordan and I were pushed suddenly inside.

Myrtle Wilson's body, wrapped in a blanket, and then in another blanket, as though she suffered from a chill in the hot night, lay on a work-table by the wall, and Tom, with his back to us, was bending over it, motionless. Next to him stood a motorcycle policeman taking down names with much sweat and correction in a little book. At first I couldn't find the source of the high, groaning words that echoed clamorously through the bare garage—then I saw Wilson standing on the raised threshold of his office, swaying back and forth and holding to the doorposts with both hands. Some man was talking to him in a low voice and attempting, from time to time, to lay a hand on his shoulder, but Wilson [139/140] neither heard nor saw. His eyes would drop slowly from the swinging light to the laden table by the wall, and then jerk back to the light again, and he gave out incessantly his high, horrible call:

"Oh, my Ga-od! Oh, my Ga-od! Oh, Ga-od! Oh, my Ga-od!"

Presently Tom lifted his head with a jerk and, after staring around the garage with glazed eyes, addressed a mumbled incoherent remark to the policeman.

"M-a-v—" the policeman was saying, "—o——"

"No, r—" corrected the man, "M-a-v-r-o——"

"Listen to me!" muttered Tom fiercely.

"r" said the policeman, "o——"

"g——"

"g—" He looked up as Tom's broad hand fell sharply on his shoulder. "What you want, fella?"

"What happened?—that's what I want to know."

"Auto hit her. Ins'antly killed."

"Instantly killed," repeated Tom, staring.

"She ran out ina road. Son-of-a-bitch didn't even stopus car."

"There was two cars," said Michaelis, "one comin', one goin', see?"

"Going where?" asked the policeman keenly.

"One goin' each way. Well, she"—his hand rose toward the blankets but stopped half way and fell to his side—"she ran out there an' the one comin' from N'York knock right into her, goin' thirty or forty miles an hour."

"What's the name of this place here?" demanded the officer.

"Hasn't got any name."

A pale well-dressed negro stepped near. **[140/141]**

"It was a yellow car," he said, "big yellow car. New."

"See the accident?" asked the policeman.

"No, but the car passed me down the road, going faster'n forty. Going fifty, sixty."

"Come here and let's have your name. Look out now. I want to get his name."

Some words of this conversation must have reached Wilson, swaying in the office door, for suddenly a new theme found voice among his gasping cries:

"You don't have to tell me what kind of car it was! I know what kind of car it was!"

Watching Tom, I saw the wad of muscle back of his shoulder tighten under his coat. He walked quickly over to Wilson and, standing in front of him, seized him firmly by the upper arms.

"You've got to pull yourself together," he said with soothing gruffness.

Wilson's eyes fell upon Tom; he started up on his tiptoes and then would have collapsed to his knees had not Tom held him upright.

"Listen," said Tom, shaking him a little. "I just got here a minute ago, from New York. I was bringing you that coupé we've been talking about. That yellow car I was driving this afternoon wasn't mine—do you hear? I haven't seen it all afternoon."

Only the negro and I were near enough to hear what he said, but the policeman caught something in the tone and looked over with truculent eyes.

"What's all that?" he demanded.

"I'm a friend of his." Tom turned his head but kept his hands firm on Wilson's body. "He says he knows the car that did it. . . . It was a yellow car." **[141/142]**

Some dim impulse moved the policeman to look suspiciously at Tom.

"And what color's your car?"

"It's a blue car, a coupé."

"We've come straight from New York," I said.

Someone who had been driving a little behind us confirmed this, and the policeman turned away.

"Now, if you'll let me have that name again correct——"

Picking up Wilson like a doll, Tom carried him into the office, set him down in a chair, and came back.

"If somebody'll come here and sit with him," he snapped authoritatively. He watched while the two men standing closest glanced at each other and went unwillingly into the room. Then Tom shut the door on them and came down the single step, his eyes avoiding the table. As he passed close to me he whispered: "Let's get out."

Self-consciously, with his authoritative arms breaking the way, we pushed through the still gathering crowd, passing a hurried doctor, case in hand, who had been sent for in wild hope half an hour ago.

Tom drove slowly until we were beyond the bend—then his foot came down hard, and the coupé raced along through the night. In a little while I heard a low husky sob, and saw that the tears were overflowing down his face.

"The God damned coward!" he whimpered. "He didn't even stop his car."

The Buchanans' house floated suddenly toward us through the dark rustling trees. Tom stopped beside the [142/143] porch and looked up at the second floor, where two windows bloomed with light among the vines.

"Daisy's home," he said. As we got out of the car he glanced at me and frowned slightly.

"I ought to have dropped you in West Egg, Nick. There's nothing we can do to-night."

A change had come over him, and he spoke gravely, and with decision. As we walked across the moonlight gravel to the porch he disposed of the situation in a few brisk phrases.

"I'll telephone for a taxi to take you home, and while you're waiting you and Jordan better go in the kitchen and have them get you some supper—if you want any." He opened the door. "Come in."

"No, thanks. But I'd be glad if you'd order me the taxi. I'll wait outside."

Jordan put her hand on my arm.

"Won't you come in, Nick?"

"No, thanks."

I was feeling a little sick and I wanted to be alone. But Jordan lingered for a moment more.

"It's only half-past nine," she said.

I'd be damned if I'd go in; I'd had enough of all of them for one day, and suddenly that included Jordan too. She must have seen something of this in my expression, for she turned abruptly away and ran up the porch steps into the house. I sat down for a few minutes with my head in my hands, until I heard the phone taken up inside and the butler's voice calling a taxi. Then I walked slowly down the drive away from the house, intending to wait by the gate.

I hadn't gone twenty yards when I heard my name and Gatsby stepped from between two bushes into the [143/144] path. I must have felt pretty weird by that time, because I could think of nothing except the luminosity of his pink suit under the moon.

"What are you doing?" I inquired.

"Just standing here, old sport."

Somehow, that seemed a despicable occupation. For all I knew he was going to rob the house in a moment; I wouldn't have been surprised to see sinister faces, the faces of "Wolfsheim's people," behind him in the dark shrubbery.

"Did you see any trouble on the road?" he asked after a minute.

"Yes."

He hesitated.

"Was she killed?"

"Yes."

"I thought so; I told Daisy I thought so. It's better that the shock should all come at once. She stood it pretty well."

He spoke as if Daisy's reaction was the only thing that mattered.

"I got to West Egg by a side road," he went on, "and left the car in my garage. I don't think anybody saw us, but of course I can't be sure."

I disliked him so much by this time that I didn't find it necessary to tell him he was wrong.

"Who was the woman?" he inquired.

"Her name was Wilson. Her husband owns the garage. How the devil did it happen?"

"Well, I tried to swing the wheel—" He broke off, and suddenly I guessed at the truth.

"Was Daisy driving?"

"Yes," he said after a moment, "but of course I'll say I was. You see, when we left New York she was very [**144/145**] nervous and she thought it would steady her to drive—and this woman rushed out at us just as we were passing a car coming the other way. It all happened in a minute, but it seemed to me that she wanted to speak to us, thought we were somebody she knew. Well, first Daisy turned away from the woman toward the other car, and then she lost her nerve and turned back. The second my hand reached the wheel I felt the shock—it must have killed her instantly."

"It ripped her open——"

"Don't tell me, old sport." He winced. "Anyhow—Daisy stepped on it. I tried to make her stop, but she couldn't, so I pulled on the emergency brake. Then she fell over into my lap and I drove on.

"She'll be all right tomorrow," he said presently. "I'm just going to wait here and see if he tries to bother her about that unpleasantness this afternoon. She's locked herself into her room, and if he tries any brutality she's going to turn the light out and on again."

"He won't touch her," I said "He's not thinking about her."

"I don't trust him, old sport."

"How long are you going to wait?"

"All night, if necessary. Anyhow, till they all go to bed."

A new point of view occurred to me. Suppose Tom found out that Daisy had been driving. He might think he saw a connection in it—he might think anything. I looked at the house; there were two or three bright windows downstairs and the pink glow from Daisy's room on the second floor.

"You wait here," I said. "I'll see if there's any sign of a commotion."

I walked back along the border of the lawn, traversed [**145/146**] the gravel softly, and tiptoed up the veranda steps. The drawing-room curtains were open, and I saw that the room was empty. Crossing the porch where we had dined that June night three months before, I came to a small rectangle of light which I guessed was the pantry window. The blind was drawn, but I found a rift at the sill.

Daisy and Tom were sitting opposite each other at the kitchen table, with a plate of cold fried chicken between them, and two bottles of ale. He was talking intently across the table at her, and in his earnestness his hand had fallen upon and covered her own. Once in a while she looked up at him and nodded in agreement.

They weren't happy, and neither of them had touched the chicken or the ale—and yet they weren't unhappy either. There was an unmistakable air of natural intimacy about the picture, and anybody would have said that they were conspiring together.

As I tiptoed from the porch I heard my taxi feeling its way along the dark road toward the house. Gatsby was waiting where I had left him in the drive.

"Is it all quiet up there?" he asked anxiously.

"Yes, it's all quiet." I hesitated. "You'd better come home and get some sleep."

He shook his head.

"I want to wait here till Daisy goes to bed. Good night, old sport."

He put his hands in his coat pockets and turned back eagerly to his scrutiny of the house, as though my presence marred the sacredness of the vigil. So I walked away and left him standing there in the moonlight—watching over nothing. [**146/147**]

CHAPTER VIII

I couldn't sleep all night; a fog-horn was groaning incessantly on the Sound, and I tossed half-sick between grotesque reality and savage, frightening dreams. Toward dawn I heard a taxi go up Gatsby's drive, and immediately I jumped out of bed and began to dress—I felt that I had something to tell him, something to warn him about, and morning would be too late.

Crossing his lawn, I saw that his front door was still open and he was leaning against a table in the hall, heavy with dejection or sleep.

"Nothing happened," he said wanly. "I waited, and about four o'clock she came to the window and stood there for a minute and then turned out the light."

His house had never seemed so enormous to me as it did that night when we hunted through the great rooms for cigarettes. We pushed aside curtains that were like pavilions, and felt over innumerable feet of dark wall for electric light switches—once I tumbled with a sort of splash upon the keys of a ghostly piano. There was an inexplicable amount of dust everywhere, and the rooms were musty, as though they hadn't been aired for many days. I found the humidor on an unfamiliar table, with two stale, dry cigarettes inside. Throwing open the French windows of the drawing-room, we sat smoking out into the darkness.

"You ought to go away," I said. "It's pretty certain they'll trace your car."

"Go away *now*, old sport?" [147/148]

"Go to Atlantic City for a week, or up to Montreal."

He wouldn't consider it. He couldn't possibly leave Daisy until he knew what she was going to do. He was clutching at some last hope and I couldn't bear to shake him free.

It was this night that he told me the strange story of his youth with Dan Cody —told it to me because "Jay Gatsby" had broken up like glass against Tom's hard malice, and the long secret extravaganza was played out. I think that he would have acknowledged anything now, without reserve, but he wanted to talk about Daisy.

She was the first "nice" girl he had ever known. In various unrevealed capacities he had come in contact with such people, but always with indiscernible barbed wire between. He found her excitingly desirable. He went to her house, at first with other officers from Camp Taylor, then alone. It amazed him—he had never been in such a beautiful house before. But what gave it an air of breathless intensity was that Daisy lived there—it was as casual a thing to her as his tent out at camp was to him. There was a ripe mystery about it, a hint of bedrooms upstairs more beautiful and cool than other bedrooms, of gay and radiant activities taking place through its corridors, and of romances that were not musty and laid away already in lavender, but fresh and breathing and redolent of this year's shining motor-cars and of dances whose flowers were scarcely withered. It excited him, too, that many men had already loved Daisy—it increased her value in his eyes. He felt their presence all about the house, pervading the air with the shades and echoes of still vibrant emotions. [148/149]

But he knew that he was in Daisy's house by a colossal accident. However, glorious might be his future as Jay Gatsby, he was at present a penniless young man without a past, and at any moment the invisible cloak of his uniform might slip from his shoulders. So he made the most of his time. He took what he could get, ravenously and unscrupulously—eventually he took Daisy one still October night, took her because he had no real right to touch her hand.

He might have despised himself, for he had certainly taken her under false pretenses. I don't mean that he had traded on his phantom millions, but he had deliberately given Daisy a sense of security; he let her believe that he was a person from much the same stratum as herself—that he was fully able to take care of her. As a matter of fact, he had no such facilities—he had no comfortable family standing behind him, and he was liable at the whim of an impersonal government to be blown anywhere about the world.

But he didn't despise himself and it didn't turn out as he had imagined. He had intended, probably, to take what he could and go—but now he found that he had committed himself to the following of a grail. He knew that Daisy was extraordinary, but he didn't realize just how extraordinary a "nice" girl could be. She vanished into her rich house, into her rich, full life, leaving Gatsby—nothing. He felt married to her, that was all.

When they met again, two days later, it was Gatsby who was breathless, who was, somehow, betrayed. Her porch was bright with the bought luxury of starshine; the wicker of the settee squeaked fashionably as she turned toward him and he kissed her curious and lovely mouth. She had caught a cold, and it made her [149/150] voice huskier and more charming than ever, and Gatsby was overwhelmingly aware of the youth and mystery that wealth imprisons and preserves, of the freshness of many clothes, and of Daisy, gleaming like silver, safe and proud above the hot struggles of the poor.

"I can't describe to you how surprised I was to find out I loved her, old sport. I even hoped for a while that she'd throw me over, but she didn't, because she was in love with me too. She thought I knew a lot because I knew different things from her . . . Well, there I was, 'way off my ambitions, getting deeper in love every minute, and all of a sudden I didn't care. What was the use of doing great things if I could have a better time telling her what I was going to do?"

On the last afternoon before he went abroad, he sat with Daisy in his arms for a long, silent time. It was a cold fall day, with fire in the room and her cheeks flushed. Now and then she moved and he changed his arm a little, and once he kissed her dark shining hair. The afternoon had made them tranquil for a while, as if to give them a deep memory for the long parting the next day promised. They had never been closer in their month of love, nor communicated more profoundly one with another, than when she brushed silent lips against his coat's shoulder or when he touched the end of her fingers, gently, as though she were asleep.

He did extraordinarily well in the war. He was a captain before he went to the front, and following the Argonne battles he got his majority and the command of the divisional machine-guns. After the Armistice he [150/151] tried frantically to get home, but some complication or misunderstanding sent him to Oxford instead. He was worried now—there was a quality of nervous despair in Daisy's letters. She didn't see why he couldn't come. She was feeling the pressure of the world outside, and she wanted to see him and feel his presence beside her and be reassured that she was doing the right thing after all.

For Daisy was young and her artificial world was redolent of orchids and pleasant, cheerful snobbery and orchestras which set the rhythm of the year, summing up the sadness and suggestiveness of life in new tunes. All night the saxophones wailed the hopeless comment of the *Beale Street Blues* while a hundred pairs of golden and silver slippers shuffled the shining dust. At the gray tea hour there were always rooms that throbbed incessantly with this low, sweet fever, while fresh faces drifted here and there like rose petals blown by the sad horns around the floor.

Through this twilight universe Daisy began to move again with the season; suddenly she was again keeping half a dozen dates a day with half a dozen men, and drowsing asleep at dawn with the beads and chiffon of an evening dress tangled among dying orchids on the floor beside her bed. And all the time something within her was crying for a decision. She wanted her life shaped now, immediately —and the decision must be made by some force—of love, of money, of unquestionable practicality—that was close at hand.

That force took shape in the middle of spring with the arrival of Tom Buchanan. There was a wholesome bulkiness about his person and his position, and Daisy [151/152] was flattered. Doubtless there was a certain struggle and a certain relief. The letter reached Gatsby while he was still at Oxford.

It was dawn now on Long Island and we went about opening the rest of the windows downstairs, filling the house with gray-turning, gold-turning light. The shadow of a tree fell abruptly across the dew and ghostly birds began to sing among the blue leaves. There was a slow, pleasant movement in the air, scarcely a wind, promising a cool, lovely day.

"I don't think she ever loved him," Gatsby turned around from a window and looked at me challengingly. "You must remember, old sport, she was very excited this afternoon. He told her those things in a way that frightened her—that made it look as if I was some kind of cheap sharper. And the result was she hardly knew what she was saying."

He sat down gloomily.

"Of course she might have loved him just for a minute, when they were first married—and loved me more even then, do you see?"

Suddenly he came out with a curious remark.

"In any case," he said, "it was just personal."

What could you make of that, except to suspect some intensity in his conception of the affair that couldn't be measured?

He came back from France when Tom and Daisy were still on their wedding trip, and made a miserable but irresistible journey to Louisville on the last of his army pay. He stayed there a week, walking the streets where their footsteps had clicked together through the [152/153] November night and revisiting the out-of-the-way places to which they had driven in her white car. Just as Daisy's house had always seemed to him more mysterious and gay than other houses, so his idea of the city itself, even though she was gone from it, was pervaded with a melancholy beauty.

He left feeling that if he had searched harder, he might have found her—that he was leaving her behind. The day-coach —he was penniless now—was hot. He went out to the open vestibule and sat down on a folding-chair, and the station slid away and the backs of unfamiliar buildings moved by. Then out into the spring fields, where a yellow trolley raced them for a minute with the people in it who might once have seen the pale magic of her face along the casual street.

The track curved and now it was going away from the sun, which, as it sank lower, seemed to spread itself in benediction over the vanishing city where she had drawn her breath. He stretched out his hand desperately as if to snatch only a wisp of air, to save a fragment of the spot that she had made lovely for him. But it was all going by too fast now for his blurred eyes and he knew that he had lost that part of it, the freshest and the best, forever.

It was nine o'clock when we finished breakfast and went out on the porch. The night had made a sharp difference in the weather and there was an autumn flavor in the air. The gardener, the last one of Gatsby's former servants, came to the foot of the steps.

"I'm going to drain the pool today, Mr. Gatsby. Leaves'll start falling pretty soon, and then there's always trouble with the pipes." [153/154]

"Don't do it today," Gatsby answered. He turned to me apologetically. "You know, old sport, I've never used that pool all summer?"

I looked at my watch and stood up.

"Twelve minutes to my train."

I didn't want to go to the city. I wasn't worth a decent stroke of work, but it was more than that—I didn't want to leave Gatsby. I missed that train, and then another, before I could get myself away.

"I'll call you up," I said finally.

"Do, old sport."

"I'll call you about noon."

We walked slowly down the steps.

"I suppose Daisy'll call too." He looked at me anxiously, as if he hoped I'd corroborate this.

"I suppose so."

"Well, good-by."

We shook hands and I started away. Just before I reached the hedge I remembered something and turned around.

"They're a rotten crowd," I shouted across the lawn. "You're worth the whole damn bunch put together."

I've always been glad I said that. It was the only compliment I ever gave him, because I disapproved of him from beginning to end. First he nodded politely, and then his face broke into that radiant and understanding smile, as if we'd been in ecstatic cahoots on that fact all the time. His gorgeous pink rag of a suit made a bright spot of color against the white steps, and I thought of the night when I first came to his ancestral home, three months before. The lawn and drive had been crowded with the faces of those who guessed at his corruption— [154/155] and he had stood on those steps, concealing his incorruptible dream, as he waved them good-by.

I thanked him for his hospitality. We were always thanking him for that—I and the others.

"Good-by," I called. "I enjoyed breakfast, Gatsby."

Up in the city, I tried for a while to list the quotations on an interminable amount of stock, then I fell asleep in my swivel-chair. Just before noon the phone woke me, and I started up with sweat breaking out on my forehead. It was Jordan Baker; she often called me up at this hour because the uncertainty of her own movements between hotels and clubs and private houses made her hard to find in any other way. Usually her voice came over the wire as something fresh and cool, as if a divot from a green golf-links had come sailing in at the office window, but this morning it seemed harsh and dry.

"I've left Daisy's house," she said. "I'm at Hempstead, and I'm going down to Southampton this afternoon."

Probably it had been tactful to leave Daisy's house, but the act annoyed me, and her next remark made me rigid.

"You weren't so nice to me last night."

"How could it have mattered then?"

Silence for a moment. Then:

"However—I want to see you."

"I want to see you, too."

"Suppose I don't go to Southampton, and come into town this afternoon?"

"No—I don't think this afternoon."

"Very well." [155/156]

"It's impossible this afternoon. Various——"

We talked like that for a while, and then abruptly we weren't talking any longer. I don't know which of us hung up with a sharp click, but I know I didn't care. I couldn't have talked to her across a tea-table that day if I never talked to her again in this world.

I called Gatsby's house a few minutes later, but the line was busy. I tried four times; finally an exasperated central told me the wire was being kept open for long distance from Detroit. Taking out my time-table, I drew a small circle around the three-fifty train. Then I leaned back in my chair and tried to think. It was just noon.

When I passed the ashheaps on the train that morning I had crossed deliberately to the other side of the car. I supposed there'd be a curious crowd around there all day with little boys searching for dark spots in the dust, and some garrulous man telling over and over what had happened, until it became less and less real even to him and he could tell it no longer, and Myrtle Wilson's tragic achievement was forgotten. Now I want to go back a little and tell what happened at the garage after we left there the night before.

They had difficulty in locating the sister, Catherine. She must have broken her rule against drinking that night, for when she arrived she was stupid with liquor and unable to understand that the ambulance had already gone to Flushing. When they convinced her of this, she immediately fainted, as if that was the intolerable part of the affair. Someone, kind or curious, took her in his car and drove her in the wake of her sister's body.

Until long after midnight a changing crowd lapped up against the front of the garage, while George Wilson [156/157] rocked himself back and forth on the couch inside. For a while the door of the office was open, and every one who came into the garage glanced irresistibly through it. Finally some one said it was a shame, and closed the door. Michaelis and several other men were with him; first, four or five men, later two or three men. Still later Michaelis had to ask the last stranger to wait there fifteen minutes longer, while he went back to his own place and made a pot of coffee. After that, he stayed there alone with Wilson until dawn.

About three o'clock the quality of Wilson's incoherent muttering changed—he grew quieter and began to talk about the yellow car. He announced that he had a way of finding out whom the yellow car belonged to, and then he blurted out that a couple of months ago his wife had come from the city with her face bruised and her nose swollen.

But when he heard himself say this, he flinched and began to cry "Oh, my God!" again in his groaning voice. Michaelis made a clumsy attempt to distract him.

"How long have you been married, George? Come on there, try and sit still a minute and answer my question. How long have you been married?"

"Twelve years."

"Ever had any children? Come on, George, sit still—I asked you a question. Did you ever have any children?"

The hard brown beetles kept thudding against the dull light, and whenever Michaelis heard a car go tearing along the road outside it sounded to him like the car that hadn't stopped a few hours before. He didn't like to go into the garage, because the work bench was stained where the body had been lying, so he moved uncomfortably around the office—he knew every object in it [157/158] before morning—and from time to time sat down beside Wilson trying to keep him more quiet.

"Have you got a church you go to sometimes, George? Maybe even if you haven't been there for a long time? Maybe I could call up the church and get a priest to come over and he could talk to you, see?"

"Don't belong to any."

"You ought to have a church, George, for times like this. You must have gone to church once. Didn't you get married in a church? Listen, George, listen to me. Didn't you get married in a church?"

"That was a long time ago."

The effort of answering broke the rhythm of his rocking—for a moment he was silent. Then the same half-knowing, half-bewildered look came back into his faded eyes.

"Look in the drawer there," he said, pointing at the desk.

"Which drawer?"

"That drawer—that one."

Michaelis opened the drawer nearest his hand. There was nothing in it but a small, expensive dog-leash, made of leather and braided silver. It was apparently new.

"This?" he inquired, holding it up.

Wilson stared and nodded.

"I found it yesterday afternoon. She tried to tell me about it, but I knew it was something funny."

"You mean your wife bought it?"

"She had it wrapped in tissue paper on her bureau."

Michaelis didn't see anything odd in that, and he gave Wilson a dozen reasons why his wife might have bought the dog-leash. But conceivably Wilson had heard some of these same explanations before, from [158/159] Myrtle, because he began saying "Oh, my God!" again in a whisper —his comforter left several explanations in the air.

"Then he killed her," said Wilson. His mouth dropped open suddenly.

"Who did?"

"I have a way of finding out."

"You're morbid, George," said his friend. "This has been a strain to you and you don't know what you're saying. You'd better try and sit quiet till morning."

"He murdered her."

"It was an accident, George."

Wilson shook his head. His eyes narrowed and his mouth widened slightly with the ghost of a superior "Hm!"

"I know," he said definitely, "I'm one of these trusting fellas and I don't think any harm to *no*body, but when I get to know a thing I know it. It was the man in that car. She ran out to speak to him and he wouldn't stop."

Michaelis had seen this too, but it hadn't occurred to him that there was any special significance in it. He believed that Mrs. Wilson had been running away from her husband, rather than trying to stop any particular car.

"How could she of been like that?"

"She's a deep one," said Wilson, as if that answered the question. "Ah-h-h——"

He began to rock again, and Michaelis stood twisting the leash in his hand.

"Maybe you got some friend that I could telephone for, George?"

This was a forlorn hope—he was almost sure that Wilson had no friend: there was not enough of him for [159/160] his wife. He was glad a little later when he noticed a change in the room, a blue quickening by the window, and realized that dawn wasn't far off. About five o'clock it was blue enough outside to snap off the light.

Wilson's glazed eyes turned out to the ashheaps, where small gray clouds took on fantastic shapes and scurried here and there in the faint dawn wind.

"I spoke to her," he muttered, after a long silence. "I told her she might fool me but she couldn't fool God. I took her to the window"—with an effort he got up and walked to the rear window and leaned with his face pressed against it—"and I said 'God knows what you've been doing, everything you've been doing. You may fool me, but you can't fool God!' "

Standing behind him, Michaelis saw with a shock that he was looking at the eyes of Doctor T. J. Eckleburg, which had just emerged, pale and enormous, from the dissolving night.

"God sees everything," repeated Wilson.

"That's an advertisement," Michaelis assured him. Something made him turn away from the window and look back into the room. But Wilson stood there a long time, his face close to the window pane, nodding into the twilight.

By six o'clock Michaelis was worn out, and grateful for the sound of a car stopping outside. It was one of the watchers of the night before who had promised to come back, so he cooked breakfast for three, which he and the other man ate together. Wilson was quieter now, and Michaelis went home to sleep; when he awoke four hours later and hurried back to the garage, Wilson was gone. [160/161]

His movements—he was on foot all the time—were afterward traced to Port Roosevelt and then to Gad's Hill, where he bought a sandwich that he didn't eat, and a cup of coffee. He must have been tired and walking slowly, for he didn't reach Gad's Hill until noon. Thus far there was no difficulty in accounting for his time— there were boys who had seen a man "acting sort of crazy," and motorists at whom he stared oddly from the side of the road. Then for three hours he disappeared from view. The police, on the strength of what he said to Michaelis, that he "had a way of finding out," supposed that he spent that time going from garage to garage thereabout, inquiring for a yellow car. On the other hand, no garage man who had seen him ever came forward, and perhaps he had an easier, surer way of finding out what he wanted to know. By half-past two he was in West Egg, where he asked some one the way to Gatsby's house. So by that time he knew Gatsby's name.

At two o'clock Gatsby put on his bathing-suit and left word with the butler that if any one phoned word was to be brought to him at the pool. He stopped at the garage for a pneumatic mattress that had amused his guests during the summer, and the chauffeur helped him pump it up. Then he gave instructions that the open car wasn't to be taken out under any circumstances—and this was strange, because the front right fender needed repair.

Gatsby shouldered the mattress and started for the pool. Once he stopped and shifted it a little, and the chauffeur asked him if he needed help, but he shook his [161/162] head and in a moment disappeared among the yellowing trees.

No telephone message arrived, but the butler went without his sleep and waited for it until four o'clock—until long after there was any one to give it to if it came. I have an idea that Gatsby himself didn't believe it would come, and perhaps he no longer cared. If that was true he must have felt that he had lost the old warm world, paid a high price for living too long with a single dream. He must have looked up at an unfamiliar sky through frightening leaves and shivered as he found what a grotesque thing a rose is and how raw the sunlight was upon the scarcely created grass. A new world, material without being real, where poor ghosts, breathing dreams like air, drifted fortuitously about . . . like that ashen, fantastic figure gliding toward him through the amorphous trees.

The chauffeur—he was one of Wolfsheim's protégés—heard the shots—afterward he could only say that he hadn't thought anything much about them. I drove from the station directly to Gatsby's house and my rushing anxiously up the front steps was the first thing that alarmed any one. But they knew then, I firmly believe. With scarcely a word said, four of us, the chauffeur, butler, gardener, and I, hurried down to the pool.

There was a faint, barely perceptible movement of the water as the fresh flow from one end urged its way toward the drain at the other. With little ripples that were hardly the shadows of waves, the laden mattress moved irregularly down the pool. A small gust of wind that scarcely corrugated the surface was enough to disturb its accidental course with its accidental burden. [162/163] The touch of a cluster of leaves revolved it slowly, tracing, like the leg of transit, a thin red circle in the water.

It was after we started with Gatsby toward the house that the gardener saw Wilson's body a little way off in the grass, and the holocaust was complete. [163/164]

CHAPTER IX

After two years I remember the rest of that day, and that night and the next day, only as an endless drill of police and photographers and newspaper men in and out of Gatsby's front door. A rope stretched across the main gate and a policeman by it kept out the curious, but little boys soon discovered that they could enter through my yard, and there were always a few of them clustered open-mouthed about the pool. Some one with a positive manner, perhaps a detective, used the expression "madman" as he bent over Wilson's body that afternoon, and the adventitious authority of his voice set the key for the newspaper reports next morning.

Most of those reports were a nightmare —grotesque, circumstantial, eager, and untrue. When Michaelis's testimony at the inquest brought to light Wilson's suspicions of his wife I thought the whole tale would shortly be served up in racy pasquinade—but Catherine, who might have said anything, didn't say a word. She showed a surprising amount of character about it too—looked at the coroner with determined eyes under that corrected brow of hers, and swore that her sister had never seen Gatsby, that her sister was completely happy with her husband, that her sister had been into no mischief whatever. She convinced herself of it, and cried into her handkerchief, as if the very suggestion was more than she could endure. So Wilson was reduced to a man "deranged by grief" in order that the [164/165] case might remain in its simplest form. And it rested there.

But all this part of it seemed remote and unessential. I found myself on Gatsby's side, and alone. From the moment I telephoned news of the catastrophe to West Egg Village, every surmise about him, and every practical question, was referred to me. At first I was surprised and confused; then, as he lay in his house and didn't move or breathe or speak, hour upon hour, it grew upon me that I was responsible, because no one else was interested—interested, I mean, with that intense personal interest to which every one has some vague right at the end.

I called up Daisy half an hour after we found him, called her instinctively and without hesitation. But she and Tom had gone away early that afternoon, and taken baggage with them.

"Left no address?"

"No."

"Say when they'd be back?"

"No."

"Any idea where they are? How I could reach them?"

"I don't know. Can't say."

I wanted to get somebody for him. I wanted to go into the room where he lay and reassure him: "I'll get somebody for you, Gatsby. Don't worry. Just trust me and I'll get somebody for you——"

Meyer Wolfsheim's name wasn't in the phone book. The butler gave me his office address on Broadway, and I called Information, but by the time I had the number it was long after five, and no one answered the phone.

"Will you ring again?"

"I've rung them three times." [165/166]

"It's very important."

"Sorry. I'm afraid no one's there."

I went back to the drawing-room and thought for an instant that they were chance visitors, all these official people who suddenly filled it. But, as they drew back the sheet and looked at Gatsby with unmoved eyes, his protest continued in my brain:

"Look here, old sport, you've got to get somebody for me. You've got to try hard. I can't go through this alone."

Some one started to ask me questions, but I broke away and going upstairs looked hastily through the unlocked parts of his desk—he'd never told me definitely that his parents were dead. But there was nothing—only the picture of Dan Cody, a token of forgotten violence, staring down from the wall.

Next morning I sent the butler to New York with a letter to Wolfsheim, which asked for information and urged him to come out on the next train. That request seemed superfluous when I wrote it. I was sure he'd start when he saw the newspapers, just as I was sure there'd be a wire from Daisy before noon—but neither a wire nor Mr. Wolfsheim arrived; no one arrived except more police and photographers and newspaper men. When the butler brought back Wolfsheim's answer I began to have a feeling of defiance, of scornful solidarity between Gatsby and me against them all.

Dear Mr. Carraway. This has been one of the most terrible shocks of my life to me I hardly can believe it that it is true at all. Such a mad act as that man did should make us all think. I cannot come down now as I am tied up in some very important business and cannot get mixed up in this thing now. If there is anything I can do a little later let me know in a letter by Edgar. [167/168] I hardly know where I am when I hear about a thing like this and am completely knocked down and out.
Yours truly
MEYER WOLFSHEIM

and then hasty addenda beneath:

Let me know about the funeral etc do not know his family at all.

When the phone rang that afternoon and Long Distance said Chicago was calling I thought this would be Daisy at last. But the connection came through as a man's voice, very thin and far away.

"This is Slagle speaking . . ."

"Yes?" The name was unfamiliar.

"Hell of a note, isn't it? Get my wire?"

"There haven't been any wires."

"Young Parke's in trouble," he said rapidly. "They picked him up when he handed the bonds over the counter. They got a circular from New York giving 'em the numbers just five minutes before. What d'you know about that, hey? You never can tell in these hick towns——"

"Hello!" I interrupted breathlessly. "Look here—this isn't Mr. Gatsby. Mr. Gatsby's dead."

There was a long silence on the other end of the wire, followed by an exclamation . . . then a quick squawk as the connection was broken.

I think it was on the third day that a telegram signed Henry C. Gatz arrived from a town in Minnesota. It said only that the sender was leaving immediately and to postpone the funeral until he came.

It was Gatsby's father, a solemn old man, very helpless and dismayed, bundled up in a long cheap ulster [167/168] against the warm September day. His eyes leaked continuously with excitement, and when I took the bag and umbrella from his hands he began to pull so incessantly at his sparse gray beard that I had difficulty in getting off his coat. He was on the point of collapse, so I took him into the music room and made him sit down while I sent for something to eat. But he wouldn't eat, and the glass of milk spilled from his trembling hand.

"I saw it in the Chicago newspaper," he said. "It was all in the Chicago newspaper. I started right away."

"I didn't know how to reach you."

His eyes, seeing nothing, moved ceaselessly about the room.

"It was a madman," he said. "He must have been mad."

"Wouldn't you like some coffee?" I urged him.

"I don't want anything. I'm all right now, Mr. ——"

"Carraway."

"Well, I'm all right now. Where have they got Jimmy?"

I took him into the drawing-room, where his son lay, and left him there. Some little boys had come up on the steps and were looking into the hall; when I told them who had arrived, they went reluctantly away.

After a little while Mr. Gatz opened the door and came out, his mouth ajar, his face flushed slightly, his eyes leaking isolated and unpunctual tears. He had reached an age where death no longer has the quality of ghastly surprise, and when he looked around him now for the first time and saw the height and splendor [168/169] of the hall and the great rooms opening out from it into other rooms, his grief began to be mixed with an awed pride. I helped him to a bedroom upstairs; while he took off his coat and vest I told him that all arrangements had been deferred until he came.

"I didn't know what you'd want, Mr. Gatsby——"

"Gatz is my name."

"—Mr. Gatz. I thought you might want to take the body West."

He shook his head.

"Jimmy always liked it better down East. He rose up to his position in the East. Were you a friend of my boy's, Mr. ——?"

"We were close friends."

"He had a big future before him, you know. He was only a young man, but he had a lot of brain power here."

He touched his head impressively, and I nodded.

"If he'd of lived, he'd of been a great man. A man like James J. Hill. He'd of helped build up the country."

"That's true," I said, uncomfortably.

He fumbled at the embroidered coverlet, trying to take it from the bed, and lay down stiffly—was instantly asleep.

That night an obviously frightened person called up, and demanded to know who I was before he would give his name.

"This is Mr. Carraway," I said.

"Oh!" He sounded relieved. "This is Klipspringer."

I was relieved too, for that seemed to promise another friend at Gatsby's grave. I didn't want it to be [169/170] in the papers and draw a sight-seeing crowd, so I'd been calling up a few people myself. They were hard to find.

"The funeral's tomorrow," I said. "Three o'clock, here at the house. I wish you'd tell anybody who'd be interested."

"Oh, I will," he broke out hastily. "Of course I'm not likely to see anybody, but if I do."

His tone made me suspicious.

"Of course you'll be there yourself."

"Well, I'll certainly try. What I called up about is——"

"Wait a minute," I interrupted. "How about saying you'll come?"

"Well, the fact is—the truth of the matter is that I'm staying with some people up here in Greenwich, and they rather expect me to be with them tomorrow. In fact, there's a sort of picnic or something. Of course I'll do my very best to get away."

I ejaculated an unrestrained "Huh!" and he must have heard me, for he went on nervously:

"What I called up about was a pair of shoes I left there. I wonder if it'd be too much trouble to have the butler send them on. You see, they're tennis shoes, and I'm sort of helpless without them. My address is care of B. F.——"

I didn't hear the rest of the name, because I hung up the receiver.

After that I felt a certain shame for Gatsby—one gentleman to whom I telephoned implied that he had got what he deserved. However, that was my fault, for he was one of those who used to sneer most bit- [170/171] terly at Gatsby on the courage of Gatsby's liquor, and I should have known better than to call him.

The morning of the funeral I went up to New York to see Meyer Wolfsheim; I couldn't seem to reach him any other way. The door that I pushed open, on the advice of an elevator boy, was marked "The Swastika Holding Company," and at first there didn't seem to be any one inside. But when I'd shouted "hello" several times in vain, an argument broke out behind a partition, and presently a lovely Jewess appeared at an interior door and scrutinized me with black hostile eyes.

"Nobody's in," she said. "Mr. Wolfsheim's gone to Chicago."

The first part of this was obviously untrue, for some one had begun to whistle "The Rosary," tunelessly, inside.

"Please say that Mr. Carraway wants to see him."

"I can't get him back from Chicago, can I?"

At this moment a voice, unmistakably Wolfsheim's, called "Stella!" from the other side of the door.

"Leave your name on the desk," she said quickly. "I'll give it to him when he gets back."

"But I know he's there."

She took a step toward me and began to slide her hands indignantly up and down her hips.

"You young men think you can force your way in here any time," she scolded. "We're getting sickantired of it. When I say he's in Chicago, he's in Chicago."

I mentioned Gatsby.

"Oh-h!" She looked at me over again. "Will you just — What was your name?"

She vanished. In a moment Meyer Wolfsheim stood [171/172] solemnly in the doorway, holding out both hands. He drew me into his office, remarking in a reverent voice that it was a sad time for all of us, and offered me a cigar.

"My memory goes back to when first I met him," he said. "A young major just out of the army and covered over with medals he got in the war. He was so hard up he had to keep on wearing his uniform because he couldn't buy some regular clothes. First time I saw him was when he come into Winebrenner's poolroom at Forty-third Street and asked for a job. He hadn't eat anything for a couple of days. 'Come on have some lunch with me,' I sid. He ate more than four dollars' worth of food in half an hour."

"Did you start him in business?" I inquired.

"Start him! I made him."

"Oh."

"I raised him up out of nothing, right out of the gutter. I saw right away he was a fine-appearing, gentlemanly young man, and when he told me he was an Oggsford I knew I could use him good. I got him to join up in the American Legion and he used to stand high there. Right off he did some work for a client of mine up to Albany. We were so thick like that in everything"—he held up two bulbous fingers—"always together."

I wondered if this partnership had included the World's Series transaction in 1919.

"Now he's dead," I said after a moment. "You were his closest friend, so I know you'll want to come to his funeral this afternoon."

"I'd like to come."

"Well, come then." [172/173]

The hair in his nostrils quivered slightly, and as he shook his head his eyes filled with tears.

"I can't do it—I can't get mixed up in it," he said.

"There's nothing to get mixed up in. It's all over now."

"When a man gets killed I never like to get mixed up in it in any way. I keep out. When I was a young man it was different—if a friend of mine died, no matter how, I stuck with them to the end. You may think that's sentimental, but I mean it—to the bitter end."

I saw that for some reason of his own

he was determined not to come, so I stood up.

"Are you a college man?" he inquired suddenly.

For a moment I thought he was going to suggest a "gonnegtion," but he only nodded and shook my hand.

"Let us learn to show our friendship for a man when he is alive and not after he is dead," he suggested. "After that my own rule is to let everything alone."

When I left his office the sky had turned dark and I got back to West Egg in a drizzle. After changing my clothes I went next door and found Mr. Gatz walking up and down excitedly in the hall. His pride in his son and in his son's possessions was continually increasing and now he had something to show me.

"Jimmy sent me this picture." He took out his wallet with trembling fingers. "Look there."

It was a photograph of the house, cracked in the corners and dirty with many hands. He pointed out every detail to me eagerly. "Look there!" and then sought admiration from my eyes. He had shown it so often that I think it was more real to him now than the house itself. [173/174]

"Jimmy sent it to me. I think it's a very pretty picture. It shows up well."

"Very well. Had you seen him lately?"

"He come out to see me two years ago and bought me the house I live in now. Of course we was broke up when he run off from home, but I see now there was a reason for it. He knew he had a big future in front of him. And ever since he made a success he was very generous with me."

He seemed reluctant to put away the picture, held it for another minute, lingeringly, before my eyes. Then he returned the wallet and pulled from his pocket a ragged old copy of a book called *Hopalong Cassidy*.

"Look here, this is a book he had when he was a boy. It just shows you."

He opened it at the back cover and turned it around for me to see. On the last fly-leaf was printed the word schedule, and the date September 12, 1906. And underneath:

Rise from bed	6.00	A.M.
Dumbbell exercise and wall-scaling	6.15–6.30	"
Study electricity, etc.	7.15–8.15	"
Work	8.30–4.30	P.M.
Baseball and sports	4.30–5.00	"
Practice elocution, poise and how to attain it	5.00–6.00	"
Study needed inventions	7.00–9.00	"

GENERAL RESOLVES

No wasting time at Shafters or [a name, indecipherable]
No more smokeing or chewing.
Bath every other day
Read one improving book or magazine per week
Save $5.00 [crossed out] $3.00 per week
Be better to parents [174/175]

"I come across this book by accident," said the old man. "It just shows you, don't it?"

"It just shows you."

"Jimmy was bound to get ahead. He always had some resolves like this or something. Do you notice what he's got about improving his mind? He was always great for that. He told me I et like a hog once,. and I beat him for it."

He was reluctant to close the book, reading each item aloud and then looking eagerly at me. I think he rather expected me to copy down the list for my own use.

A little before three the Lutheran minister arrived from Flushing, and I began to look involuntarily out the windows for other cars. So did Gatsby's father. And as the time passed and the servants came in and stood waiting in the hall, his eyes began to blink anxiously, and he spoke of the rain in a worried, uncertain way. The minister glanced several times at his watch, so I took him aside and asked him to wait for half an hour. But it wasn't any use. Nobody came.

About five o'clock our procession of three cars reached the cemetery and stopped in a thick drizzle beside the gate—first a motor hearse, horribly black and wet, then Mr. Gatz and the minister and I in the limousine, and a little later four or five servants and the postman from West Egg, in Gatsby's station wagon, all wet to the skin. As we started through the gate into the cemetery I heard a car stop and then the sound of some one splashing after us over the soggy ground. I looked around. It was the man with owl-eyed glasses whom I had found marvelling over Gatsby's books in the library one night three months before.

I'd never seen him since then. I don't know how he [175/176] knew about the funeral, or even his name. The rain poured down his thick glasses, and he took them off and wiped them to see the protecting canvas unrolled from Gatsby's grave.

I tried to think about Gatsby then for a moment, but he was already too far away, and I could only remember, without resentment, that Daisy hadn't sent a message or a flower. Dimly I heard some one murmur "Blessed are the dead that the rain falls on," and then the owl-eyed man said "Amen to that," in a brave voice.

We straggled down quickly through the rain to the cars. Owl-eyes spoke to me by the gate.

"I couldn't get to the house," he remarked.

"Neither could anybody else."

"Go on!" He started. "Why, my God! they used to go there by the hundreds."

He took off his glasses and wiped them again, outside and in.

"The poor son-of-a-bitch," he said.

One of my most vivid memories is of coming back West from prep school and later from college at Christmas time. Those who went farther than Chicago would gather in the old dim Union Station at six o'clock of a December evening, with a few Chicago friends, already caught up into their own holiday gayeties, to bid them a hasty good-by. I remember the fur coats of the girls returning from Miss This-or-That's and the chatter of frozen breath and the hands waving overhead as we caught sight of old acquaintances, and the matchings of invitations: "Are you going to the Ordways'? the Herseys'? the Schultzes'?" and the long green tickets [176/177] clasped tight in our gloved hands. And last the murky yellow cars of the Chicago, Milwaukee & St. Paul railroad looking cheerful as Christmas itself on the tracks beside the gate.

When we pulled out into the winter night and the real snow, our snow, began to stretch out beside us and twinkle against the windows, and the dim lights of small Wisconsin stations moved by, a sharp wild brace came suddenly into the air. We drew in deep breaths of it as we walked back from dinner through the cold vestibules, unutterably aware of our identity with this country for one strange hour, before we melted indistinguishably into it again.

That's my Middle West—not the wheat or the prairies or the lost Swede towns, but the thrilling returning trains of my youth, and the street lamps and sleigh bells in the frosty dark and the shadows of holly wreaths thrown by lighted windows on the snow. I am part of that, a little solemn with the feel of those long winters, a little complacent from growing up in the Carraway house in a city where dwellings are still called through decades by a family's name. I see now that this has been a story of the West, after all— Tom and Gatsby, Daisy and Jordan and I, were all Westerners, and perhaps we possessed some deficiency in common which made us subtly unadaptable to Eastern life.

Even when the East excited me most, even when I was most keenly aware of its superiority to the bored, sprawling, swollen towns beyond the Ohio, with their interminable inquisitions which spared only the children and the very old—even then it had always for me a quality of distortion. West Egg, especially, still figures [177/178] in my more fantastic dreams. I see it as a night scene by El Greco: a hundred houses, at once conventional and grotesque, crouching under a sullen, overhanging sky and a lustreless moon. In the foreground four solemn men in dress suits are walking along the sidewalk with a stretcher on which lies a drunken woman in a white evening dress. Her hand, which dangles over the side, sparkles cold with jewels. Gravely the men turn in at a house—the wrong house. But no one knows the woman's name, and no one cares.

After Gatsby's death the East was haunted for me like that, distorted beyond my eyes' power of correction. So when the blue smoke of brittle leaves was in the air and the wind blew the wet laundry stiff on the line I decided to come back home.

There was one thing to be done before I left, an awkward, unpleasant thing that perhaps had better have been let alone. But I wanted to leave things in order and not just trust that obliging and indifferent sea to sweep my refuse away. I saw Jordan Baker and talked over and around what had happened to us together, and what had happened afterward to me, and she lay perfectly still, listening, in a big chair.

She was dressed to play golf, and I remember thinking she looked like a good illustration, her chin raised a little jauntily, her hair the color of an autumn leaf, her face the same brown tint as the fingerless glove on her knee. When I had finished she told me without comment that she was engaged to another man. I doubted that, though there were several she could have married at a nod of her head, but I pretended to be surprised. For just a minute I wondered if I wasn't [178/179] making a mistake, then I thought it all over again quickly and got up to say good-by.

"Nevertheless you did throw me over," said Jordan suddenly. "You threw me over on the telephone. I don't give a damn about you now, but it was a new experience for me, and I felt a little dizzy for a while."

We shook hands.

"Oh, and do you remember"—she added —"a conversation we had once about driving a car?"

"Why—not exactly."

"You said a bad driver was only safe until she met another bad driver? Well, I met another bad driver, didn't I? I mean it was careless of me to make such a wrong guess. I thought you were rather an honest, straightforward person. I thought it was your secret pride."

"I'm thirty," I said. "I'm five years too old to lie to myself and call it honor."

She didn't answer. Angry, and half in love with her, and tremendously sorry, I turned away.

One afternoon late in October I saw Tom Buchanan. He was walking ahead of me along Fifth Avenue in his alert, aggressive way, his hands out a little from his body as if to fight off interference, his head moving sharply here and there, adapting itself to his restless eyes. Just as I slowed up to avoid overtaking him he stopped and began frowning into the windows of a jewelry store. Suddenly he saw me and walked back, holding out his hand.

"What's the matter, Nick? Do you object to shaking hands with me?" [179/180]

"Yes. You know what I think of you."

"You're crazy, Nick," he said quickly. "Crazy as hell. I don't know what's the matter with you."

"Tom," I inquired, "what did you say to Wilson that afternoon?"

He stared at me without a word, and I knew I had guessed right about those missing hours. I started to turn away, but he took a step after me and grabbed my arm.

"I told him the truth," he said. "He came to the door while we were getting ready to leave, and when I sent down word that we weren't in he tried to force his way upstairs. He was crazy enough to kill me if I hadn't told him who owned the car. His hand was on a revolver in his pocket every minute he was in the house—" He broke off defiantly. "What if I did tell him? That fellow had it coming to him. He threw dust into your eyes just like he did in Daisy's, but he was a tough one. He ran over Myrtle like you'd run over a dog and never even stopped his car."

There was nothing I could say, except the one unutterable fact that it wasn't true.

"And if you think I didn't have my share of suffering—look here, when I went to give up that flat and saw that damn box of dog biscuits sitting there on the sideboard, I sat down and cried like a baby. By God it was awful——"

I couldn't forgive him or like him, but I saw that what he had done was, to him, entirely justified. It was all very careless and confused. They were careless people, Tom and Daisy—they smashed up things and creatures and then retreated back into their money or their vast carelessness, or whatever it was that kept [180/181] them together, and let other people clean up the mess they had made. . . .

I shook hands with him; it seemed silly not to, for I felt suddenly as though I were talking to a child. Then he went into the jewelry store to buy a pearl necklace—or perhaps only a pair of cuff buttons—rid of my provincial squeamishness forever.

Gatsby's house was still empty when I left—the grass on his lawn had grown as long as mine. One of the taxi drivers in the village never took a fare past the entrance gate without stopping for a minute and pointing inside; perhaps it was he who drove Daisy and Gatsby over to East Egg the night of the accident, and perhaps he had made a story about it all his own. I didn't want to hear it and I avoided him when I got off the train.

I spent my Saturday nights in New York because those gleaming, dazzling parties of his were with me so vividly that I could still hear the music and the laughter, faint and incessant, from his garden, and the cars going up and down his drive. One night I did hear a material car there, and saw its lights stop at his front steps. But I didn't investigate. Probably it was some final guest who had been away at the ends of the earth and didn't know that the party was over.

On the last night, with my trunk packed and my car sold to the grocer, I went over and looked at that huge incoherent failure of a house once more. On the white steps an obscene word, scrawled by some boy with a piece of brick, stood out clearly in the moonlight, and I erased it, drawing my shoe raspingly along the stone. Then I wandered down to the beach and sprawled out on the sand. [181/182]

Most of the big shore places were closed now and there were hardly any lights except the shadowy, moving glow of a ferryboat across the Sound. And as the moon rose higher the inessential houses began to melt away until gradually I became aware of the old island here that flowered once for Dutch sailors' eyes—a fresh, green breast of the new world. Its vanished trees, the trees that had made way for Gatsby's house, had once pandered in whispers to the last and greatest of all human dreams; for a transitory enchanted moment man must have held his breath in the presence of this continent, compelled into an æsthetic contemplation he neither understood nor desired, face to face for the last time in history with something commensurate to his capacity for wonder.

And as I sat there brooding on the old, unknown world, I thought of Gatsby's wonder when he first picked out the green light at the end of Daisy's dock. He had come a long way to this blue lawn, and his dream must have seemed so close that he could hardly fail to grasp it. He did not know that it was already behind him, somewhere back in that vast obscurity beyond the city, where the dark fields of the republic rolled on under the night.

Gatsby believed in the green light, the orgiastic future that year by year recedes before us. It eluded us then, but that's no matter—tomorrow we will run faster, stretch out our arms farther. . . . And one fine morning—— *we achieve our goal*

So we beat on, boats against the current, borne back ceaselessly into the past.

Fine morning - - -

PART TWO

INTENTION AND GENESIS:
THE AUTHOR'S VIEW

Absolution *

F . S C O T T   F I T Z G E R A L D (1896–1940) intended "Absolution" at one time to be the opening chapter of an early version of *The Great Gatsby*. Referring to this version, or an even earlier one, he told his editor at Scribners, Maxwell Perkins, that it would be about the Mid-West during the boom years of the 1880's and would have "a catholic element." In April, 1924, he recast the novel in its final form, discarding most of what he had written thus far with the exception of "Absolution," which he revised and sold as a short story to his friend H. L. Mencken, editor of *The American Mercury*. Mencken published it in the June, 1924 issue.

There was once a priest with cold, watery eyes, who, in the still of the night, wept cold tears. He wept because the afternoons were warm and long, and he was unable to attain a complete mystical union with our Lord. Sometimes, near four o'clock, there was a rustle of Swede girls along the path by his window, and in their shrill laughter he found a terrible dissonance that made him pray aloud for the twilight to come. At twilight the laughter and the voices were quieter, but several times he had walked past Romberg's Drug Store when it was dusk and the yellow lights shone inside and the nickel taps of the soda-fountain were gleaming, and he had found the scent of cheap toilet soap desperately sweet upon the air. He passed that way when he returned from hearing confessions on Saturday nights, and he grew careful to walk on the other side of the street so that the smell of the soap would float upward before it reached his nostrils as it drifted, rather like incense, toward the summer moon.

But there was no escape from the hot madness of four o'clock. From his window, as far as he could see, the Dakota wheat thronged the valley of the Red River. The wheat was terrible to look upon and the carpet pattern to which in agony he bent his eyes sent his thought brooding through grotesque labyrinths, open always to the unavoidable sun.

One afternoon when he had reached the point where the mind runs down like an old clock, his housekeeper brought into his study a beautiful, intense little boy of eleven named Rudolph Miller. The little [136/137] boy sat down in a patch of sunshine, and the priest, at his walnut desk, pretended to be very busy. This was to conceal his relief that some one had come into his haunted room.

Presently he turned around and found himself staring into two enormous, staccato eyes, lit with gleaming points of cobalt light. For a moment their expression startled him—then he saw that his visitor was in a state of abject fear.

"Your mouth is trembling," said Father Schwartz, in a haggard voice.

The little boy covered his quivering mouth with his hand.

"Are you in trouble?" asked Father Schwartz, sharply. "Take your hand away from your mouth and tell me what's the matter."

The boy—Father Schwartz recognized him now as the son of a parishoner, Mr.

* F. Scott Fitzgerald, "Absolution" (Copyright 1924 American Mercury, Inc.; renewal copyright 1952 Frances Scott Fitzgerald Lanahan) from *All the Sad Young Men* (New York: Charles Scribner's Sons, 1926). Reprinted with the permission of Charles Scribner's Sons.

Miller, the freight-agent—moved his hand reluctantly off his mouth and became articulate in a despairing whisper.

"Father Schwartz—I've committed a terrible sin."

"A sin against purity?"

"No, Father . . . worse."

Father Schwartz's body jerked sharply.

"Have you killed somebody?"

"No—but I'm afraid—" the voice rose to a shrill whimper.

"Do you want to go to confession?"

The little boy shook his head miserably. Father Schwartz cleared his throat so that he could make his voice soft and say some quiet, kind thing. In this moment he should forget his own agony, and try to act like God. He repeated to himself a devotional phrase, hoping that in return God would help him to act correctly.

"Tell me what you've done," said his new soft voice.

The little boy looked at him through his tears, and was reassured by the impression of moral resiliency which the distraught priest had created. Abandoning as much of himself as he was able to this man, Rudolph Miller began to tell his story.

"On Saturday, three days ago, my father he said I had to go to confession, because I hadn't been for a month, and the family they go every week, and I hadn't been. So I just as leave go, I didn't care. So I put it off till after supper because I was playing with a bunch of kids and father asked me if I went, and I said 'no,' and he took me by the neck and he said 'You go now,' so I said 'All right,' so I [137/138] went over to church. And he yelled after me: 'Don't come back till you go.' . . ."

II

"On Saturday, Three Days Ago."

The plush curtain of the confessional rearranged its dismal creases, leaving exposed only the bottom of an old man's old shoe. Behind the curtain an immortal soul was alone with God and the Reverend Adolphus Schwartz, priest of the parish. Sound began, a labored whispering, sibilant and discreet, broken at intervals by the voice of the priest in audible question.

Rudolph Miller knelt in the pew beside the confessional and waited, straining nervously to hear, and yet not to hear what was being said within. The fact that the priest was audible alarmed him. His own turn came next, and the three or four others who waited might listen unscrupulously while he admitted his violations of the Sixth and Ninth Commandments.

Rudolph had never committed adultery, nor even coveted his neighbor's wife—but it was the confession of the associate sins that was particularly hard to contemplate. In comparison he relished the less shameful fallings away—they formed a grayish background which relieved the ebony mark of sexual offenses upon his soul.

He had been covering his ears with his hands, hoping that his refusal to hear would be noticed, and a like courtesy rendered to him in turn, when a sharp movement of the penitent in the confessional made him sink his face precipitately into the crook of his elbow. Fear assumed solid form, and pressed out a lodging between his heart and his lungs. He must try now with all his might to be sorry for his sins—not because he was afraid, but because he had offended God. He must convince God that he was sorry and to do so he must first convince himself. After a tense emotional struggle he achieved a tremulous self-pity, and decided that he was now ready. If, by allowing no other thought to enter his head, he could preserve this state of emotion unimpaired until he went into that large coffin set on end, he would have survived another crisis in his religious life.

For some time, however, a demoniac notion had partially possessed [138/139] him. He could go home now, before his turn came, and tell his mother that he had arrived too late, and found the priest gone. This, unfortunately, involved the risk of being caught in a lie. As an alternative he could say that he *had* gone to confession, but this meant that he must avoid communion next day, for communion taken upon an uncleansed soul would turn to poison in his mouth, and he would crumple limp and damned from the altar-rail.

Again Father Schwartz's voice became audible.

"And for your——"

The words blurred to a husky mumble, and Rudolph got excitedly to his feet. He felt that it was impossible for him to go to confession this afternoon. He hesitated tensely. Then from the confessional came a tap, a creak, and a sustained rustle. The slide had fallen and the plush curtain trembled. Temptation had come to him too late. . . .

"Bless me, Father, for I have sinned. . . . I confess to Almighty God and to you, Father, that I have sinned. . . . Since my last confession it has been one month and three days. . . . I accuse myself of—taking the Name of the Lord in vain. . . ."

This was an easy sin. His curses had been but bravado—telling of them was little less than a brag.

". . . of being mean to an old lady."

The wan shadow moved a little on the latticed slat.

"How, my child?"

"Old lady Swenson," Rudolph's murmur soared jubilantly. "She got our baseball that we knocked in her window, and she wouldn't give it back, so we yelled 'Twenty-three, Skidoo,' at her all afternoon. Then about five o'clock she had a fit, and they had to have the doctor."

"Go on, my child."

"Of—of not believing I was the son of my parents."

"What?" The interrogation was distinctly startled.

"Of not believing that I was the son of my parents."

"Why not?"

"Oh, just pride," answered the penitent airily.

"You mean you thought you were too good to be the son of your parents?"

"Yes, Father." On a less jubilant note.

"Go on." [139/140]

"Of being disobedient and calling my mother names. Of slandering people behind their back. Of smoking——"

Rudolph had now exhausted the minor offenses, and was approaching the sins it was agony to tell. He held his fingers against his face like bars as if to press out between them the same in his heart.

"Of dirty words and immodest thoughts and desires," he whispered very low.

"How often?"

"I don't know."

"Once a week? Twice a week?"

"Twice a week."

"Did you yield to these desires?"

"No, Father."

Were you alone when you had them?"

"No, Father. I was with two boys and a girl."

"Don't you know, my child, that you should avoid the occasions of sin as well as the sin itself? Evil companionship leads to evil desires and evil desires to evil actions. Where were you when this happened?"

"In a barn in back of——"

I don't want to hear any names," interrupted the priest sharply.

"Well, it was up in the loft of this barn and this girl and—a fella, they were saying things—saying immodest things, and I stayed."

"You should have gone—you should have told the girl to go."

He should have gone! He could not tell Father Schwartz how his pulse had bumped in his wrist, how a strange, romantic excitement had possessed him when those curious things had been said. Perhaps in the houses of delinquency among the dull and hard-eyed incorrigible girls can be found those for whom has burned the whitest fire.

"Have you anything else to tell me?"

"I don't think so, Father."

Rudolph felt a great relief. Perspiration had broken out under his tight-pressed fingers.

"Have you told any lies?"

The question startled him. Like all those who habitually and instinctively lie, he had an enormous respect and awe for the truth. Something almost exterior to himself dictated a quick, hurt answer. "Oh, no, Father, I never tell lies." [140/141]

For a moment, like the commoner in the king's chair, he tasted the pride of the situation. Then as the priest began to murmur conventional admonitions he realized that in heroically denying he had told lies, he had committed a terrible sin—he had told a lie in confession.

In automatic response to Father Schwartz's "Make an act of contrition," he began to repeat aloud meaninglessly:

"Oh, my God, I am heartily sorry for having offended Thee. . . ."

He must fix this now—it was a bad mistake—but as his teeth shut on the last words of his prayer there was a sharp sound, and the slat was closed.

A minute later when he emerged into the twilight the relief in coming from the muggy church into an open world of wheat and sky postponed the full realization of what he had done. Instead of worrying he took a deep breath of the crisp air and began to say over and over to himself the words "Blatchford Sarnemington, Blatchford Sarnemington!"

Blatchford Sarnemington was himself, and these words were in effect a lyric. When he became Blatchford Sarnemington a suave nobility flowed from him. Blatchford Sarnemington lived in great sweeping triumphs. When Rudolph half closed his eyes it meant that Blatchford had established dominance over him and, as he went by, there were envious mutters in the air: "Blatchford Sarnemington! There goes Blatchford Sarnemington."

He was Blatchford now for a while as he strutted homeward along the staggering road, but when the road braced itself in macadam in order to become the main street of Ludwig, Rudolph's exhilaration faded out and his mind cooled, and he felt the horror of his lie. God, of course, already knew of it—but Rudolph reserved a corner of his mind where he was safe from God, where he prepared the subterfuges with which he often tricked God. Hiding now in this corner he considered how he could best avoid the consequences of his misstatement.

At all costs he must avoid communion next day. The risk of angering God to such an extent was too great. He would have to drink water "by accident" in the morning, and thus, in accordance with a church law, render himself unfit to receive communion that day. In spite of its flimsiness this subterfuge was the most feasible that oc- [141/142] curred to him. He accepted its risks and was concentrating on how best to put it into effect, as he turned the corner by Romberg's Drug Store and came in sight of his father's house.

III

Rudolph's father, the local freight-agent, had floated with the second wave of German and Irish stock to the Minnesota-Dakota country. Theoretically, great opportunities lay ahead of a young man of energy in that day and place, but Carl Miller had been incapable of establishing either with his superiors or his subordinates the reputation for approximate immutability which is essential to success in a hierarchic industry. Somewhat gross, he was, nevertheless, insufficiently hard-headed and unable to take fundamental relationships for granted, and this inability made him suspicious, unrestful, and continually dismayed.

His two bonds with the colorful life were his faith in the Roman Catholic Church and his mystical worship of the Empire Builder, James J. Hill. Hill was the apotheosis of that quality in which

Miller himself was deficient—the sense of things, the feel of things, the hint of rain in the wind on the cheek. Miller's mind worked late on the old decisions of other men, and he had never in his life felt the balance of any single thing in his hands. His weary, sprightly, undersized body was growing old in Hill's gigantic shadow. For twenty years he had lived alone with Hill's name and God.

On Sunday morning Carl Miller awoke in the dustless quiet of six o'clock. Kneeling by the side of the bed he bent his yellow-gray hair and the full dapple bangs of his mustache into the pillow, and prayed for several minutes. Then he drew off his night-shirt—like the rest of his generation he had never been able to endure pajamas—and clothed his thin, white, hairless body in woollen underwear.

He shaved. Silence in the other bedroom where his wife lay nervously asleep. Silence from the screened-off corner of the hall where his son's cot stood, and his son slept among his Alger books, his collection of cigar-bands, his mothy pennants—"Cornell," "Hamlin," and "Greetings from Pueblo, New Mexico"—and the other possessions of his private life. From outside Miller could hear the shrill birds and the whirring movement of the poultry, and, as an under- [142/143] tone, the low, swelling click-a-tick of the six-fifteen through-train for Montana and the green coast beyond. Then as the cold water dripped from the wash-rag in his hand he raised his head suddenly—he had heard a furtive sound from the kitchen below.

He dried his razor hastily, slipped his dangling suspenders to his shoulder, and listened. Some one was walking in the kitchen, and he knew by the light footfall that it was not his wife. With his mouth faintly ajar he ran quickly down the stairs and opened the kitchen door.

Standing by the sink, with one hand on the still dripping faucet and the other clutching a full glass of water, stood his son. The boy's eyes, still heavy with sleep, met his father's with a frightened, re-proachful beauty. He was barefooted, and his pajamas were rolled up at the knees and sleeves.

For a moment they both remained motionless—Carl Miller's brow went down and his son's went up, as though they were striking a balance between the extremes of emotion which filled them. Then the bangs of the parent's mustache descended portentously until they obscured his mouth, and he gave a short glance around to see if anything had been disturbed.

The kitchen was garnished with sunlight which beat on the pans and made the smooth boards of the floor and table yellow and clean as wheat. It was the centre of the house where the fire burned and the tins fitted into tins like toys, and the steam whistled all day on a thin pastel note. Nothing was moved, nothing touched—except the faucet where beads of water still formed and dripped with a white flash into the sink below.

"What are you doing?"

"I got awful thirsty, so I thought I'd just come down and get——"

"I thought you were going to communion."

A look of vehement astonishment spread over his son's face.

"I forgot all about it."

"Have you drunk any water?"

"No——"

As the word left his mouth Rudolph knew it was the wrong answer, but the faded indignant eyes facing him had signalled up the truth before the boy's will could act. He realized, too, that he should never have come down-stairs; some vague necessity for verisimilitude had [143/144] made him want to leave a wet glass as evidence by the sink; the honesty of his imagination had betrayed him.

"Pour it out," commanded his father, "that water!"

Rudolph despairingly inverted the tumbler.

"What's the matter with you, anyways?" demanded Miller angrily.

"Nothing."

"Did you go to confession yesterday?"

"Yes."

"Then why were you going to drink water?"

"I don't know—I forgot."

"Maybe you care more about being a little bit thirsty than you do about your religion."

"I forgot." Rudolph could feel the tears streaming in his eyes.

"That's no answer."

"Well, I did."

"You better look out!" His father held to a high, persistent, inquisitory note: "If you're so forgetful that you can't remember your religion something better be done about it."

Rudolph filled a sharp pause with:

"I can remember it all right."

"First you begin to neglect your religion," cried his father, fanning his own fierceness, "the next thing you'll begin to lie and steal, and the *next* thing is the *reform* school!"

Not even this familiar threat could deepen the abyss that Rudolph saw before him. He must either tell all now, offering his body for what he knew would be a ferocious beating, or else tempt the thunderbolts by receiving the Body and Blood of Christ with sacrilege upon his soul. And of the two the former seemed more terrible—it was not so much the beating he dreaded as the savage ferocity, outlet of the ineffectual man, which would lie behind it.

"Put down that glass and go up-stairs and dress!" his father ordered, "and when we get to church, before you go to communion, you better kneel down and ask God to forgive you for your carelessness."

Some accidental emphasis in the phrasing of this command acted like a catalytic agent on the confusion and terror of Rudolph's mind. A wild, proud anger rose in him, and he dashed the tumbler passionately into the sink. [**144/145**]

His father uttered a strained, husky sound, and sprang for him. Rudolph dodged to the side, tipped over a chair, and tried to get beyond the kitchen table.

He cried out sharply when a hand grasped his pajama shoulder, then he felt the dull impact of a fist against the side of his head, and glancing blows on the upper part of his body. As he slipped here and there in his father's grasp, dragged or lifted when he clung instinctively to an arm, aware of sharp smarts and strains, he made no sound except that he laughed hysterically several times. Then in less than a minute the blows abruptly ceased. After a lull during which Rudolph was tightly held, and during which they both trembled violently and uttered strange, truncated words, Carl Miller half dragged, half threatened his son up-stairs.

"Put on your clothes!"

Rudolph was now both hysterical and cold. His head hurt him, and there was a long, shallow scratch on his neck from his father's finger-nail, and he sobbed and trembled as he dressed. He was aware of his mother standing at the doorway in a wrapper, her wrinkled face compressing and squeezing and opening out into new series of wrinkles which floated and eddied from neck to brow. Despising her nervous ineffectuality and avoiding her rudely when she tried to touch his neck with witch-hazel, he made a hasty, choking toilet. Then he followed his father out of the house and along the road toward the Catholic church.

IV

They walked without speaking except when Carl Miller acknowledged automatically the existence of passers-by. Rudolph's uneven breathing alone ruffled the hot Sunday silence.

His father stopped decisively at the door of the church.

"I've decided you'd better go to confession again. Go in and tell Father Schwartz what you did and ask God's pardon."

"You lost your temper, too!" said Rudolph quickly.

Carl Miller took a step toward his son,

who moved cautiously backward.

"All right, I'll go."

"Are you going to do what I say?" cried his father in a hoarse whisper. [145/146]

"All right."

Rudolph walked into the church, and for the second time in two days entered the confessional and knelt down. The slat went up almost at once.

"I accuse myself of missing my morning prayers."

"Is that all?"

"That's all."

A maudlin exultation filled him. Not easily ever again would he be able to put an abstraction before the necessities of his ease and pride. An invisible line had been crossed, and he had become aware of his isolation—aware that it applied not only to those moments when he was Blatchford Sarnemington but that it applied to all his inner life. Hitherto such phenomena as "crazy" ambitions and petty shames and fears had been but private reservations, unacknowledged before the throne of his official soul. Now he realized unconsciously that his private reservations were himself—and all the rest a garnished front and a conventional flag. The pressure of his environment had driven him into the lonely secret road of adolescence.

He knelt in the pew beside his father. Mass began. Rudolph knelt up—when he was alone he slumped his posterior back against the seat—and tasted the consciousness of a sharp, subtle revenge. Beside him his father prayed that God would forgive Rudolph, and asked also that his own outbreak of temper would be pardoned. He glanced sidewise at this son, and was relieved to see that the strained, wild look had gone from his face and that he had ceased sobbing. The Grace of God, inherent in the Sacrament, would do the rest, and perhaps after Mass everything would be better. He was proud of Rudolph in his heart, and beginning to be truly as well as formally sorry for what he had done.

Usually, the passing of the collection box was a significant point for Rudolph in the services. If, as was often the case, he had no money to drop in he would be furiously ashamed and bow his head and pretend not to see the box, lest Jeanne Brady in the pew behind should take notice and suspect an acute family poverty. But to-day he glanced coldly into it as it skimmed under his eyes, noting with casual interest the large number of pennies it contained.

When the bell rang for communion, however, he quivered. There was no reason why God should not stop his heart. During the past [146/147] twelve hours he had committed a series of mortal sins increasing in gravity, and he was now to crown them all with a blasphemous sacrilege.

"*Domine, non sum dignus; ut intres sub tectum meum; sed tantum dic verbo, et sanabitur anima mea. . . .*"

There was a rustle in the pews, and the communicants worked their ways into the aisle with downcast eyes and joined hands. Those of larger piety pressed together their finger-tips to form steeples. Among these latter was Carl Miller. Rudolph followed him toward the altar-rail and knelt down, automatically taking up the napkin under his chin. The bell rang sharply, and the priest turned from the altar with the white Host held above the chalice:

"*Corpus Domini nostri Jesu Christi custodiat animam tuam in vitam æternam.*"

A cold sweat broke out on Rudolph's forehead as the communion began. Along the line Father Schwartz moved, and with gathering nausea Rudolph felt his heart-valves weakening at the will of God. It seemed to him that the church was darker and that a great quiet had fallen, broken only by the inarticulate mumble which announced the approach of the Creator of Heaven and Earth. He dropped his head down between his shoulders and waited for the blow.

Then he felt a sharp nudge in his side. His father was poking him to sit up, not to slump against the rail; the priest was only two places away.

"Corpus Domini nostri Jesu Christi cus-todiat animam tuam in vitam æternam."

Rudolph opened his mouth. He felt the sticky wax taste of the wafer on his tongue. He remained motionless for what seemed an interminable period of time, his head still raised, the wafer undissolved in his mouth. Then again he started at the pressure of his father's elbow, and saw that the people were falling away from the altar like leaves and turning with blind downcast eyes to their pews, alone with God.

Rudolph was alone with himself, drenched with perspiration and deep in mortal sin. As he walked back to his pew the sharp taps of his cloven hoofs were loud upon the floor, and he knew that it was a dark poison he carried in his heart. **[147/148]**

V

"Sagitta Volante in Dei"

The beautiful little boy with eyes like blue stones, and lashes that sprayed open from them like flower-petals had finished telling his sin to Father Schwartz—and the square of sunshine in which he sat had moved forward half an hour into the room. Rudolph had become less fright-ened now; once eased of the story a reaction had set in. He knew that as long as he was in the room with this priest God would not stop his heart, so he sighed and sat quietly, waiting for the priest to speak.

Father Schwartz's cold watery eyes were fixed upon the carpet pattern on which the sun had brought out the swastikas and the flat bloomless vines and the pale echoes of flowers. The hall-clock ticked insistently toward sunset, and from the ugly room and from the afternoon outside the window arose a stiff monotony, shat-tered now and then by the reverberate clapping of a far-away hammer on the dry air. The priest's nerves were strung thin and the beads of his rosary were crawling and squirming like snakes upon the green felt of his table top. He could not remember now what it was he should say.

Of all the things in this lost Swede town he was most aware of this little boy's eyes —the beautiful eyes, with lashes that left them reluctantly and curved back as though to meet them once more.

For a moment longer the silence per-sisted while Rudolph waited, and the priest struggled to remember something that was slipping farther and farther away from him, and the clock ticked in the broken house. Then Father Schwartz stared hard at the little boy and remarked in a peculiar voice:

"When a lot of people get together in the best places things go glimmering."

Rudolph started and looked quickly at Father Schwartz's face.

"I said—" began the priest, and paused, listening. "Do you hear the hammer and the clock ticking and the bees? Well, that's no good. The thing is to have a lot of people in the centre of the world, wherever that happens to be. Then"—his watery eyes widened knowingly—"things go glimmering." **[148/149]**

"Yes, Father," agreed Rudolph, feeling a little frightened.

"What are you going to be when you grow up?"

"Well, I was going to be a baseball-player for a while," answered Rudolph nervously, "but I don't think that's a very good ambition, so I think I'll be an actor or a Navy officer."

Again the priest stared at him.

"I see *exactly* what you mean," he said, with a fierce air.

Rudolph had not meant anything in particular, and at the implication that he had, he became more uneasy.

"This man is crazy," he thought, "and I'm scared of him. He wants me to help him out some way, and I don't want to."

"You look as if things went glimmer-ing," cried Father Schwartz wildly. "Did you ever go to a party?"

"Yes, Father."

"And did you notice that everybody was properly dressed? That's what I mean. Just as you went into the party there was a moment when everybody was properly dressed. Maybe two little girls were standing by the door and some boys were leaning over the banisters, and there were bowls around full of flowers."

"I've been to a lot of parties," said Rudolph, rather relieved that the conversation had taken this turn.

"Of course," continued Father Schwartz triumphantly, "I knew you'd agree with me. But my theory is that when a whole lot of people get together in the best places things go glimmering all the time."

Rudolph found himself thinking of Blatchford Sarnemington.

"Please listen to me!" commanded the priest impatiently. "Stop worrying about last Saturday. Apostasy implies an absolute damnation only on the supposition of a previous perfect faith. Does that fix it?"

Rudolph had not the faintest idea what Father Schwartz was talking about, but he nodded and the priest nodded back at him and returned to his mysterious preoccupation.

"Why," he cried, "they have lights now as big as stars—do you realize that? I heard of one light they had in Paris or somewhere that was as big as a star. A lot of people had it—a lot of gay people. They have all sorts of things now that you never dreamed of."

"Look here—" he came nearer to Rudolph, but the boy drew away, so Father Schwartz went back and sat down in his chair, his eyes dried out and hot. "Did you ever see an amusement park?" [149/150]

"No, Father."

"Well, go and see an amusement park." The priest waved his hand vaguely. "It's a thing like a fair, only much more glittering. Go to one at night and stand a little way off from it in a dark place—under dark trees. You'll see a big wheel made of lights turning in the air, and a

long slide shooting boats down into the water. A band playing somewhere, and a smell of peanuts—and everything will twinkle. But it won't remind you of anything, you see. It will all just hang out there in the night like a colored balloon—like a big yellow lantern on a pole."

Father Schwartz frowned as he suddenly thought of something.

"But don't get up close," he warned Rudolph, "because if you do you'll only feel the heat and the sweat and the life."

All this talking seemed particularly strange and awful to Rudolph, because this man was a priest. He sat there, half terrified, his beautiful eyes open wide and staring at Father Schwartz. But underneath his terror he felt that his own inner convictions were confirmed. There was something ineffably gorgeous somewhere that had nothing to do with God. He no longer thought that God was angry at him about the original lie, because He must have understood that Rudolph had done it to make things finer in the confessional, brightening up the dinginess of his admissions by saying a thing radiant and proud. At the moment when he had affirmed immaculate honor a silver pennon had flapped out into the breeze somewhere and there had been the crunch of leather and the shine of silver spurs and a troop of horsemen waiting for dawn on a low green hill. The sun had made stars of light on their breastplates like the picture at home of the German cuirassiers at Sedan.

But now the priest was muttering inarticulate and heart-broken words, and the boy became wildly afraid. Horror entered suddenly in at the open window, and the atmosphere of the room changed. Father Schwartz collapsed precipitously down on his knees, and let his body settle back against a chair.

"Oh, my God!" he cried out, in a strange voice, and wilted to the floor.

Then a human oppression rose from the priest's worn clothes, and mingled with the faint smell of old food in the corners. Rudolph gave a sharp cry and ran in a panic from the house—while the collapsed man lay there quite still, filling his room, filling it with voices and [150/151] faces until it was crowded with echolalia, and rang loud with a steady, shrill note of laughter.

Outside the window the blue sirocco trembled over the wheat, and girls with yellow hair walked sensuously along roads that bounded the fields, calling innocent, exciting things to the young men who were working in the lines between the grain. Legs were shaped under starchless gingham, and rims of the necks of dresses were warm and damp. For five hours now hot fertile life had burned in the afternoon. It would be night in three hours, and all along the land there would be these blonde Northern girls and the tall young men from the farms lying out beside the wheat, under the moon.

The Untrimmed Christmas Tree: The Religious Background of The Great Gatsby *

HENRY DAN PIPER (1918–   ) is a professor of English and former dean of the College of Liberal Arts and Sciences, Southern Illinois University, Carbondale. He is the author of F. Scott Fitzgerald: A Critical Portrait (1965) and edited American Literary Manuscripts (1960), Dimensions in Drama (1962) and Think Back On Us (1967), selected essays of Malcolm Cowley.

Scott Fitzgerald began planning his third novel, The Great Gatsby, sometime during the late spring of 1922. "I've been lazy this month trying to outline a new novel," he wrote Maxwell Perkins, his editor at Scribners, in mid-June. Several months earlier Scribners had published his second novel, The Beautiful and Damned; and although it was selling well, it was currently getting harsh treatment from the critics and reviewers—treatment Fitzgerald privately admitted that it deserved. When The Beautiful had started running as a serial in the Metropolitan Magazine the previous autumn, he had at first been so embarrassed by its obvious shortcomings that for a time he had considered delaying publication of the book version until he could rewrite it entirely. But, this proving impractical, he had reluctantly let it come out between hard covers with few major revisions of any kind. Nonetheless, he had learned a lesson and was determined that his next [321/322] novel, unlike The Beautiful and Damned, should be written slowly and with care. "I want to write something new," he had written Max Perkins that summer of 1922, "—something extraordinary and beautiful and simple and intricately patterned."[1]

This next novel, he told Perkins, would differ from his previous fiction in several other respects. "It's locale will be the Middle West and New York of 1885, I think. It will contain less superlative beauties than I run to usually and will be centered in a smaller period of time. It will have a Catholic element." As things turned out, however, he was to make little headway with it for the next two years. Instead, spurred on by the encouragement of Edmund Wilson and George Jean Nathan, and by his own hope of making a financial killing on Broadway, he spent the next eighteen months trying to write a successful play for the New York stage. Although Nathan openly predicted a promising future for him in the theatre, and Wilson called The Vegetable "the best American comedy ever written," it flopped deservedly during its Atlantic City tryout in November, 1923, leaving Fitzgerald $5000 in debt. Again the manuscript of his novel was put aside while he

[1] Two letters to Max Perkins, no date (ca. mid-June, and July, 1922), files of Charles Scribner's Sons Inc. All material from these files quoted with Scribner's permission.

spent the next six months grinding out a total of eighteen short stories and articles for the slick magazines. It was discouraging work, especially since none of these pieces amounted to anything, and it left him exhausted. But by April, 1924, he had paid off all his debts and had enough cash on hand so that he could take his wife and daughter to the south of France and devote the next ten months to finishing his novel.[2]

By now, however, his conception of that novel had altered radically. Back in 1922 when he had first begun thinking about *The Great Gatsby,* he had been living in St. Paul, Minnesota, the [322/323] Middle Western city in which he had been born and where he had spent his early childhood. Actually, after his departure from St. Paul for boarding school in 1911 at the age of fourteen, he had lived the greater part of the next ten years in the East. But in 1921, after the success of his first novel, *This Side of Paradise,* and his marriage to Zelda Sayre, he had felt a compulsion to return, a triumphant celebrity, to the scene of so many childhood frustrations and disappointments. Zelda was expecting their first child, and Fitzgerald felt it was important that it should be born where he had been born.

But after a year in St. Paul they had moved East again in the autumn of 1922. This time they rented a house in Great Neck, Long Island, in hopes this proximity to Broadway would help in the search for a producer for *The Vegetable.* By April, 1924, when Fitzgerald was again in a position to work on *The Great Gatsby,* he had decided to shift its setting from the 1880's to the immediate present, and from the Middle West to the vicinity of Great Neck. At this time he also decided to abandon the conventional third-person method of narration he had used in his preceding two novels, and to adopt

instead the device of a first-person narrator named Nick Carraway.

Just before he sailed to France he wrote Max Perkins explaining some of these new intentions. "Much of what I wrote last summer is good," he said, "but it was so interrupted that it was ragged and in approaching it from a new angle I've had to discard a lot of it—in one case 18,000 [words] (part of which will appear in the *Mercury* as a short story)." The story mentioned was "Absolution," which his friend H. L. Mencken published in the June issue of the *American Mercury.* "I'm glad you like it," Fitzgerald wrote Perkins after it appeared. "As you know it was to have been the prologue of the novel but it interfered with the neatness of my plan."[3]

Ten years later, in a letter to one of *The Great Gatsby's* ad- [323/324] mirers, Fitzgerald again mentioned the connection between his novel and "Absolution," saying this time that the latter had been "intended to be a picture of his [i.e., Gatsby's] early life, but . . . I cut it because I preferred to preserve the sense of mystery." Any attempt to come to terms with *The Great Gatsby,* therefore, cannot afford to overlook its relationship to "Absolution." The short story is especially important because it makes explicit the religious considerations that served its author as the basis for the moral judgments that he made so conspicuously in its sequel, *The Great Gatsby.*[4]

"Absolution" is the story of a ten-year-old boy's first encounter with evil, whereas *The Great Gatsby* is the story of the consequences of that boyhood encounter, Rudolph Miller, the hero of the short story, is the son of pious, hard-working Roman Catholic immigrants living in a drab farm community on the Middle Western prairie. A lonely child endowed with a lively imagination, his closest playmate is a companion of his imagination with the elegant name of Blatchford Sarneming-

[2] To Perkins, n.d. (ca. June 20, 1922), Scribner files; E. Wilson to FSF, May 26, 1922 (Fitzgerald Papers, Princeton University Library); George Jean Nathan, *The Theatre, The Drama, The Girls* (New York, 1921), 16, 72.

[3] To Perkins, n.d. (ca. April 16, 1924) Scribner files.
[4] To John Jamieson, April 15, 1934, quoted in Arthur Mizener, *The Far Side of Paradise* (Boston: Houghton Mifflin and Co., 1951), p. 172.

ton. Blatchford is Rudolph's alter ego, the romantic superman he would like to be. Where Rudolph is expected to mind his parents, school teachers, and parish priest, Blatchford soars above such mundane obligations. He is beyond good and evil, responsible only to his own imagination. When Rudolph does something he shouldn't, his first impulse is to pretend that it is not himself, Rudolph, who has done wrong, but Blatchford. Unfortunately, however, his well-developed conscience will not allow him to indulge this fiction for very long.[5]

The story commences one Saturday afternoon when Rudolph impulsively tells a lie to his priest during confession. He has been reciting his usual catalogue of petty sins, and wishing that he could liven up the occasion by confessing something really spectacular, when the priest unexpectedly asks if he hasn't some lies [324/325] to confess, too. Of course, he tells lies. But instead, Rudolph unthinkingly seizes the opportunity to make a dramatic gesture. Drawing himself up to his full height, he proudly assures the priest that he *never* tells lies. It is a convincing performance, and afterwards, walking home, Rudolph savors to the full the esthetic satisfaction of a dramatic action brilliantly executed. But before long his conscience reminds him of the terrible thing he has done. Not only has he lied to the priest but, by telling a lie during confession, he has nullified the value of the priest's subsequent act of absolution. He has trouble convincing himself, however, that an action which has been so unpremeditated and the source of such intense pleasure could be displeasing to God. His first thought is to excuse the lie by pretending that Blatchford said it, for it is the kind of performance of which Blatchford would have approved. But eventually his religious training reasserts itself. After several unhappy days during which he expects momentarily to be stricken down by the hand of an angry God, Rudolph finally seeks out the priest and confesses everything.

At this point, however, the priest fails him. Father Schwartz is also an incurable romantic. In Rudolph's actions he sees mirrored his own frustrated desires for a fuller, more esthetically satisfying life. Instead of disciplining the child, exacting the penance he expects as his punishment, and then absolving him, Father Schwartz offhandedly excuses his conduct by mumbling a technical expiatory formula over Rudolph's head. Then the priest launches out into a crazy speech that Rudolph understands as justification of what he has done. Leaving the unhappy old man, Rudolph now believes that all his previous suspicions about God and His Church have been confirmed. Somewhere there is a glittering world where he can exist apart from God and his priests, morally responsible only to the promptings of his own imagination. This is the world of Blatchford Sarnemington, a world that he can enter merely by shedding his everyday identity and becoming Blatchford. Henceforth, as Blatchford Sarnemington, he would dwell "in that small corner of his mind where he [325/326] was safe from God, where he prepared the subterfuges with which he often tricked God."[6]

In *The Great Gatsby* Rudolph Miller reappears as Jimmie Gatz while Blatchford Sarnemington has been renamed Jay Gatsby. Jimmie's decision to change his name, Fitzgerald tells us, was "the specific moment that witnessed the beginning of his career." And that career began, as we know from "Absolution," when ten-year-old Jimmie Gatz decided to commit himself to the moral world of his private imagination "where he was safe from God." "The truth was," Fitzgerald says, "that Jay Gatsby of West Egg, Long Island, sprang from his Platonic conception of himself. He was a Son of God—a

[5] *The Short Stories of F. Scott Fitzgerald*, ed., Malcolm Cowley, (New York: Charles Scribner's Sons, 1951), pp. 159-172.

[6] *Ibid.*, p. 163.

phrase which, if it means anything, means just that—and he must be about His Father's business, the service of a vast, vulgar, and meretricious beauty."[7]

The source of "Absolution," as we might expect, was its author's own childhood. At the age of eleven Fitzgerald had told a lie during confession and endured several subsequent days of terror before he finally mustered up the courage to tell the priest what he had done. Many years later he still remembered it distinctly as having been "a very chilling experience." Moreover, although he never went so far as to formally change his name, he had gone around the neighborhood as a child claiming that he was not the son of his parents but had been found on the Fitzgerald doorstep one cold morning wrapped in a blanket to which was pinned a paper bearing on it the regal name of "Stuart." These were merely manifestations of his passionate desire to escape from the drab, everyday world into the more exciting one of his imagination. He was convinced that the latter was a better world, esthetically as well as morally. But when he told grown-ups about the adventures he had in that other world they merely scolded him and accused him of "telling lies."[8] [326/327]

By the time Fitzgerald was twenty-two, that is, by the time he had decided to become a professional writer and had begun to write his first novel, he had renounced his moral responsibility both to his parents and to their church—the Church of Rome—and had committed himself to the realization of his own romantic dreams. In his Ledger opposite September, 1917, (his twenty-first birthday) he noted "last year as a Catholic." For the next several years this new philosophy paid off handsome dividends. He completed the autobiographical novel, "The Romantic Ego-

tist," which, rewritten and retitled *This Side of Paradise*, made him rich and famous. He married the elusive, much-sought-after Alabama girl, Zelda Sayre, who (as he proudly noted in his Ledger) has been voted "prettiest and most attractive" by her high school graduating class.[9]

But by 1922, when Fitzgerald began to plan his third novel, *The Great Gatsby*, the romantic idealism which had supported him so well at the beginning of his career was beginning to wear thin. By hard work and single-minded devotion to his adolescent dreams, he had made every single one of them come true: fame, money, success, marriage to a popular girl. Yet one by one as he had reached out and seized them, they had literally turned to ashes in his grasp. Now looking back from a more mature vantage point, he saw how much he had enthralled himself in the service of a spurious set of ideals. In "Absolution," we find Fitzgerald scrutinizing his own past, trying to locate where it was that he had gone wrong. He was by no means ready to discount completely the value of his romantic egotism. "That's the whole burden of this novel," he would write Ludlow Fowler while he was still working on it during the summer of 1924, "—the loss of those illusions that give such color to the world that you don't care whether things are true or false so long as they partake of the imagined glory." But he was nonetheless keenly aware of the limitations of this philosophy as a guide to what was actually "true and false." In "Absolution" we see Fitzgerald struggling awk- [327/328] wardly to judge it from the only other moral point of view at his disposal, that of the childhood religious faith in which he had been reared.[10]

The trouble with "Absolution", however, is that Fitzgerald's personal history so muddied up the narrative that the story failed to make its point effectively. Fitz-

---

[7] F. Scott Fitzgerald, *The Great Gatsby*, The Scribner Library Edition (New York: Charles Scribner's Sons, 1960), p. 99.
[8] See unpublished ms. of Chap. I of "The Romantic Egotist," and Fitzgerald's unpublished autobiographical Ledger, Princeton Library.

[9] Ledger, Princeton University Library.
[10] To Ludlow Fowler, n.d. (ca. August 1924), Princeton Library.

gerald was so sentimentally involved in his private dislike for Father Schwartz (probably based on someone he had once known) that the reader easily misses the point that Rudolph, who is a much more attractive character, is being judged by the standards of the church served so badly by its crazy priest. To Fitzgerald's chagrin, after "Absolution" appeared in the *American Mercury*, he was accused by some of his Catholic friends of having written a sacrilegious story. We can see from its sequel, *The Great Gatsby*, however, that Rudolph by his choice is irretrievably damned.

One of the things that saved Fitzgerald, in *Gatsby*, from the subjective pitfalls of "Absolution," was his decision to approach his material "from a new angle" by presenting it through the eyes of a narrator, Nick Carraway. Nick is a marked improvement over Father Schwartz because although, like the priest, he both sympathizes with and judges the hero, he is capable of a much wider sympathy as well as a more universal and less dogmatic kind of judgment. Fortunately Fitzgerald saved the first draft of *The Great Gatsby* that was written from this new approach. And from it we can see that at the beginning Fitzgerald was almost as confused and uncertain about Nick's relationship to Gatsby as he had been about that of Father Schwartz to Rudolph Miller. This is especially true of the opening chapter, in which Nick is first introduced. But as the new version of *Gatsby* took shape, especially after the first draft was finished and Fitzgerald had gone back and carefully revised it, Nick gradually developed a clear relationship to the hero as well as a definite personality all his own.[11] **[328/329]**

During this process the specifically Catholic framework of "Absolution" disappeared and Nick's judgment of his neighbor, Gatsby, was established on other terms. Nick and Gatsby, like Rudolph Miller and Blatchford Sarnemington,

[11] Pencil draft, *Gatsby* ms., Princeton, Chap. I.

were originally doubles — projections of two different aspects of Fitzgerald's own personality. How much Nick and Gatsby at first were almost identical characters we can see by turning back to this first draft of the novel; but gradually, after extensive revision, they assumed separate identities. What distinguishes Nick from Gatsby most conspicuously, of course, is the fact that despite his deeply-rooted self-identification with Gatsby, Nick is capable of judging him—and so is saved from a similar fate.

What is it that saves Nick from following in his gaudy neighbor's footsteps? What has taken the place of the Catholic framework that served for "Absolution"? Nick survives because he possesses two kinds of knowledge that Gatsby lacks. The first is that heritage of traditional moral values that he has learned from his father. He is indebted to Mr. Carraway, he says at the beginning, both for that "habit of reserving all judgments" which allows him (alone of all of Gatsby's acquaintances) to value his neighbor's romantic idealism, and for that "sense of the fundamental decencies of life" which makes it possible for him to see the shabby limitations of Gatsby's dreams. At the start of the story, you recall, Nick was ready to reject this moral heritage, along with the Carraway name. That is, Nick refused to take the job awaiting him in the Middle Western wholesale hardware business that had been in his family for three generations. Instead he left the "bored, sprawling, swollen towns beyond the Ohio" and came East to take a job in a Wall Street brokerage firm. But by the end of the novel it is the values represented for Nick by the image of his father that have saved him from Gatsby's terrible mistake. Realizing this, Nick is ready at last to come home.

The second kind of knowledge that Nick possesses, in contrast to his neighbor, is his ever-present awareness of man's mortality. **[329/330]** For Nick the fact of death stands inexorably between man's dreams and the chances of realizing them during his brief lifetime. Not only is Nick continually aware of death, and his narrative strewn with death images, but the entire novel seems to have been conceived by Fitzgerald as the expression of a death wish—a wish that, in his first draft, he actually has Nick express at the conclusion of Chapter I. At this initial stage of his conception of *The Great Gatsby,* Nick resembled Gatsby not only in his Mid-Western origins and his romantic setting off for the East, but by the fact that Nick had also been in love with Daisy Buchanan before her marriage to Tom. In this earliest version that we have of Chapter I, Nick has not yet seen Daisy since her marriage. So, when he learns the facts about that marriage he is profoundly disturbed. It is bad enough to find Tom having an affair with another woman. What shocks Nick even more is Daisy's amoral attitude toward her situation, her "basic insincerity," as he calls it. Discovering this, it is as though the virginal Daisy of Nick's dreams has been contaminated by an evil so palpable that everything surrounding him has been corrupted by it—not only Long Island, but the whole American continent stretching out to the Western sea. Indeed so intense is Nick's mood of disillusion in this earliest version of Chapter I that Fitzgerald was inspired at this point to write the long, oft-quoted threnody to the memory of the continent's lost innocence (that "fresh, green breast of the new world . . .") that he eventually made the coda-like conclusion to the entire novel.

At this point also, in this earliest version that we have of Chapter I, Nick also said (in a passage later altered):[12]

It was already deep summer on roadhouse roofs and on the dark murmurous little porches and around the garages where new red gas-pumps sat out in pools of light—and summer always promised fulfillment of my old childish dreams. I wanted something definite to happen to *me,* something that would wear me out a little—for

[330/331] I suppose the urge to adventure is one and the same with the obscure craving of our bodies for a certain death.

Then, looking out across the bay, Nick notices for the first time the shadowy silhouette of his mysterious neighbor, Gatsby, standing on the beach nearby. Thus, everything that is still to happen—all of Gatsby's subsequent history—is to serve Nick as a kind of moral exemplum, a cautionary tale illustrating the kind of fate Nick himself might have suffered if his love for Daisy had blinded him, as it did Gatsby, to the evil that is as much a part of her nature as it is of any other mortal being.

But Nick, unlike Gatsby, is continually aware of the fact that man must die. Indeed the odor of mortality is everywhere in the novel, even more in the early drafts than in the published version of the text. In one draft, when Gatsby proudly shows Nick his oversized yellow sports car ("the death car," as the New York newspapers will later call it after Myrtle's death), Nick is automatically reminded of a hearse. Indeed, a few paragraphs further on, when Nick is riding in Gatsby's car to New York, he actually passes a funeral and is confronted with the image of "a dead man . . . in a hearse heaped full of flowers." Undoubtedly the most conspicuous death image in the novel is that of the waste land of dust and ashes over which Gatsby and his neighbors must pass every time they go to New York. From this limbo blows that "foul dust" that, Nick reminds us, "floated in the wake of Gatsby's dreams." It is typical of Tom Buchanan's inverted sense of values that, after having helped to contrive Gatsby's murder, he arrogantly tells Nick "He [Gatsby] threw dust in your eyes just like he did Daisy's." At one time Fitzgerald even planned to call his novel "Among the Ash-Heaps and Millionaires."[13]

Over this portentous waste land brood the sightless eyes of Dr. T. J. Eckleburg—

[12] The quoted passage will be found in the pencil draft, *Gatsby* ms., at a point corresponding to line 19, p. 25, of the 1925 pub. text.

[13] The deleted reference to the hearse (pencil draft) comes at line 6, p. 77, of the 1925 text; see letter of Maxwell Perkins to FSF, April 4, 1924 (Princeton).

rooted (as Fitzgerald says in another deleted [**331/332**] passage) "in a spot that reeks of death." Nearby stands the squalid, ash-covered garage of George Wilson, the insane agent of Gatsby's doom. (In his manuscript Fitzgerald carefully changed the color of Wilson's hair from "yellow" to the more deathly hue of "pale.")[14]

At the end, the simple fact of Gatsby's death is quickly stated in a sentence. But the implications of that death necessitate a long, concluding chapter. No one besides Nick is willing to confront those implications. Gatsby's fatuous father (an obvious contrast to Nick's father) consoles himself with the sordid lie of his dead son's "success." Gatsby's other friends all stay away presumably following the corrupt Wolfsheim's maxim that in matters connected with death "it is better to leave everything alone." Only Nick is incapable of letting things alone. The fact of his neighbor's death rouses Nick—the hitherto passive onlooker—to one of the few positive actions of his career.

As he lay in his house and didn't move or breathe or speak, hour upon hour, it grew upon me that I was responsible because no one else was interested—interested, I mean, with that intense personal interest to which every one has some vague right at the end.

Whereupon Nick sees that his dead friend has a decent funeral and then, taking up one more responsibility, goes back home.[15]

Nick's vicarious involvement in Gatsby's destiny, in other words, has permitted him to see the world for a brief space through the glasses of Dr. T. J. Eckleburg. What he sees is a waste land without moral sanctions of any kind, an anarchy in which romantic idealists like Gatsby are the most vulnerable of all. "After Gatsby's death," Nick says, "the East was haunted for me . . . distorted beyond my eyes' power of correction. So . . . I decided to come back home." Dr. Eckleburg is the symbol of a world without the idea of God, a kind of anti-God. When George Wil- [**332/333**] son discovers that his wife has been unfaithful he drags her to the window of his garage and there, in front of the eyes of Dr. Eckleburg, tells her: "God knows what you've been doing. You may fool me but you can't fool God." "God sees everything," the vengeance-crazed husband tells Michaelis after Myrtle's death, just before setting off on his quest for vengeance. As we might expect, he only succeeds in killing the wrong man.[16]

The evidence of "Absolution" thus serves to emphasize the crucial role played by Nick Carraway in *The Great Gatsby*. Nick is one aspect of Fitzgerald judging another aspect of himself. To do this Nick must possess not only sympathy but also the capacity for moral judgment. As the basis for this judgment, Fitzgerald initially tried to draw upon the framework of his own Catholic childhood; but his feelings about the Church of Rome had become so confused that he was unable to make objective use of them. In one sense his first novel, *This Side of Paradise*, had been the chronicle of his loss of religious faith. His subsequent feelings about the Church probably had not changed materially from those he attributed to his hero, Amory Blaine, at the end of that novel:

The idea was strong in him that there was an intrinsic lack in those to whom religion was necessary, and religion to Amory meant the Church of Rome. Quite conceivably it was an empty ritual, but it was seemingly the only assimilative traditionary bulwark against the decay of morals. . . . Yet, acceptance was, for the present, impossible. He wanted time and the absence of pressure. He wanted to keep the tree without the ornaments.[17]

Fitzgerald's solution, in *The Great Gatsby*, was to retain the tree—the residual tradition of moral values represented by the advice given Nick by his father—without the sectarian dogma. Underlying this was

---

[14] The deleted reference to Dr. Eckleburg's eyes (pencil draft) comes at line 3, p. 28, of the 1925 text.
[15] *Gatsby*, 178 (Scribner Library Edition).

[16] *Ibid.*, 178, 160.
[17] F. Scott Fitzgerald, *This Side of Paradise* (New York: Charles Scribner's Sons, 1920, 1948), p. 281.

his profound, perhaps unconscious, awareness of death.

The result was a moral position that permitted Fitzgerald to [333/334] value the romantic impulse he shared in common with Nick and Gatsby (a "heightened sensitivity to the promises of life"), as well as to see its limitations. Thus, *The Great Gatsby* became a criticism of the romantic egotism Fitzgerald had celebrated in *This Side of Paradise*. It was a retreat toward, though by no means into, the bosom of Mother Church. How desperately Nick longed for such a moral absolute by the end of *Gatsby* is suggested by his remark, "When I came back from the East last summer I wanted the world to be in uniform and at a sort of moral attention forever." The closest Nick can come to such an absolute, however, is to go back home and take up his responsibilities as a member of the Carraway clan.[18]

Several months after *Gatsby* was published, Fitzgerald complained in letters to both Edmund Wilson and John Peale Bishop that (as he wrote Wilson) "of all the reviews, even the most enthusiastic, no one has the slightest idea what the book is about." What it was about, he told Bishop, was himself. To this Bishop objected strenuously. "I can't understand your resentment of the critics' failure to perceive your countenance behind Gatsby's mask. . . . It seems to me to be interesting, if at all, privately only." What Fitzgerald meant, however, was not his literal, but rather his moral countenance. Like T. S. Eliot's *The Waste Land, The Great Gatsby* is a religious work because it has as its source a deeply felt religious emotion. This, perhaps, was what Mr. Eliot had in mind when, soon after it was published, he called it "the first step the American novel has taken since Henry James."[19]

[18] *Gatsby*, 2.

[19] FSF to Edmund Wilson, n.d. (ca. autumn, 1925) reprinted in *The Crack-Up*, ed. by Wilson, (New York 1945), 270; Bishop to FSF, n.d. (ca. Jan. 1926) Princeton University; T. S. Eliot to FSF, Dec. 31, 1925, reprinted in *The Crack-Up*, 310.

Letters about *The Great Gatsby*

SCOTT FITZGERALD mailed the completed manuscript of *The Great Gatsby* to Maxwell E. Perkins, his editor at Scribners, in October, 1924. The letters that follow record some of his afterthoughts during the next few months as well as some of the changes that he made in the galley and page proofs that Perkins sent him for correction and approval. The last letter included here, written more than a year after the novel had been published, was to John Peale Bishop (1891–1944), Fitzgerald's roommate at Princeton and later a poet and literary critic. Fitzgerald portrayed Bishop as Thomas Parke D'Invilliers in his first novel, *This Side of Paradise* (1920).

Villa Marie, Valescure
St. Raphael, France
(After Nov. 3d care of
American Express Co., Rome, Italy)
October 27, 1924[*]

Dear Max:

Under separate cover I'm sending you my third novel, *The Great Gatsby*. (I think that at last I've done something really my own, but how good "my own" is remains to be seen.)

I should suggest the following contract.

> 15% up to 50,000
> 20% after 50,000

The book is only a little over fifty thousand words long but I believe, as you know, that Whitney Darrow [1] has the wrong psychology about prices (and about what class constitute the book-buying public now that the lowbrows go to the movies) and I'm anxious to charge two dollars for it and have it a *full-size book*. [168/169]

Of course I want the binding to be absolutely uniform with my other books—the stamping too—and the jacket we discussed before. This time I don't want any signed blurbs on the jacket—not Mencken's or Lewis' or Howard's [2] or anyone's. I'm tired of being the author of *This Side of Paradise* and I want to start over.

About serialization. I am bound under contract to show it to *Hearst's*, but I am asking a prohibitive price, Long [3] hates me, and it's not a very serialized book. If they should take it—they won't—it would put publication in the fall. Otherwise you can publish it in the spring. When Hearst turns it down, I'm going to offer it to *Liberty* for $15,000 on condition that they'll publish it in ten weekly installments before April 15th. If they don't want it, I shan't serialize. *I am absolutely positive Long won't want it.*

I have an alternative title: *Gold-hatted Gatsby*.

After you've read the book, let me know what you think about the title. Naturally I won't get a night's sleep until I hear from you, but do tell me the absolute truth, *your first impression of the book*, and tell me anything that bothers you in it.

As ever,

Scott

[1] Sales manager at Scribners.

[2] Playwright Sidney Howard.
[3] Ray Long, editor of *Hearst's International*.

[*] Two letters [October 27, 1924, and circa November 7, 1924] from *The Letters of F. Scott Fitzgerald*, ed. Andrew Turnbull (New York: Charles Scribner's Sons, 1963), pp. 168-70. Copyright © 1963 Charles Scribner's Sons; reprinted with the permission of Charles Scribner's Sons.

I'd rather you wouldn't call Reynolds as he might try to act as my agent.

Hotel Continental
St. Raphael, France
(leaving Tuesday)
[circa *November 7, 1924*]

Dear Max:

By now you've received the novel. There are things in it I'm not satisfied with, in the middle of the book—Chapters 6 and 7. And I may write in a complete new scene in proof. I hope you got my telegram.

I have now decided to stick to the title I put on the book: *Trimalchio in West Egg.*

The only other titles that seem to fit it are *Trimalchio* and *On the Road to West Egg.* I had two others, *Gold-hatted Gatsby* and *The High-bouncing Lover,* but they seemed too light.

We leave for Rome as soon as I finish the short story I'm working on.

As ever,

Scott

I was interested that you've moved to New Canaan. It sounds wonderful. Sometimes I'm awfully anxious to be home.

But I am confused at what you say about Gertrude Stein. I thought it was one purpose of critics and publishers to educate the public up to original work. The first people who risked Conrad certainly didn't do it as a commercial venture. Did the evolution of startling work into accepted work cease twenty years ago?

Do send me Boyd's (Ernest's) book when it comes out. I think the Lardner ads are wonderful. Did the *Dark Cloud* flop? [169/170]

Would you ask the people downstairs to keep sending me my monthly bill for the encyclopedia?

November 20, 1924*

Dear Scott:

I think you have every kind of right to be proud of this book. It is an extraordinary book, suggestive of all sorts of thoughts and moods. You adopted exactly the right method of telling it, that of employing a narrator who is more of a spectator than an actor: this puts the reader upon a point of observation on a higher level than that on which the characters stand and at a distance that gives perspective. In no other way could your irony have been so immensely effective, nor the reader have been enabled so strongly to feel at times the strangeness of human circumstance in a vast heedless universe. In the eyes of Dr. Eckleberg various readers will see different significances; but their presence gives a superb touch to the whole thing: great unblinking eyes, expressionless, looking down upon the human scene. It's magnificent!

I could go on praising the book and speculating on its various elements, and means, but points of criticism are more important now. I think you are right in feeling a certain slight sagging in chapters six and seven, and I don't know how to suggest a remedy. I hardly doubt that you will find one and I am only writing to say that I think it does need something to hold up here to the pace set, and ensuing. I have only two actual criticisms:

One is that among a set of characters marvelously palpable [38/39] and vital—I would know Tom Buchanan if I met him on the street and would avoid him—Gatsby is somewhat vague. The reader's eyes can never quite focus upon him, his outlines are dim. Now everything about Gatsby is more or less a mystery, i.e. more or less vague, and this may be somewhat of an artistic intention, but I think it is mistaken. Couldn't *he* be physically de-

From Editor to Author: The Letters of Maxwell E. Perkins, ed. John Hall Wheelock (New York: Charles Scribner's Sons, 1950), pp. 38-41. Copyright 1950 Charles Scribner's Sons; reprinted with the permission of Charles Scribner's Sons.

scribed as distinctly as the others, and couldn't you add one or two characteristics like the use of that phrase "old sport"—not verbal, but physical ones, perhaps. I think that for some reason or other a reader—this was true of Mr. Scribner[1] and of Louise[2]—gets an idea that Gatsby is a much older man than he is, although you have the writer say that he is little older than himself. But this would be avoided if on his first appearance he was seen as vividly as Daisy and Tom are, for instance—and I do not think your scheme would be impaired if you made him so.

The other point is also about Gatsby: his career must remain mysterious, of course. But in the end you make it pretty clear that his wealth came through his connection with Wolfsheim. You also suggest this much earlier. Now almost all readers numerically are going to be puzzled by his having all this wealth and are going to feel entitled to an explanation. To give a distinct and definite one would be, of course, utterly absurd. It did occur to me, though, that you might here and there interpolate some phrases, and possibly incidents, little touches of various kinds, that would suggest that he was in some active way mysteriously engaged. You do have him called on the telephone, but couldn't he be seen once or twice consulting at his parties with people of some sort of mysterious significance, from the political, the gambling, the sporting world, or whatever it may be. I know I am floundering, but that fact may help you to see [**39/40**] what I mean. The *total* lack of an explanation through so large a part of the story does seem to me a defect—or not of an explanation, but of the suggestion of an explanation. I wish you were here so I could talk about it to you, for then I know I could at least make you understand what I mean. What Gatsby did ought never to be definitely imparted,

even if it could be. Whether he was an innocent tool in the hands of somebody else, or to what degree he was this, ought not to be explained. But if some sort of business activity of his were simply adumbrated, it would lend further probability to that part of the story.

There is one other point: in giving deliberately Gatsby's biography, when he gives it to the narrator, you do depart from the method of the narrative in some degree, for otherwise almost everything is told, and beautifully told, in the regular flow of it, in the succession of events or in accompaniment with them. But you can't avoid the biography altogether. I thought you might find ways to let the truth of some of his claims like "Oxford" and his army career come out, bit by bit, in the course of actual narrative. I mention the point anyway, for consideration in this interval before I send the proofs.

The general brilliant quality of the book makes me ashamed to make even these criticisms. The amount of meaning you get into a sentence, the dimensions and intensity of the impression you make a paragraph carry, are most extraordinary. The manuscript is full of phrases which make a scene blaze with life. If one enjoyed a rapid railroad journey I would compare the number and vividness of pictures your living words suggest, to the living scenes disclosed in that way. It seems, in reading, a much shorter book than it is, but it carries the mind through a series of experiences that one would think would require a book of three times its length.

The presentation of Tom, his place, Daisy and Jordan, and [**40/41**] the unfolding of their characters is unequaled so far as I know. The description of the valley of ashes adjacent to the lovely country, the conversation and the action in Myrtle's apartment, the marvelous catalogue of those who came to Gatsby's house —these are such things as make a man famous. And all these things, the whole pathetic episode, you have given a place

---

[1] Charles Scribner, Senior (1854-1930), president of Charles Scribner's Sons.
[2] Mrs. Maxwell E. Perkins.

in time and space, for with the help of T. J. Eckleberg and by an occasional glance at the sky, or the sea, or the city, you have imparted a sort of sense of eternity. You once told me you were not a *natural writer*—my God! You have plainly mastered the craft, of course; but you needed far more than craftsmanship for this.

As ever,

Max

Hotel des Princes
Piazza di Spagna
Rome, Italy
[circa *December 1, 1924*]*

Dear Max:

Your wire and your letters made me feel like a million dollars—I'm sorry I could make no better response than a telegram whining for money. But the long siege of the novel winded me a little and I've been slow on starting the stories on which I must live.

I think all your criticisms are true.

(a) About the title. I'll try my best but I don't know what I can do. Maybe simply *Trimalchio*[1] or *Gatsby*. In the former case, I don't see why the note shouldn't go on the back.
(b) Chapters VI and VII I know how to fix.
(c) Gatsby's business affairs I can fix. I get your point about them.
(d) His vagueness I can repair by *making more pointed*—this doesn't sound good but wait and see. It'll make him clear.
(e) But his long narrative in Chapter VIII will be difficult to split up. Zelda also thought it was a little out of key, but it is good writing and I

don't think I could bear to sacrifice any of it.
(f) I have 1000 minor corrections which I will make on the proof and several more large ones which you didn't mention.

Your criticisms were excellent and most helpful, and you picked out all my favorite spots in the book to praise as high spots. Except you didn't mention my favorite of all—the chapter where Gatsby and Daisy meet.

Two more things. Zelda's been reading me the cowboy book[1] aloud to spare my mind and I love it—tho I think he learned the American language from Ring[2] rather than from his own ear.

Another point—in Chapter II of my book when Tom and Myrtle [**170/171**] go into the bedroom while Carraway reads *Simon Called Peter*—is that raw? Let me know. I think it's pretty necessary.

I made the royalty smaller because I wanted to make up for all the money you've advanced these two years by leting it pay a sort of interest on it. But I see by calculating I made it too small—a difference of 2000 dollars. Let us call it 15% up to 40,000 and 20% after that. That's a good fair contract all around.

By now you have heard from a smart young French woman who wants to translate the book. She's equal to it intellectually and linguistically, I think—had read all my others—if you'll tell her how to go about it as to royalty demands, etc.

Anyhow thanks and thanks and thanks for your letters. I'd rather have you and Bunny[2] like it than anyone I know. And I'd rather have you like it than Bunny. If it's as good as you say, when I finish with the proof it'll be perfect.

[1] *Cowboys North and South* by Will James.
[2] Ring Lardner (1885-1933), author of *You Know Me, Al, How to Write Short Stories* and other volumes of short stories, and a friend of Fitzgerald's.
[2] Edmund Wilson.

[1] Trimalchio, the hero of *the Satiricon*, a satire on Roman society by Gaius Petronius, who died ca. 66 A.D.

Remember, by the way, to put by some cloth for the cover uniform with my other books.

As soon as I can think about the title, I'll write or wire a decision. Thank Louise[3] for me, for liking it. Best regards to Mr. Scribner. Tell him Galsworthy is here in Rome.

As ever,

Scott

Hotel des Princes
Piazza di Spagna
Rome, Italy
[circa *December 20, 1924*]*

Dear Max:

I'm a bit (not very—not dangerously) stewed tonight and I'll probably write you a long letter. We're living in a small, unfashionable but most comfortable hotel at $525.00 a month, including tips, meals, etc. Rome does *not* particularly interest me but it's a big year here, and early in the spring we're going to Paris. There's no use telling you my plans because they're usually just about as unsuccessful as to work as [**171/172**] religious prognosticators are as to the End of the World. I've got a new novel to write—title and all—that'll take about a year.[1] Meanwhile, I don't want to start it until this is out and meanwhile I'll do short stories for money (I now get $2000 a story but I hate worse than hell to do them) and there's the never-dying lure of another play.

Now! Thanks enormously for making up the $5000. I know I don't technically deserve it, considering I've had $3000 or $4000 for as long as I can remember. But since you force it on me (inexecrable [or is it execrable] joke) I will accept it.

I hope to Christ you get 10 times it back on *Gatsby*—and I think perhaps you will. For:

I can now make it perfect but the proof (I will soon get the immemorial letter with the statement "We now have the book in hand and will soon begin to send you proof." What is "in hand?" I have a vague picture of everyone in the office holding the book in the right hand and reading it.) will be one of the most expensive affairs since *Madame Bovary*. *Please* charge it to my account. If it's possible to send a second proof over here I'd love to have it. Count on 12 days each way—four days here on first proof and two days on the second. I hope there are other good books in the spring because I think now the public interest in *books* per se rises when there seems to be a group of them, as in 1920 (spring and fall), 1921 (fall), 1922 (spring). Ring's and Tom's (first) books,[1] Willa Cather's *Lost Lady*, and in an inferior cheap way Edna Ferber's are the only American fiction in over two years that had a really excellent press (say, since *Babbitt*).

With the aid you've given me I can make *Gatsby* perfect. The Chapter 7 (the hotel scene) will never quite be up to mark—I've worried about it too long and I can't quite place Daisy's reaction. But I can improve it a lot. It isn't imaginative energy that's lacking—it's because I'm automatically prevented from thinking it out over again *because I must get all those characters to New York* in order to have the catastrophe on the road going back, and I must have it pretty much that way. So there's no chance of bringing the freshness to it that a new free conception sometimes gives.

The rest is easy and I see my way so clear that I even see the mental quirks

---

[3] Mrs. Maxwell Perkins.
[1] *Tender Is the Night* (1934).

[1] Thomas Boyd, best known for his war novel, *Through the Wheat*.

*From *The Letters of F. Scott Fitzgerald*, ed. Andrew Turnbull (New York: Charles Scribner's Sons, 1963), pp. 171-175. Copyright © 1963 Charles Scribner's Sons; reprinted with the permission of Charles Scribner's Sons.

that queered it before. Strange to say, my notion of Gatsby's vagueness was O.K. What you and Louise and Mr. Charles Scribner found wanting was that:

I myself didn't know what Gatsby looked like or was engaged in [172/173] and you felt it. If I'd known and kept it from you you'd have been *too impressed with my knowledge to protest.* This is a complicated idea but I'm sure you'll understand. But I know now—and as a penalty for not having known first, in other words to make sure, I'm going to tell more.

It seems of almost mystical significance to me that you thought he was older—the man I had in mind, half-unconsciously, *was* older (a specific individual) and evidently, without so much as a definite word, I conveyed the fact. Or rather I must qualify this Shaw Desmond trash by saying that I conveyed it without a word that I can at present or for the life of me trace. (I think Shaw Desmond was one of your bad bets—I was the other.)

Anyhow after careful searching of the files (of a man's mind here) for the Fuller Magee case and after having had Zelda draw pictures until her fingers ache I know Gatsby better than I know my own child. My first instinct after your letter was to let him go and have Tom Buchanan dominate the book (I suppose he's the best character I've ever done—I think he and the brother in *Salt*[1] and Hurstwood in *Sister Carrie*[2] are the three best characters in American fiction in the last twenty years, perhaps and perhaps not) but Gatsby sticks in my heart. I had him for awhile, then lost him, and now I know I have him again. I'm sorry Myrtle is better than Daisy. Jordan of course was a great idea (perhaps you know it's Edith Cummings[3]) but she fades out. It's Chapter VII that's the trouble with Daisy and it may hurt the book's popularity that it's *a man's book.*

Anyhow I think (for the first time since *The Vegetable*[4] failed) that I'm a wonderful writer and it's your always wonderful letters that help me to go on believing in myself.

Now some practical, very important questions. Please answer every one.

1. Montenegro has an order called the Order of Danilo. Is there any possible way you could find out for me there what it would look like—whether a courtesy decoration given to an American would bear an English inscription—or anything to give verisimilitude to the medal which sounds horribly amateurish?

2. Please have *no blurbs of any kind on the jacket!!!* No Mencken or Lewis or Sid Howard or anything. I don't believe in them *one bit* any more.

3. Don't forget to change name of book in list of works. [173/174]

4. Please shift exclamation point from end of third line to end of fourth line in title page poem. *Please!* Important!

5. I thought that the whole episode (2 paragraphs) about their playing the "Jazz History of the World" at Gatsby's first party was rotten. Did you? Tell me your frank *reaction—personal.* Don't *think!* We can all think!

Got a sweet letter from Sid Howard—rather touching. I wrote him first I thought *Transatlantic* was great stuff—a really gorgeous surprise. Up to that I never believed in him specially and I was sorry because he did in me. Now I'm tickled silly to find he has power, and his own power. It seemed tragic too to see *Mrs. Vietch* wasted in a novelette when, despite Anderson, the short story is at its lowest ebb as an art form. (Despite Ruth Suckow, Gertrude Stein, Ring, there is a horrible impermanence on it *because* the overwhelming number of short stories are impermanent.)

[1] A recent novel by Charles Norris
[2] By Theodore Dreiser
[3] A girl Fitzgerald had known

[4] Fitzgerald's play, *The Vegetable: or From President to Postman* (1923)

Poor Tom Boyd! His cycle sounded so sad to me—perhaps it'll be wonderful but it sounds to me like sloughing in a field whose first freshness has gone.

See that word:[2] The ambition of my life is to make that use of it correct. The temptation to use it as a neuter is one of the vile fevers in my still insecure prose.

Tell me about Ring! About Tom—is he poor? He seems to be counting on his short story book, frail cane! About Biggs[3]—did he ever finish the novel? About Peggy Boyd[4]—I think Louise might have sent us her book!

I thought *The White Monkey*[4] was stinko. On second thoughts I didn't like *Cowboys, West and South* either. What about *Bal du Comte d'Orgel?*[5] and Ring's set? and his new book? and Gertrude Stein? and Hemingway?

I still owe the store almost $700.00 on my encyclopedia, but I'll pay them on about January 10th—all in a lump as I expect my finances will then be on a firm footing. Will you ask them to send me Ernest Boyd's book?[6] Unless it has about my drinking in it that would reach my family. However, I guess it'd worry me more if I hadn't seen it [174/175] than if I had. If my book is a big success or a great failure (financial—no other sort can be imagined I hope) I *don't* want to publish stories in the fall. If it goes between 25,000 and 50,000 I have an excellent collection for you. This is the longest letter I've written in three or four years. Please thank Mr. Scribner for me for his exceeding kindness.

Always yours,

Scott Fitz—

14 rue de Tilsitt
Paris, France
*[August 9, 1925]**

Dear John:[1]

Thank you for your most pleasant, full, discerning and helpful letter about *The Great Gatsby*. It is about the only criticism that the book has had which has been intelligible, save a letter from Mrs. Wharton.[2] I shall duly ponder, or rather I have pondered, what you say about accuracy—I'm afraid I haven't quite reached the ruthless artistry which would let me cut out an exquisite bit that had no place in the context. I can cut out the almost exquisite, the adequate, even the brilliant—but a true accuracy is, as you say, still in the offing. Also you are right about Gatsby being blurred and patchy. I never at any one time saw him clear myself—for he started as one man I knew and then changed into myself—the amalgam was never complete in my mind.

Your novel sounds fascinating and I'm crazy to see it. I am beginning a new novel next month on the Riviera. I understand that MacLeish[3] is there, among other people (at Antibes where we are going). Paris has been a mad-house this spring and, as you can imagine, we were in the thick of it. I don't know when we're coming back—maybe never. We'll be here till January (except for a month in Antibes), and then we go Nice for the spring, with Oxford for next summer. Love to Margaret and many thanks for the kind letter.

Scott

---

[2] Fitzgerald had encircled "whose" in the sentence before.
[3] Fitzgerald's college friend, John Biggs.
[4] Mrs. Thomas Boyd.
[4] By John Galsworthy
[5] By the young French novelist, Pierre Radiguet
[6] *Portraits Real and Imaginary*

[1] John Peale Bishop
[2] Edith Wharton, the well-known novelist
[3] Archibald MacLeish, the poet

[An Introduction to *The Great Gatsby*] *

F. SCOTT FITZGERALD wrote the following introduction for the Modern Library edition of his novel that was published in 1934.

To one who has spent his professional life in the world of fiction the request to "write an introduction" offers many facets of temptation. The present writer succumbs to one of them; with as much equanimity as he can muster, he will discuss the critics among us, trying to revolve as centripetally as possible about the novel which comes hereafter in this volume.

To begin with, I must say that I have no cause to grumble about the "press" of any book of mine. If Jack (who liked my last book) didn't like this one—well then John (who despised my last book) *did* like it; so it all mounts up to the same total. But I think the writers of my time were spoiled in that regard, living in generous days when there was plenty of space on the page for endless ratiocination about fiction—a space largely created by Mencken because of his disgust for what passed as criticism before he arrived and made his public. They were encouraged by his bravery and his tremendous and profound love of letters. In his [165/166] case, the jackals are already tearing at what they imprudently regard as a moribund lion, but I don't think many men of my age can regard him without reverence, nor fail to regret that he got off the train. To any new effort by a new man he brought an attitude; he made many mistakes—such as his early undervaluation of Hemingway—but he came equipped; he never had to go back for his tools.

And now that he has abandoned American fiction to its own devices, there is no one to take his place. If the present writer had seriously to attend some of the efforts of political diehards to tell him the values of a métier he has practised since boyhood—well, then, babies, you can take this number out and shoot him at dawn.

But all that is less discouraging, in the past few years, than the growing cowardice of the reviewers. Underpaid and overworked, they seem not to care for books, and it has been saddening recently to see young talents in fiction expire from sheer lack of a stage to act on: West, McHugh and many others.

I'm circling closer to my theme song, which is: that I'd like to communicate to such of them who read this novel a healthy cynicism toward contemporary reviews. Without undue vanity one can permit oneself a suit of chain mail in any profession. Your pride is all you have, and if you let it be tampered with by a man who has a dozen prides to tamper with before lunch, you are promising yourself a lot of disappointments that a hard-boiled professional has learned to spare himself.

This novel is a case in point. Because the pages weren't loaded with big names of big things and the subject not concerned with farmers (who were the heroes of the moment), there was easy judgment exercised that had nothing to do with criticism but was simply an attempt on the part of men who had few chances of self-

*F. Scott Fitzgerald, Introduction to the Modern Library Edition of *The Great Gatsby* (New York: Random House, Inc., 1934. Copyright 1934 by The Modern Library, Inc. Reprinted by permission of Random House, Inc. Reprinted in *The Great Gatsby: A Study*, ed. Frederick J. Hoffman (New York: Charles Scribner's Sons, 1962).

expression to express themselves. How anyone could take up the responsibility of being a novelist without a sharp and concise attitude about life is a puzzle to me. How a critic could assume a [**166/167**] point of view which included twelve variant aspects of the social scene in a few hours seems something too dinosaurean to loom over the awful loneliness of a young author.

To circle nearer to this book, one woman, who could hardly have written a coherent letter in English, described it as a book that one read only as one goes to the movies around the corner. That type of criticism is what a lot of young writers are being greeted with, instead of any appreciation of the world of imagination in which they (the writers) have been trying, with greater or lesser success, to live—the world that Mencken made stable in the days when he was watching over us.

Now that this book is being reissued, the author would like to say that never before did one try to keep his artistic conscience as pure as during the ten months put into doing it. Reading it over one can see how it could have been improved —yet without feeling guilty of any discrepancy from the truth, as far as I saw it; truth or rather the *equivalent* of the truth, the attempt at honesty of imagination. I had just re-read Conrad's preface to *The Nigger,* and I had recently been kidded half haywire by critics who felt that my material was such as to preclude all dealing with mature persons in a mature world. But, my God! it was my material, and it was all I had to deal with.

What I cut out of it both physically and emotionally would make another novel!

I think it is an honest book, that is to say, that one used none of one's virtuosity to get an effect, and, to boast again, one

soft-pedalled the emotional side to avoid the tears leaking from the socket of the left eye, or the large false face peering around the corner of a character's head.

If there is a clear conscience, a book can survive—at least in one's feelings about it. On the contrary, if one has a guilty conscience, one reads what one wants to hear out of reviews. In addition, if one is young and willing to learn, almost all reviews have a value, even the ones that seem unfair. [**167/168**]

The present writer has always been a "natural" for his profession, in so much that he can think of nothing he would have done as efficiently as to have lived deeply in the world of imagination. There are plenty other people constituted as he is, for giving expression to intimate explorations, the:

—Look—this is here!

—I saw this under my eyes.

—*This* is the way it was!

—No, it was like this.

"Look! Here is that drop of blood I told you about."

—"Stop everything! Here is the flash of that girl's eyes, here is the reflection that will always come back to me from the memory of her eyes.

—"If one chooses to find that face again in the non-refracting surface of a washbowl, if one chooses to make the image more obscure with a little sweat, it should be the business of the critic to recognize the intention.

—"No one felt like this before—says the young writer—but *I* felt like this; I have a pride akin to a soldier going into battle; without knowing whether there will be anybody there, to distribute medals or even to record it."

But remember, also, young man: you are not the first person who has ever been alone and alone.

The Craft of Revision: *The Great Gatsby* *

KENNETH EBLE (1923–   ) is a professor of English at the University of Utah. He is the author of *The Profane Comedy: American Higher Education in the Sixties* (1962) and *F. Scott Fitzgerald* (1963) and recently edited a collection of essays on the fiction of William Dean Howells.

"With the aid you've given me," Fitzgerald wrote Maxwell Perkins in December, 1924, "I can make *Gatsby* perfect."[1] Fitzgerald had sent the manuscript of the novel to Scribner's in late October, but the novel achieved its final form only after extensive revisions Fitzgerald made in the next four months. The pencil draft and the much revised galley proofs now in the Fitzgerald collection at Princeton library show how thoroughly and expertly Fitzgerald practiced the craft of revision.[2]

I

The pencil draft both reveals and masks Fitzgerald's struggles. The manuscript affords a complete first version, but the pages are not numbered serially from beginning to end, nor are the chapters and sections of chapters all tied together. There are three segments (one a copy of a previous draft) designated "Chapter III," two marked "Chapter VI." The amount of revising varies widely from page to page and chapter to chapter; the beginning and end are comparatively clean, the middle most cluttered. Fitzgerald's clear, regular hand, however, imposes its own sense of order throughout the text. For all the revisions, the script goes about its business with a straightness of line, a regularity of letter that approaches formal elegance. When he is striking out for the first time, the writing tends to be large, seldom exceeding eight words per line or twenty-five lines per page. When he is copying or reworking from a previous draft the writing becomes compressed—but never crabbed—and gets half again as much on a page. [315/316]

An admirer of Fitzgerald—of good writing, for that matter—reads the draft with a constant sense of personal involvement, a sensation of small satisfied longings as the right word gets fixed in place, a feeling of strain when the draft version hasn't yet found its perfection of phrase, and a nagging sense throughout of how precariously the writer dangles between the almost and the attained. "All good writing," Fitzgerald wrote his daughter, "is *swimming under water* and holding your breath."[3]

At the beginning of the draft, there appears to have been little gasping for air. There at the outset, virtually as published, is that fine set piece which establishes the tone of the novel with the

[1] *The Letters of F. Scott Fitzgerald*, ed. Andrew Turnbull (New York, 1963), p. 172.

[2] This study is based on an examination of the original pencil draft and the galley proofs in the Fitzgerald collection in the Princeton Library and subsequent work with a microfilm copy of this material. I am indebted to the University of Utah Research Fund for a grant which enabled me to study the materials at Princeton, to Alexander P. Clark, curator of manuscripts, for his indispensable help in making this material available, and to Mr. Ivan Von Auw and the Fitzgerald estate for permission to use this material.

[3] *The Crack-Up*, p. 304.

*Kenneth Eble, "The Craft of Revision: The Great Gatsby," *American Literature* XXXVI (Autumn, 1964), 315-26. Reprinted with the permission of Duke University Press and the author.

creation of Nick Carraway and his heightened sense of the fundamental decencies. As one reads the first chapter, however, the satisfaction of seeing the right beginning firmly established soon changes to surprise. The last page of the novel— "gradually I became aware of the old island here that flowered once for Dutch sailors' eyes—a fresh, green breast of the new world."[4]—was originally written as the conclusion of Chapter I. Some time before the draft went into the submission copy, Fitzgerald recognized that the passage was too good for a mere chapter ending, too definitive of the larger purposes of the book, to remain there. By the time the pencil draft was finished, that memorable paragraph had been put into its permanent place, had fixed the image of man holding his breath in the presence of the continent, "face to face for the last time in history with something commensurate to his capacity for wonder."

The three paragraphs which come immediately after, the last paragraphs of the novel, grew out of one long fluid sentence which was originally the final sentence of Chapter I in the draft: "And as I sat there brooding on the old unknown world I too held my breath and waited, until I could feel the motion of America as it turned through the hours—my own blue lawn and the tall incandescent city on the water and beyond that, the dark fields of the republic rolling on under the night." Fitzgerald expanded this suggestion into a full paragraph, crossed out the first attempt, and then rewrote it into three paragraphs on the final page of the draft. There, almost as it appears in the novel, is the green light on Daisy's dock ("green [**316/317**] glimmer" in the draft), the orgiastic future (written "orgastic"),[5] and that ultimate sentence, "So we beat on, a boat [changed to "boats"] against

the current, borne back ceaselessly into the past." So the draft ends, the last lines written in a "bold, swooping hand," as Fitzgerald described Gatsby's signature, a kind of autograph for the completed work.

The green light (there were originally two) came into the novel at the time of Daisy's meeting with Gatsby. "If it wasn't for the mist," he tells her, we could see your house across the bay. You always have two green lights that burn all night at the end of your dock." Fitzgerald not only made the green light a central image of the final paragraph, but he went back to the end of the first chapter and added it there: "Involuntarily I glanced seaward— and distinguished nothing except a single green light, minute and far away, that might have been the end of a dock" (pp. 21-22).

II

Throughout the pencil draft, Fitzgerald made numerous revisions which bring out his chief traits as a reviser: he seldom threw anything good away, and he fussed endlessly at getting right things in the right places. The two parties at Gatsby's house, interesting as illustrations of Fitzgerald's mastery of the "scenic method," are equally interesting as examples of how he worked.

The purpose of the first party as it appears in the draft (Chapter III in the book) was chiefly that of creating the proper atmosphere. Though Gatsby makes his first appearance in this section, it is Gatsby's world that most glitters before our eyes. The eight servants (there were only seven in the draft), the five crates (only three in the draft) of oranges and lemons, the caterers spreading the canvas,

---

[4] All citations hereafter are from the Scribner Library edition of *The Great Gatsby*.

[5] Arthur Mizener points out that Fitzgerald corrected the spelling from "orgastic" to "orgiastic" in his own copy of the book (*The Far Side of Paradise*, Boston, 1951,

p. 336, n. 22). Yet Fitzgerald's letter to Maxwell Perkins, January 24, 1925, defends the original term: " 'Orgastic' is the adjective for 'orgasm' and it expresses exactly the intended ecstasy. It's not a bit dirty" (*Letters*, p. 175). The word appears as "orgiastic" in most editions of the novel, including the current Scribner's printings.

the musicians gathering, the Rolls-Royce carrying party-goers from the city, are the kind of atmospherics Fitzgerald could always do well. The party itself as it unfolds in the draft reveals a number of intentions that Fitzgerald abandoned as he saw the pos- [**317/318**] sibilities of making the party vital to the grander design of the novel.

Originally, whether from strong feelings or in response to his readers' expectations, he took pains to bring out the wild and shocking lives being lived by many of Gatsby's guests. Drug addiction was apparently commonplace, and even more sinister vices were hinted at. A good deal of undergraduate party chatter was also cut from the draft. What a reader of the novel now remembers is what Fitzgerald brought into sharp relief by cutting out the distracting embellishments. "The Jazz History of the World" by Vladimir Tostoff (it was Leo Epstien [*sic*] originally; Fitzgerald deleted a number of "Jewish" remarks from the draft) was described in full. When Fitzgerald saw the galleys he called the whole episode "rotten" and reduced the page-and-a-half description to a single clause: "The nature of Mr. Tostoff's composition eluded me . . ." (p. 50). By the time the party scene had been cut and reworked, almost all that remained was the introduction of Gatsby's physical presence into the novel and the splendid scene of Owl-Eyes in Gatsby's high Gothic library.

Among the many excisions in this party scene, one seemed far too good to throw away. In the draft, it began when Jordan Baker exchanges a barbed remark with another girl:

"You've dyed your hair since then," remarked Miss Baker and I started but the girls had moved casually on and were talking to an elaborate orchid of a woman who sat in state under a white plum tree.
"Do you see who that is?" demanded Jordan Baker interestly. [I use Fitzgerald's spelling here and elsewhere in quoting from the draft.]
Suddenly I did see, with the peculiar unreal feeling which accompanies the recognition of a hitherto ghostly celebrity of the movies.

"The man with her is her director," she continued. "He's just been married."
"To her?"
"No."
She laughed. The director was bending over his pupil so eagerly that his chin and her mettalic black hair were almost in juxtaposition.
"I hope he doesn't slip," she added. "And spoil her hair."
It was still twilight but there was already a moon, produced no doubt like the turkey and the salad out of a caterer's basket. With her hard, slender golden arm drawn through mine we descended the steps. . . . [**318/319**]

It is a fine scene, and the girl with the dyed hair, the moon, and the caterer's basket can be found on page 43 of the novel, so smoothly joined together that no one could suspect, much less mourn, the disappearance of that "elaborate orchid" of a woman. But, of course, she did not disappear. The scene was merely transported to the second party where the actress defined the second party as Owl-Eyes defined the first:

"Perhaps you know that lady," Gatsby indicated a gorgeous, scarcely human orchid of a woman who sat in state under a white-plum tree. Tom and Daisy stared, with the particularly unreal feeling that accompanies the recognition of a hitherto ghostly celebrity of the movies.
"She's lovely," said Daisy.
"The man bending over her is her director." (p. 106)

Two pages later, at the end of the second party, we see her again:

It was like that. Almost the last thing I remember was standing with Daisy and watching the movie-picture director and his Star. They were still under the white-plum tree and their faces were touching except for a pale, thin ray of moonlight between. It occurred to me that he had been very slowly bending toward her all evening to attain this proximity, and even while I watched I saw him stoop one ultimate degree and kiss at her cheek.
"I like her," said Daisy. "I think she's lovely."
But the rest offended her. . . . (p. 108)

One can almost see the writer's mind in action here. The scene was first created, almost certainly, from the rightness of having a "ghostly celebrity of the movies" at the party. It first served merely as scenery and as a way of hinting at the moral laxity of Gatsby's guests. The need to compress and focus probably brought Fitzgerald to consider cutting it out entirely though it was obviously too good to throw away. By that time, perhaps, the second party scene had been written, another possibility had been opened up. Maybe at once, maybe slowly, Fitzgerald recognized that the scene could be used to capture Daisy's essential aloofness which was to defy even Gatsby's ardor. It may well be that this developed and practiced ability to use everything for its maximum effect, to strike no note, so to speak, without anticipating all its vibrations, is what separates Fitzgerald's work in *The Great Gatsby* from his earlier writing, what makes it seem such a leap from his first novels. [319/320]

Among the many lessons Fitzgerald applied between the rough draft and the finished novel was that of cutting and setting his diamonds so that they caught up and cast back a multitude of lights. In so doing, he found it unnecessary to have an authorial voice gloss a scene. The brilliance floods in upon the reader; there is no necessity for Nick Carraway to say, as he did at one point in the pencil draft: "I told myself that I was studying it all like a philosopher, a sociologist, that there was a unity here that I could grasp after or would be able to grasp in a minute, a new facet, elemental and profound." The distance Fitzgerald traveled from *This Side of Paradise* and *The Beautiful and Damned* to *The Great Gatsby* is in the rewriting of the novel. There the sociologist and philosopher were at last controlled and the writer assumed full command.

III

Rewriting was important to Fitzgerald because, like many other good writers, he had to see his material assume its form—not in the *idea* of a character or a situation—but in the way character and situation and all the rest got down on paper.

Once set down, they began to shape everything else in the novel, began to raise the endless questions of emphasis, balance, direction, unity, impact.

The whole of Chapter II in the finished novel (Chapter III in the draft) is illustration of how the material took on its final form. That chapter begins with Dr. T. J. Eckleburg's eyes brooding over the ash heaps and culminates in the quarrel in Myrtle's apartment where "making a short deft movement, Tom Buchanan broke her nose with his open hand." Arthur Mizener first pointed out that the powerful symbol introduced in this chapter—Dr. Eckleburg's eyes—was the result of Fitzgerald's seeing a dust jacket portraying Daisy's eyes brooding over an amusement park world. "For Christ's sake," he wrote to Perkins, "don't give anyone that jacket you're saving for me. I've written it into the book."[6] The pencil draft indicates that the chapter—marked Chapter III in the manuscript—was written at a different period of time from that of the earlier chapters. The consecutive numbering of the first sixty-two pages of the novel (the first two chapters) shows that for a long time Fitzgerald intended Chapter II as it now stands in the novel to be the third chapter. [320/321]

In substance, the chapter remained much the same in the finished novel as it was in the draft. But, in addition to moving the chapter forward, Fitzgerald transposed to the next chapter a four-page section at the end describing Nick's activities later in the summer. Summing up Nick's character at the end of the third chapter gave more point to his concluding remark: "I am one of the few honest ["decent" in the draft] people that I have ever known" (p. 60). Bringing the Eckleburg chapter forward meant that the reader could never travel to or from Gatsby's house without traversing the valley of ashes. And ending the second chapter where it now ends meant that the reader could never get to Gatsby's blue gardens where "men and

---

6 Mizener, p. 170. The entire letter is to be found in *Letters*, pp. 165-167.

girls came and went like moths among the whisperings and the champagne and the stars" without waking up waiting for a four o'clock train in Penn Station.

But putting a brilliant chapter in place was only part of the task Fitzgerald could see needed to be done once the material was down on paper. Within that chapter, Fitzgerald's pencil was busily doing its vital work. The substance was all there: Tom and Myrtle and Nick going up to New York, the buying of the dog, the drinking in the apartment, the vapid conversations between the McKees and sister Catherine and Myrtle, the final violence. But some little things were not. The gray old man with the basket of dogs did not look like John D. Rockefeller until Fitzgerald pencilled it in between lines; the mongrel "undoubtedly had Airedale blood" until Fitzgerald made it "an Airedale concerned in it somewhere"; and finally, the pastoral image of Fifth Avenue on a summer Sunday—"I wouldn't have been surprised to see a great flock of white sheep turn the corner"—this didn't arrive until the galleys.

IV

The appearances of Gatsby, as might be expected, are among the most worked-over sections in the draft. Even when the manuscript was submitted, the characterization was not quite satisfactory, either to Fitzgerald or to Maxwell Perkins. The "old sport" phrase which fixes Gatsby as precisely as his gorgeous pink rag of a suit is to be found in only one section of the pencil draft, though it must have been incorporated fully into his speech before Fitzgerald sent off the manuscript. "Couldn't you add one or two characteristics like the use of that phrase 'old sport' —not verbal, but physical ones, per- [321/ 322] haps," Perkins suggested.[7] Fitzgerald chose the most elusive of physical characteristics—Gatsby's smile. How he worked it up into a powerfully suggestive bit of characterization can be seen by comparing the pencil draft and the final copy. Gatsby is telling Nick about his experiences during the war:

Rough Draft

"I was promoted to be a major/ and every Allied government gave me a decoration—/even ~~But~~ Montenegro little Montenegro down on the Adriatic/Sea!"

~~He lifted up the w~~ Little Montenegro! He lifted up the words/
them
and nodded at ~~it~~ with a faint smile. My incredulity had/had turned to fascination now; ~~Gatsby was no longer a~~ it was/~~person he was a magazine I had picked up on~~
like
~~the casually train and I was~~ reading only
the climaxes of all the stories/~~it contained~~ in a magazine.

Final Version

"I was promoted to be a major, and every Allied government gave me a decoration—even Montenegro, little Montenegro down on the Adriatic Sea!"

Little Montenegro! He lifted up the words and nodded at them—with his smile. The smile comprehended Montenegro's troubled history and sympathized with the brave struggles of the Montenegrin people. It appreciated fully the chain of national circumstances which had elicited this tribute from Montenegro's warm little heart. My incredulity was submerged in fascination now; it was like skimming hastily through a dozen magazines. (pp. 66-67)

. [7] *Editor to Author: The Letters of Maxwell E. Perkins,* ed. John Hall Wheelock (New York, 1950) p. 39.

The smile is described in even fuller detail in a substantial addition to galley 15 (page 48 of the novel). One can virtually see Fitzgerald striking upon the smile as a characteristic which could give Gatsby substance without destroying his necessary insubstantiality.

Gatsby is revised, not so much into a real person as into a mythical one; what he *is* is not allowed to distract the reader from what he stands for. Without emphasizing the particulars of Gatsby's past, Fitzgerald wanted to place him more squarely before the reader.[8] [322/323] Many of the further changes made in the galley proofs were directed toward that end. In the first five chapters of the galleys, the changes are the expected ones: routine corrections, happy changes in wording or phrasing, a few deletions, some additions. But at Chapter VI the galley proofs become fat with whole paragraphs and pages pasted in. Whole galleys are crossed out as the easiest way to make the extensive changes Fitzgerald felt were necessary. Throughout this section, he cut passages, tightened dialogue, reduced explicit statements in order to heighten the evocative power of his prose.

The major structural change brought the true story of Gatsby's past out of Chapter VIII and placed it at the beginning of Chapter VI. Chapter V, the meeting between Gatsby and Daisy, was already at the precise center of the novel.[9] That scene is the most static in the book. For a moment, after the confusion of the meeting, the rain, and his own doubts, Gatsby holds past and present together. The revision of Chapter VI, as if to prolong this scene in the reader's mind, leaves the narrative, shifts the scene to the reporter inquiring about Gatsby, and fills in Gatsby's real past. "I take advantage of this short halt," Nick Carraway says, "while Gatsby, so to speak, caught his breath" (p. 102). The deliberate pause illustrates the care with which the novel is constructed. The Gatsby of his self-created present is contrasted with the Gatsby of his real past, and the moment prolonged before the narrative moves on. The rest of Chapter VI focuses on the first moment of disillusion, Gatsby's peculiar establishment seen through Daisy's eyes.

The rewriting so extensive in this chapter is as important as the shifting of material. The draft at this point has five different sets of numbers, and these pieces are fitted only loosely together. The Gatsby who finally emerges from the rewritten galleys answers the criticisms made by Maxwell Perkins and, more important, satisfies Fitzgerald's own critical sense. "ACTION IS CHARACTER," Fitzgerald wrote in his notes for *The Last Tycoon*. His revisions of dialogue, through which the novel often makes its vital disclosures and confrontations, shows his adherence to that precept. The truth of Gatsby's connection with Oxford was originally revealed to Nick Carraway in a somewhat flat, overly detailed conversation in which Gatsby tries to define his feeling for Daisy. Most of that conversa- [323/324] tion was cut out and the Oxford material worked into the taut dialogue between Tom Buchanan and Gatsby in the Plaza Hotel which prefaces the sweep of the story to its final action.[10]

In the draft, Gatsby reveals his sentimentality directly; he even sings a poor song he had composed as a boy. In the novel, a long passage of this sort is swept away, a good deal of the dialogue is put into exposition and the effect is preserved

---

[8] Fitzgerald wrote in response to Perkins's criticism: "His [Gatsby's] vagueness I can repair by *making more pointed*—this doesn't sound good but wait and see. It'll make him clear." In a subsequent letter, he wrote: ". . . Gatsby sticks in my heart. I had him for awhile, then lost him, and now I know I have him again" (*Letters*, pp. 170, 173).

[9] Fitzgerald called this chapter his "favorite of all" (To Maxwell Perkins, *circa* Dec. 1, 1924, *Letters*, p. 170).

[10] Mizener points out that Fitzgerald was revising almost up to the day of publication. The revision of this section came some time around February 18, 1925, when Fitzgerald cabled Maxwell Perkins: "Hold Up Galley Forty For Big Change" (*The Far Side of Paradise*, p. 164; p. 335, n. 63). Fitzgerald returned the proofs about February 18th. In a letter to Perkins, he listed what he had done: "1) I've brought Gatsby to life. 2) I've accounted for his money. 3) I've fixed up the two weak chapters (VI and VII). 4) I've improved his first party. 5) I've broken up his long narrative in Chapter VIII" (*Letters*, p. 177).

by Nick's comment at the end: "Through all he said, even through his appalling sentimentality . . ." (p. 112). In the draft, Gatsby carefully explains to Nick why he cannot run away. " 'I've got to,' he announced with conviction, 'That's what I've got to do—live the past over again.' " Substance and dialogue are cleared away here, but the key idea is kept, held for a better place, and then shaped supremely right, as a climactic statement in a later talk with Nick: " 'Can't repeat the past?' he cried incredulously. 'Why of course you can!' " (p. 111). In the draft, much of Gatsby's story is told in dialogue as he talks to Nick. It permits him to talk too much, to say, for example: " 'Jay Gatsby!' he cried suddenly in a ringing voice. 'There goes the great Jay Gatsby! That's what people are going to say—wait and see.' " In the novel even the allusion to the title is excised. Gatsby's past is compressed into three pages of swift exposition punctuated by the images of his Platonic self, of his serving "a vast, vulgar, and meretricious beauty," and of Dan Cody and "the savage violence of the frontier brothel and saloon" from which he had come. Finally, in the draft, the undercurrent of passion and heat and boredom which sweeps all of them to the showdown in the Plaza is almost lost. Instead of going directly to the Plaza that fierce afternoon, they all went out to the Polo Grounds and sat through a ball game.

Of the changes in substance in this section—and in the novel—the most interesting is the dropping of a passage in which Gatsby reveals to Nick that Daisy wants them to run away. Daisy, elsewhere in the draft, reveals the same intentions. Perhaps Fitzgerald [324/325] felt this shifted too much responsibility upon Daisy and made Gatsby more passive than he already was. Or perhaps his cutting here was part of a general intention of making Daisy less guilty of any chargeable wrong. Earlier in the draft, Fitzgerald removed a number of references to a previous romance between Daisy and Nick, and at other points he excised uncomplimentary remarks. The result may be contrary to expectation—that a writer ordinarily reworks to more sharply delineate a character—but it was not contrary to Fitzgerald's extraordinary intention. Daisy moves away from actuality into an idea existing in Gatsby's mind and ultimately to a kind of abstract beauty corrupted and corrupting in taking on material form.

V

After Chapter VI and the first part of Chapter VII, to judge both from the draft and the galleys, the writing seemed to go easier. The description of the accident with its tense climax—"her left breast was swinging loose like a flap"—is in the novel almost exactly as in the pencil draft. "I *want* Myrtle Wilson's breast ripped off"— he wrote to Perkins, "it's exactly the thing, I think, and I don't want to chop up the good scenes by too much tinkering."[11] Wilson and his vengeance needed little reworking, and though the funeral scene is improved in small ways, as is the conversation with Gatsby's father, no great changes occur here. The last ten pages, the epilogue in which Nick decides to go back West, are much the same, too.

In these last pages, as in the rest of the manuscript, one can only guess at how much writing preceded the version Fitzgerald kept as the pencil draft. "What I cut out of it both physically and emotionally," he wrote later, "would make another novel!"[12] The difference in hand, in numbering of pages, in the paper and pencils used, suggest that much had preceded that draft. Few of the pages have the look of Fitzgerald's hand putting first thoughts to paper, and fewer still—except those obviously recopied—are free of the revision

[11] *Letters*, p. 175.
[12] Introduction to Modern Library edition of *The Great Gatsby* (New York, 1934), p. x.

in word and line which show the craftsman at work.

These marks of Fitzgerald at work, the revelation they give of his ear and his eye and his mind forcing language to do more than it will willingly do, run all through the manuscript. [325/326]

The best way of summarizing what Fitzgerald did in shaping *The Great Gatsby* from pencil draft to galley to book is to take him at his word in the introduction he wrote in 1934 for the Modern Library edition of the novel. "I had just re-read Conrad's preface to *The Nigger,* and I had recently been kidded half haywire by critics who felt that my material was such as to preclude all dealing with mature persons in a mature world. But, my God! it was my material, and it was all I had to deal with." What he did with it was what Conrad called for in his Preface, fashioned a work which carried "its justification in every line," and which "through an unremitting, never-discouraged care for the shape and ring of sentences" aspired to "the magic suggestiveness of music."

PART THREE

ACHIEVEMENT: THE CRITICS' VIEWS

The Great Gatsby *

H. L. MENCKEN (1880–1956) was one of the leading literary critics of the 1920's. As editor successively of *The Smart Set* Magazine (1908–1923) and *The American Mercury* (1924–1933) he exercised an especially important influence on American literary taste. Among his many books were *George Bernard Shaw* (1900), *The Philosophy of Friedrich Nietzsche* (1908), *A Book of Prefaces* (1917), *Prejudices* (1919–1927) and *The American Language* (1917–1948).

Scott Fitzgerald's new novel, *The Great Gatsby,* is in form no more than a glorified anecdote, and not too probable at that. The scene is the Long Island that hangs precariously on the edges of the New York city ash dumps—the Long Island of gaudy villas and bawdy house parties. The theme is the old one of a romantic and preposterous love—the ancient *fidelis ad urrum* motif reduced to a macabre humor. The principal personage is a bounder typical of those parts—a fellow who seems to know everyone and yet remains unknown to all—a young man with a great deal of mysterious money, the tastes of a movie actor and, under it all, the simple sentimentality of a somewhat sclerotic fat woman.

This clown Fitzgerald rushes to his death in nine short chapters. The other performers in the Totentanz are of a like, or even worse quality. One of them is a rich man who carries on a grotesque intrigue with the wife of a garage keeper. Another is a woman golfer who wins championships by cheating. A third, a sort of chorus to the tragic farce, is a bond salesman—symbol of the New America! Fitzgerald clears them all off at last by a triple [9/10] butchery. The garage keeper's wife, rushing out upon the road to escape her husband's third degree, is run down and killed by the wife of her

lover. The garage keeper, misled by the lover, kills the lover of the lover's wife—the Great Gatsby himself. Another bullet, and the garage keeper is also reduced to offal. Choragus fades away. The crooked lady golfer departs. The lover of the garage keeper's wife goes back to his own consort. The immense house of the Great Gatsby stands idle, its bedrooms given over to the bat and the owl, its cocktail shakers dry. The curtain lurches down.

This story is obviously unimportant, and though, as I shall show, it has its place in the Fitzgerald canon, it is certainly not to be put on the same shelf, with, say, *This Side of Paradise.* What ails it, fundamentally, is the plain fact that it is simply a story—that Fitzgerald seems to be far more interested in maintaining its suspense than in getting under the skins of its people. It is not that they are false; it is that they are taken too much for granted. Only Gatsby himself genuinely lives and breathes. The rest are mere marionettes—often astonishingly lifelike, but nevertheless not quite alive.

What gives the story distinction is something quite different from the management of the action or the handling of the characters; it is the charm and beauty of the writing. In Fitzgerald's first days it seemed almost unimaginable that he could

*H.L. Mencken, "The Great Gatsby," Baltimore *Evening Sun* (May 2, 1925) p. 9. Reprinted by permission of *The Evening Sun*, Baltimore, Md.

ever show such qualities. His writing, then, was extraordinarily slipshod—at times almost illiterate. He seemed to be devoid of any feeling for the color and savor of words. He could see people clearly and he could devise capital situations, but as writer qua writer he was apparently little more than a bright college boy. The critics of the Republic were not slow to discern the fact. They praised *This Side of Paradise* as a story, as a social document, but they were almost unanimous in denouncing it as a piece of writing.

It is vastly to Fitzgerald's credit that he appears to have taken their caveats seriously and pondered them to good effect. In *The Great Gatsby* the highly agreeable fruits of that pondering [10/11] are visible. The story, for all its basic triviality, has a fine texture, a careful and brilliant finish. The obvious phrase is simply not in it. The sentences roll along smoothly, sparklingly, variously. There is evidence in every line of hard and intelligent effort. It is a quite new Fitzgerald who emerges from this little book and the qualities that he shows are dignified and solid. *This Side of Paradise,* after all, might have been merely a lucky accident. But *The Great Gatsby*, a far inferior story at bottom, is plainly the product of a sound and stable talent, conjured into being by hard work.

I make much of this improvement because it is of an order not often witnessed in American writers, and seldom indeed in those who start off with a popular success. The usual progression, indeed, is in the opposite direction. Every year first books of great promise are published—and every year a great deal of stale drivel is printed by the promising authors of year before last. The rewards of literary success in this country are so vast that, when they come early, they are not unnaturally somewhat demoralizing. The average author yields to them readily. Having struck the bull's-eye once, he is too proud to learn new tricks. Above all, he is too proud

to tackle hard work. The result is a gradual degeneration of whatever talent he had at the beginning. He begins to imitate himself. He peters out.

There is certainly no sign of petering out in Fitzgerald. After his first experimenting he plainly sat himself down calmly to consider his deficiencies. They were many and serious. He was, first of all, too facile. He could write entertainingly without giving thought to form and organization. He was, secondly, somewhat amateurish. The materials and methods of his craft, I venture, rather puzzled him. He used them ineptly. His books showed brilliancy in conception, but they were crude and even ignorant in detail. They suggested, only too often, the improvisations of a pianist playing furiously by ear but unable to read notes.

These are the defects that he has now got rid of. *The Great Gatsby*, I seem to recall, was announced a long while ago. It [11/12] was probably several years on the stocks. It shows on every page the results of that laborious effort. Writing it, I take it, was painful. The author wrote, tore up, rewrote, tore up again. There are pages so artfully contrived that one can no more imagine improvising them than one can imagine improvising a fugue. They are full of little delicacies, charming turns of phrase, penetrating second thoughts. In other words, they are easy and excellent reading—which is what always comes out of hard writing.

Thus Fitzgerald, the stylist, arises to challenge Fitzgerald, the social historian, but I doubt that the latter ever quite succumbs to the former. The thing that chiefly interests the basic Fitzgerald is still the florid show of modern American life—and especially the devil's dance that goes on at the top. He is unconcerned about the sweatings and sufferings of the nether herd; what engrosses him is the high carnival of those who have too much money to spend and too much time for the spending of it. Their idiotic pursuit of sensation, their almost incredible stupidity and triviality, their glittering swinishness—these are the things that go into his notebook.

In *The Great Gatsby,* though he does not go below the surface, he depicts this rattle and hullabaloo with great gusto and, I believe, with sharp accuracy. The Long Island he sets before us is no fanciful Alsatia; it actually exists. More, it is worth any social historian's study, for its influence upon the rest of the country is immense and profound. What is vogue among the profiteers of Manhattan and their harlots today is imitated by the flappers of the Bible Belt country clubs weeks after next. The whole tone of American society, once so highly formalized and so suspicious of change, is now taken largely from frail ladies who were slinging hash a year ago.

Fitzgerald showed the end products of the new dispensation in *This Side of Paradise.* In *The Beautiful and Damned* he cut a bit lower. In *The Great Gatsby* he comes near the bottom. Social leader and jailbird, grand lady and kept woman, are here almost indistinguishable. We are in an atmosphere grown increasingly levantine. The Paris of the Second Empire pales to a sort of snobbish chautauqua; the New York of Ward McAllister becomes the scene of a convention of Gold Star Mothers. To find a parallel for the grossness and debauchery that now reign in New York one must go back to the Constantinople of Basil I.

The Great Gatsby *

JOHN M. KENNY, JR. (ca. 1902–1958) was a member of the staff of *Commonweal*, the well-known Catholic weekly magazine, when he wrote the following review of *The Great Gatsby*. For several years he served as the magazine's circulation manager. He was an alumnus of Vanderbilt University, Class of 1924.

One has a feeling of exasperation after reading a novel of Scott Fitzgerald's that is not easy to overcome. His very real talent for writing sparkles throughout the book, on scattered pages, as does the sheer beauty of isolated phrases and the vividness of some of his description. The occasional insights into character stand out as very green oases on an all too arid desert of waste paper.

Fitzgerald's development as a writer has not been all that was expected of him, after his sudden burst into literary fame and financial fortune with This Side of Paradise. In the first three-quarters of the earlier book, he wrote well and entertainingly as the interpreter of the new jazz age that followed on the heels of the Armistice. Amory, the flappers, and would-be philosophers he loved and drank with, had not been pictured before—and everyone but Princeton graduates read and enjoyed the tale. Then came The Beautiful and Damned—a very weak novel without point or promise. Now he has written The Great Gatsby—a singular improvement over his last novel, but an improvement which fails to realize the hopes held out in his first success. Taken alone, The Great Gatsby is a mediocre novel. In the light of his former books, it marks an important stepping-stone toward a literary excellence which Scott Fitzgerald ought some day to achieve.

The Great Gatsby wasn't great at all—just a sordid, cheap, little crook whose gawdy palace on the Sound with its Saturday night parties, his glittering motor cars, speed boats, and hydroplanes, and his tawdry friends would classify him as what is called, in the Broadway vernacular, "a butter and egg man." For Fitzgerald he provides a convenient, if hackneyed, background upon which to weave his tale. Throughout the first half of the book the author shadows his leading character in mystery, but when in the latter part he unfolds his life story we fail to find the brains, the cleverness, and the glamor that countless melodramatic writers have taught us to expect of these romantic crooks.

The other characters in the book are of flimsy material, and when the author sets a real warm human emotion in their frail bodies the strain is too great, and they are left a smoking sacrifice on the altar of Fitzgerald's development of character insight. One feels he might better have pictured the unnatural types one has been taught to expect from him.

It is not beyond probability that Mr. Fitzgerald may have had one eye cocked on the movie lots while writing this last novel. The movie type of wild Bacchanalian revel, with the drunken ladies in the swimming-pool and garden fêtes that just drip expensiveness, are done to perfection—and who knows but that they will offer some soulful Hollywood director a chance to display his art? But for a writer in whom there is the spark at least of real distinction to be so palpably under suspicion of catering to Hollywood is a grievous thing.

*John M. Kenny, Jr., "The Great Gatsby," Commonweal, II (June 3, 1925), 110. Reprinted with the permission of Commonweal.

New York Chronicle *

GILBERT SELDES (1893–   ), one of the pioneers in the new science of mass communications and a distinguished critic of popular culture, was managing editor of the *Dial* and contributed regularly for many years to the New York *Journal* and T. S. Eliot's London-based journal, *The New Criterion*. He has also been director of television programs for the Columbia Broadcasting Company and professor and dean of the Annenberg School of Communications, the University of Pennsylvania. Among his books are *The Seven Lively Arts* (1924), *The Stammering Century* (1928), and *The Public Arts* (1956).

The Great Gatsby, by F. Scott Fitzgerald, has given me an extraordinary pleasure; even if Sinclair Lewis' *Arrowsmith* and Mrs. Wharton's *The Mother's Recompense* are as good as their admirers believe them to be, I should still feel that Fitzgerald's novel is more important. Lewis and Mrs. Wharton are known quantities and one can predict their line of development; Fitzgerald is much younger, his talent is only beginning to mature; and, until now, it has appeared to be the most abundant talent, most casually wasted, in American fiction. For Fitzgerald's person I have long had an affectionate regard, and it annoyed me not to find wholly admirable his first two novels, *This Side of Paradise* and *The Beautiful and Damned*. The first was an American step-child of *Sinister Street,* the collegiate portions, with traces of H. G. Wells; the second, a much better work, influenced by Mrs. Wharton and Joseph Conrad, had, although I was too obtuse to discover it for myself, a strong satiric strain, and this appeared again in *The Diamond as Big as the Ritz,* one of Fitzgerald's few good shorter pieces, and in *The Vegetable,* a play with a central episode like that of *Beggar on Horseback,* which it anticipated, but without success on the stage. The first novel had a fabulous success; Fitzgerald had just left

Princeton and must have been about twenty-one at the time. It was treated as an *exposé* of love-making at our colleges; and, because of it, the word 'petting', soon to be displaced by 'necking', supplanted its almost-synonym, flirting, in our vocabulary. The second novel, too, was successful, and Fitzgerald began to write endlessly for the popular magazines, stories and travel-sketches and even an article on 'How to Live on $30,000 a Year'. It was after this last had been written, after the experience for it had been gained at the price named, that Fitzgerald [170/171] took his enchanting household and the unfinished manuscript of *The Great Gatsby* to the south of France.

I mention these small details because they are the normal circumstances of American authorship, only multiplied a hundred times. They are the prelude, usually, to extremely bad novels; and they form the prelude, in this case, to an extremely good one. *The Great Gatsby* is a brilliant work, and it is also a sound one; it is carefully written, and vivid; it has structure, and it has life. To all the talents, discipline has been added. The form is again derived from James through Mrs. Wharton, and there are cadences direct from the pages of Conrad; but I feel that Fitzgerald has at last made his borrowings

*Gilbert Seldes, "New York Chronicle," *The New Criterion* (London), IV (June 1926), 170-171. Reprinted with the permission of the author.

his own, and that they nowhere diminish the vitality of his work. The subject, too, ought to be of interest outside America; it is a drama of an intense passion played on Long Island, the summer home of wealth, and even, in spots, of Society, near New York. Fitzgerald has no feeling for Main Street; his satire is not that of a reformer; and he has certainly the best chance, at this moment, of becoming our finest artist in fiction. The press has not been too enthusiastic about *The Great Gatsby;* Mencken has notably discovered its virtues, but so intense is our preoccupation with the drab as subject, that this story of a Long Island Trimalchio has been compared to the preposterous stories of high-life written by Robert W. Chambers. At the moment of writing, *The Constant Nymph* is the best-seller, and, in addition, is receiving unlimited critical praise. I am not concerned with Fitzgerald's royalties; but he stands at this time desperately in need of critical encouragement, and temporarily I shall agitate for an outrageous import tax on English novels.

[The Great Gatsby] *

ARTHUR MIZENER (1907–   ) is a professor of English at Cornell University. His life of Fitzgerald, *The Far Side of Paradise*, is one of the notable biographies of a twentieth-century American author. He has also written *The Sense of Life in the Modern Novel* (1964) and edited *The Fitzgerald Reader* (1963) and a collection of critical essays, *F. Scott Fitzgerald: Twentieth Century Views* (1963).

The Great Gatsby is usually considered Fitzgerald's finest novel. Established opinion is represented by Lionel Trilling: "Except once, Fitzgerald did not fully realize his powers. . . . But [his] quality was a great one and on one occasion, in *The Great Gatsby*, it was as finely crystallized in art as it deserved to be." [1] Perhaps people are so sure of this judgment, despite *Tender Is the Night's* claim to consideration, because it was quickly reached when the book was published and became a commonplace during the late twenties as time passed and Fitzgerald published no new novel. *The Dial* called *Gatsby* "one of the finest of contemporary novels," the *Saturday Review* said it revealed "thoroughly matured craftsmanship" and had "high occasions of felicitous, almost magic craftmanship." Even Mencken, though he thought that it was "in form no more than a glorified anecdote" and that Fitzgerald did not get "under the skin of its people," was deeply impressed by "the charm and beauty of the writing." [2]

Fitzgerald thought he knew what bothered Mencken. "I gave no account (and had no feeling about or knowledge of) the emotional relations between Gatsby and Daisy from the time of their reunion to the catastrophe. However the lack is so astutely concealed by the retrospect of Gatsby's past and by blankets of excellent prose that no one has noticed it. . . . I felt that what [Mencken] really missed was the lack of any emotional backbone at the very height of it." [3] He was also capable of sharp detailed criticism of the book: "I thought that the whole episode (2 paragraphs) about their playing the Jazz History of the [185/186] world at Gatsby's first party [Chapter III] was rotten," he wrote Perkins. "Did you? Tell me frank *reaction*—PERSONAL. Don't THINK. We can all think!" [4]

But whatever its limitations, *The Great Gatsby* was a leap forward for him. He had found a story which allowed him to exploit much more of his feeling about experience, and he had committed himself to an adequate and workable form which he never betrayed. "I want to write something *new*," he told Perkins, "—something extraordinary and beautiful and simple and intricately patterned." [5] Where

[1] *The Great Gatsby*, New Directions, n.d., p. xiv.
[2] The reviews quoted are by Gilbert Seldes, *The Dial*, August, 1925; S. V. Benét, *The Saturday Review of Literature*, May 9, 1925; H. L. Mencken, *The Baltimore Sun*, May 3, 1925.
[3] To EW; CU, p. 270. Mr. Wilson dates this letter "1925." It states that they have just moved into their apartment in the rue de Tilsitt. That move was made May 12, 1925.
[4] To MP, December 20, 1924.
[5] To MP, July, 1922.

*Arthur Mizener, The Far Side of Paradise: A Biography of F. Scott Fitzgerald (New York: Houghton Mifflin Co., 1950; rev. ed., New York: Vintage Books, 1959, copyright 1959, Houghton Mifflin Co.) pp. 185-194 (rev. ed.). Reprinted with the permission of Houghton Mifflin Co.

he learned how to make that pattern is not easy to say. He was never very conscious of his literary debts, and it is typical of his intuitive way of working that one of the best symbols in *Gatsby,* the grotesque eyes of Doctor T. J. Eckleburg's billboard, was an accident. Perkins had had a dust jacket designed for the book before Fitzgerald went abroad; it is a very bad picture intended to suggest—by two enormous eyes—Daisy brooding over an amusement-park version of New York. In August, 1924, as soon as Fitzgerald got back to the book, he wrote Perkins: "For Christ's sake don't give anyone that jacket you're saving for me. I've written it into the book."

The dust jacket was not, of course, the real source of that symbol, but it was the only source Fitzgerald consciously understood, and he was hardly more aware of his literary sources. Gilbert Seldes said that the book was written in "a series of scenes, a method which Fitzgerald derived from Henry James through Mrs. Wharton"; and Seldes had talked to Fitzgerald about the book. Moreover, Wilson had been urging James on him. He had also been reading Conrad. His use of a narrator and the constant and not always fortunate echoes of Conrad's phrasing—e.g., "the abortive sorrows and short-winded elations of men"—show the extent of this influence. Yet when a correspondent of *Hound & Horn* ventured the guess that Thackeray had been an important influence on the book, Fitzgerald replied, "I never read a French author, except the usual prep-school classics, until I was twenty, but Thackeray I [**186/187**] had read over and over by the time I was sixteen, so as far as I am concerned you guessed right." [6]

His use of a narrator allowed Fitzgerald to keep clearly separated for the first time in his career the two sides of his nature, the middle-western Trimalchio and the spoiled priest who disapproved of but grudgingly admired him. Fitzgerald shuffled back and forth between their attitudes in his attempt to find a title for the book. His first suggestion, *Among Ash Heaps and Millionaires,* soon gave way to *The Great Gatsby;* but he kept experimenting with others which would suggest a more satiric attitude toward Gatsby, such as *Trimalchio in West Egg.* "The only other titles that seem to fit it are *Trimalchio* and *On the Road to West Egg.* I had two others *Gold-Hatted Gatsby* and *The High-Bouncing Lover* but they seemed too light," he wrote Perkins. A month later he had returned to *The Great Gatsby,* but by January he was saying, "My heart tells me I should have named it *Trimalchio*"; and on March 25, two weeks before publication, he cabled: CRAZY ABOUT TITLE UNDER THE RED WHITE AND BLUE WHAT WOULD DELAY BE.[7]

Perhaps the formal ordering of the Gatsby material was easier for him because, at least in its externals, it was not so close to him as his material usually was. Wolfsheim, for instance, was based on Arnold Rothstein, and about him Fitzgerald knew only the ordinary rumors of the day.[8] Gatsby himself—once again in externals—was based on a Long Island bootlegger whom Fitzgerald knew only [**187/188**] slightly. After one visit at his place Fitzgerald told Edmund Wilson all about this man and Wilson put his description into "The Crime in the Whistler Room." (Opposite Wilson's description, in his own copy of *This Room and This*

[6] John Jamieson, *Hound & Horn,* October–December, 1932; to John Jamieson, April 17, 1934. Shortly after he had written B & D, Fitzgerald made a list of the ten most important novels for *The Chicago Tribune;* in it he called *Nostromo* "the greatest novel since 'Vanity Fair' (possibly excluding 'Madame Bovary')." (Clipping in Album III.) In 1940 he told Perkins that "I read [Spengler] the same summer I was writing 'The Great Gatsby,' and I don't think I ever quite recovered from

him." What Spengler meant to him he then makes clear: "Spengler prophesied gang rule, 'young people hungry for soil,' and more particularly 'the world as soil' as an idea, a dominant, supersessive idea." (To MP, June 6, 1940.)

[7] To MP, April 7, October 11, December 16, 1924, January 24, March 25, 1925.

[8] Compare Fitzgerald's description with the summary of the rumors about Rothstein given by Lloyd Morris, *A Postscript to Yesterday,* pp. 66–7 and 75.

Gin and These Sandwiches, Fitzgerald wrote: "I had told Bunny my plan for Gatsby.")

He's a gentleman bootlegger: his name is Max Fleischman. He lives like a millionaire. Gosh, I haven't seen so much to drink since Prohibition. . . . Well, Fleischman was making a damn ass of himself bragging about how much his tapestries were worth and how much his bath-room was worth and how he never wore a shirt twice— and he had a revolver studded with diamonds. . . . And he finally got on my nerves—I was a little bit stewed—and I told him I wasn't impressed by his ermine-lined revolver: I told him he was nothing but a bootlegger, no matter how much money he made. . . . I told him I never would have come into his damn house if it hadn't been to be polite and that it was a torture to stay in a place where everything was in such terrible taste.[9]

Again, however, these details account only for the externals of Gatsby; the vulgar and romantic young man Fitzgerald found somewhere inside himself to fill this outline of a character is what matters. About this young man he could only say, "He was perhaps created in the image of some forgotten farm type of Minnesota that I have known and forgotten, and associated at the same moment with some sense of romance . . . a story of mine, called "Absolution" . . . was intended to be a picture of his early life, but . . . I cut it because I preferred to preserve the sense of mystery."[10] Because the form of *Gatsby* keeps Fitzgerald's assertions of the romance and of the vulgarity clearly separated, he was able to make out of those unworn shirts of Max Fleischman the fine episode of Gatsby's many shirts, to blend without confusion the elements of bad taste and [188/189] idealism implied by that pile of material with "stripes and scrolls and plaids in coral and apple green and lavender and faint orange, with monograms of Indian blue" on which Daisy suddenly bowed her head and cried."[11]

Nick Carraway, Fitzgerald's narrator, is, for the book's structure, the most important character. Quite apart from his power to concentrate the story and its theme into a few crucial scenes and thus increase its impact, a great deal of the book's color and subtlety comes from the constant play of Nick's judgment and feelings over the events. Fitzgerald had struggled awkwardly with all sorts of devices in his earlier books to find a way to get these things in without intervening in his own person and destroying our dramatic perception of them. Nick, as one of the characters in the story, not only allows but requires him to imply feelings everywhere.

[Daisy] turned her head as there was a light dignified knocking at the front door. I went out and opened it. Gatsby, pale as death, with his hands plunged like weights in his coat pockets, was standing in a puddle of water glaring tragically into my eyes.

With his hands still in his coat pockets he stalked by me into the hall, turned sharply as if he were on a wire, and disappeared into the living-room. It wasn't a bit funny.[12]

Nick has come east after the war to be a real Easterner, but his moral roots are in the Middle West. He is prepared, in the book's very first scene, to respond to the beauty and charm of Daisy, adrift like some informal goddess in that "bright, rosy-colored space" which is the Buchanans' drawing room. But he is humorously aware of their difference: " 'You make me feel uncivilized, Daisy,' I confessed. . . . 'Can't you talk about crops or something?' " A moment later, when Daisy has confessed her unhappiness with Tom, he has an uncomfortable glimpse of what is really involved in this difference. "The instant her voice broke off, ceasing to compel my attention, my [189/190] belief, I felt the basic insincerity of what she had said. It made me uneasy, as though the whole evening had been a trick of some sort to exact a contributory emotion from me. I waited, and sure enough in a moment she looked at me with an absolute smirk on her

---

[9] *This Room and This Gin and These Sandwiches,* pp. 75–76. Zelda said late in her life that this was a Teutonic-featured man named von Guerlach (ZSF to H. D. Piper.)
[10] To John Jamieson, April 15, 1934.
[11] *Gatsby,* p. 112.

[12] *Gatsby,* pp. 103–4.

lovely face, as if she had asserted her membership in a rather distinguished secret society to which she and Tom belonged."[13]

It is a secret society distinguished by more than he had supposed, for Nick is learning that the rich are different from you and me in more than their habituation to the appurtenances of wealth which give their lives such a charmed air for the outsider like Gatsby. What astonished Gatsby was the way Daisy's beautiful house in Louisville "was as casual a thing to her as his tent out at camp was to him." For Gatsby "there was a ripe mystery about it, a hint of bedrooms up-stairs more beautiful and cool than other bedrooms, of gay and radiant activities taking place through its corridors, and of romances that were not musty and laid away already in lavender but fresh and breathing and redolent of this year's shining motor-cars and of dances whose flowers were scarcely withered."[14]

But while Nick is humorously aware of this charm, he is a Carraway and he has grown up "in the Carraway house in a city where dwellings are still called through decades by a family's name." When at the end of the book he unexpectedly runs into Tom in front of a jewelry store on Fifth Avenue, he thinks:

> I couldn't forgive him or like him, but I saw what he had done was, to him, entirely justified. It was all very careless and confused. They were careless people, Tom and Daisy—they smashed up things and creatures and then retreated back into their money or their vast carelessness, or whatever it was that kept them together, and let other people clean up the mess they had made. . . .
> I shook hands with him; it seemed silly not to, for I felt suddenly as if I were talking to a child. Then we went into the jewelry store to buy a pearl necklace [190/191]—or perhaps only a pair of cuff buttons—rid of my provincial squeamishness forever.[15]

It is characteristic of Fitzgerald's control of his material that he can sum up all he

wants to say about Tom in that last sentence with Nick's ironic glance at the "string of pearls valued at three hundred and fifty thousand dollars" which had been the symbol of Daisy's surrender to Tom's world. "A pearl necklace—or perhaps only a pair of cuff buttons." "I see you're looking at my cuff buttons," Meyer Wolfsheim says to Nick. "I hadn't been looking at them, but I did now. They were composed of oddly familiar pieces of ivory. 'Finest specimens of human molars,' he informed me." This kind of control is everywhere in the book. Gatsby, giving Nick his cheap-magazine version of his life, says that he "lived like a young rajah in all the capitals of Europe—Paris, Venice, Rome—collecting jewels, chiefly rubies, hunting big game, painting a little. . . ." Nick is disgusted by this image "of a turbaned 'character' leaking sawdust at every pore as he pursued a tiger through the Bois de Boulogne." But when Gatsby is showing Daisy his house and Nick sees the pictures of Dan Cody and Gatsby in yachting costume, he is on the verge of seriously "[asking] Gatsby to see the rubies." In the same way Nick makes a little joke about Daisy's chauffeur, Ferdie, when he brings Daisy to tea. "Does the gasoline affect his nose?" he asks. "I don't think so," Daisy answers innocently. "Why?" But her innocence is only assumed, for it was her own joke; she had told Nick in the book's first scene about her butler whose nose had been permanently injured because he had to polish silver from the morning till night.[16]

So Nick, having learned just how much brutal stupidity and carelessness exist beneath the charm and even the pathos of Tom and Daisy, goes back to the West, to the country he remembers from the Christmas vacations of his boyhood, to "the thrilling returning trains of my youth, and the street lamps and the sleigh bells in the frosty dark and the shadows of holly wreaths thrown by lighted win-

[13] The quotations in this paragraph are from *Gatsby*, pp. 15 and 21-2.
[14] *Gatsby*, p. 178.
[15] *Gatsby*, p. 216.
[16] The quotations in this paragraph are from *Gatsby*, pp. 92-3, 87, 79, 113, 103, and 17.

dows on the snow. I am part of that. . . ." The [191/192] East remains for him "a night scene from El Greco" in which "in the foreground four solemn men in dress suits are walking along the sidewalk with a stretcher on which lies a drunken woman in a white evening dress. Her hand, which dangles over the side, sparkles cold with jewels. Gravely the men turn in at a house —the wrong house. But no one knows the woman's name, and no one cares."[17]

Thus, though Fitzgerald would be the last to have reasoned it out in such terms, *The Great Gatsby* becomes a kind of tragic pastoral, with the East exemplifying urban sophistication and culture and corruption, and the Middle West, "the bored, sprawling, swollen towns beyond the Ohio," the simple virtues. This contrast is summed up in the title to which Fitzgerald came with such reluctance. In so far as Gatsby represents the simplicity of heart Fitzgerald associated with the Middle West, he is really a great man; in so far as he achieves the kind of notoriety the East accords success of his kind and imagines innocently that because his place is right across from the Buchanans' he lives in Daisy's world, he is great about as Barnum was. Out of Gatsby's ignorance of his real greatness and his misunderstanding of his notoriety, Fitzgerald gets most of the book's direct irony.

Gatsby himself is a romantic who, as his creator nearly did, has lost his girl because he had no money. On her he had focused all his "heightened sensitivity to the promises of life." For him money is only the means for the fulfillment of "his incorruptible dream." "I wouldn't ask too much of her. You can't repeat the past," Nicks says to him of Daisy. " 'Can't repeat the past?' he cried incredulously. 'Why of course you can!' " For Gatsby the habits of wealth have preserved and heightened Daisy's charm. No one understood that better than he.

"She's got an indiscreet voice," I remarked. "It's full of —" I hesitated.

"Her voice is full of money," [Gatsby] said suddenly.

That was it. I'd never understood before. It was full of money—that was the inexhaustible charm [192/193] that rose and fell in it, the jingle of it, the cymbals' song of it. . . . High in a white palace the king's daughter, the golden girl. . . . [18]

But if a lifetime of wealth colors Daisy's charm in a way that Gatsby's new wealth cannot imitate, it has also given her the habit of retreating with Tom "into their money or their vast carelessness" whenever she has to face responsibility. So, as Gatsby watches anxiously outside their house after the accident in order to protect Daisy, she sits with Tom over a plate of cold fried chicken and two bottles of ale in the kitchen. "There was an unmistakable air of natural intimacy about the picture, and anybody would have said they were conspiring together." After looking through the window at them, Nick returns to Gatsby. "He put his hands in his coat pockets and turned back eagerly to his scrutiny of the house, as though my presence marred the sacredness of the vigil. So I walked away and left him standing there in the moonlight—watching over nothing."[19] The next day, waiting for a telephone message from Daisy which never comes, he is shot by Wilson.

In contrast to the grace of Daisy's world, Gatsby's fantastic mansion, his incredible car, his absurd clothes, "his elaborate formality of speech [which] just missed being absurd" all appear ludicrous. But in contrast to the corruption which underlies Daisy's world, Gatsby's essential incorruptibility is heroic. Because of the skilful construction of *The Great Gatsby* the eloquence and invention with which Fitzgerald gradually reveals this heroism are given a concentration and therefore a power he was never able to achieve again. The art of the book is nearly perfect.

Its limitation is the limitation of Fitzgerald's own nearly complete commitment

[17] *Gatsby*, pp. 211-13.

[18] The quotations in this paragraph are from *Gatsby*, pp. 133 and 144.

[19] *Gatsby*, p. 175.

to Gatsby's romantic attitude. "That's the whole burden of this novel," he wrote a friend, "—the loss of those illusions that give such color to the world so that you don't care whether things are true or false as long as they partake of the magical glory."[20] Fitzgerald's irony touches only the surface of Gatsby and the [193/194] book never suggests a point of view which might bring seriously into question the adequacy to experience of "a heightened sensitivity to the promises of life" The world of Tom and Daisy, which is set over against Gatsby's dream of a world, is superficially beautiful and appealing but indefensible: Tom's muddled attempts to defend it, his impassioned gibberish" about " 'The Rise of the Colored Empires' by this man Goddard," prove how indefensible it is.[21]

"They're a rotten bunch," Nick shouts back to Gatsby as he leaves him for the last time. "You're worth the whole damn bunch put together." Then he thinks: "I've always been glad I said that. It was the only compliment I ever gave him, because I disapproved of him from beginning to end. First he nodded politely, and then his face broke into that radiant and understanding smile, as if we'd been in ecstatic cahoots on that fact all the time. His gorgeous pink rag of a suit made a bright spot of color. . . ." But though the tone of this passage is perfect, even down to the irony of the colloquial "rag of a

suit," it does not seriously qualify Nick's—and Fitzgerald's—commitment to Gatsby, to the romantic "capacity for wonder" and its belief "in the green light, the orgiastic future," which justifies by its innocent faith Gatsby's corruption.

The last two pages of the book make overt Gatsby's embodiment of the American dream as a whole by identifying his attitude with the awe of the Dutch sailors when, "for a transitory enchanted moment," they found "something commensurate to [their] capacity for wonder" in the "fresh, green breast of the new world." Though this commitment to the wonder and the enchantment of a dream is qualified by the dream's unreality, by its "year by year reced[ing] before us," the dream is still the book's only positive good; the rest is a world of "foul dust," like the "valley of ashes—a fantastic farm where ashes grow like wheat in ridges and hills and gardens"—through which one passed every evening on his way to the night world of East and West Egg.[22]

[20] To Ludlow Fowler, ca. August, 1924.
[21] Gatsby, p. 16. Fitzgerald was thinking of Lothrop Stoddard"s The Rising Tide of Color, Scribner's, 1921.

[22] The phrases quoted in these two paragraphs are from Gatsby, pp. 185, 217–18, 3, 27. The first edition reads "orgastic future." In his own copy of the book Fitzgerald corrected this spelling to "orgiastic." It was one of the few proof errors in the book, perhaps because Scribner's worked harder over Gatsby than over Fitzgerald's earlier books, perhaps because Lardner read the final proofs. The only other proof error Fitzgerald found was the reading of "eternal" for "external" on p. 58, and this mistake was caused by a confusing revision of his in the proofs. It is characteristic of the fate of Fitzgerald's texts that both these misprints remained uncorrected in the reprints by The Modern Library, New Directions, Bantam Books, and Grosset and Dunlap. Edmund Wilson's reprint in his edition of The Last Tycoon corrects all it could without access to Fitzgerald's personally corrected copy.

The Romance of Money *

MALCOLM COWLEY (1898–   ), one of the nation's leading critics, was literary editor of *The New Republic* for many years and is now a consulting editor to The Viking Press. He is the author of *Exile's Return* (1934, rev. ed. 1951), *The Literary Situation* (1954), *The Faulkner-Cowley File: Letters and Memories* (1966), *Think Back on Us . . . A Contemporary Chronicle of the 1930's* (1967), and *Blue Juniata: Collected Poems* (1968), and has edited many books, including *After the Genteel Tradition* (1937, rev. ed. 1964), *Books That Changed Our Minds* (1939), and *The Short Stories of F. Scott Fitzgerald* (1950).

Although Fitzgerald regarded himself, and was regarded by others, as a representative figure of the age, there was one respect in which he did not represent most of its serious writers. In that respect he was much closer to the men of his college year who were trying to get ahead in the business world; like them he was fascinated by the process of earning and spending money. The young businessmen of his time were bitterly determined to be successful and, much more than their successors of a later generation, they had been taught to measure success, failure, and even virtue in monetary terms. They had learned in school and Sunday school that virtue was rewarded with money and that viciousness was punished by the loss of money; apparently their only problem was to earn lots of it fast. Yet money was merely a convenient and inadequate symbol for what they dreamed of earning. The best of them were like Jay Gatsby in having "some heightened sensitivity to the promise of life"; or they were like another Fitzgerald hero, Dexter Green—of "Winter Dreams"—who "wanted not association with glittering things and glittering people—he wanted the glittering things themselves." Their real dream was that of achieving a new status and a new essence, of rising to a loftier place in the mysterious hierarchy of human worth.

The serious writers also dreamed of rising to a loftier status, but—except for Fitzgerald—they felt that money-making was the wrong way to rise. They liked money if it reached them in the form of gifts or legacies or publishers' advances, but they were afraid of high earned incomes because of what the incomes stood for: obligations, respectability, time lost from their own work, expensive habits that would drive them to earn still higher incomes; in short, a series of involvements in the commercial culture that was hostile to art. "If you want to ruin a writer," I used to hear them saying, "just give him a big magazine contract or a job at ten thousand a year." Many [ix-x] of them tried to preserve their independence by earning only enough to keep them alive while writing; a few liked to regard themselves as heroes of poverty and failure.

Their attitude toward money went into the texture of their work, which was noncommercial in the sense of being written in various new styles that the public was slow to accept. The 1920s were the great age of literary experiment, when the new writers were moving in all directions simultaneously. Some of them tried to capture in words the effects of modern painting (like E. E. Cummings); some used the older literary language with Shakespearean orotundity (like Thomas Wolfe) ; some worked at developing a new language based on Midwestern speech (like Hemingway). Some tried to omit all but the simplest adjectives (again like Hemingway); some used five or six long adjectives in a row (like Faulkner); some ran adjectives and adverbs together in a hurryconfusing fashion (like Dos Passos). Some approached their characters only from the outside, some gave only their inmost thoughts, their streams of subconsciousness, some broke a story into fragments, some told it backwards, some tried to dispense with stories. They were all showing the same spirit of adventure and exploration in fiction that their contemporaries were showing in the business world. That spirit made them part of the age, but at the same time they were trying to criticize and escape from it, and many of them looked back longingly to other ages when, so they liked to think, artists had wealthy patrons and hence were able to live outside the economic system.

Fitzgerald, on the other hand, immersed himself in the age and always remained close to the business world which the others were trying to evade. That world was the background of his stories and they performed a business function in themselves, by supplying the narration that readers followed like a thread through the labyrinth of advertising in the slick-paper magazines. He did not divorce himself from readers by writing experimental prose or by inventing new methods of telling or refusing to tell a story. His very real originality was a matter of mood and subject rather than form and it was more evident in his novels than in his stories, good as the stories often were. Although he despised the trade of writing for magazines—or despised it with part of his mind —he worked at it honestly. It yielded him

a [x-xi] large income that he couldn't have earned in any other fashion and the income was necessary to his self-respect.

Fitzgerald kept an accurate record of his earnings—in the big ledger where he also recorded his deeds and misdeeds, as if to strike a book-keeper's balance between them—but he was always vague about his expenditures and was usually vague about his possessions, including his balance in the bank. Once he asked the cashier, "How much money have I got?" The cashier looked in a big book and answered without even scowling, "None." Fitzgerald resolved to be more thrifty, knowing that he would break the resolution. He had little interest in money for itself and less in the physical objects it would buy. On the other hand, he had a great interest in earning money, lots of it fast, because that was a sort of gold medal awarded with the blue ribbon for competitive achievement. Once the money was earned he and Zelda liked to spend lots of it fast, usually for impermanent things: not for real estate, fine motorcars, or furniture, but for traveling expenses, the rent of furnished houses, the wages of nurses and servants; for entertainments, party dresses, and feather fans of five colors. Zelda was as proudly careless about money as an eighteenth-century nobleman's heir. Scott was more practical and had his penny-pinching moments, as if in memory of his childhood, but at other times he liked to spend without counting in order to enjoy a sense of careless potency.

In his attitude toward money he revealed the new spirit of an age when conspicuous accumulation was giving way to conspicuous earning and spending. It was an age when gold was melted down and became fluid; when wealth was no longer measured in possessions—land, houses, livestock, machinery—but rather in dollars per year, as a stream is measured by its flow; when for the first time the expenses of government were being met by income taxes more than by property and excise taxes. There were still old solid fortunes at the hardly accessible peak of the social system, which young men dreamed of reaching, but the romantic figures of the age were not capitalists properly speaking. They were hired executives, promoters, salesmen, stock gamblers, or racketeers, and they were millionaires in a new sense—not men each of whom owned a million dollars' worth of property, but men who lived in rented apartments and had [xi/xii] nothing but stock certificates and life-insurance policies (or nothing but credit and the proper connections), while spending more than the income of the old millionaires.

All these changes and survivals, as refracted through different personalities, are mirrored in Fitzgerald's work. In dealing with the romance of money, he chose the central theme of his American age. "Americans," he liked to say, "should be born with fins, and perhaps they were—perhaps money was a form of fin."

2

One of his remarks about his work has always puzzled his critics. "D. H. Lawrence's great attempt to synthesize animal and emotional—things he left out," Fitzgerald wrote in his notebook, then added the comment, "Essential pre-Marxian. Just as I am essentially Marxian." He was never Marxian in any sense of the word that Marxians of whatever school would be willing to accept. It is true that he finally read *Das Kapital* and was impressed by "the terrible chapter," as he called it, "on 'The Working Day' "; but it left in him not so much as a trace of Marx's belief in the mission of the proletariat.

His picture of proletarian life was of something alien to his background, mysterious and even criminal. It seems to have been symbolized in some of his stories by the riverfront strip in St. Paul that languished in the shadow of the big houses on the bluff; he described the strip as a gridiron of mean streets where consumptive or pugilistic youths lounged in front of poolrooms, their skins turned livid by the neon lights. In *The Great Gatsby* he must have been thinking about the lower levels of American society when he described the valley of ashes between West Egg and New York—"A fantastic farm," he called it, "where ashes grow like wheat into ridges and hills and grotesque gardens; where ashes take the forms of houses and chimneys and rising smoke and, finally, with a transcendent effort, of men who move dimly and always crumbling through the powdery air." One of his early titles for the novel was "Among Ash Heaps and Millionaires"—as if he were setting the two against each other while suggesting a vague affinity between [xii-xiii] them. Tom Buchanan, the brutalized millionaire, found a mistress in the valley of ashes.

In Fitzgerald's stories there could be no real struggle between this dimly pictured ash-gray proletariat and the bourgeoisie. On the other hand, there could be a different struggle that the author must have regarded, for a time, as essentially Marxian. It was the struggle that I have already suggested, between wealth as fluid income and wealth as a solid possession—or rather, since Fitzgerald is not an essayist but a story-teller, it is between a man and a woman as representatives of the new and the old moneyed classes.

We are not allowed to forget that they are representatives. The man comes from a family with little or no money, but he manages to attend an Eastern university—often Harvard or Yale, to set a distance between the hero and the Princeton author. He then sets out to earn a fortune equal to those of his wealthy classmates. Usually what he earns is not a fortune but an impressively large income, after he has become a success in his chosen profession —which may be engineering or architecture or advertising or the laundry business or bootlegging or real estate or even, in one story, frozen fish; the heroes are never writers like himself, although one of them is described as a popular dramatist. When the heroes are halfway to success, they fall in love.

The woman—or rather the girl—in a Fitzgerald story is younger and richer than the man and the author makes it even clearer that she represents her social class. "She was a stalk of ripe corn," he says of one heroine, "but bound not as cereals are but as a rare first edition, with all the binder's art. She was lovely and expensive and about nineteen." Of another heroine he says when she first appears that "Her childish beauty was wistful and sad about being so rich and sixteen." Later, when her father loses his money, the hero pays her a visit in London. "All around her," Fitzgerald says, "he could feel the vast Mortmain fortune melting down, seeping back into the matrix whence it had come." The hero thinks that she might marry him, now that she has fallen almost to his financial level; but he finds that the Mortmain (or dead-hand) fortune, even though lost, is still a barrier between them. Note that the man is not attracted by the fortune in itself. He is not seeking money so much as position at the [xiii/xiv] peak of the social hierarchy and the girl becomes the symbol of that position, the incarnation of its mysterious power. That is Daisy Buchanan's charm for the great Gatsby, and it is the reason why he directs his whole life toward winning back her love.

"She's got an indiscreet voice," Nick Carraway says of her. "It's full of—" and he hesitates.

"Her voice is full of money," Gatsby says suddenly.

And Nick, the narrator, thinks to himself, "That was it. I'd never understood before. It was full of money—that was the inexhaustible charm that rose and fell in it, the cymbals' song of it. . . . High in a white palace the king's daughter, the golden girl."

In Fitzgerald's stories a love affair is like secret negotiations between the diplomats of two countries which are not at peace and not quite at war. For a moment they forget their hostility, find it transformed into mutual curiosity, attraction, even passion (though the passion is not physical); but the hostility will survive even in marriage, if marriage is to be their future. I called the lovers diplomats, ambassadors, and that is another way of saying that they are representatives. When they meet it is as if they were leaning toward each other from separate high platforms—the man from a platform built up of his former poverty, his ambition, his competitive triumphs, his ability to earn and spend always more, more; the girl from another platform covered with cloth of gold and feather fans of many colors, but beneath them a sturdy pile of stock certificates representing the ownership of mines, forests, factories, villages—all of Candy Town.

She is the embodied spirit of wealth, as can be clearly seen in one of the best of Fitzgerald's early stories, "Winter Dreams." A rising young man named Dexter Green takes home the daughter of a millionaire for whom he used to be a caddy. She is Judy Jones, "a slender enamelled doll in cloth of gold: gold in a band at her head, gold in two slipper points at her dress's hem." The rising young man stops his coupé, Fitzgerald says, "in front of the great white bulk of the Mortimer Jones house, somnolent, gorgeous, drenched with the splendor of the damp moonlight. Its solidity startled him. The strong walls, the steel of the girders, the breadth and beam and pomp of it were there only to bring out the contrast with the young beauty beside him. It was sturdy to accentuate her slightness —as if to show [xiv-v] what a breeze could be generated by a butterfly's wing." Butterflies used to be taken as symbols of the soul. The inference is clear that, holding Judy in his arms, Dexter is embracing the spirit of a great fortune.

Nicole Warren, the heroine of *Tender*

Is the Night, is the spirit of an even greater fortune. Fitzgerald says of her:

> Nicole was the product of much ingenuity and toil. For her sake trains began their run at Chicago and traversed the round belly of the continent to California; chicle factories fumed and link belts grew link by link in factories; men mixed toothpaste in vats and drew mouthwash out of copper hogsheads; girls canned tomatoes quickly in August or worked rudely at the five-and-tens on Christmas Eve; half-breed Indians toiled on Brazilian coffee plantations and dreamers were muscled out of patent rights in new tractors—these were some of the people who gave a tithe to Nicole, and as the whole system swayed and thundered onward it lent a feverish bloom to such processes of hers as wholesale buying [of luxuries], like the flush of a fireman's face holding his post before a spreading blaze.

Sometimes Fitzgerald's heroines are candid, even brutal, about class relationships. "Let's start right," the heroine of "Winter Dreams" says to Dexter Green on the first evening they spend alone together. "Who are you?"

"I'm nobody," Dexter tells her, without adding that he had been her father's caddy. "My career is largely a matter of futures."

"Are you poor?"

"No," he says frankly, "I'm probably making more money than any man my age in the Northwest. I know that's an obnoxious remark, but you advised me to start right."

"There was a pause," Fitzgerald adds. "Then she smiled and the corners of her mouth drooped and an almost imperceptible sway brought her closer to him, looking up into his eyes." Money brings them together, but later they are separated by something undefined—a mere whim of Judy's, it seems on one's first reading of the story, though one comes to feel that the whim was based on her feeling that she should marry a man of her own caste. Dexter, as he goes East to earn a still larger income, is filled with regret for "the coun- [**xv-xvi**] try of illusions, of youth, of the richness of life, where his winter dreams had flourished." It seems likely that Judy Jones, like Josephine Perry

in a series of later stories, was a character suggested by Fitzgerald's memories of a debutante with whom he was desperately in love during his first years at Princeton; afterward she made a more sensible marriage and Fitzgerald, too, regretted his winter dreams. As for the general attitude toward the rich that began to be expressed in the story, it is perhaps connected with his experiences in 1919, when Zelda broke off their engagement because they couldn't hope to live on his salary as a junior copywriter. Later he said of the time:

> During a long summer of despair I wrote a novel instead of letters, so it came out all right; but it came out all right for a different person. The man with the jingle of money in his pocket who married the girl a year later would always cherish an abiding distrust, an animosity, toward the leisure class—not the conviction of a revolutionist but the smoldering hatred of a peasant.

His mixture of feelings toward the very rich, which included curiosity and admiration as well as distrust, is revealed in his treatment of a basic situation that reappears in many of his stories. Of course he presented other situations that were not directly concerned with the relationship between social classes. He wrote about the problem of adjusting oneself to life, which he thought was especially difficult in the case of self-indulgent American women. He wrote about the manners of flappers and slickers. He wrote engagingly about his own boyhood. He wrote about the attempt to recapture youthful dreams, about the patching-up of broken marriages, about the contrast between Northern and Southern manners, about Americans going to pieces in Europe, about the self-tortures of gifted alcoholics, and in much of his later work —as notably in *The Last Tycoon*—he would be expressing his admiration for supremely great technicians, such as brain surgeons and movie directors. But a great number of his stories, especially the early ones, start with the basic situation I have mentioned: a rising young man of the middle class in love with the daughter of a very rich family. (Sometimes the family is Southern, in which case it needn't be so rich, since a high social status can exist in the South without great wealth.) [xvi/xvii]

From that beginning the story may take any one of several turns. The hero may marry the girl, but only after she loses her fortune or (as in "Presumption" and " 'The Sensible Thing' ") he gains an income greater than hers. He may lose the girl (as in "Winter Dreams") and always remember that she represented his early aspirations. In "The Bridal Party" he resigns himself to the loss after being forced to recognize that the rich man she married is stronger and more capable than himself. In "More Than Just a House" he learns that the girl is empty and selfish and ends by marrying her good sister; in "The Rubber Check" he marries Ellen Mortmain's quiet cousin. There is, however, still another development out of the Fitzgerald situation that comes closer to revealing his ambiguous feelings toward the very rich. To state it simply— too simply—the rising young man wins the rich girl and then is destroyed by her wealth or her relatives.

The plot is like that of "Young Lochinvar," but with a tragic ending—as if fair Ellen's armed kinsmen had overtaken the pair, or as if they had slain the hero by treachery. Fitzgerald used it for the first time in a fantasy, "The Diamond as Big as the Ritz," which he wrote in St. Paul in the winter of 1921-22. Like many other fantasies it reveals more of the author's mind than does his more realistic work. It deals with the adventures of a boy named John T. Unger (we might read "Hunger"), who was born in a town on the Mississippi called Hades, though it might also be called St. Paul. He is sent away to St. Midas', which is "the most expensive and most exclusive boys' preparatory school in the world," and there he meets a classmate named Percy Washington, who invites him to spend the summer at his home in the West. On the train Percy confides to him that his father is the richest man alive and owns a diamond bigger than the Ritz-Carlton Hotel (solid as opposed to fluid wealth).

The description of the Washington mansion, in its hidden valley that wasn't even shown on the maps of the U. S. Geodetic Survey, is fantasy mingled with burlesque; but then the familiar Fitzgerald note appears. John falls in love with Percy's younger sister, Kismine. After an idyllic summer Kismine tells him accidentally—she had meant to keep the secret —that he will very soon be murdered, like all the former guests of the Washingtons. "It was done very nicely," [xvii/xviii] Kismine explains to him. "They were drugged while they were asleep—and their families were always told that they died of scarlet fever in Butte. . . . I shall probably have visitors too—I'll harden up to it. We can't let such an inevitable thing as death stand in the way of enjoying life while we have it. Think how lonesome it'd be out here if we never had *anyone*. Why, father and mother have sacrificed some of their best friends just as we have."

Tom and Daisy Buchanan also sacrificed some of their best friends. "They were careless people, Tom and Daisy— they smashed up things and creatures and then retreated back into their money on their vast carelessness, or whatever it was that kept them together, and let other people clean up the mess they had made." "The Diamond as Big as the Ritz" can have a happy ending for the two lovers because it is fantasy; but the same plot reappears in *The Great Gatsby*, where it is surrounded by the real world of the 1920s and for the first time it is carried through to its logical conclusion.

3

There is a moment in any real author's career when he suddenly becomes capable of doing his best work. He has found a fable that expresses his central truth and everything falls into place around it, so that his whole experience of life is available for use in his fiction. Something like that happened to Fitzgerald when he invented the story of Jimmy Gatz, otherwise known as Jay Gatsby, and it explains the amazing richness and scope of a very short novel.

To put facts on record, *The Great Gatsby* is a book of about fifty thousand words, a small structure built of nine chapters like big blocks. The fifth chapter—Gatsby's meeting with Daisy Buchanan—is the center of the narrative, as is proper; the seventh chapter is the climax. Each chapter consists of one or more dramatic scenes, sometimes with intervening passages of straight narration. The "scenic" method is one that Fitzgerald probably learned from Edith Wharton, who in turn learned it from Henry James; at any rate the book is technically in the Jamesian tradition (and Daisy Buchanan is named for James's heroine, Daisy Miller). [**xviii/xix**]

Part of the tradition is the device of having the story told by a single observer, who stands somewhat apart from the action and whose vision "frames" it for the reader. In this case the observer plays a special role. Although Nick Carraway doesn't save or ruin Gatsby, his personality in itself provides an essential comment on all the other characters. Nick stands for the older values that prevailed in the Middle West before the First World War. His family isn't tremendously rich, like the Buchanans, but it has a long established and sufficient fortune, so that Nick is the only person in the book who hasn't been corrupted by seeking or spending money. He is so certain of his own values that he hesitates to criticize others, but when he does pass judgment—on Gatsby, on Jordan Baker, on the Buchanans—he speaks as if for ages to come.

All the other characters belong to their own brief era of confused and dissolving standards, but they are affected by the era in different fashions. Each of them, we note on reading the book a second time, represents some particular variety of moral failure; Lionel Trilling says that they are "treated as if they were ideographs," a true observation; but the treatment does not detract from their reality as persons. Tom Buchanan is wealth brutalized by selfishness and arrogance; he looks for a mistress in the valley of ashes and finds an ignorant woman, Myrtle Wilson, whose raw vitality is like his own. Daisy Buchanan is the spirit of wealth and offers a continual promise "that she had done gay, exciting, things just a while since and that there were gay, exciting things hovering in the next hour"; but it is a false promise, since at heart she is as self-centered as Tom and even colder. Jordan Baker apparently lives by the old standards, but she uses them only as a subterfuge. Aware of her own cowardice and dishonesty, she feels "safer on a plane where any divergence from a code would be thought impossible."

All these, except Myrtle Wilson, are East Egg people, that is, they are part of a community where wealth takes the form of solid possessions. Set against them are the West Egg people, whose wealth is fluid income that might cease overnight. The West Egg people, with Gatsby as their archetype and tragic hero, have worked furiously to rise in the world, but they will never reach East Egg for all the money they spend; at most they can sit at the water's edge and [**xix/xx**] look across the bay at the green light that shines and promises at the end of the Buchanans' dock. The symbolism of place has a great part in Fitzgerald's novel, as has that of motorcars. The characters are visibly represented by the cars they drive: Nick has a conservative old Dodge, the Buchanans, too rich for ostentation, have an "easy-going blue coupé," while Gatsby's car is "a rich cream color, bright with nickel, swollen here and there in its monstrous length with triumphant hat-boxes and supper-boxes and tool-boxes, and terraced with a labyrinth of wind-shields that mirrored a dozen suns"—it is West Egg on wheels. When Daisy drives through the valley of ashes in Gatsby's car, she causes the two deaths that end the story.

The symbols are not synthetic or contrived, like those in so many recent novels; they are images that Fitzgerald instinctively found to represent his characters and their destiny. When he says, "Daisy took her face in her hands as if feeling its lovely shape," he is watching her act the charade of her self-love. When he says, "Tom would drift on forever seeking, a little wistfully, for the dramatic turbulence of some irrecoverable football game,"

he suggests the one appealing side of Tom's nature. He is so familiar with the characters and their background, so absorbed in their fate, that the book has an admirable unity of texture; we can open it to any page and find another of the touches that illuminate the story. We end by feeling that *Gatsby* has a double virtue. Except for *The Sun Also Rises* it is the best picture we possess of the age in which it was written and it also achieves a sort of moral permanence. Fitzgerald's story of the innocent murdered suitor for wealth is a compendious fable of the 1920s that will survive as a legend for other times.

F. Scott Fitzgerald's *The Great Gatsby*: Legendary Bases and Allegorical Significances *

JOHN HENRY RALEIGH (1920–   ) is professor of English and chairman of the Department of English at the University of California at Berkeley. He is the author of *Matthew Arnold and American Culture* (1957) and *The Plays of Eugene O'Neill* (1965), and edited *History and the Individual* (1962).

F. Scott Fitzgerald's character Gatsby, as has often been said, represents the irony of American history and the corruption of the American dream. While this certainly is true, yet even here, with this general legend, Fitzgerald has rung in his own characteristic changes, doubling and redoubling ironies. At the center of the legend proper there is the relationship between Europe and America and the ambiguous interaction between the contradictory impulses of Europe that led to the original settling of America and its subsequent development: mercantilism and idealism. At either end of American history, and all the way through, the two impulses have a way of being both radically exclusive and mutually confusing, the one melting into the other: the human faculty of wonder, on the one hand, and the power and beauty of things, on the other.

The Great Gatsby dramatizes this continuing ambiguity directly in the life of Gatsby and retrospectively by a glance at history at the end of the novel. Especially does it do so in the two passages in the novel of what might be called the ecstatic moment, the moment when the human imagination seems to be on the verge of entering the earthly paradise. The two passages are (1) the real Gatsby looking on the real Daisy, and (2) the imaginary Dutchmen, whom Nick conjures up at the end of the novel, looking on the "green breast" of Long Island.

Here is the description of Gatsby and Daisy:

> Out of the corner of his eye Gatsby saw that the blocks of the sidewalk really formed a ladder and mounted to a secret place above the trees— he could climb to it, if he climbed alone, and once there he could suck on the pap of life, gulp down the incomparable milk of wonder.
>
> His heart beat faster and faster as Daisy's white face came up to his own. He knew that when he kissed this girl, and forever wed his unutterable visions to her perishable breath, his mind would never romp again like the mind of God. So he waited, listening for a moment longer to the tuning-fork that had been struck upon a star. Then he kissed her. At his lips' touch she blossomed for him like a flower and the incarnation was complete.

And below is Nick's imaginative reconstruction of the legendary Dutchman. He is sprawled on the sand at night, with Gatsby's mansion behind him and Long Island Sound in front of him:

> And as the moon rose higher the inessential houses began to melt away until gradually I became aware of the old Island that flowered once for Dutch eyes—a fresh green breast of the new world. Its vanished trees, the trees that had made way for Gatsby's house, had once pandered in whispers to the last and greatest of all human dreams; for a transitory enchanted moment man must have held his breath in the presence of this

*John Henry Raleigh, "F. Scott Fitzgerald's *The Great Gatsby:* Legendary Bases and Allegorical Significances," *University of Kansas City Review*, XXIV (October 1957), 55-58. Reprinted with the permission of the author and the *University Review*, University of Missouri at Kansas City.

continent, compelled into an aesthetic contempla- tion he [55/56] neither understood nor desired, face to face for the last time in history with something commensurate to his capacity for wonder.

The repetition in the two passages of the words "wonder" and "flower" hardly need comment, or the sexuality, illicit in the Dutchmen's and both infantile and mature in Gatsby's—or the star-lit, moon- lit setting in both. For these are the cen- tral symbols in the book: the boundless imagination trying to transfigure under the stars the endlessly beautiful object. Now, of course, the Dutchmen and Gatsby are utterly different types of being and going in different directions. The Dutch- men are pure matter, momentarily and unwillingly raised into the realms of the spirit, while Gatsby is pure spirit coming down to earth. They pass one another, so to speak, at the moment when ideal and reality seem about to converge. Histori- cally, the Dutch, legendarily stolid, pur- sued their mercantile ways and produced finally a Tom Buchanan but also, it should be remembered, a Nick Carraway. But their ecstatic moment hung on in the air, like an aroma, intoxicating prophets, sages, poets, even poor farm boys in twen- tieth-century Dakota. The heady insub- stantiability of the dream and the heavy intractability of the reality were expressed by Van Wyck Brooks (who could well have been Fitzgerald's philosopher in these matters) in his *The Wine of the Puritans* as follows:

You put the old wine [Europeans] into new bottles [American continent] . . . and when the explosion results, one may say, the aroma passes into the air and the wine spills on the floor. The aroma or the ideal, turns into transcendentalism and the wine or the real, becomes commercial- ism.

No one knew better than Gatsby that nothing could finally match the splendors of his own imagination, and the novel would suggest finally that not only had the American dream been corrupted but that it was, in part anyway, necessarily

corrupted, for it asked too much. Nothing of this earth, even the most beautiful of earthly objects, could be anything but a perversion of it.

The Great Gatsby, then, begins in a dramatization, as suggested, of the basic thesis of the early Van Wyck Brooks: that America had produced an idealism so im- palpable that it had lost touch with re- ality (Gatsby) and a materialism so heavy that it was inhuman (Tom Buchanan). The novel as a whole is another turn of the screw on this legend, with the im- possible idealism trying to realize itself, to its utter destruction, in the gross materiality. As Nick says of Gatsby at the end of the novel:

. . . his dream must have seemed so close that he could hardly fail to grasp it. He did not know that it was already behind him back in that vast obscurity beyond the city, where the dark fields of the republic rolled on under the night.

Yet he imagines too that Gatsby, before his moment of death, must have had his "realization" of the intractable brutish- ness of matter:

. . . he must have felt that he had lost the old warm world, paid a high price for living too long with a single dream. He must have looked up at an unfamiliar sky through fright- ening leaves and shivered as he found what a grotesque thing a rose is and how raw the sun- light was upon the scarcely created grass.

Thus Fitzgerald multiples the [56/57] ironies of the whole legend: that the mer- cantile Dutchmen should have been se- duced into the esthetic; that Gatsby's wondrous aspirations should attach them- selves to a Southern belle and that in pursuit of her he should become a gang- ster's lieutenant; that young Englishmen ("agonizingly aware of the easy money in the vicinity") should scramble for crumbs at Gatsby's grandiose parties (the Dutch- men once more); that idealism, beauty, power, money should get all mixed up; that history should be a kind of parody of itself, as with the case of the early

Dutch and the contemporary English explorers.

Still *The Great Gatsby* would finally suggest, at a level beyond all its legends and in the realm of the properly tragic, that it is right and fitting that the Jay Gatzes of the world should ask for the impossible, even when they do so as pathetically and ludicrously as does Gatsby himself. Writing to Fitzgerald about his novel, Maxwell Perkins, after enumerating some specific virtues, said:

> . . . these are such things as make a man famous. And all the things, the whole pathetic episode, you have given a place in time and space, for which the help of T. J. Eckleburg, and by an occasional glance at the sky, or the city, you have imparted a sort of sense of eternity.

A "sense of eternity"—this is indeed high praise, but I think that Perkins, as he often was, was right.

For at its highest level *The Great Gatsby* does not deal with local customs or even national and international legends but with the permanent realities of existence. On this level nothing or nobody is to blame, and people are what they are and life is what it is, just as, in Bishop Butler's words, "things are what they are." At this level, too, most people don't count; they are merely a higher form of animality living out its mundane existence: the Tom Buchanans, the Jordan Bakers, the Daisy Fays. Only Nick and Gatsby count. For Gatsby, with all his absurdities and his short, sad, pathetic life, is still valuable; in Nick's parting words to him: "You're worth the whole damn bunch put together." Nick, who in his way is as much of this world as Daisy is in hers, still sees, obscurely, the significance of Gatsby. And although he knows that the content of Gatsby's dream is corrupt, he senses that its form is pristine. For, in his own fumbling, often gross way, Gatsby was obsessed with the wonder of human life and driven by the search to make that wonder actual. It is the same urge that motivates visionaries and prophets, the urge to make

the facts of life measure up to the splendors of the human imagination, but it is utterly pathetic in Gatsby's case because he is trying to do it so subjectively and so uncouthly, and with dollar bills. Still Nick's obscure instinct that Gatsby is essentially all right is sound. It often seems as if the novel is about the contrast between the two, but the bond between them reveals that they are not opposites but rather complements, opposed together, to all the other characters in the novel.

Taken together they contain most of the essential polarities that go to make up the human mind and its existence. Allegorically considered, Nick is reason, experience, waking, reality, and history, while Gatsby is imagination, innocence, sleeping, dream, and eternity. Nick is like [57/58] Wordsworth listening to "the still sad music of humanity," while Gatsby is like Blake seeing hosts of angels in the sun. The one can only look at the facts and see them as tragic; the other tries to transform the facts by an act of the imagination. Nick's mind is conservative and historical, as is his lineage; Gatsby's is radical and apocalyptic—as rootless as his heritage. Nick is too much immersed in time and in reality; Gatsby is hopelessly out of it. Nick is always withdrawing, while Gatsby pursues the green light. Nick can't be hurt, but neither can he be happy. Gatsby can experience ecstasy, but his fate is necessarily tragic. They are generically two of the best types of humanity: the moralist and the radical.

One may well ask why, if their mental horizons are so lofty, is one a bond salesman and the other a gangster's lieutenant, whose whole existence is devoted to a love affair that has about it the unmistakable stamp of adolescence? The answer is, I think, that Fitzgerald did not know enough of what a philosopher or revolutionary might really be like, that at this point in his life he must have always thought of love in terms of a Princeton Prom, and that, writing in the twenties, a bond salesman and a gangster's functionary would seem more representative anyway. Van Wyck Brooks might have said, at one time, that his culture gave him nothing more to work with. A lesser writer might have attempted to make Nick a literal sage and Gatsby a literal prophet. But it is certain that such a thought would never have entered Fitzgerald's head, as he was only dramatizing the morals and manners of the life he knew. The genius of the novel consists precisely in the fact that, while using only the stuff, one might better say the froth and flotsam of its own limited time and place, it has managed to suggest, as Perkins said, a sense of eternity.

Color-Symbolism in *The Great Gatsby* *

DANIEL J. SCHNEIDER is a professor of English and chairman of the Department of English at Windham College, in Vermont. He has published a number of essays on the fiction of Fielding, Henry James, Conrad, Hemingway, and Hawthorne in various journals of literary criticism and is writing a book on symbolism in the fiction of Henry James.

The vitality and beauty of F. Scott Fitzgerald's writing are perhaps nowhere more strikingly exhibited than in his handling of the color-symbols in *The Great Gatsby*. We are all familiar with "the green light" at the end of Daisy's dock—that symbol of the "orgiastic future," the limitless promise of the dream Gatsby pursues to its inevitably tragic end; familiar, too, with the ubiquitous yellow—symbol of the money, the crass materialism that corrupts the dream and ultimately destroys it. What apparently has escaped the notice of most readers, however, is both the range of the color-symbols and their complex operation in rendering, at every stage of the action, the central conflict of the work. This article attempts to lay bare the full pattern.

The central conflict of *The Great Gatsby*, announced by Nick in the fourth paragraph of the book, is the conflict between Gatsby's dream and the sordid reality—the foul dust which floats "in the wake of his dreams." Gatsby, Nick tells us, "turned out all right in the end"; the dreamer remains as pure, as inviolable, at bottom, as his dream of a greatness, an attainment "commensurate to [man's] capacity for wonder." What does *not* turn out all right at the end is of course the reality: Gatsby is slain, the enchanted universe is exposed as a world of wholesale corruption and predatory violence, and Nick returns to the Midwest in disgust. As we shall see, the color-symbols render, with a close and delicate discrimination, both the dream and the reality—and these both in their separateness and in their tragic intermingling.

Now the most obvious representation, by means of color, of the novel's basic conflict is the pattern of contrasting lights and darks. Gatsby, Nick tells us, is "like an ecstatic patron of recurrent light." His imagination has created a "universe of ineffable gaudiness," of "a vast, vulgar, and meretricious beauty"—a world of such stirring vividness that it may be represented now by all the colors of the rainbow (Gatsby's shirts are appropriately "coral and apple-green and lavender and faint orange, with monograms of Indian blue"), now simply by light itself, by glitter, by flash. In his innocence, Gatsby of course sees only the pure light of the grail which he has "committed himself" to follow. The reader, however, sees a great deal more: sees, for example, the grotesque "valley of ashes," "the gray land and the spasms of bleak dust which drift endlessly over it"— the sordid reality lying beneath the fictions of the American dream of limitless Opportunity and Achievement.

If for a time "the whole front" of Gatsby's mansion "catches the light," if

*Daniel J. Schneider, "Color-Symbolism in *The Great Gatsby*," *University Review* (formerly *University of Kansas City Review*), XXXI (Autumn 1964), 13-18. Reprinted with the permission of the author and the *University Review*, University of Missouri at Kansas City.

the house, "blazing with light" at two o'clock in the morning, "looks like the World's Fair," the reader understands why it comes to be filled with an inexplicable amount of dust everywhere and why "the white steps" are sullied by "an obscene word, scrawled by some boy with a piece of brick." Fair and foul is the intermingling of [13/14] dream and reality; as Nick observes in Chapter VIII, there is a "gray-turning, gold-turning light" in the mansion, and the moral problem for the young Mid-westerner is to prevent himself from mistaking the glittering appearance for the true state of things.

The light-dark symbolism is employed with great care. It is not accidental, for example, that Daisy and Jordan, when they are introduced to the reader in the first scene of the novel, are dressed in white. In this scene, in which almost all of the color symbols are born, Nick tells us that "the only completely stationary object in the room was an enormous couch on which two young women were buoyed up as though upon an anchored balloon. They were both in white, and their dresses were rippling and fluttering as if they had just been blown back in after a short flight around the house."

White traditionally symbolizes purity, and there is no doubt that Fitzgerald wants to underscore the ironic disparity between the ostensible purity of Daisy and Jordan and their actual corruption. But Fitzgerald is not content with this obvious and facile symbolism. White, in this early appearance in the novel, is strongly associated with airiness, buoyancy, levitation. One is reminded of the statement in Chapter VI that for Gatsby "the rock of the world was founded securely on a fairy's wing." Daisy and Jordan seem about to float off into the air because they are—to both Gatsby and Nick—a bit unreal, like fairies (Daisy's maiden name is Fay); and they are in white because, as we learn in Chapter VII, to wear white is to be "an absolute little dream":

[Daisy's] face bent into the single wrinkle of the small white neck. "You dream, you. You absolute little dream."

"Yes," admitted the child calmly. "Aunt Jordan's got on a white dress too."

The white Daisy embodies the vision which Gatsby (who, like Lord Jim, usually wears white suits) seeks to embrace—but which Nick, who discovers the corrupt admixture of dream and reality, rejects in rejecting Jordan. For, except in Gatsby's extravagant imagination, the white does not exist pure: it is invariably stained by the money, the yellow. Daisy is the white flower—with the golden center. If in her virginal beauty she "dressed in white, and had a little white roadster," she is, Nick realizes, "high in a white palace the king's daughter, the golden girl." Her voice is "like money"; she carries a "little gold pencil"; when she visits Gatsby there are "two rows of brass buttons on her dress."

As for the "incurably dishonest" Jordan, she displays a "slender golden arm" and "a golden shoulder"; her fingers are "powdered white over their tan"; the lamp-light shines "bright on . . . the autumn-leaf yellow of her hair." When she enters the hotel with Daisy, both are wearing "small tight hats of metallic cloth"; and when Nick sees them both lying on the couch a second time, they are "like silver idols weighing down their own white dresses against the singing breeze of the fans"—the silver, of course, symbolizing both the dream and the reality, since as the color of the romantic stars and the moon (the first time we observe Gatsby he is gazing up at the "silver pepper of the stars") it is clearly associated with the romantic hope and promise that govern Gatsby's life, and as the color of money it is obviously a symbol of corrupt materialism. [14/15]

Both Jordan and Daisy are enchanting—but false. And Nick's attitude toward them is identical with his attitude toward life in the East. In the apartment in New York with Tom and Myrtle, he tells us that he is like the "casual watcher in the darkening streets" looking up and wondering" at "our line of yellow windows" in the "long white cake of apartmenthouses": "I was within and without, simultaneously enchanted and repelled by the inexhaustible variety of life." Viewed from "without," the windows glow with all the beauty and potency of the Dream; but "within" the apartment, Nick observes only greed, irresponsibility, conspicuous waste: he recognizes that the glow of the windows is that of money, not of enchantment. If, like Gatsby, he has tasted "the incomparable milk of wonder," he discovers that the milk will presently sour: turn yellow.

These conjunctions of white and yellow in contexts exhibiting the contrast between the dream and the reality are so numerous that most readers are likely to perceive the symbolic functioning of the colors. The symbolism of blue and red is less obvious.

The first striking reference to blue occurs at the beginning of Chapter II, where Fitzgerald describes the eyes of Doctor T. J. Eckleburg peering out over the Valley of Ashes, "*above* the gray land and the spasms of bleak dust." (italics mine)

> The eyes of Doctor T. J. Eckleburg are blue and gigantic—their retinas are one yard high. They look out of no face, but, instead, from a pair of enormous yellow spectacles which pass over a non-existent nose.

When, later in the novel, Wilson, staring at these same eyes, says, "God sees everything," and Michaelis contradicts him, "That's an advertisement," it is clear that Fitzgerald wants us to view T. J. Eckleburg as a symbol of the corruption of spirit in the Waste Land—as if even God has been violated by materialism and hucksterism—reduced to an advertisement. This might suggest that blue symbolizes a certain ideality; but the meaning of the symbol is not defined until we reach Chapter III, which begins: "There was music from my neighbor's house through the summer nights. In his blue gardens men

and women came and went like moths among the whisperings and the champagne and the stars."

The romantic blue is obviously associated with the promise, the dream, that Gatsby has mistaken for reality. Fitzgerald is even more explicit in Chapter VII: "Our eyes lifted over the rose-beds and the hot lawn and the weedy refuse of the dog-days along shore. Slowly the white wings of the boat moved against the blue cool limit of the sky. Ahead lay the scalloped ocean and the abounding blessed isles."

Here blue and white become the symbols of the ultimate bliss, the ideal perfection which Gatsby's parties in the blue gardens seem to promise. If, later on when the parties are over, it is necessary to repair "the ravages of the night before"; if the "five crates of oranges and lemons" that arrive every Friday, leave the back door "in a pyramid of pulpless halves"; if the parties degenerate into ugliness and violence and "a sudden emptiness" falls upon the house—that is, after all, no more than we have already learned to expect: the white and the blue of the dream are inevitably sullied by the yellow. So T. J. Eckleburg's blue eyes are surrounded by yellow spectacles; so the music in the blue gardens is "yellow [15/16] cocktail music"; so the chauffeur in a uniform of "robin's-egg-blue" turns out to be "one of Wolfsheim's protégés." Gatsby begins his ascent toward Greatness when Dan Cody takes the young man to Duluth and buys him "a blue coat, six pairs of white duck trousers, and a yachting cap." But on the day of his death his clothes change color symbolically—as we shall see after examining the symbolism of red.

The first striking reference to red occurs in Chapter I, where Nick tells us that he "bought a dozen volumes on banking and credit and investment securities, and they stood on my shelf in red and gold like new money from the mint, promising to unfold the shining secrets that Midas and Morgan and Mæcenas knew." It is possible that Fitzgerald's choice of red in this context is arbitrary, but a study of the many appearances of the color in the novel, and especially of its appearances in conjunction with yellow and white, suggests strongly that red should be interpreted not merely as image but as symbol. In fact it has, I believe, the same signification as yellow: that is, it may represent either the "ineffable gaudiness" of the dream or the ugliness of the reality.

It stands for the dream because it is one of the glittering colors of Gatsby's romantic universe. We remember that Gatsby describes himself as a collector of jewels, "chiefly rubies," and in Chapter VI Nick remarks ironically: "I saw him opening a chest of rubies to ease, with their crimson-lighted depths, the gnawings of his broken heart." Gatsby's bedazzlement by the crimson rubies is matched by the awed Nick's wonder at what is to him, at the beginning of the novel, the *almost* enchanted world of the Buchanans. Entering this world of the rich, Nick is dazzled by the glowing light, the reds, and the rosiness: he walks "through a high hallway into a bright rosy-colored space"; there is "a rosy-colored porch, open toward the sunset, where four candles flickered on the table in the diminished wind"; the French windows are "glowing . . . with reflected gold"; there is "a half acre of deep, pungent roses"; later on, "the crimson room bloomed with light," and on his way home he observes how "new red gas-pumps sat out in pools of light."

Red, in these passages, is glitter, is enchantment, is dream; but there is another and a more interesting reason for the frequent occurrence of the color. As the color of blood, it is inevitably associated with the violence caused by the human animals who prey upon Gatsby—not merely the Hornbeams and the Blackbucks and Beavers and Ferrets and Wolfsheims, but also the respectable Tom and Daisy, the "careless people" who smashed up things and creatures and then retreated back into their money or their vast carelessness . . . and let other people clean up the mess they had made." Thus Tom breaks Myrtle's nose and there are "bloody towels upon the bathroom floor." (He is also involved in an accident in which "the girl who was with him," a hotel chambermaid, has her arm broken.) Daisy runs down Myrtle, whose "thick dark blood" mingles with the dust of the Valley of Ashes—the foul dust which floats in the wake of Gatsby's dreams. And Wilson murders Gatsby, whose blood leaves "a thin red circle in the water." The beautiful reds become the color of carnage, and, as Nick tells us, perhaps even Gatsby, discovering the truth about Daisy, [16/17] would find "what a grotesque thing a rose is."

On the hypothesis that red symbolizes the violent reality as well as the glittering dream, it is not surprising to find that just as yellow is inextricably joined to white, so red is wedded to both white and yellow, to reveal, simultaneously, both the dreamlike enchantment and the actual brutality. Thus it is appropriate that the Buchanans' house is a "cheerful red-and-white Georgian Colonial mansion"; and (though I may be guilty of forcing the symbolism here) I find it significant that Gatsby, when he enters the Buchanan house for the first time, "stood in the center of the crimson carpet and gazed around him with fascinated eyes. Daisy watched him and laughed, her sweet, exciting laugh; a tiny gust of powder rose from her bosom into the air."

Equally appropriate is the fact that Myrtle's sister, one of the careless people who attend Gatsby's parties and who ironically share in the dream, is a "slender worldly girl of about thirty, with a solid, sticky bob of red hair and a complexion powdered milky white." And the red and gold of Nick's dozen books appear again at one of Gatsby's parties—those strange tributes to the Dream which end always in violence—where "one of the girls in yellow was playing the piano, and beside her stood a tall, red-haired young lady from a famous chorus, engaged in song"; the violence occurs only moments later when Nick discovers, in a ditch beside the road, a new coupé shorn of one wheel.

So much for the basic color-symbols, the four primaries. But since, as we have already seen, one of Fitzgerald's techniques is to call attention to the conjunctions of his colors, that tragic and pervasive mingling of dream and reality, we are not surprised to find the writer refining his palette so as to exhibit, in a single word, the wedding of the pure and the corrupt. White and red, for example, may blend to produce pink, the color of the dream stained by violence—or, again, (a simpler interpretation) one of the colors of Gatsby's adolescent universe. In Chapter V, when Daisy excitedly summons Gatsby to observe "a pink and golden billow of foamy clouds above the sea," the pink is obviously part of the picture-postcard Fairyland; but when, after Myrtle's death, Nick, visiting Gatsby in the mansion which contains the "inexplicable amount of dust," sees the dreamer no longer in his customary white but in pink —"His gorgeous pink rag of a suit made a bright spot of color against the white steps"—the suit would seem to be not merely gaudy but blood-stained. Gatsby remains incorruptible, but his house and his clothes reveal the sordidness of the reality. Similarly, in the charged context of events following the murder, it is scarcely surprising to observe, with Nick, the "pink glow from Daisy's room on the second floor" of the Buchanans' house— the glow of enchantment and of blood, of princess and murderess.

Another blending of the primaries is exhibited in Gatsby's car: "I'd seen it. Everybody had seen it. It was a rich cream color, bright with nickel, swollen here and there in its monstrous length with triumphant hat-boxes and supper-boxes and tool boxes, and terraced with a labyrinth of wind-shields that mirrored a dozen suns. . . . With fenders spread like wings we scattered light through half Astoria. . . ." [17/18]

The glitter of the car is exactly that of the white palaces of East Egg glittering along the water, and like the dresses of Jordan and Daisy, the car possesses a buoyancy, a penchant for levitation. But the white and the shine of the dream fuse inevitably with the yellow of materialism: the car is "a rich cream color." It is only much later, after the slaughter of Myrtle, when the limousine is described as "the death car," that the color of the dream disappears. "It was a yellow car," a witness reports. For the dream is dead, and Daisy's self-seeking has given its unmistakable color to Gatsby's colossal vision.

A similar change of color occurs in the scene in which Nick accompanies Tom and Myrtle to the apartment in New York. Arriving in New York, Myrtle wears a dress of brown muslin—the brown being, of course, a color from the valley of ashes, where among other things one finds "hard brown beetles . . . thudding against the dull light." But when she reaches the apartment she changes into a "dress of cream-colored chiffon, which gave out a continual rustle as she swept about the room." Nick observes that "with the influence of the dress her personality had also undergone a change. The intense vitality that had been so remarkable in the garage was converted into impressive hauteur." She is transformed into the money-stained dream-girl, the Daisy or the Jordan, "high in a white palace, the king's daughter, the golden girl . . ."

There is, finally, the green light at the end of Daisy's dock, that symbol which Fitzgerald explicitly identifies with "the orgiastic future that year by year recedes before us." Being green, the light summons Gatsby and his fellow Americans to Go Ahead—to "run faster, stretch out our arms farther. . . ." Yet the covert symbolism of the light should by this time be clear: green, as the mixture of yellow and blue, is once again the tragic commingling of dream and reality. Gatsby, seeking the blue, is blind to the sordid yellow. For him the money does not matter, does not exist; it is finally only the white or the blue that enchants him. But it is in the pursuit of an adulterated grail that he is destroyed.

The Greatness of "Gatsby" *

CHARLES THOMAS SAMUELS (1936–   ) is an associate professor of English at Williams College and the author of *John Updike* (1969). He has just completed editing a book on the cinema and is writing a book on the art of Henry James. His essays and reviews have appeared in the *New Republic*, the *Atlantic Monthly* and other magazines and journals. He won the Newton Arvin Award of the *Massachusetts Review* for distinguished criticism in 1966.

The Great Gatsby's excellence was immediately seen, but soon the carping began. Mencken wrote "a most enthusiastic letter" to Fitzgerald, in which he complained that "the central story was trivial and a sort of anecdote. . . ." In a characteristic blend of modesty, temerity and odd spelling, Fitzgerald replied: "Without making any invidious comparisons between Class A and Class C, if my novel is an anecdote so is *The Brothers Karamazoff*."

Nevertheless, Fitzgerald granted Mencken's point and agreed that it had been a mistake to becloud the relationship between Gatsby and Daisy from the time of their reunion until Gatsby's death. Yet Fitzgerald's error was his triumph. Had he dramatized that relationship he would have been validating a sham. There could be no fulfillment of Gatsby's tragic dream. Fitzgerald shows all that happens or could have happened. Daisy joyfully crying into Gatsby's shirts; Gatsby realizing, at last, that her siren's voice was merely full of money; Daisy's failure in the hotel room and in the accident; Myrtle's mangled body and Gatsby's on the float, turned from its "accidental course" by the "touch of a cluster of leaves."

Fitzgerald gave his critics more than their due, and some such imbalance has always marred appraisal of his work. What Owl-eyes declared at Gatsby's grave and Dorothy Parker so affectingly repeated over Fitzgerald's has sounded a flat note in the chorus of praise: "the poor son of a bitch." However great the work, the man's life was a fiasco—perhaps the work is not so great as we thought. Can we ignore the life in the writing? Surely Fitzgerald is Gatsby, as he admitted. What else is Nick but a shield against the blinding rays of too easy, too complete resemblance? If Fitzgerald was, in the words of an early and sensitive critic, "the Authority of Failure," can he ever have succeeded? Isn't there some softness at the heart of his masterpiece just as there was, notoriously, the glaring sentimentalism in his life—the liquor, the mad wife? Could so bad a risk be a great writer? [783/784]

We have not been willing to leave his life alone. The current monument in Fitzgerald studies, *The Far Side of Paradise*, contains page after page of Scott and Zelda in Paris and New York but only eight on the art in *Gatsby*. It sees Nick as a structural device and an author's therapy. The novel's meaning is reduced to a neat dichotomy between East and West. We are told that the book's relevance was limited by Fitzgerald's total commitment to romantic ideals and that the Eyes of Dr.

*Charles Thomas Samuels, "The Greatness of 'Gatsby'," *The Massachusetts Review*, VII (Autumn 1966), 783-794. Reprinted from *The Massachusetts Review*, © 1966, The Massachusetts Review, Inc. By permission of the author.

Eckleburg are merely an accidental gift from Max Perkins' premature dust jacket. Such are the uses of scholarship.

Since Mizener's biography, criticism has shot nearer the mark. Nick's importance has been, at least, recognized; and the neat dichotomy between East and West has been qualified so that the novel's profound criticism of American life seems, at last, clear. We need to show now that Fitzgerald's most successful book is a great novel.

2

Its fundamental achievement is a triumph of language.

I do not speak merely of the "flowers," the famous passages: Nick's description of Gatsby yearning toward the green light on Daisy's dock, Gatsby's remark that the Buchanans' love is "only personal," the book's last page. Throughout, *The Great Gatsby* has the precision and splendor of a lyric poem, yet well-wrought prose is merely one of its triumphs. Fitzgerald's distinction in this novel is to have made language celebrate itself. Among other things, *The Great Gatsby* is about the power of art.

This celebration of literary art is inseparable from the novel's second great achievement—its management of point of view, the creation of Nick. With his persona, Fitzgerald obtained more than objectivity and concentration of effect. Nick describes more than the experience which he witnesses; he describes the act and consequences of telling about it. The persona is—as critics have been seeing—a character, but he is more than that: he is a character engaged in a significant action.

Nick is writing a book. He is recording Gatsby's experience; in the act of recording Gatsby's experience he discovers himself.

Though his prose has all along been creating for us Gatsby's "romantic readiness," almost until the very end Nick insists that he deplores Gatsby's "appalling sentimentality." This is not a reasoned judgment. Nick disapproves because he cannot yet affirm. He is a Jamesian spectator, a fastidious intelligence ill-suited to profound engagement of life. But writing does profoundly engage life. In writing about Gatsby, Nick alters his attitude toward his subject and ultimately toward his own life. [784/785] As his book nears completion his identification with Gatsby grows. His final affirmation is his sympathetic understanding of Gatsby and the book which gives his sympathy form: both are a celebration of life; each is a gift of language. This refinement on James's use of the persona might be the cause of Eliot's assertion that *The Great Gatsby* represented the first advance which the American novel had made since James.

In Nick's opening words we find an uncompleted personality. There are contradictions and perplexities which (when we first read the passage) are easily ignored, because of the characteristic suavity of his prose. He begins the chronicle, whose purpose is an act of judgment and whose title is an evaluation, by declaring an inclination "to reserve all judgments." The words are scarcely digested when we find him judging:

The abnormal mind is quick to detect and attach itself to this quality [tolerance] when it appears in a normal person, and so it came about that in college I was unjustly accused of being a politician, because I was privy to the secret griefs of wild, unknown men.

The tone is unmistakable—a combination of moral censure, self-protectiveness, and final saving sympathy that marks Nick as an outsider who is nonetheless drawn to the life he is afraid to enter. So when he tells us a little later in the passage that "Reserving judgments is a matter of infinite hope," we know that this and not the *noblesse oblige* he earlier advanced explains his fear of judging. Nick cannot help judging, but he fears a world in which he is constantly beset by objects worthy of rejection. He is "a little afraid of missing something"; that is why he hears the promise in Daisy's voice, half-heartedly entertains the idea of loving Jordan Baker, and becomes involved with the infinite hope of Jay Gatsby—"Gatsby, who represented everything for which [Nick had] an unaffected scorn."

When Nick begins the book he feels the same ambivalence toward Gatsby that characterizes his attitude toward life: a simultaneous enchantment and revulsion which places him "within and without." When he has finished, he has become united with Gatsby, and he judges Gatsby great. Finally he has something to admire; contemplating Gatsby redeems him from the "foul dust [which had] temporarily closed out [his] interest in the abortive sorrows and short-winded elations of men."

The economy with which Fitzgerald presents those sorrows and short-winded elations is another of the book's major achievements. In *The Great Gatsby* Fitzgerald contrived to develop a story by means of symbols while at the same time investing those symbols with vivid [785/786] actuality. Everything in the book is symbolic, from Gatsby's ersatz mansion to the wild and aimless parties which he gives there, yet everything seems so "true to life" that some critics continue to see that novel primarily as a recreation of the 20's. *The Great Gatsby* is about the 20's only in the sense that *Moby Dick* is about whaling or that *The Scarlet Letter* is about Puritan Boston. Comparing the liveliness of Fitzgerald's book with Melville's or, better still, with Hawthorne's (which resembles its tight dramatic structure and concentration), you have a good indication of the peculiar distinction in Fitzgerald's work.

Of the novel's symbols, only the setting exists without regard to verisimilitude, purely to project meaning. *The Great Gatsby* has four locales: East Egg, home of the rich Buchanans and their ultra-traditional Georgian Colonial mansion; West Egg where the once-rich and the parvenus live and where Gatsby apes the splendor of the Old World; the wasteland of the average man; and New York, where Nick labors, ironically, at the "Probity Trust." East and West Egg are 'crushed flat at the contact end"; they represent the collision of dream and dreamer which is dramatized when Gatsby tries to establish his "universe of ineffable gaudiness" through the crass materials of the real world. The wasteland is a valley of ashes in which George Wilson dispenses gasoline to the irresponsible drivers from East and West Egg, eventually yielding his wife to their casual lust and cowardly violence.

Fitzgerald's world represents iconographically a sterile, immoral society. Over this world brood the blind eyes of Dr. T. J. Eckleburg: the sign for an oculist's business which was never opened, the symbol of a blindness which can never be corrected. Like other objects in the book to which value might be attached, the eyes of Dr. Eckleburg are a cheat. They are not a sign of God, as Wilson thinks, but only an advertisement—like the false promise of Daisy's moneyed voice, or the green light on her dock, which is invisible in the mist.

These monstrous eyes are the novel's major symbol. The book's chief characters are blind, and they behave blindly. Gatsby does not see Daisy's vicious emptiness, and Daisy, deluded, thinks she will reward her gold-hatted lover until he tries to force from her an affirmation she is too weak to make. Tom is blind to his hypocrisy; with "a short deft movement" he breaks Myrtle's nose for daring to mention the name of the wife she is helping him to deceive. Before her death, Myrtle mistakes Jordan for Daisy. Just as she had always mistaken Tom for salvation from the ash-heap, she blindly rushes for his car in her need to escape her lately informed husband, and is struck down. Moreover, [786/787] Daisy is driving the car; and the man with her is Gatsby, not Tom. The final act of blindness is specifically associated with Dr. Eckleburg's

eyes. Wilson sees them as a sign of right-
eous judgment and righteously proceeds
to work God's judgment on earth. He
kills Gatsby, but Gatsby is the wrong man.
In the whole novel, only Nick sees. And
his vision comes slowly, in the act of writing the book.

The act of writing the book is, as I have
said, an act of judgment. Nick wants to
know why Gatsby "turned out all right
in the end," despite all the phoniness and
crime which fill his story, and why Gatsby
was the only one who turned out all right.
For, in writing about the others, Nick discovers the near ubiquity of folly and despair.

The novel's people are exemplary types
of the debasement of life which is Fitzgerald's subject. Daisy, Tom, and Jordan
lack the inner resources to enjoy what
their wealth can give them. They show
the peculiar folly of the American dream.
At the pinnacle, life palls. Daisy is almost unreal. When Nick first sees her
she seems to be floating in midair. Her
famous protestation of grief ("I'm sophisticated. God, I'm sophisticated") is accompanied by an "absolute smirk." Her
extravagant love for Gatsby is a sham, less
real than the unhappy but fleshly bond
with Tom which finally turns them into
"conspirators." Her beauty is a snare.
Like Tom's physical prowess, it neither
pleases her nor insures her pleasure in
others. Tom forsakes Daisy for Myrtle
and both for "stale ideas." Jordan's
balancing act is a trick; like her sporting reputation, a precarious lie. They are
all rich and beautiful—and unhappy.

Yearning toward them are Myrtle and
Gatsby. Like Gatsby, Myrtle desires "the
youth and mystery that wealth imprisons and preserves . . . gleaming . . .
above the hot struggles of the poor."
Unlike him, her "panting vitality" is
wholly physical, merely pathetic; whereas
Gatsby's quest is spiritual and tragic.
Myrtle is maimed and victimized by
Daisy's selfish fear of injury (Daisy could
have crashed into another car but, at the

last minute, loses heart and runs Myrtle
down); Gatsby's death is but the final
stage of disillusionment, and he suffers
voluntarily.

Gatsby is, of course, one of the major
achievements I have been noting. Although we see little of him and scarcely
ever hear him speak, his presence is continually with us; and he exists, as characters in fiction seldom do, as a life force.
He recalls the everlasting yea of Carlyle,
as well as the metaphysical rebellion of
Camus. His "heightened sensitivity to the
promise of life" is but one half of his
energy; the other being a passionate denial of life's limitations. Gatsby's devotion to Daisy is an implicit assault on the
human condition. His passion would
defy time and [787/788] decay to make
the glorious first moment of wonder,
which is past, eternally present. His passion is supra-sexual, even super-personal.
In his famous remark to Nick about
Daisy's love for Tom, he is making two
assertions: that the "things between Daisy
and Tom [which Tom insists] he'll never
know" are merely mundane and that the
Daisy which he loves is not the Daisy
which Tom had carried down from the
Punch Bowl but the Daisy who "blossomed for him like a flower," incarnating
his dream, the moment he kissed her.
Gatsby's love for life is finally an indictment of the life he loves. Life does not
reward such devotion, nor, for that reason, does it deserve it. Gatsby is great for
having paid life the compliment of believing its promise.

When Hamlet dies amidst the carnage
of his bloody quest for justice, he takes
with him the promise that seeming will
coincide with being and the hope that
man can strike a blow for truth and save
a remnant of the universe. When Ahab
dies a victim to his own harpoon, he kills
the promise that man may know his life
and the hope that knowledge will absolve
him. When Gatsby dies, more innocently
than they (since, though a "criminal,"
he lacks utterly their taste for destruc-

tion), he kills a promise more poignant and perhaps more precious, certainly more inclusive than theirs: Gatsby kills the promise that desire can ever be gratified.

In addition to the story of Gatsby and Daisy and the parable of America which that story suggests and which finds its marvelous adumbration in Nick's last words, *The Great Gatsby* tells another tale: a tale of the blindness of desire and of the rock-like indifference of the universe. Nothing lives up to your image of it. This romantic agony, formerly expressed by Fitzgerald's beloved Keats, is the major theme which animates Fitzgerald's masterpiece. In the uneven novel which immediately preceded *Gatsby*, Fitzgerald clearly articulated what had always been his tragic sense of life. The epigraph to *The Beautiful and the Damned*, "written" by its hero, dourly observes that "the Victor belongs to the spoils." Midway in the fable which exemplifies this sad moral, its author, Anthony Patch, cries out:

. . . desire just cheats you. It's like a sunbeam skipping here and there about a room. It stops and gilds some inconsequential object, and we poor fools try to grasp it—but when we do the sunbeam moves on to something else, and you've got the inconsequential part, but the glitter that made you want it is gone.

Anthony's observation is the donnée of Fitzgerald's fiction. *The Great Gatsby's* characters respond in one of three ways to this un- [788/789] fortunate truth. The Buchanans and Jordan avoid deep attachments (Daisy thinks to make Nick fall in love with Jordan by accidentally locking them in linen closets), and drift "unrestfully wherever people played polo and were rich together." Wilson and Nick escape the phantom of desire by not desiring. Myrtle, stupidly, and Gatsby, grandly, take life's gambit, are cheated, and destroyed. Whatever their *modus vivendi*, all of these people are unhappy.

Hamlet is a tragedy of the moral sense. *Moby Dick* is a tragedy of the intelligence. *The Great Gatsby* is a tragedy of the will. Intensity of will makes Gatsby a great man. Despite the barrenness of his beginnings, despite the evil world of Dan Cody which was his first reward, despite Daisy's selfish denial and final treason, Gatsby believes in the promise of life. He *will* believe—this is his tragedy and vindication—despite his knowledge that life cannot repay his devotion.

Gatsby knows that desire is a cheat, yet he persists in his aspirations. I do not think that this fact has been properly appreciated. In the magnificent passage which ends the sixth chapter and which forms a climatic stage in Nick's growing comprehension of Gatsby, Nick imagines the scene in which Gatsby first kisses the girl of his dreams. The night is suitably bathed in moonlight. (In *The Beautiful and Damned* Fitzgerald concludes Anthony's rumination on the nature of desire by remarking how "the moon, at its perennial labor of covering the bad complexion of the world, showered its illicit honey over the drowsy street.") The entire universe seems to participate in Gatsby's passion. There is "a stir and bustle among the stars"; there is the equinox with its "mysterious excitement." Then Gatsby imagines

that the blocks of the sidewalks really formed a ladder and mounted to a secret place above the trees—he could climb to it, if he climbed alone, and once there he could suck on the pap of life, gulp down the incomparable milk of wonder.

If Gatsby remained unattached, if he had not grown up to adult sexuality, he could have gained the mystical ecstasy which his imagination sought. "He knew that when he kissed [Daisy], and forever wed his unutterable visions to her perishable breath, his mind would never romp again like the mind of God." Despite this knowledge, Gatsby chooses life. He hesitates, "listening for a moment longer to the tuning-fork that had struck upon a star." Finally, he renounces the innocent, pre-sexual, other-worldliness which alone brings one in contact with ideality to marry the temporal, perishable, sexual world. Like God, he renounces unlimited promise for love of humanity. He [789/790] permits the incarnation, and from that moment he is weaned from the "milk of wonder" and born into the world of sex, cash, and ashes.

Gatsby's choice is made in the fullness of knowledge. Moreover, he comprehends his subsequent ordeal. On the book's second page, Nick compares Gatsby to a seismograph, a wonderfully responsive machine. When Daisy comes to the mansion which Gatsby purchased only for her, he has become another machine—a clock. But since Gatsby's desire to confound time and return to the source of wonder has reached "an inconceivable pitch of intensity," the clock is running down. When Daisy puts her arm through Gatsby's, she loses the enchantment of distance, and Nick notes that her green light is no longer a star to Gatsby but merely "a green light on a dock." Throughout the novel, Nick hears promise in Daisy's voice; Gatsby realizes that it is full only of money.

Gatsby knows the desperate game he is playing, and his fervent passion is controlled by form (for all his vulgarity, Gatsby is elegant, a figure in a ritual). He represents, in short, a formed attempt to reorder reality, to wrest for the will a hitherto impossible victory. Gatsby is also a kind of artist; but whereas Nick works with words, Gatsby works with life. Life is the more recalcitrant.

Through a special discipline, Gatsby ignores what he knows in order to pursue his quest. Only before he dies can he understand that "he had lost the old warm world"; only then will he look at the sky "through frightening leaves" and see "what a grotesque thing a rose is and how raw the sunlight was upon the scarcely created grass."

Through the greater discipline of art, Nick is able to see the real landscape and affirm the glory of life. He can see Gatsby's vulgarity as well as his greatness. Words save Nick from Gatsby's catastrophe for they hold life at bay and permit contemplation, but Gatsby gives Nick a life worth celebrating in language and therefore the will to write as well as the will to live.

Which brings me back where I started. Nick. Nick and Gatsby. They are the novel's subject. Their relationship. We follow Nick's development in the novel— Gatsby is static—and we reach the first stage in his growth when he meets Gatsby. Writing the first chapter, Nick is still a divided, deluded man. He writes not out of knowledge possessed, conclusions reached, but in an attempt to know and to conclude. This, more even than the superb prose, gives the book its air of happening now. Though Nick tells us he reserves judgments, though he brags about his tolerance, he is quickly revolted by Tom Buchanan. Before Tom even speaks, Nick recalls that "there were men at New Haven [790/791] who had hated [Tom's] guts." Though Nick comes ultimately to understand Daisy's moral squalor, he is initially taken in. He sees her insincerity, but he expects her to run from the house, baby in arms, and ask him to take her away from Tom. His reaction to Buchanan's sterility is naive. He wants to flee Tom's love nest with its middle class pretension (Myrtle's furniture tapestried with scenes of ladies swinging in the gardens of Versailles, her "impressive hauteur" which results from a change of costume). After seeing that, he can only get drunk. The sophistication he came East to attain has begun to produce inner deadening. When Nick meets Gatsby, everything changes. Gatsby involves him in life. Gatsby wins his admiration. Gatsby dies, and Nick lives.

From the first, Gatsby is contrasted with Daisy. Daisy's voice is calculated to make you lean toward her. Her grief is "a trick of some sort to exact a contributory emotion." Gatsby "faced—or seemed to face— the whole external world for an instant, and then concentrated on *you* with an irresistible prejudice in your favor." Totally self-absorbed as he is, Gatsby nevertheless brings life to others. He is the incarnating God. He fails with Daisy; but, by the way and without plan, he succeeds in bringing life to Nick. When once Gatsby is "delivered [to Nick] from the womb of his purposeless splendor," Nick finds a *raison d'etre*.

Nick had not been reserving judgment; he had been denying life. He came East to flee home and the girl who was to help him settle down there. After the war, the Mid-West bored him. Unable to find a place where he belongs, he comes East to find a new life, but finds only a wasteland. Gatsby saves him from cynical withdrawal, and, suitably, at the end of the book Nick goes home once more; not because home is better but because it *is* home. Gatsby enables Nick to accept his own imperfect life.

But before that final acceptance Nick has to tell himself the truth. Throughout the novel, Nick half-heartedly courts Jordan Baker, explaining his indecisiveness with a characteristic bit of self-justification:

> . . . I am slow-thinking and full of interior rules that act as brakes on my desires, and I knew that first I had to get myself definitely out of that tangle back home.

However, when Jordan calls Nick after Myrtle's death, he refuses to see her because he is more interested in Gatsby than in the woman he thinks he might love. Before the end of the book Jordan tells Nick that he never loved her and that his whole treatment of her had been, despite his protestations, dishonest. Tauntingly, she accuses him: [**791/792**]

> ". . . I thought you were rather an honest, straightforward person. I thought it was your secret pride."
> "I'm thirty," [Nick replies] "I'm five years too old to lie to myself and call it honor."

This is the measure of Nick's growth. Discovering Gatsby in the act of writing about him, Nick discovers that he had deluded himself, that he had been dishonest, and that he had better go back and start all over.

Like everything else in this great novel, Nick's spiritual growth is symbolically represented rather than discussed. In the last chapter the stages in his identification with Gatsby are clearly depicted. After the murder, Nick stands by Gatsby simply because "no one else was interested—interested, I mean, with that intense personal interest to which everyone has some vague right at the end." But when the others refuse to come to Gatsby's funeral, Nick begins to feel "defiance, scornful solidarity between Gatsby and me against them all." When Gatsby's father arrives, Nick admits that he and Gatsby "were close friends." In the famous last scene Nick affirms Gatsby's greatness by seeing him as the prototype of the dreamers who established the new world.

This famous passage shows the greatness of *Gatsby*. It is richer and more beautiful than has been remarked.

> Most of the big shore places were closed now and there were hardly any lights except the shadowy, moving glow of a ferryboat across the Sound. And as the moon rose higher the inessential houses began to melt away until gradually I became aware of the old island here that flowered once for Dutch sailors' eyes—a fresh, green breast of the new world. Its vanished trees, the trees that had made way for Gatsby's house, had once pandered in whispers to the last and greatest of all human dreams; for a transitory enchanted moment man must have held his breath in the presence of this continent, compelled into an aesthetic contemplation he neither understood nor desired, face to face for the last time in history with something commensurate to his capacity for wonder.
> And as I sat there brooding on the old, unknown world, I thought of Gatsby's wonder when he first picked out the green light at the end of Daisy's dock. He had come a long way to this blue lawn, and his dream must have seemed so close that he could hardly fail to grasp it. He did not know that it was already behind him, somewhere back in that vast obscurity beyond the city, where the dark fields of the republic rolled on under the night.
> Gatsby believed in the green light, the orgiastic future that year by year recedes before us. It eluded us then, but that's no matter—tomorrow we will run faster, stretch out our arms farther. . . . And one fine morning—
> So we beat on, boats against the current, borne back ceaselessly into the past. [**792/793**]

Nick's final vision carefully parallels his other sympathetic vision of Gatsby in chapter six. Taken together they figuratively combine all of the novel's themes. Gatsby and Daisy pass beyond the trees into a moonlit scene where wonder lurked; Nick sees through the "inessential" world of Long Island to the trees which were cleared away to make a place for that world. Like Gatsby who saw "the secret place above the trees" where he could suck the pap of life, Nick sees the "green breast of the world" which "pandered in whispers" to the Dutch sailors who sailed to find the promised land of America. But Nick also sees that the promised land had been a cheat. Its greenness became Daisy's green light; not the fecund green of the forest but the green of machines and the money which buys them. Like the sailors, Gatsby tried to return to the source of life, to imbibe wonder at its breast. But man ages, time goes on, and life is a slow dying. Renouncing the secret place above the trees, Gatsby embraces the flower Daisy; but daisies die. When Gatsby loved Daisy he lost his dream; when the sailors took the new world they began the degradation of America's promise; when God saw what he had incarnated he went back to Heaven leaving only a blind sign of the business he would not now open. The past is our future. We have come to the end of possibility.

3

The theme of Fitzgerald's novel is more inclusive and more shocking than we have known. Its subject is atrophy; the wasting away of the self as one grows into the world of sex and money and time; the wasting away of America as it grows from wilderness to civilization, of the universe as it grows by its impossible plan.

Humanly, the novel reflects the disillusionment and the failure of youthful dreams which is so marked a feature of man's lot. Culturally, it dramatizes, perhaps more cogently than any other American novel, the cause and cost of America's identification with eternal beginnings. Cosmically, it suggests the apocalyptic vision with which we have become familiar in our literature, our intellectuals, and our newspapers.

It is the novel's greatest achievement to have painted this bleak picture with the brightest of colors. Never has the dying swan sung so sweetly or so surely.

What gives the book its vitality, these words about death which are not dead (surely, in our time, at once the greatest and the most difficult of literary effects)? First, there is the style. In it, everything is heightened; by sheer audacity, sheer refusal to be tight-lipped about a [793/794] world that sets one's teeth on edge (what Hemingway, the brave, lacked the courage to do), Fitzgerald is able to color the face of death, to turn the death agony into a gorgeous dance.

Then there is Nick, who is more than just a clever manipulation of point of view. When we finish the last page we have no certainty that Nick will escape the blind desire which drives the others, but we are sure that he has, at least, seen life and glory. And that, surely, is no small achievement, for he has made us see it too.

Finally, there is the incredible tightness in plotting, characterization and detail. In Joyce's sense of the word, *The Great Gatsby* is one of the few novels *written* in our language. In concentration of meaning, nuance, and effect, there are few books in any language with which to compare it. In haunting scenes, there are few literary works which live so long in one's memory: Jordan and Daisy floating through the air on a stationary couch; the overturned auto with Owl-Eyes slowly climbing out to proclaim that he does not know how it happened, that he doesn't drive, and that he wasn't trying to drive; the director endlessly bending to kiss the starlet at Gatsby's party, thrilling Daisy with arrested sexuality; Daisy crying into

Gatsby's shirts; the scene in the hotel room where Daisy can only say that she "loved [Gatsby] *too.*"

Fitzgerald's life, indeed we know by now, was wasteful. He cracked up in the full glare of publicity in the pages of *Esquire.* His wife went mad, and he drank quantities of liquor. Moreover, he died young, and left one unfinished, not very interesting novel, and more trash than any author of equal gifts. His work was fragmentary, frequently self-indulgent, too often frivolous. He was the "authority of failure"; but that is after all, not so small a portion of reality. When he had learned enough about his subject, he had the craft to make a masterpiece of it.

The Great Gatsby is a novel for which a writer might give his life.

Patterns in *The Great Gatsby* *

VICTOR A. DOYNO (1937–   ) is an associate professor of English at the State University of New York at Buffalo. He has published essays on Milton, Mark Twain, Robert Lowell, and the art of the film and is completing a critical edition of a Renaissance sonnet-sequence. This essay grew out of a freshman class in which the author was teaching *The Great Gatsby*.

When Fitzgerald was revising a scene at the end of the second chapter of *The Great Gatsby*, he added some phrases which have no apparent relevance to the novel. The scene involves a photographer showing an album to the narrator, Nick Carraway. Fitzgerald inserted four picture titles: "Beauty and the Beast . . . Loneliness . . . Old Grocery Horse . . . Brook'n Bridge. . . ." Why did he, when preparing the novel for the printer, wish to insert these titles? What function does this seemingly irrelevant list have? A clue to the answer lies, I think, in two letters from Fitzgerald to his editor, Maxwell Perkins. In 1922, after he began planning his third novel, Fitzgerald wrote that he wanted "to write something *new*—something extraordinary and beautiful and simple & intricately patterned." And in 1924, speaking about his difficulties in composition, Fitzgerald said:

So in my new novel I'm thrown directly on purely creative work—not trashy imaginings as in my stories but the sustained imagination of a sincere yet radiant world. So I tread slowly and carefully & at times in considerable distress. This book will be a consciously artistic achievement & must depend on that as the 1st books did not.[1]

These statements suggest that a careful study of the text might reveal *The Great*

Gatsby to be indeed "a consciously artistic achievement" that is "intricately patterned."

Fortunately, this close study of the patterning can draw upon a wealth of material: the holograph pencil version, the galley proofs, and the extensive galley revisions. Portions of the holograph text include several stages of composition: some parts of this version, usually those written in a large hand, are extensively revised early drafts; those parts written in a small, precise hand with fewer revisions seem to be transcriptions of earlier drafts. The holograph text was revised, presumably in a lost typescript; the revised readings can be found in the galley proofs. This material, with the galley [415/416] revisions, allows us to see that the patterns which appear in the final text are often the result of laborious revisions.[2]

Several patterns in the novel are obvious. The first three chapters present the different settings and social groupings of three evenings: dinner and strained

[2] I am very grateful to the Firestone Library of Princeton University and to Mr. Alexander P. Clark, curator of manuscripts, for aiding my study, and to Mrs. Samuel J. Lanahan and Mr. Ivan Von Auw, her agent, for permitting manuscript and galley proof quotation. Similarly, I am indebted to Charles Scribner's Sons, publishers of *The Great Gatsby* (New York, 1925), for permission to quote the text of the first edition. As a convenience I shall also cite in italics the page number of the corresponding section of the widely available Scribner's paperback edition. All references will be included parenthetically.

[1] Both letters are quoted by Andrew Turnbull, *Scott Fitzgerald* (New York, 1962) pp. 146-147.

*Victor A. Doyno, "Patterns in *The Great Gatsby*," *Modern Fiction Studies*, XII (Winter 1966-67), 415-426. *Modern Fiction Studies*, © 1969 by Purdue Research Foundation, Lafayette, Indiana. Reprinted with the permission of the author and the publisher.

conversation at Tom Buchanan's house, drinks and a violent argument at Myrtle's apartment, a party and loutish behavior at Gatsby's mansion. Fitzgerald calls attention to this pattern when he has Nick say, "Reading over what I have written so far, I see I have given the impression that the events of three nights several weeks apart were all that absorbed me" (p. 68, *56*). Similarly, through Nick, Fitzgerald emphasizes the patterning of situation which presents two very different characters, George Wilson and Tom Buchanan, as cuckolded husbands: "I stared at him and then at Tom, who had made a parallel discovery less than an hour before" (p. 148, *124*). Clearly Fitzgerald is aware of these patterns and wishes the reader to share this awareness.

There are, moreover, numerous less obvious patterns in the novel which have the important functions of deepening characterization, shaping the reader's attitudes toward events and major themes, and creating and controlling unity and emphasis. Those patternings which affect characterization include the repetition of dialogue, gesture, and detail. For example, Daisy's speech is used to characterize her in two comparable scenes which are far apart. Fitzgerald indicates the relation between the scenes by presenting the same tableau as Nick enters: Daisy and Jordan Baker, both in white, wind-blown dresses, lounge on a couch on a wine or crimson rug. The first scene (in Chapter I) occurs as Nick renews his acquaintance with Daisy; the second (in Chapter VII) when Gatsby intends to reclaim Daisy. In the latter scene Jordan and Daisy say together, "We can't move," and the speech is perfectly appropriate to the hot weather. In the first scene Daisy says, as her first direct statement in the novel, "I'm p-paralyzed with happiness." This statement, however, was inserted after the second scene was written, since it first occurs in the galley proof. This inserted statement, besides presenting an apt characterization of Daisy, likens her feelings at

the beginning to those which she has shortly before the argument about leaving Tom. Through this repetition Fitzgerald emphasizes Daisy's lack of growth within the novel. [416/417]

Fitzgerald also deepens characterization by the repetition of gesture. Nick says that when he first saw Gatsby, "he gave a sudden intimation that he was content to be alone—he stretched out his arms toward the dark water in a curious way, and, far as I was from him, I could have sworn he was trembling" (p. 26, *21*). This picture of Gatsby in the coda of Chapter I presents him with an air of mystery, and in the reader's memory he stands etched reaching for the green light. Gatsby's mysteriousness is transformed later in the novel when he tells Nick that as he was leaving Louisville he went to the open vestibule of the coach and "stretched out his hand desperately as if to snatch only a wisp of air, to save a fragment of the spot that she had made lovely for him" (p. 183, *153*). This repetition of the reaching gesture explains the first picture of Gatsby, establishes the durability of his devotion, and thereby evokes sympathy for one who loves so fervently.

The characterization of Gatsby's rival, Tom Buchanan, is influenced by the repetition of details. Arthur Mizener has noted that Fitzgerald can "sum up all he wants to say about Tom" in his last meeting with Nick.[3] An examination of the composition of the passage leads to a fuller explanation of Mizener's insight and an increased respect for Fitzgerald's craftsmanship. The manuscript version reads: "Then he went into the jewellry store *for a* to buy a *pair of c* pearl necklace *and* or pair of cuff buttons," (MS. VIII, 42).[4] The evidence indicates that Fitzgerald probably planned for a moment simply to mention the cuff links, then decided to begin with the necklace. What is gained by the inclusion of a pearl

---

[3] *The Far Side of Paradise* (Boston, 1949), p. 174.
[4] The cancelled *c* is followed by what appears to be the first vertical curve of a *u*.

necklace? Tom's wife, Daisy, already has the pearl necklace which was her wedding gift; the necklace is probably not for Daisy; perhaps Tom has found a replacement for his dead mistress. This meeting, which also associates Tom with cuff buttons, occurs directly after Nick's condemnation of the Buchanans for their callous inhumanity: "they smashed up things and creatures and then retreated back into their money or their vast carelessness . . ." (p. 216, *180*). Fitzgerald may have realized that the inhumanity of their attitude could be subtly reinforced by an unfavorable association with the cuff buttons. At any rate he decided to introduce an anterior reference to cuff buttons. Accordingly the galley proofs contain a passage not in the manuscript version in which Meyer Wolfsheim mentions his cuff buttons and calls them "Finest specimens of human molars." The attitude of gross inhumanity latent in this remark carries over to Tom. With the insertion of this unfavorable association for cuff buttons, Fitzgerald decided to alter **[417/418]** the syntax of the later reference. The galley proof version is: "Then he went into the jewelry store to buy a pearl necklace, or perhaps only a pair of cuff buttons,". This version, which created a deceptively casual tone while subordinating the cuff links, was modified when Fitzgerald, in revising the galleys, changed the commas to dashes and raised the importance of the alternative (Galley sheet 57). The final elaborated version conveys, in a devastatingly casual tone, oblique references of approximately equal emphasis to Tom's lust and to his inhumanity.

And this passage is not the only implicit character assassination of Tom brought about by a patterning of details. While leaving Gatsby's first party, Nick observes the aftermath of a car accident in which the vehicle is "violently shorn of one wheel." The confusion and discordant noise of the scene create an unfavorable impression which is intensified when Nick tells of the driver's stupid, irresponsible drunkenness. With this scene in mind we can easily visualize an accident which Jordan Baker describes only briefly in the next chapter:

A week after I left Santa Barbara Tom ran into a wagon on the Ventura road one night, and ripped a front wheel off his car. The girl who was with him got into the papers, too, because her arm was broken—she was one of the chambermaids in the Santa Barbara Hotel. (p. 93, *78*)

The accident is primarily another indictment of Tom's lust, but the repetition of detail—the loss of a wheel in a night accident—associates Tom with the irresponsible drunken driver.

Besides adding depth to characterization, patterning also shapes the reader's attitudes toward events and themes in the novel. As it happens, this kind of repetition also includes a case of poor driving. Surprisingly few commentators have criticized Fitzgerald for the highly improbable plot manipulation whereby Daisy runs down her husband's mistress. The reader's uncritical acceptance of the accident is influenced, I suggest, by something Nick says in the coda of Chapter III about his relationship with Jordan Baker: "It was on that same house party that we had a curious conversation about driving a car. It started because she passed so close to some workmen that our fender flicked a button on one man's coat" (p. 71, *59*). This near-accident subliminally prepares the reader to think of Daisy's hitting Myrtle not as an unbelievable wrenching of probability but as a possible event. After all, Jordan nearly did a similar thing. Nick's ensuing conversation with Jordan reveals his attitude toward carelessness. This dialogue seems to be relevant only to Nick and Jordan's friendship, but the casual banter presents the same diction and attitude found in Nick's final condemnation of Daisy and Tom for their **[418/419]** carelessness. In this case patterning leads the reader to accept both an improbable event and the narrator's final judgment of it.

The reader's attitude is more frequently shaped by an ironic juxtaposition of such themes as romantic idealization and realistic disillusionment.[5] For example, Nick learns from Myrtle of her first meeting with Tom Buchanan on the train to New York, and as she relates the story her limited word choice, additive syntax, and rushing narration establish both her character and her attitude toward the pickup:

"It was on the two little seats facing each other that are always the last ones left on the train. I was going up to New York to see my sister and spend the night. He had on a dress suit and patent leather shoes, and I couldn't keep my eyes off him, but every time he looked at me I had to pretend to be looking at the advertisement over his head. When we came into the station he was next to me, and his white shirt-front pressed against my arm, and so I told him I'd have to call a policeman, but he knew I lied. I was so excited that when I got into a taxi with him I didn't hardly know I wasn't getting into a subway train. All I kept thinking about, over and over, was 'You can't live forever; you can't live forever.'" (p. 43, *36*)

The style and growing desperation of tone suggest that Myrtle is a socially and morally limited character who acted in an understandable way because of her romantic expectation. But her romantic opinion of her meeting with Tom contrasts with another version of the same situation which is told in a realistic style from a masculine and definitely unromantic point of view when Nick tells this tale of the commuter train:

The next day was broiling, almost the last, certainly the warmest, of the summer. As my train emerged from the tunnel into sunlight, only the hot whistles of the National Biscuit Company broke the simmering hush at noon. The straw seats of the car hovered on the edge of combustion; the woman next to me perspired delicately for a while into her white shirtwaist, and then, as her newspaper dampened under her fingers, lapsed despairingly into deep heat with a desolate cry. Her pocket-book slapped to the floor.

"Oh, my!" she gasped.

I picked it up with a weary bend and handed it back to her, holding it at arm's length and by the extreme tip of the corners to indicate that I had no designs upon it—but every one near by, including the woman, suspected me just the same.

"Hot!" said the conductor to familiar faces. "Some weather! . . . Hot! . . . Hot! . . . Hot! . . . Is it hot enough for you? Is it hot? Is it . . .?"

My commutation ticket came back to me with a dark stain from his hand. That any one should care in this heat whose flushed lips he kissed, whose head made damp the pajama pocket over his heart! (pp. 136-137, *114-115*) [419/420]

Nick's scornful attitude toward romance refers, in context, primarily to the love of Gatsby for Daisy, but the situation parallels Myrtle's first meeting with Tom and reflects a disillusioned view of such an event. Fitzgerald has controlled his material to make each of the attitudes—Myrtle's desperate romanticism and Nick's uncomfortable realism—valid in its own moment of presentation; but in the context of the novel each thematic attitude toward love is juxtaposed to and qualifies the other.

A similar attempt to influence the reader's attitudes occurs with the use of analogous scenes in the codas of Chapters V and VII. And, as shall later become clear, the positioning of the scenes lends them importance. In each case Nick sees a tableau of Daisy sitting and talking with a man who is holding her hand. In Chapter V, of course, the man is Gatsby, who has just re-won Daisy and is experiencing sublime happiness. Nick says:

As I watched him he adjusted himself a little, visibly. His hand took hold of hers, and as she said something low in his ear he turned toward her with a rush of emotion. I think that voice held him most, with its fluctuating, feverish warmth, because it couldn't be over-dreamed—that voice was a deathless song.

They had forgotten me, but Daisy glanced up and held out her hand; Gatsby didn't know me now at all. I looked once more at them and they looked back at me, remotely, possessed by intense life. Then I went out of the room and down the marble steps into the rain, leaving them there together. (p. 116, *97*)

However, Fitzgerald balances this moment of romantic bliss with a parallel but decidedly realistic description of Daisy after the auto accident:

Daisy and Tom were sitting opposite each other at the kitchen table, with a plate of cold

---

[5] For a discussion of the importance of these themes throughout Fitzgerald's career see the unpubl. diss. (Columbia, 1958) by John R. Kuehl, "Scott Fitzgerald: Romantic and Realist" (L. C. card no. Mic. 59-747).

fried chicken between them, and two bottles of ale. He was talking intently across the table at her, and in his earnestness his hand had fallen upon and covered her own. Once in a while she looked up at him and nodded in agreement.

They weren't happy, and neither of them had touched the chicken or the ale—and yet they weren't unhappy either. There was an unmistakable air of natural intimacy about the picture, and anybody would have said that they were conspiring together. (pp. 174-175, *146*)

This second scene signals, of course, Gatsby's loss of Daisy. In addition, the repetition destroys the uniqueness of Gatsby's moment of happiness and thereby makes the reader question the validity of his romantic idealization.

The reader's attitude toward romantic idealization and realistic disillusionment is also shaped by the elaborate patterning of a natural enough event—a man and woman kissing. In Chapter VI Nick tells of the movie director bending over his star, who had been described [**420/421**] as "a scarcely human orchid of a woman": "They were still under the white-plum tree and their faces were touching except for a pale, thin ray of moonlight between. It occurred to me that he had been very slowly bending toward her all evening to attain this proximity, and even while I watched I saw him stoop one ultimate degree and kiss at her cheek" (p. 129, *108*). Although the setting is described romantically, the event itself is narrated with touches of sarcasm in the involved syntax, elevated diction ("attain this proximity"), and precision of word choice ("kiss *at* her cheek"). The presentation of this kiss, which does not involve any of the major characters, prepares the reader to adopt a complex attitude toward the other kisses. In the coda of the same chapter, Nick relates Gatsby's description of kissing Daisy. Once more Nick's incongruous word choice, e.g., "romp," helps give the passage a peculiar texture.[6] The dominant tone of the passage is, however, cer-

---

[6] The complete passage, which begins with the setting and is too long to quote, has several complicating aspects; it also includes allusions to such religious matters as Jacob's ladder and the incarnation.

tainly one of romantic idealization, culminating in the flower simile:

> His heart beat faster and faster as Daisy's white face came up to his own. He knew that when he kissed this girl, and forever wed his unutterable visions to her perishable breath, his mind would never romp again like the mind of God. So he waited, listening for a moment longer to the tuning-fork that had been struck upon a star. Then he kissed her. At his lips' touch she blossomed for him like a flower and the incarnation was complete. (p. 134, *112*)

The idealization of Gatsby's description is touching, but Nick's sarcastic insertions are not the only means of qualifying the romantic point of view. The reader's attitude toward the kiss has already been influenced by the movie star's kiss and, more importantly, by a similar incident described from a less romantic point of view. In the coda of Chapter IV Nick says:

> We passed a barrier of dark trees, and then the façade of Fifty-ninth Street, a block of delicate pale light, beamed down into the park. Unlike Gatsby and Tom Buchanan, I had no girl whose disembodied face floated along the dark cornices and blinding signs, and so I drew up the girl beside me, tighteninig my arms. Her wan, scornful mouth smiled, and so I drew her up again closer, this time to my face. (p. 97, *81*)

Throughout this sardonic description Nick has certainly reserved his emotional commitment; neither his motivation nor his choice of words like "scornful" conveys idealistic enthusiasm. As in the other passages the setting is described, and Nick even calls attention to the relation between the kisses by saying "Unlike Gatsby. . . ." Furthermore, the [**421/422**] relationship between the kisses in the codas of Chapter IV and VI is subtly emphasized early in Chapter VII, when Tom goes out to make drinks and leaves Daisy alone with Gatsby in front of Nick and Jordan:

> . . . she got up and went over to Gatsby and pulled his face down, kissing him on the mouth.
> "You know I love you," she murmured.
> "You forget there's a lady present," said Jordan.

Daisy looked around doubtfully.
"You kiss Nick too."
"What a low, vulgar girl!" (p. 139, *116*)

In this patterning Fitzgerald has presented in order Nick's disenchanted personal account, his sarcastic third-person narration, and Gatsby's romantic, personal version of a kiss; in addition, Fitzgerald includes a scene which draws a parallel between the kisses involving major characters. The sheer idealization of Gatsby's love is qualified by this elaborate repetition, and the reader develops a complex attitude toward a major theme.

With all this evidence of patterning in mind, we may establish still a third function by returning to our original question. Beyond combining the romantic and the mundane, what possible relevance have the picture titles, "Beauty and the Beast . . . Loneliness . . . Old Grocery Horse . . . Brook'n Bridge . . ."? The first title, of course, refers to the well-known fairy tale or folk tale in which a lowly creature regains his former princely condition by the transforming power of a beautiful girl's kiss.[7] Gatsby's background is analogous to this tale, since he was "a son of God" (p. 118, *99*) whose imagination had never accepted his mother and father as his real parents. The transformation of James Gatz to Jay Gatsby was, of course, gradual, but when Gatsby kissed Daisy "the incarnation was complete" (p. 134, *112*): she embodied his dreams, and his princely status was confirmed by the love of "the king's daughter" (p. 144, *120*). And Gatsby's casual remark that in Europe he "lived like a young rajah" (p. 79, *66*) seems quite appropriate to the prince motif.

The next title, "Loneliness," calls to mind Nick's first sight of Gatsby, when "he gave a sudden intimation that he was content to be alone." Several references to Gatsby's loneliness follow: he is "standing alone on the marble steps" (p. 60, *50*)

during his party, and Nick mentions the "complete isolation" of the host (p. 68, *56*). The scenes of Gatsby's vigil outside the Buchanans' and of his body's [422/ 423] floating in the pool also reinforce the motif of loneliness. Gatsby, when alive, seems quite content with his isolation, but Nick, in a contrapuntal fashion, frequently refers to his own loneliness in terms of discomfort or unhappiness. Nick's dissatisfaction with loneliness makes Gatsby's satisfaction in isolation more striking, more mystic.

Since these motifs sufficiently account for the insertion, admittedly very tenuous suggestions about the last two titles may be offered. The word *grocery* occurs twice in connection with financial necessity. Nick, when he is preparing to leave for the Midwest, sells his car to the grocer. And Tom Buchanan scoffs at Gatsby's financial and social inferiority when he first knew Daisy by saying, "and I'll be damned if I see how you got within a mile of her unless you brought the groceries to the back door" (pp. 157-158, *132*). The other two words of the title also possess some relevance to Gatsby's inferiority. Tom's wealth, of course, is old and established, while Gatsby's richness is quite *nouveau*. Tom's wealth and aristocratic background are indicated by his transportation of his string of polo ponies, and Gatsby's social ineptitude appears in Chapter VI when Tom and the haughty Mr. Sloane dispose of a dinner invitation Gatsby should have refused by riding away without him. There is, then, some evidence that the third title may be a complex and subtle reference to the financial and social differences between Tom and Gatsby.

The last of the titles, "Brook'n Bridge," is even less obvious and has no relevance—unless we consider Fitzgerald's aural imagination and the context of the title within the novel. The brilliance of the catalogue of guests' names at the beginning of Chapter IV is a critical commonplace, but the person who reads these

---

[7] For another example of the use of folklore in the novel see Tristram P. Coffin, "Gatsby's Fairy Lover," *Midwest Folklore* X (Summer 1960), 79-85.

names silently misses a good bit. One must read aloud to appreciate names such as "the Dancies," "Gus Waize," "young Brewer," "Miss Haag," and "Miss Claudia Hip." That Fitzgerald's imagination upon occasion worked aurally is beyond question. The title "Brook'n Bridge" occurs just after Tom has broken Myrtle's nose and may be a punning reference to this incident and thus to the leitmotif of violence in the novel. Each chapter from the first, with Daisy's bruised finger, to the last, with Tom's story of Wilson's forced entry, includes some sort of violence. The only exception to this, of course, is the more or less idyllic Chapter V, in which Daisy and Gatsby are reunited.

Fitzgerald's decision to insert these picture titles in the version used for type setting is quite significant. The titles serve as an index of leitmotifs within the novel. By picking these motifs from the many others in the book, Fitzgerald has singled them out for emphasis, and the presentation in one group subtly helps create unity in the novel. [423/424]

In addition, the placing of this index in the coda of Chapter II contributes to the structural patterning for unity and emphasis. The conclusion of Chapter III, we remember, is also of particular importance, since by presenting Jordan's near-accident with the discussion of carelessness it prepares for what is to follow. Fitzgerald consciously uses this emphatic position at each chapter's end to call attention to major elements of the novel and frequently creates relations between the structural units.

For example, the codas of Chapters IV and VI present Nick's and Gatsby's versions of a kiss. Fitzgerald's awareness of this patterning is implied in the extensive revisions which brought Gatsby's story to its present parallel position. The story appears in manuscript in the beginning of an early version of Chapter VI and in galley proof at the beginning of Chapter VII (MS. VI. 3; Galley 35). In the galley version Fitzgerald has added a paragraph

about a forgotten phrase in Nick's mind. This paragraph dealing with the forgotten phrase was originally written to follow Gatsby's singing of a song he composed in his youth, and Fitzgerald shifted the paragraph, with only a minor change, to its present position after Gatsby's kiss. This shift serves two purposes: it comments upon Gatsby's story, and it creates another analogy to Nick's narration of a kiss, because Nick also had a phrase in mind when he kissed Jordan. The similarities of the events and the phrases were then put into an unmistakable relationship when, in revising the galleys, Fitzgerald shifted Gatsby's narration and the paragraph about the forgotten phrase to a position parallel to Nick's. Thus the codas of IV and VI help unify the book by treating two similar events, and control thematic emphasis by presenting contrasting points of view toward romance. And, of course, the codas of V and VII, which picture first Gatsby and then Tom holding Daisy's hand, also function in this way.

The patterning of alternate codas is tightened to one of direct connection in the last three chapters. In VII and VIII, Gatsby is pictured as alone, first on his vigil and then in his pool. In the one chapter Gatsby is the faithful, devoted, vigilant protector of his lady. In the next he is dead. This contrast, a commentary on romantic idealization, works within the leitmotif of "Loneliness." A similar commentary also links the eighth with the ninth and final coda. At the novel's conclusion Nick likens the human struggle to "boats against the current." And the previous coda presents the image of Gatsby, his struggle over, on a boat going against the current, as the faint wind and a cluster of leaves disturb the course of his mattress in the current of the pool.

The last coda must be discussed in conjunction with the first, since [424/425] their composition is related. The conclusion of the first chapter was once very different. For example, the manuscript version does not mention that Gatsby was "content to be alone," nor does it include the symbolic green light. Both these insertions were made, however, by the time the novel was ready for typesetting. The insertion of the green light picks up other uses of green as a symbol of romance which occur later in the novel, such as the "green card" which Daisy jokes about as entitling Nick to a kiss, the "long green tickets" which carried young Nick to Midwestern parties, and the "fresh, green breast of the new world" of the conclusion. The description of Gatsby reaching out was not, however, the original end of the chapter. The manuscript first chapter ends with a passage we now find at the novel's conclusion. Only by cutting away this material did Fitzgerald raise the importance of the picture of Gatsby on his lawn, reaching toward Daisy.

It is crucial to a complete understanding of the novel that we realize that this portion of the conclusion was composed early in the writing process:

And as the moon rose higher the inessential houses began to melt away until gradually I became aware of the old island here that flowered once for Dutch sailors' eyes—a fresh, green breast of the new world. Its vanished trees, the trees that had made way for Gatsby's house, had once pandered in whispers to the last and greatest of all human dreams; for a transitory enchanted moment man must have held his breath in the presence of this continent, compelled into an aesthetic contemplation he neither understood nor desired, face to face for the last time in history with something commensurate to his capacity for wonder. (pp. 217-218, *182*)

The references to the past in this section and in the remainder of the conclusion raise the thematic importance of Gatsby's "can't repeat the past? . . . Why of course

you can!" (pp. 133, *111*) and of Tom's conversion of a garage into a stable. Both Gatsby and Tom are, each in his own way, borne back into the past. From the early composition of this section we can also surmise that several of the leitmotifs mentioned in the conclusion, such as the notion of pandering and the Edenic conception of America, may have been in Fitzgerald's mind from the beginning.

Similarly, the "new world" seen by the Dutch sailors was already in Fitzgerald's mind when he wrote of the "new world" which Gatsby had seen shortly before being killed by Wilson in the coda of Chapter VIII:

He must have looked up at an unfamiliar sky through frightening leaves and shivered as he found what a grotesque thing a rose is and how raw the sunlight was upon the scarcely created grass. A new world, material without being real, [425/426] where poor ghosts, breathing dreams like air, drifted fortuitously about . . . like that ashen, fantastic figure gliding toward him through the amorphous trees. (p. 194, *162*)

Fitzgerald's decision to present these radically different "new worlds"—Nick's imputation of Gatsby's realistic disillusionment and the Dutch sailors' romantic idealization—in the codas to the last two chapters reveals once more his consummate use of patterning.

It is clear, I think, that Fitzgerald fulfilled his intention to write a "consciously artistic achievement." And a knowledge of the ways in which the novel is "intricately patterned," from minor details up to large structural units, partially explains how Fitzgerald created a novel that is "something extraordinary and beautiful and simple."

II. THE AMERICAN DREAM

[The Fuller-McGee Case] *

HENRY DAN PIPER (1918–   ). For biographical information see "The Untrimmed Christmas Tree," p. 93.

Almost every Sunday the society columns and rotogravure sections of the New York newspapers carried accounts of wealthy young Mid-westerners like the Buchanans who had moved to Long Island to enjoy the yachting, polo, and other expensive pastimes of the very rich. The financial sections of the same papers almost as regularly reported the mysterious appearance of Gatsby-like figures who had suddenly emerged from the West with millions of dollars at their command. A typical example was Charles Victor Bob, who turned up in Wall Street from Colorado, claiming to be the owner of tin mines in South America and copper mines in Canada. He spent money like water, throwing lavish parties for Broadway celebrities who had never heard of him before, and selling gilt-edged mining securities. He was finally indicted on a six-million-dollar mail fraud charge, but, in spite of the evidence, three successive juries refused to convict him. So far as the Twenties were concerned, anyone as rich, colorful, and successful as Charles Victor Bob deserved a better fate than jail.[5]

Knowing of Fitzgerald's interest in "success" stories like this, his friends collected them for him. The outskirts of Great Neck, where palatial estates fronted on Long Island Sound, made an especially good hunting ground. "He [Ring Lardner] told me of a newcomer who'd made money in the drug business—not dope but the regular line," Max Perkins wrote the Fitzgeralds shortly after they went to France:[6]

This gentleman had evidently taken to Ring. One morning he called early with another man and a girl and Ring was not dressed. [114/115] But he hurried down, unshaven. He [Ring] introduced to the *girl only*, and said he was sorry to appear that way but didn't want to keep them waiting while he shaved.

At this point the drug man signals to the other, who goes to the car for a black bag and from it produces razors, strops, etc., etc., and publicly shaves Ring. *This* was the drug man's private barber; the girl was his private manicurist. But as he was lonely he had made them also his companions. Ring declares this is true!

Lardner himself sent the Fitzgeralds an account of a Fourth of July celebration that might have come from the pages of *The Great Gatsby*:[7]

On the Fourth of July, Ed Wynn gave a fireworks display at his new estate in the Grenwolde division. After the children had been sent home, everybody got pie-eyed and I never enjoyed a night so much. All the Great Neck professionals did their stuff, the former chorus girls danced, Blanche Ring kissed me and sang, etc. The party lasted through the next day and wound up next evening at Tom Meighan's where the principal entertainment was provided by Lila Lee and another dame, who did some very funny imitations (really funny) in the moonlight on the tennis court. We would ask them to imitate Houdini, or Leon Errol, or Will Rogers or Elsie

[5] *Time*, December 11, 1944, 84.

[6] MP to FSF, August 8, 1924, PF.
[7] Ring Lardner to FSF, August 8, 1925, PF.

*From Chapter VII, "The Great Gatsby: Finding a Hero," in Henry Dan Piper, F. Scott Fitzgerald: A Critical Portrait (New York: Holt, Rinehart and Winston, Inc.), copyright © 1962, 1965 by Henry Dan Piper. Reprinted with permission of Holt, Rinehart and Winston, Inc.

Janis; the imitations were all the same, consisting of an aesthetic dance which ended with an unaesthetic fall onto the tennis court.

Of all Fitzgerald's Long Island neighbors, the one whose outlines are most clearly discernible in *The Great Gatsby* was a certain Great Neck resident by the name of Edward M. Fuller. This was the Fuller of the "Fuller-McGee" case which Fitzgerald told Perkins he had studied until he felt he knew Gatsby better than he knew his own child. A thirty-nine-year-old bachelor and man about town, Fuller was president of the New York brokerage firm of E.M. Fuller and Co., with offices at 50 Broad Street. Of obscure origins, he had emerged suddenly on Wall Street in 1916 as a member of the Consolidated Stock Exchange and the head of his own company. Before long, he was being mentioned in the newspapers as one of a fashionable set that included Gertrude Vanderbilt, Charles A. Stoneham, the owner of the New York Giants baseball team, and Walter B. Silkworth, prominent clubman and president of the Consolidated Exchange. Fuller, an aviation enthusiast, was one of the first Long Island residents to commute weekly by airplane [115/ 116] from his Great Neck estate to Atlantic City while the horse-racing season was on.[8]

On June 22, 1922, however, E.M. Fuller and Co. declared itself bankrupt, with some six million dollars in debts and assets of less than seventy thousand dollars. Fuller and his vice-president, William F. McGee, were promptly indicted on a twelve-count charge that included operating a "bucket shop"—i.e., illegally gambling with their customers' funds. It took four trials to put them behind prison bars, and it is significant that the first opened two months after the Fitzgeralds moved to Great Neck, and ended several days later with a hung jury. The second trial,

[8] The histories of E.M. Fuller and Co., of Euward Fuller, and of his business associates, can be traced through the New York *Times Annual Index*, 1920–28 and the annual index, 1922–24, of the *Commercial and Financial Chronicle*; for Fuller's flying exploits see New York *Times*, July 11, 1921, 11:3.

in December, ended in a mistrial after the state admitted its inability to produce a key witness, who had unaccountably disappeared. The third, which began the following April, 1923, also resulted in a hung jury. During this trial it was revealed that Fuller's lawyer, a prominent New York attorney named William J. Fallon, had tried to bribe one of the jurors. For this Fallon was subsequently convicted and imprisoned, disgraced for life.

During this third trial, a leading state's witness was temporarily kidnapped by another of Fuller's attorneys, and vital records and other evidence also disappeared. By now the "Fuller-McGee" case was being featured on the front pages of the New York newspapers, and the fourth trial opened on June 11, 1923, amid a rash of rumors that Fuller and McGee were going to throw themselves on the mercy of the court and make a full confession. A deal had been arranged, it was reported, whereby they were to receive light sentences in exchange for confessions implicating a number of prominent New York officials, politicians, and businessmen with whom they had been associated in their financial ventures. Instead, however, both Fuller and McGee merely pleaded guilty to the more innocuous charges and were promptly sentenced to five years in Sing Sing—a sentence that was subsequently reduced to twelve months for "good behavior."

By coincidence, McGee's wife, a former New York showgirl named Louise Groody, arrived in Paris the same day that Fuller and her husband confessed their guilt. According to the Paris newspapers, Mrs. McGee disembarked from the liner at Cherbourg covered with diamonds and other jewels valued at several hundred thousand dollars. It was subsequently revealed that she had cashed a check of her husband's for $300,000 just a few hours before E.M. Fuller and Company went bankrupt.

Actually, the state of New York had

difficulty establishing conclusive proof for most of the charges brought against Fuller and McGee. None- [116/117] theless, it was obvious that they were part of a tangled web of corruption that included some of New York's wealthiest and most powerful business and political leaders. Fuller, according to his testimony, owed his business success mainly to his friendship with Charles A. Stoneham, another mysterious Gatsby-like figure who began life as a board boy in a broker's office and rose swiftly in the Wall Street financial hierarchy, emerging eventually as president of the brokerage house of C.A. Stoneham and Company. In 1921, he had sold out his firm's interest to E.M. Fuller and Co. and three other investment houses (E.D. Dier and Co., E.H. Clarke and Co., and Dillon and Co.) and plunged heavily into big-time gambling and sporting enterprises. Besides his controlling interest in the New York Giants baseball club, Stoneham owned a race track, a gambling casino, a newspaper, and other associated interests in Havana. By 1923, all four of the firms which had bought the assets of Stoneham and Co. had gone bankrupt, with debts totaling more than twenty million dollars.[9]

Fuller testified under oath that, after the dissolution of Stoneham and Co., Charles Stoneham had become a silent partner in the Fuller firm; he further claimed that his friend had advanced some two hundred thousand dollars in checks drawn against the Giants club, in a fruitless attempt to stave off Fuller and Co.'s impending bankruptcy. Stoneham insisted, however, that the money had merely been a private loan to Fuller, which he had advanced at the request of his friend Thomas F. Foley, former New York sheriff and Tammany Hall official. Foley, who had himself loaned Fuller $15,000, explained that he had come to Fuller's

assistance purely out of friendship for one of McGee's former wives, a certain Nellie Sheean, who had remarried and was now living in Paris (the residence, also, of the current Mrs. McGee).

Fuller and Company, it turned out, had a rather dubious financial history. In 1920, the firm was indicted for having systematically defrauded its customers over the past three years by sale of worthless oil securities, but the case was thrown out of court on the grounds of insufficient evidence. On February 24, 1923, while awaiting his third bankruptcy trial, Fuller was arrested on another charge along with seven other men and women, most of whom had criminal records. They were seized in a suite of the Hotel Embassy, where they were accused of having attempted to sell fraudulent securities over the telephone. It was further claimed by the police that Fuller and his friends were planning to organize a new securities firm for the purpose of selling worthless stocks. This case, however, was also dismissed by the court because of lack of evidence. [117/118]

On June 13, 1922, Fuller had again been involved with the police, but under more romantic circumstances. On this occasion, his Broad Street offices had been invaded by "a fashionably dressed young lady" who, according to the New York Times, had threatened Fuller with severe bodily harm. Later, in the police court, the woman identified herself as Nellie Burke, twenty-seven, of 245 West Seventy-fifth Street. Miss Burke, who at the time of her arrest was wearing $20,000 worth of what she told newspaper reporters was "borrowed" jewelry, testified that she had become acquainted with Fuller in 1915, in the bar of the Hotel Knickerbocker. Their subsequent friendship had terminated in a breach-of-promise suit which she had brought against him in 1921. On June sixth of that year, she said, she had been visited by Fuller's friend and business associate, the notorious Arnold Rothstein, who had promised her $10,000 if

[9] Feature article on Charles Stoneham, New York Times, September 9, 1923, VIII:2:1, see also Gene Fowler, The Great Mouthpiece: A Life Story of William J. Fallon (New York, Blue Ribbon Books, 1931), 326-340.

she would sign a paper dropping the suit and agreeing not to pester Fuller any more. She had signed the paper and received $5,000 from Rothstein, but the rest of the money had been withheld. Her visit to Fuller's office the following June had, she claimed, been merely to collect the $5,000 in cash still due her. The magistrate found her guilty of assault but agreed to suspend sentence if she would promise not to give Fuller any more trouble. (Fuller's failure to pay her the additional $5,000 was explained several days later, on June twenty-second, when his firm went into bankruptcy!)

Many intimations of a mysterious tie between Fuller and the gambler, Arnold Rothstein, appeared during the Fuller trials, but the precise nature of this relationship was never fully clarified. Rothstein—"the walking bank, the pawnbroker of the underworld, the fugitive, unhealthy man who sidled along doorways," as Stanley Walker has described him in *The Night Club Era*—testified that Fuller owed him $336,768, most of which consisted of unpaid gambling debts. Fuller countered this statement with the charge that Rothstein personally owed him some $385,000. In subsequent testimony, Rothstein admitted having borrowed $187,000 at one time from Fuller and Co., for which he had put up $25,000 worth of collateral. But Fuller and Co.'s financial records (those that could be located) were so confused that this testimony was of little significance. More informative was Rothstein's statement that Fuller was a shrewd gambler who usually won his bets. Beyond this, Rothstein refused to testify. It was generally suspected that the firm's assets had been squandered by Fuller, McGee, Rothstein, and their friends on racing, baseball, boxing, and other sporting interests. Rothstein was believed to have "fixed" the World Series in 1919, although, again, nothing conclusive was ever proved against him. He was [118/119] also reputed to be engaged in numerous other criminal activities, including the operation of gambling houses, shops selling stolen gems, brothels, and a lucrative bootlegging business—enterprises which did not affect his social standing. Like Fuller, he was frequently seen in the company of respected New York business and society figures, whom' he entertained lavishly in his expensive Park Avenue apartment.[10]

Another interesting friendship disclosed during the trials was that between Edward Fuller and William S. Silkworth, the president of the Consolidated Stock Exchange. For months prior to the collapse of Fuller and Company, Silkworth had repeatedly ignored requests from Fuller's customers that Fuller and Co. be suspended from the exchange for fraudulent practices. Silkworth's brother was one of Fuller's employees, and during the trial Silkworth himself was unable to account for $133,000 in his private banking account—$55,175 of which had been deposited in cash. After Fuller's and McGee's convictions, Silkworth was obliged to resign from his presidency of the Consolidated Exchange.

Fitzgerald borrowed heavily from the newspaper accounts of Fuller's business affairs in creating Gatsby than he had from the details of Fuller's personality. For example, it seems unlikely that Fuller's friendship with Nellie Burke inspired Gatsby's idealistic attachment to Daisy Buchanan. However, Charles Stoneham's paternal interest in young Fuller, as it came out during the trial, is paralleled in the novel by Dan Cody's friendship for Gatsby, and Meyer Wolfshiem obviously was suggested by Fuller's friend, Arnold Rothstein. From the newspaper accounts of Fuller's career Fitzgerald also borrowed such details as Gatsby's airplane, the young stock-and-bond salesmen who haunted his parties, his mysterious connections with "the oil business" as well as his efforts to find a "small town" in which to start up some new and un-

[10] Stanley Walker, *The Night Club Era* (New York, Fred A. Stokes Co., 1933), 10; Lloyd Morris, *Postscript to Yesterday* (New York, Random House, 1947), 75.

mistakably shady enterprise, and his connections with New York society people like Tom Buchanan's friend Walter Chase. "That drug store business was just small change," Tom says after he has investigated Gatsby's business connections with Chase, "but you've got something on now that Walter's afraid to tell me about." What that "something" was Fitzgerald had spelled out in more detail in one of the earlier drafts of *The Great Gatsby*. "Until last summer when Wolfshiem was tried (but not convicted) on charges of grand larceny, forgery, bribery, and dealing in stolen bonds," Nick Carraway says, "I wasn't sure what it all included." Later, however, Fitzgerald omitted this passage, preferring to leave most of the facts about his hero's business affairs to the reader's imagination.[11]

For after all, in a world where people like Tom and Daisy and Jordan [119/ 120] Baker survived and continued to be admired, what difference did it make what crimes Gatsby had committed? Besides, who in the real world of the Twenties, or in the novel that mirrored it, was free of the universal stain? The files of the Fuller-McGee case prove concretely what *The Great Gatsby* implies indirectly: that society leaders, financial tycoons, politicians, magistrates, pimps, jurors, lawyers, baseball players, sheriffs, bond salesmen, debutantes, and prostitutes—all shared in some degree the responsibility for Gatsby's fate.

Gatsby's murder was a grimmer fate than that meted out to Edward Fuller, who successfully delayed going to Sing

Sing for several years and who was then paroled at the end of a year. Even so, Fitzgerald's premonition that careers like Fuller's and Rothstein's were destined to end violently was borne out by later history. Rothstein was fated to die in almost exactly the same manner as Meyer Wolfshiem's friend Rosy Rosenthal, who was shot "three times in his full belly" at four A.M. in the morning outside the old Metropole, where he had spent the night plotting with five of his mobsters. Rothstein was finally killed by an anonymous gunman in 1928 just as he was leaving a conference of big-time bootleggers and gangsters in the Park Central Hotel. In Rothstein's case, however, there were no witnesses to eulogize the manner of his passing, as Wolfshiem did so lyrically for Rosy Rosenthal. Afterwards, the New York police were not only reluctant to investigate Rothstein's murder, but devoted their efforts instead to seizing and suppressing his papers, lest his connections with other prominent New Yorkers be brought to light. Ultimately it was the public hue and cry over the police's inability to solve the mystery of the Rothstein slaying that triggered the historic Seabury investigation into New York City politics a year later, in 1929. As Judge Seabury gradually compiled enough evidence to force the resignation of Mayor Jimmy Walker and his top officials, intimate ties were disclosed between money, politics, sports, crime, and business—ties which Fitzgerald had already described in *Gatsby* some years earlier. The further the 1920's recede, the more that novel emerges as one of the most penetrating criticisms of that incredible decade.

[11] *Gatsby*, 161; pencil draft of *Gatsby* manuscript, 206, Princeton University Library.

[The New York *Times* reports the "Fuller-McGee Case"]

THE NEW YORK TIMES was founded in 1851 as a conservative newspaper but during the 1870's it became famous for its support of reform measures and its exposure of graft and corruption. In 1896 it was purchased by Adolph Ochs and continues to be owned and edited by his descendants and heirs. Since then it has become internationally respected as the most eminent American newspaper.

E. M. FULLER & CO. FAIL; BROKERS OWE OVER A MILLION*

Suspended From Consolidated Stock Exchange for "Reckless Methods."

BOOKS ARE HURRIED AWAY

Reported Turned Over to Receiver Only After Making Condition as to Use.

FULLER A MEX. PETE. LOSER

Concern Has 1,500 Customers Here and 2,100 in Chicago—Branches in Other Cities.

E. M. Fuller & Co., stock brokers, of 50 Broad Street, members of the Consolidated Stock Exchange, failed yesterday.

In a petition in bankruptcy filed in the United States District Court here, assets were tentatively estimated at $250,000 and liabilities at $500,000. No more definite estimate is expected for several days.

Information current in Chicago, following the crash here, was that there were only negligible assets to offset the claims of customers there totaling $1,250,000. This outlook, coupled with the fact that the firm also has branches with many customers in Boston, Cleveland, Pittsburgh and Uniontown, Pa., gave rise to a belief in Wall Street that total losses might be much greater than those intimated in the original petition.

The firm had accounts on its books here of from 1,500 to 1,800 men and women. In Chicago there were 2,100 customers. The number trading with other branches was not disclosed.

"Propaganda against Consolidated Exchange houses," with its resulting "pressure," was the cause assigned for the failure by James Louis Moore of Hays, St. John & Moore, 43 Exchange Place, attorneys for the firm. Added to this was a story circulated immediately after the failure became known, to the effect that an enemy of the concern had broken into its private files, rifled them of a list of customers and circulated an anonymous circular which frightened its traders. This story, attributed to a clerk employed by the firm, was furnished with the added details that since the files were pillaged a night watchman had guarded them.

Suspended From Exchange.

This general explanation of the cause of the failure, however, was flatly disputed by William S. Silkworth, President of the Consolidated Exchange, from which the Fuller concern was suspended yesterday. Public announcement from the rostrum of the Exchange attributed the dropping of the firm to failure to meet commitments and "reckless and unbusinesslike methods."

To that Mr. Silkworth added last night the declaration that one of the two partners, Edward M. Fuller, had been hard hit in Mexican Petroleum stock. Mr. Silkworth said that Fuller had speculated on the short side of the market. Within the last two weeks "Mex Pete" has undergone a sensational rise.

*The New York *Times*, June 28, 1922, pp. 1, 5. © 1922-1923 by The New York Times Company. Reprinted by permission.

Mr. Fuller, who lives at Great Neck, L. I., refused to make any comment on the situation for himself. The other partner, William F. McGee, lived until recently at 55 East Seventy-third Street, the home of Miss Louise Groody, star of "Good Morning, Dearie," with whom McGee entered into a runaway marriage in Greenwich, Conn., on Feb. 20 last. Mr. McGee made no statement after the failure and could not be reached last night.

The house closed its doors yesterday under sensational circumstances. A big corps of clerks, stenographers, telegraphers, messengers and other employes reported to find the suite bare of virtually everything except furniture.

Books, papers and records had been removed so that the place resembled an office just being furnished in anticipation of doing business instead of one in which hundreds of customers had been trading daily. The employes milled around, at a loss to understand what had overtaken them. They were all the more puzzled when they found that the executives who could have explained the situation to them were not on hand.

Gradually the idea that they were out of a job began to filter through the minds of the staff and there was some good natured rejoicing that they all had been paid up to Saturday night, even if the customary formality of informing them that they were through had been omitted. Mixed with the philosophic chaff was the dismay of some to whom the sudden loss of employment was a serious if not an overwhelming happening.

Things were in that state and the excitement was growing when word came that an involuntary petition in bankruptcy had been filed, that the firm had consented to being adjudged bankrupt [1/5] and that a receiver had been appointed. While the clerks and other employes were dispersing there came word of a most unusual procedure to explain the bareness of the offices.

The firm had taken its books, papers and records late on Monday night to the offices of its attorneys. Not until after the receiver had been appointed were their whereabouts disclosed. Then, according to Carl J. Austrian of 27 Cedar Street, who, with Francis L. Kohlman, represented the petitioning creditors, they were surrendered to the receiver under a stipulation that they were not to be the basis of court proceedings against the firm other than those normal to a liquidation.

No one could be found after the failure was made public to explain this proceeding in detail or to answer the question whether any such stipulation would operate to stay the hand of any Federal or State authorities who might believe that they had found in the circumstances of the failure cause for official action. Nor could it be learned whether the pains taken to sequester the records and to surrender them only under a protecting stipulation had any connection with the fact that an indictment was returned in the United States District Court on June 24, 1920, charging the several defendants with conspiracy to defraud by using the United States mails in exploiting and selling the capital stock of the Crown Oil Company, a California concern.

The defendants named in this indictment were: The Crown Oil Company, Charles D. Pratt, no address; Benjamin V. Hole, Burlingham, Cal.; William P. Williams, no address; B. X. Dawson, 601 West 113th Street; Edward M. Fuller and W. F. McGee, 50 Broad Street.

All of the defendants in this case appeared in court and filed pleas of not guilty to the charge before Judge Learned Hand. The Court fixed bail at $5,000 each, which was given, and the defendants were released.

Case Never Tried.

This indictment followed an investigation conducted by Jerome Simmons, then an assistant to the United States Attorney. When Mr. Simmons retired from office the indictments which had been in his care were turned over to Sampson Selig, now in charge of this branch of criminal prosecution in Colonel Hayward's office. Mr. Selig, in commenting yesterday on the fact that the case had not been brought to trial, remarked that he inherited a mass of true bills, many of which he had not had time as yet to bring to trial. The indictment, according to the records, has been on file more than two years.

These questions were not answered in court before Judge Julius M. Mayer yesterday, where the proceedings were largely of a routine nature. The petitioning creditors were Walter A. Clifford, who has a claim for $15,000, money loaned; Seminole Printing Company with a claim for $800 for printing and materials, and John G. Kinzinger, who claims $250 for services rendered.

After Hays, St. John & Moore had consented to their client being adjudicated a bankrupt, the Court appointed Samuel Strasbourger, former Judge of the City Court, receiver with a bond of $25,000.

Soon after the failure had become public and the partners had denied themselves to newpaper men, James L. Moore, on their behalf, made this statement:

"E. M. Fuller & Co., is the largest brokerage house on the Consolidated Exchange. The house is eight years old. There are only two members in the firm, Edward M. Fuller and W. F. McGee. They have two offices in New York, one at 50 Broad Street, and the other uptown. They have branch offices in Boston, Philadelphia, Chicago, Cleveland, Pittsburgh and Uniontown, Penn.

"It is impossible to give even an approximate estimate of the assets and liabilities at this time.

It is hoped that the estate will be sufficient to pay a large part of the claims but it will take an audit, perhaps of months, to determine just what the assets are.

"The cause of the failure is due to the pressure which has been brought to bear upon Consolidated Stock Exchange houses in the past few months. Owing to propaganda which has appeared in the newspapers and magazines concerning houses connected with this exchange, customers have transferred accounts or closed out entirely, causing a steady drain on the brokerage houses. Fuller & Co. have paid out enormous sums since the first of the year, but at last it was found necessary to put themselves in the hands of the court for the protection of the remaining creditors. We shall work in co-operation with the receiver and his counsel, Francis L. Kohlman, to realize all that we possibly can from the assets for the benefit of the creditors."

Tells of Losses in Mex. Pete.

With Mr. Moore's version of the reasons for the collapse of the partnership in hand, information was sought from Mr. Silkworth after the Consolidated had acted to bar the E. M. Fuller & Company from further trading there. Amplifying his declaration that Fuller had lost heavily in "Mex Pete" in trades in other houses than his own, Mr. Silkworth said:

"Our committee of investigation has discovered that Mr. Fuller sustained some very serious losses in the shares of Mexican Petroleum Company. He was not doing this trading in his own office, but in other offices where he had connections."

Mr. Silkworth could not say the exact number of shares of stock Mr. Fuller had been short, the extent of the losses he had sustained in that security, or whether settlement of these losses had been made. Mexican Petroleum, in its recent upswing in the market advanced from the low of 133, less than two weeks ago, to 204½, the high point reached on Monday, a sheer advance of 71½ points. It is known that many sales of the stock were made on Mr. Fuller's account between $150 and $160 per share.

"The actual reason behind the suspension," said the President of the Consolidated Stock Exchange, "was that our investigations proved that members of the firm had been reckless in their dealings. We had had many complaints of late that they had been slow in settlement with their clients. In view of these complaints that we had received, we caused an investigation to be made of the affairs of the firm, particularly the manner in which their customers have been treated of late, and we deemed it advisable, at the conclusion of the investigation, to suspend them from the privileges of the New York Consolidated Exchange. Announcement to this effect was made from the rostrum of our trading floor Tuesday morning at the opening of business."

Mr. Silkworth added that the firm had been a member of the Exchange since early in 1920, and that while he had no figures at hand, he was under the impression that the number of customers carrying accounts with the firm would aggregate between 1,500 and 1,800 men and women.

Did Business Over Telephone.

One unusual effect of the failure was that it drew to the almost deserted rooms of the concern many customers who had never been there before.

These offices are in several rooms on the seventh floor of 50 Broad Street. Unlike many other brokerage houses which recently have been obliged to suspend, they were not luxuriously furnished and did not give the appearance of "ready money" that some concerns in the financial district regard as an asset. The firm had no board room and customers were not invited to headquarters. Practically all of the business was transacted over the telephone and one entire room was given to an exchange where operators could give instant information to inquirers about the state of stocks in which they might be interested.

The office furniture was particularly plain, and consisted of a long row of wooden desks, in one large hall-like room, at which a dozen or so stenographers and other clerical assistants performed their tasks. The offices of Mr. Fuller and Mr. McGee were in the rear of this room, were glass-enclosed and, like the outer offices, were simply and modestly furnished. The firm has been a tenant at 50 Broad Street all of the time it has been a member of the Consolidated Stock Exchange.

Edward M. Fuller, the senior partner, figured in the newspapers recently when he appeared as complainant in Tombs Court against a young woman named Nellie Black of 245 West Seventy-fifth Street on June 15. He charged Miss Black with disorderly conduct. Mr. Fuller alleged that the young woman had entered his office, refused to leave when ordered to do so and had threatened him with bodily harm. Magistrate Oberwager released her on suspended sentence.

Miss Black, a movie actress, testified that she and Fuller had been friends for seven years and that she had visited Fuller's office to collect $5,000 which she alleged Fuller had agreed to pay her when she signed an agreement presented to her by Arnold Rothstein on the broker's behalf. Fuller already had paid her $5,000, she said.

The other partner, William F. McGee, has had little publicity, aside from his runaway match with Miss Groody. A month before that occurred a "Mrs. McGee" sued Miss Groody for alienation of McGee's affections. McGee denied that the plaintiff was his wife. Interviewed on the occasion of his marriage, he said that he did not know what had become of the woman's suit.

Has 2,100 Clients in Chicago.

Special to The New York Times.
CHICAGO, June 27—Hopes that Chicagoans who were clients of E. M. Fuller & Co., New York brokerage house suspended today, would realize any considerable amount on their $1,250,000 investments, seemed to be negligible tonight.

E. A. Kauffler, manager of that branch, at 309 South Lasalle Street, left for New York shortly after word of the failure was received in Chicago. He announced that he went in behalf of 2,100 clients of the Chicago branch who face losses varying from $100 to $70,000.

"The failure was not due to the activities of the Chicago office," said J. J. Wallace, assistant Chicago manager. "Our first knowledge of the trouble came Monday night, when we learned the company's deposits in Chicago banks had been withdrawn by New York."

First public information of the failure came with the announcement that the firm had been suspended by the Consolidated Stock Exchange.

It was said here that the loss to clients in Chicago, New York, Boston and Cleveland and elsewhere might total $5,000,000 and probably would not be less than $3,000,000.

The Chicago branch has experienced a rapid growth since its establishment in 1915, at which time it traded in wartime securities. Eight months ago the branch moved into the enlarged quarters closed today.

SILKWORTH RESIGNS FROM CONSOLIDATED AND SELLS HIS SEAT*

President Had Been Target of Criticism After Bucketing Revelations.

FULLER AIDED ROTHSTEIN

Lent $187,000 to Ex-Gambler, but Latter Testifies He Paid It All Back.

DODGES MANY QUESTIONS

"Perjury Has No Terror for You," Comments Attorney for 4,000 Fuller Creditors.

William S. Silkworth, President of the Consolidated Stock Exchange, yesterday resigned to take effect today, and his resignation was accepted by the Board of Directors. Announcement also was made by the Special Committee of Five of the Exchange that Silkworth had sold his seat on the Exchange, effective today, and will cease to be a member of that organization.

The resignation of Mr. Silkworth and the severing of his connection with the Consolidated Stock Exchange of New York marks another milestone in the long series of disagreements between members of the Exchange and its officials, which have developed in the investigation of member brokers of that organization, a large number of whom have been thrown into bankruptcy. The affair reached its climax with the hearings before a referee in bankruptcy on the petition of creditors attempting to recover assets of the firm of E. M. Fuller & Co., which mysteriously disappeared at the time the firm was put into bankruptcy.

During the latter part of last week, Silkworth announced that in view of the unfavorable publicity which had been brought upon the Consolidated Exchange in the last few months, he planned to resign from the Presidency of the Exchange on June 28, holding up his resignation until that time on the grounds that he would not quit under fire. No hint had been made before that Silkworth planned to sell his seat and sever all connections with the Consolidated Stock Exchange, as he now has done, according to last night's announcement.

The Special Committee of Five was named by the Board of Governors of the Consolidated Stock Exchange six weeks ago and is composed of prominent members of the Exchange, who have been independent of the factions which have grown up within the Exchange itself. It was announced that this committee would make a thorough investigation of conditions within the Exchange and would be vested with power to take summary action in case it was the judgment of the committee that summary action was necessary.

*The New York *Times*, June 26, 1923, pp. 1, 14. © 1922-1923 by The New York Times Company. Reprinted by permission.

Last night's report, issued at a late hour, was the first that the committee has made since its organization, and this brief statement was given out on behalf of the Board of Governors of the Consolidated Stock Exchange and of the Special Committee of Five:

"The Special Committee of Five made a preliminary report to the board today. W. S. Silkworth resigned as President to take effect Tuesday, June 26. His resignation was accepted. He also sold his seat to the Exchange and thereby ceases to be a member. The special committee will make a further report soon."

Arnold Rothstein, once prominent in Tenderloin gambling circles and more recently head of an insurance brokerage firm, admitted yesterday at the bankruptcy investigation of E. M. Fuller & Co., the brokerage firm which failed for $6,000,000 a year ago, that he borrowed $187,000 from Edward M. Fuller in 1921. Under a fire of questions by Referee Harold P. Coffin, Francis L. Kohlman, counsel for the trustee in bankruptcy, and William M. Chadbourne, representing the 4,000 Fuller creditors, Rothstein fell back on his constitutional rights and refused to answer certain pertinent questions. To others he replied "I don't remember."

In admitting that Fuller lent him $187,000, Rothstein declared that he had paid it all back within a day or two of the occasions on which he borrowed it, in sums ranging from $200 to $24,000. When he first applied to Fuller for a loan, in April, 1921, he said, he put up, on Fuller's demand, $25,000 in bonds and securities to cover the loans. When he paid off the last loan, in November, 1921, Rothstein said, Fuller returned the collateral.

Questioned by Mr. Kohlman, Roth- [1/4] stein could not explain why Fuller & Co. had issued a check for $525 out of the firm's mysterious "Account 600," but said later, "It is possible that Fuller asked me for a loan of $500, but you'll have to ask Fuller about that."

Referee Coffin here interposed to inform Rothstein that Fuller had refused to testify about that check on the ground that it might degrade and incriminate him, and Rothstein replied: "I wish I could induce him to tell all about it. This matter has caused me considerable embarrassment. My dealings with Fuller & Co. were straight and aboveboard. I don't want to hide anything from you."

Mr. Kohlman brought out that $75,476.08 had been paid out from "Account No. 600." The largest payment was in Liberty bonds worth $58,925.83, but there was nothing to show to whom the bonds went. Mr. Kohlman stated that $15,025.25 had been paid to "J. J. Brady." Rothstein admitted that he knew Brady, but denied that Brady received the money for him.

When the proceeding began in Referee Coffin's office at 217 Broadway, Charles A. Stoneham, owner of the Giants baseball club, and Thomas F. Foley, ex-Sheriff and for many years Tammany leader of the First Assembly District, were present under subpoena. They were followed into the referee's office by Fuller, who is a prisoner in Ludlow Street Jail for contempt of the Federal court, and who, with his partner, William F. McGee, was sentenced two weeks ago to Sing Sing for bucketing.

Stoneham and Foley were excused from giving further testimony at the inquiry until Tuesday, July 24, and Fuller was called to the witness chair. He told Referee Coffin that he no longer was represented by William J. Fallon and Eugene F. McGee, who were his attorneys in previous hearings and in the three trials of Fuller on bucketing indictments.

Harold A. Content then told the referee that he and his partner, Charles H. Griffith, had been retained by Fuller on Saturday, but that they had not had time to consult with their client about testimony he was to give in the investigation.

"This is rather surprising," interjected Referee Coffin, "Fuller's counsel stated to Judge Nott when Fuller and McGee were arraigned for sentence before Judge Nott in General Sessions that Fuller was penniless and poverty-stricken. Now he has brought in eminent counsel." Turning to Fuller, the referee added: "Do you have to consult your counsel to tell your creditors about the conduct of your business and the whereabouts of the assets of your firm?"

"I want to talk to my counsel about the case generally," replied Fuller.

"There is no generally about it," retorted the referee. "This is merely a matter of assets; there are no criminal proceedings here." Fuller replied:

Hints at Criminal Proceedings.

"But there is apt to be a criminal proceeding as the result of this hearing."

After Fuller had admitted knowing Rothstein, the referee asked: "Did he have an account with E. M. Fuller & Co.?" Before Fuller could answer Mr. Griffiths interposed with the statement that it was not fair to examine his client before he had had an opportunity to confer with him, and when the referee insisted on an answer, Fuller said: "I refuse to answer." When Fuller would not state whether his answer would degrade or incriminate him, the referee announced that he would postpone further questioning of the bucketing broker until 2 P. M. tomorrow.

Mr. Kohlman protested and explained that he had to appear in another court.

"This court is the United States Court," said

the referee, "and it must function. We cannot wait because an attorney is engaged elsewhere. If you are not satisfied with the ruling, your course is clear to you."

Stoneham and Foley had not left the room and when Mr. Kohlman said he would like to examine Foley next week, the referee declared that neither Foley nor Stoneham could be examined until July 24.

"This is an outrage," declared Mr. Kohlman.

"Watch your step," admonished the referee.

Rothstein was called to the stand, and after he had testified as to the loans from Fuller the referee asked:

"It is reported that Fuller laid considerable sums of money with you as wagers on horse races. What have you got to say about that?"

"I'll have to refuse to answer that question, on the ground that it would degrade and incriminate me," said Rothstein.

"Charges have been made that Fuller took considerable money from Fuller & Co. and lost it on the race tracks," went on the referee.

"I always thought he was a very good player," answered Rothstein. "I understood that he often won a lot of money."

"Then you refuse to give us any information on any wager on race horses made by Fuller on the ground that to do so would degrade and incriminate you?" asked Mr. Coffin.

"Yes; much as I would like to tell you," was the reply.

Denies Interest in Fuller Firm.

"Are you prepared to tell the court," interposed Mr. Chadbourne, counsel for the Fuller creditors, "that you had no interest in Fuller & Co.?"

"Absolutely none," said Rothstein.

"Did you ever talk to Stoneham or Foley about Fuller & Co. needing money!"

"Of course not," the witness replied, "I've known Stoneham a long time, but I hardly know Foley."

"Did you know that about a month before Fuller & Co. went into bankruptcy McGee settled a large amount of money on his wife!" he was asked.

"I know nothing about that," replied Rothstein.

Rothstein was questioned at length about a report that he and others had combined to defray the expenses of the criminal proceedings against Fuller and McGee, and he declared that he gave no money to either of the brokers after their indictment.

"Did anybody approach you and ask you to contribute toward their legal expenses?"

"I don't know whether they did or not," answered Rothstein.

"This witness is palpably evading your direction to answer questions," said Mr. Chadbourne. "He is assuming a bland-like attitude in professing not to understand the simplest words in the English language."

Taking a new tack, he asked: "Did you ever place any bets for Fuller at the race tracks?"

"You wouldn't call that a business, would you?" was the answer. "That would be conferring a personal favor."

"Where did you get the Liberty bonds that you put up as security?"

"You wouldn't expect a man to remember that, would you?" asked Rothstein.

Never Heard of Baseball Bribery.

"Your memory failed you miserably during your examination by Mr. Coffin," said Mr. Chadbourne. "Let me see if I can revive you from that attack of aphasia. What do you know about the Herzog case, the attempt to bribe that player into throwing a baseball game in the National League?"

"That is an unfair question," declared Rothstein. "I give you my sacred word of honor, I never heard of the Herzog case."

"It is evident from your attitude," continued Mr. Chadbourne, "that perjury has no terror for you."

Rothstein refused to say whether he introduced Fuller and McGee to Fallon & McGee, the lawyers, their previous attorneys, on the ground that his answer would "tend to degrade and incriminate me."

"Did you pay Fallon & McGee a $4,000 retainer to defend Fuller in the criminal proceedings in 1922?"

"I refuse to answer on the same ground."

It was brought out that although Rothstein said he deposited $25,000 in Liberty bonds as collateral on the loans he obtained from Fuller there was no entry found in any of the books of the firm to show the receipt or the return of this collateral. He admitted that he indemnified a bond company to the extent of $25,000 when Fuller was arrested for bucketing. Marshall E. Ward of Einstein, Ward Co., whose failure was announced on the floor of the Stock Exchange earlier in the day, then was called to the stand to explain why he had indemnified $5,000 of the bail demanded for Fuller. He said that McGee, Fuller's partner, asked his firm to go security for the bond, explaining that Fuller & Co. had done considerable business with his firm and he felt he could not decline the request.

STONEHAM FACES CRISIS IN CAREER*

HIS SPECTACULAR RISE

Sport King of Two Countries From Gains as Broker

OWNS HAVANA CASINO

Much of Large Fortune Will Go if Fuller & Co. Creditors Win.

The career of Charles A. Stoneham, who rose from the bottom of the ladder to a position of prominence in the financial and sporting worlds of two countries, has taken a new twist. For the lad who began as a board clerk in a brokerage office and achieved eventually his own brokerage business, a $2,000,000 baseball plant, a $1,000,-000 race track, a notable racing stable and a newspaper, stands today under a Federal indictment. And his plight arises from transactions that exalted him from a humble clerkship to the wealth and position of a stock broker.

If the Federal authorities and the State officials investigating the bankruptcies of houses to which Stoneham transferred accounts achieve their aims, the fortune won by the former board boy may be largely dissipated in repayments to investors of the millions of dollars lost by them. His fortune has been estimated by the authorities as about $10,000,000.

The concerns to which Stoneham transferred acounts in disposing of his business were E. M. Fuller & Co., E. D. Dier & Co., E. H. Clarke & Co. and Dillon & Co. In none of these instances have the authorities yet been able to establish an accurate estimate of losses involved in the failures. But unofficially the losses have been estimated as high as $6,000,000 in the Fuller crash, $10,000,000 in the Dier failure, $4,000,000 in the Clarke case, and $600,000 in the Dillon bankruptcy. About 10,000 investors are said to have been affected. They represent all parts of the country and many of them contributed through branch offices in various cities.

Stoneham obtained his first knowledge of brokerage as a board boy and developed this knowledge so rapidly that when still a youth he was made a stock salesman, and in that capacity for a number of years scored a financial success that led him to dream of entering business for himself.

Establishes Own Firm.

He realized his dream in 1913 when he established the brokerage firm of Charles A. Stoneham & Co., with main offices at 41 Broadway and with branch offices, in the course of time, in Chicago and other large cities. In 1921 Stoneham's firm went out of business. It had on its books at the time the accounts of thousands of investors, totaling millions of dollars. To each of these investors went a form letter, thanking the customer for his patronage and the pleasant relations between broker and customer, and urging that, in view of the impending dissolution of the firm of Charles A. Stoneham & Co., that house be permitted to transfer the patron's account to another firm.

Some of the accounts the investors were induced to transfer to the Fuller firm, others to Dillon and many to Clarke. But it was to Dier that the bulk of Stoneham's business went. The State authorities have estimated that more than $2,000,000 of Stoneham's business went into the Dier firm.

His stock interests apparently turned over to others, Stoneham turned more attention to the sporting enterprises in which for a number of years he had taken an increasing part. Most prominent of these enterprises was his acquisition, with John J. McGraw, the manager, and Magistrate Francis X. McQuade, of the ownership of the Giants. Stoneham is said to have paid $1,900,000 for his controlling interest of 61 per cent of the stock.

His entry into baseball as a magnate fitted in with his purchases in Havana. There he bought an immense race track, which he developed at a great cost and which for several years has been a sporting centre in the Winter season. At the same time he bought the famous Havana Casino, to which multitudes of Americans flocked to chance their dollars at the gaming tables. It was developed into a sumptuous gambling palace that rivals the magnificence of Monte Carlo. His third venture in Havana was the purchase of a newspaper. Stoneham thus became a figure of importance in Cuba.

Spends $250,000 on Track.

The man who had been a broker's board boy was now able to spend $250,000 on race track improvements. He added to his already large string of thoroughbreds. His amusement enterprises were centred in the Playa Corporation, capitalized at $5,000,000.

Though assailed in one newspaper in Havana as causing tragedies and failures through losses in the Casino, Stoneham for a time prospered in Havana. But, whatever the reason, he was reported some months ago to have sold the race track and the Casino.

With these interests disposed of he turned his attention to the Giants and ordered the enlargement of the capacity of the Polo Grounds stand so that his club might compete for patronage with the Yankee Stadium. Apparently his only interests of recent months have been his ball club and his racing stable. But the State and Federal authorities insist he has been interested in brokerage houses and that until the Fuller crash he was a partner in that firm, though not so recorded.

Though the Fuller case has been the most sensational of the series of failures because of its extensive ramifications and results, the Dier collapse was the first of the series and the forerunner of the troubles aired in the last year. During the official investigations into this crash, charges against Stoneham were so profuse and sensational at the referee hearings that a Federal Court order was issued demanding his presence. Stoneham was then in Havana, but, while outside the pale of the order, hastened back to the States.

Shortly afterward he offered $200,000 to a fund toward restoration of the company's assets. It is recorded that he paid this money. It was alleged by his accusers that Stoneham held back $2,400,000 worth of securities of customers whose accounts he had transferred to the books of E. D. Dier & Co. Stoneham asserted these accounts had been sold back to him through a book transaction. At the hearings he said that he could not be held accountable for the crash of the Dier house and for the loss to his own former investors whom he had urged to patronize Dier. The Dier failure on Jan. 16, 1922, came six months after Stoneham had transferred to that firm some of the business of Charles A. Stoneham & Co. Several indictments resulted from this failure. Stoneham was not indicted.

E. H. Clarke & Co. failed on March 4, 1922. In a referee's hearing, Stoneham said that the general reputation of the Clarke firm and its apparent ability to pay for the accounts transferred to it induced him to give it much of the out-of-town business of Charles A. Stoneham & Co. It came out that Clarke was to pay Stoneham 10 per cent of the equities of the accounts.

By the time Dillon & Co. had collapsed Stoneham had been named defendant in half a dozen suits brought by irate investors who charged fraud in his transfer of their accounts to firms which failed shortly afterward. Incidentally,

Magistrate McQuade, Stoneham's baseball partner, is to testify at a hearing Sept. 12 in the Dillon bankruptcy.

Troubles on the Increase.

The former board boy's troubles multiplied rapidly after the crash of E. M. Fuller & Co. in July, 1922. It was due to developments arising from this case that he was indicted the other day by the Federal Grand Jury and compelled to put up $5,000 bail for himself. It was because of the intimations and open charges in the investigation resulting from this failure that Baseball Commissioner Kenesaw M. Landis began to take a close interest in Stoneham's financial career and that President John Heydler of the National League was moved to remark that while Stoneham had been a good man in baseball his indictment had embarrassed the League.

It was known that some of the Stoneham accounts had gone to the Fuller firm. But it was not until the bankrupt partners, Edward M. Fuller and William F. McGee, while committed for contempt of court for their failure to produce certain missing records, made their sensational confessions that evidence was obtained leading United States Attorney Hayward and Referee Harold P. Coffin to charge that Stoneham was a silent partner in the firm.

Stoneham admitted at a referee's hearing that he gave checks of the National Exhibition Company, the corporate name of his ball club, totaling $147,500, to E. M. Fuller & Co. shortly before their failure, in an effort to prevent the impending collapse. The firm was then paying out heavily during a persistent run. Stoneham testified he made the loans at the urgent behest of ex-Sheriff Thomas F. Foley, a Tammany Hall lieutenant. Foley admitted asking that Stoneham make the loans. The authorities assert the loans actually totaled $172,500.

Stoneham swore that the advances constituted nothing more than loans, but the Grand Jury differed. That body averred its belief that he had arranged with the brokers to pay them $200,000 in purchase of a 25 per cent interest in the profits.

Stoneham admitted at the hearing that when Charles A. Stoneham & Co. closed its business it turned over to E. M. Fuller & Co. most of the orders received by the Stoneham branch in Boston.

Stoneham Makes Loan.

Stoneham added that he was confident that Foley would repay him in time. "Fuller never had any collateral," Stoneham went on. "I borrowed money from the National Exhibition Company and put up my own securities with the company, and these securities were accepted by the Board of Directors of the National Exhibition Company on the loan. I never knew

E. M. Fuller & Co. were in trouble until Foley came to me and said he would like to befriend Fuller by trying to stop the run then going on. Foley told me that they had told him they were solvent, or nearly so, and that if they were not forced to throw on the market some of their securities which were as liquid as cash at that time they believed that with from $50,000 to $100,000 the run would be stopped and that later the loan would be repaid. On those representations to Foley and on Foley's representations to me I made the loan. I would not have loaned the money had not Foley requested me to do so."

Asked if there was not an agreement that he was to put up $200,000 for a 25 per cent share of the profits, Stoneham exclaimed with heat, "Do you think I am a damned fool? I could have started a brokerage business myself with $150,000. Do you think I'd put money into a concern that owed $2,000,000?"

His testimony at this hearing that he had not arranged for a partnership in E. M. Fuller & Co. led to his indictment on a perjury charge, the Grand Jury averring it had received information to the contrary. This information was given to the Grand Jury by Fuller and McGee.

In the Dier failure a Supreme Court Grand Jury indicted Dier, Harry J. Lawrence, Jr., Benjamin F. Shrimpton and Adam Recklein. They were accused of bucketing.

Out of the Fuller crash developed other indictments in the Federal Grand Jury room. Fuller and William F. McGee and their former attorneys, William J. Fallon and Eugene F. McGee, were indicted on a charge of conspiring to defeat justice by concealment and destruction of certain records. The bankrupt brokers were committed for contempt of court for failure to produce books ordered before the court and their former lawyers were made the targets of contempt proceedings on similar charges.

Stoneham realized for weeks that he was to be indicted. On Broadway he told companions that evidence was being presented against him that would lead to his indictment. He was prepared for this step by the Grand Jury and within a few minutes of the indictment was in the Federal Court with a $5,000 bond.

[New York in the 1920's: Arnold Rothstein and His Circle] *

LLOYD MORRIS (1893–   ) is a well-known New York critic and social historian. He has written *The Celtic Dawn: A Survey of the Renascence in Ireland* (1917); *The Poetry of Edwin Arlington Robinson* (1923); *The Rebellious Puritan* (1927), a biography of Hawthorne; and *William James: The Message of a Modern Mind* (1950). He is also the author of several novels and collaborated with John Van Druten in the writing of the successful Broadway play *The Damask Cheek* (1943).

Behind the sparkling front of Manhattan's gay night life, resonant with jazz and running with liquor, a network of corruption spread over New York. Its citizens were in open rebellion against Prohibition. They wanted liquor; they condoned the illegal practices which assured a wet metropolis. The effect was to make crime profitable on a scale never before conceived. To an ambitious but not squeamish young man, the vocational education acquired in a reformatory was more useful than an Ivy League diploma. Crime was "big business" and the new magnates who dominated it were men whose widely diversified enterprises touched the life of the community at many salient points. Like their illustrious predecessors, the great industrialists and financiers of the late nineteenth century, these new robber barons found that the law often obstructed their projects. So they resorted to the practice which their predecessors had adopted—they bought politicians whose power procured them a high degree of immunity. Such eminent Tammany leaders as Thomas F. Foley, James J. Hines, Thomas M. Farley, Albert Marinelli and others entered into profitable alliances with them. Through these political allies, they were able to subvert, for their own ends, the civil government of New York. Indirectly, they controlled the police, the public prosecutors, many magistrates and judges in the higher courts, a large number of administrative officials. They were thus the real overlords of the largest, wealthiest city in the United States.

The magnitude of their operations, their power, wealth and extraordinary business acumen made many of these new tycoons outstanding. No mere small-scale enterpriser, with limited vision and weak nerve, could rise to head one of the great rum-running syndicates. It was a business that yielded tremendous profits, but it required an enormous investment of capital and the taking of great risks. Furthermore, operating a syndicate was an extremely complex enterprise. Fleets of speedboats and trucks manned by tough hoodlums had to be dispatched with precise accuracy. Drops, or warehouses, had to be provided. These were usually large garages, with concealed sub-basements to which access was gained by elevators. The elevator doors, when closed, appeared to be solid walls. The elevators had to be capable of receiving a loaded ten-ton truck and quickly dropping it from view. A syndicate also had to own, or control, a printing plant that turned out fake labels and counterfeit revenue stamps, and a

* Lloyd Morris, *Incredible New York, 1850-1950: High Life and Low Life of the Last Hundred Years* (New York: Random House, 1951), pp. 342-47. Copyright © 1951 by Lloyd Morris. Reprinted with the permission of the publisher.

bottle factory able to duplicate the bottles used by foreign distillers. It had to run a cutting plant. It had to employ sales and bookeeping staffs. It had to have trustworthy pay-off men, able to bribe members of the Coast Guard and rural as well as New York police. It had to have lawyers and bondsmen available at all times, in the event of unforeseen arrests; their prompt appearance was likely to prevent an arrested man from talking indiscreetly. You might have thought that co-ordinating the manifold operations of a great rum-running syndicate was a full-time job. [342/343]

But several of the tycoons who made fortunes in these enterprises were men with a genius for business organization, and they became active in other fields likewise. In 1920, Big Bill Dwyer was a longshoreman. Three years later, he rated as a magnate, maintaining suites of offices in two buildings on Times Square, occupying a handsome suburban residence on Long Island and owing the Federal Government nearly one million dollars in income taxes. In addition to his rum-running syndicate, Dwyer was a partner in several night clubs, an owner of race tracks, the proprietor of a professional hockey team, and a large investor in spectator sports. The interests of Irving Wexler—better known as Waxey Gordon—were no less diversified. Gordon had begun his career as a pickpocket on the lower East Side. After several terms in reformatories, he moved up in the professional scale, reappearing as a slugger for a gang. In this capacity he was tried for murder and discharged, but a simple case of assault and robbery brought him a term in Sing Sing. However, by the mid-nineteen-twenties, Gordon was installed in a fine suite of offices on Forty-second Street and Broadway. He had made millions out of syndicate operations, and was investing his wealth in other enterprises. He was the proprietor of two skyscraping hotels in the Roaring Forties, west of Times Square. He owned a brewery in New Jersey, and had an interest in a large distillery in upstate New York. He maintained an ornate apartment on Central Park West, a luxurious summer home on the New Jersey shore, a fleet of expensive cars. As a man of wealth, he recognized an obligation to the arts and discharged it by backing two Broadway musicals, one of which turned out to be a smash hit.

Francesco Castiglia, another great syndicate tycoon, was less flamboyant than Gordon but, in the end, far more successful. Castiglia was more widely celebrated under the name of Frank Costello. Born in Italy, he was raised in the slums of East Harlem and, with sound practical judgment, he abandoned formal education at the age of eleven. Thirteen years later, having meanwhile won a local reputation as a gunman, he was sentenced to a term in the penitentiary for illegal possession of a weapon. Subsequent ventures, some of which were in conventional lines of business, prospered notably. Costello made judicious investments in real estate; these paid off well. So he was reputed to be a wealthy man before he organized the highly profitable rum-running syndicate which he conducted from offices on Lexington Avenue, near Grand Cental Station. In this line, he was a big-shot from the outset, a close friend of Jimmy Hines, the Tammany potentate, and of Arnold Rothstein. One of Rothstein's protégés, Philip Kastel, a dapper individual known as "Dandy Phil," became Costello's partner. Kastel had operated a night club in Montreal and a bucket shop in New York; partnership with Costello lifted him into the big time. It was probably Costello, the man of imagination and vision, who first saw the possibilities in another business which eventually made him a great power in New York politics and a nationally known figure. This was the operation of slot machines, pungently described by the columnist Westbrook Pegler as "one-armed bandits." The partners organized a syndicate to place more than five thousand of these devices in speakeasies, stationery stores, [343/344] candy shops and similar establishments throughout New York. Ostensibly candy-vending machines, a simple alteration of the mechanism converted them into gambling devices which, if certain combinations were hit by players, returned coins instead of candy. Except in speakeasies, most of them responded to the dropping of a nickel in the slot, and they became so popular with children that ladders were often supplied to enable tiny tots to reach them. The gross return on the five thousand slot machines placed in New York was said to run as high as one hundred thousand dollars daily. Not all of this golden harvest was reaped by the partners; there were heavy business expenses to be met. Among them was the maintenance of an efficient private police force to "recover" machines stolen by neighborhood gangs and presumably punish the thieves.

Naturally, tycoons like Dwyer and Gordon and Costello, men of large affairs, living in costly homes, moving in the highest political circles, bitterly resented the imputation that they were racketeers. All of them insisted that they were "legitimate businessmen." This was also the contention of Larry Fay, who ran his enterprises from handsome offices in an uptown skyscraper. "I'm a businessman," Fay always protested, "just a regular businessman like any broker or merchant." You could sympathize with his annoyance, for he too was a man of vision. He revived the economic theory so notably imposed on American big business by the elder J. P. Morgan—the doctrine that "wasteful competition" among enterprisers must give way to the recognition of a "community of interest." Fay chose the milk industry, dominated in New York by two great corporations, but also served by independent producers among whom a disastrous competition prevailed. Using the persuasive talents of a corps of mobsters, Fay organized the independents

into a "trade association," for which he established a code of "fair practice." In return for his services, he received a royalty of five cents on every forty-quart can of milk which the "members" shipped into the city. Fay's concept was elaborated in spectacular fashion by a pair of breezy, rough-diamond magnates who saw that, by creating a so-called trade association, dominating a labor union and making ruthless use of a goon squad, many industries could be given a streamlined efficiency at a high profit—with the cost of their expert services passed on to the public in the form of increased prices. Louis "Lepke" Buchalter and Jacob "Gurrah" Shapiro applied this system to the garment trades and the fur industry; to the baking industry—into which they muscled by way of the flour-trucking business; to the operation of movie theaters. A combination of terrorism and economic inventiveness paid off magnificently for Lepke and Gurrah Jake. Their squad of goons, reputed to number more than two hundred and fifty, were specialists in suave methods of persuasion: extortion, bomb-throwing, miscellaneous violence and, if necessary, murder. Moreover, Lepke and Gurrah Jake always kept their minds on the main chance. So they made the services of their mob available to Tammany politicians in primaries and elections. The arrangement was mutually advantageous.

It was certainly unfortunate that the new tycoons became chiefly notorious [344/345] because of the indiscreet behavior of their cohorts and the violence inseparable from their enterprises. Economic competition often made murder imperative, and occasionally the boys showed a taste for the macabre in their choice of methods. Frankie Marlow was taken for a ride and assassinated; madcap young Vincent Coll was lured into a telephone booth in a drug store near his hotel on West Twenty-third Street and machine-gunned to death; Jack Diamond—who became known as "the clay pigeon" because he was ambushed and thoroughly shot up several times on the streets of New York, and once in his hotel bedroom, but always recovered—was finally dispatched by gunfire in an Albany lodging house: all of these were normal, or conventional, slayings. But more picturesque methods were not unknown. Some victims were beaten into a daze, then ingeniously roped so they would strangle themselves when they recovered consciousness. Others were encased in cement and tossed over the side of a boat, or securely bound and weighted, dropped into the East River from a pier, or merely burned alive in their own cars.

The activities of their gunmen produced a distorted impression of the new plutocracy in the minds of most New Yorkers. Since sudden death was an inevitable hazard of big business as they were developing it, what wonder that they elevated obsequies to a ceremonial splendor which earlier millionaires had reserved for nuptials and balls? The great public funeral of Frankie Yale, a noted Brooklyn magnate, cost fifty-two thousand dollars. Thirty-eight cars heaped with stupendous floral offerings followed the hearse. Ten thousand mourners either attended the requiem mass, or assembled at the cemetery; the streets through which the cortege passed were jammed with people. The funeral of Danny Iamascia, bodyguard and factotum of Dutch Schultz, was equally impressive. Thirty-five automobiles were required to transport the horticultural tributes, and no less than one hundred and twenty-five were used to convey the deceased's grief-stricken friends to his grave. The splendor of these funerals led the general public to conclude that the new plutocrats regarded death as their major opportunity for extravagant expenditure.

From the aftermath of Rothstein's murder, it became clear that he had been the Morgan of the new plutocracy, its banker and master of economic strategy. His fortune was estimated at from two to ten million dollars. He owned valuable real estate, maintained large accounts in excellent banks, lived in an expensive Fifth Avenue apartment. It was his opinion, as he often said, that the majority of the human race were dubs and dumbbells, and he was always ready to turn to profit the fact that they had rotten judgment and no brains. Nothing irked Rothstein more than that people thought him crooked. Only because he had learned how to do things and how to size people up and dope out methods for himself! Never, he protested, had he been connected with a crooked deal.

The mystery of Rothstein's murder was never solved. He lived for two days after being shot in a hotel suite where a card game was in progress. But, like many another of the new tycoons, he went to his grave faithful to the common code: he refused to name his assailant. The scope of his activities, the leading [345/346] role that he played in making crime big business, were quicky established. His profession of never having been connected with a crooked deal turned out to be the most memorable example of his wit. After Rothstein's death, his private files were seized by the authorities, and it appeared that some of their contents had already been removed. Most of the information which they yielded was permanently suppressed. Perhaps his papers implicated too many people of consequence in New York—politicians, public officials and others. But it was subsequently alleged that his most significant function was in acting as intermediary between the underworld and the great financial institutions that, unwittingly, furnished the capital which made possibe illicit operations of tremendous magnitude. Rothstein had large investments in real estate and prime securities. These could always be pledged with financial institutions for loans. It was Rothstein's practice to take out insurance on the lives of the underworld clients to whom he advanced money which he had borrowed on his personal collateral. If they got killed in the course of their operations, he was indemnified. If they attempted to default on their loans, the insurance policies set a profitable price on their heads that Rothstein was capable of collecting—he had trigger-men on his payroll who knew how to dispose of welchers. And if his clients pulled off their coups, Rothstein not only made more than a banker's normal interest on his loans, but also received a large share of the profits. His ruling passion was money, and his attorney, William J. Fallon gave a curious description of him. Rothstein, Fallon said, was "a man who dwells in doorways . . . a mouse standing in a doorway, waiting for his cheese." But, since no man is a hero to his lawyer, it is possible that Fallon diminished Rothstein's real stature. A taste for profits is common to bankers, yet you wouldn't have compared the elder J. P. Morgan to a mouse.

Fallon exemplified the kind of legal talent which the new tycoons required in their operations. As counsel for the major figures of the underworld, he was called "the great mouthpiece." He had an amazing ability to secure jury disagreements which freed his clients—the vote so frequently stood at eleven to one in favor of conviction that Fallon was also known as the "jail robber." Auburn-haired, handsome in a flamboyant way, Fallon was an eloquent pleader whose theatrical sense was so acute that David Belasco had once tried to persuade him to desert the law for the stage. He was among the most notorious of Broadway playboys, a familiar figure in all the best night clubs, a charter member of the odd society invented by Miss Guinan. Under his spectacular front, disguised by his extraordinary audacity, there lurked a brilliant mind. Fallon's mastery of criminal law, his command of technicalities, his knowledge of medicine and psychiatry won him the reluctant admiration of eminent jurists and honorable members of the bar who despised his character. Like Roth-

stein, he came of good stock. He had received an excellent education; the influence of religion pervaded his youth. Yet the moral climate of the festive era was registered by Fallon's peculiar ethics. He regarded the bribing of jurors as a proper professional expedient. He could hardly help doing so. [346/347] With full knowledge of the terms and the consequences of his bargain, quite freely and only for money, he had sold his services to a crime machine.

That Fallon's ethics, however peculiar, were far from unique became increasingly clear to New Yorkers during the years following Rothstein's murder. An aura of *Alice in Wonderland* seemed to envelop the administration of municipal affairs. It was charged that one magistrate had paid ten thousand dollars for his appointment; that another had received, from a corporation, a fee of one hundred and ninety thousand dollars for procuring an advantageous lease of city property. And there was the diverting case of a banquet in honor of Magistrate Albert H. Vitale held in a Bronx restaurant. Among the guests who joined in paying tribute to this eminent dispenser of justice were a leading underworld tycoon and six well-known gangsters. Also present were a police detective and two court attendants, all of whom were armed. In these circumstances, it seemed remarkable that the banquet was held up by seven gunmen, who disarmed the police detective and court attendants, and then proceeded to rob the assembled guests of their jewelry and cash. However, within three hours after this fantastic exploit, by methods never explained, Magistrate Vitale managed to retrieve the pistol of which the police detective had been relieved. But, as later became evident, Magistrate Vitale was in many ways a remarkable man. On an official salary of twelve thousand dollars a year, he had managed to deposit in his bank more than one hundred thousand dollars in a period of five years.

Jay Gatsby's Hidden Source of Wealth *

J O H N H . R A N D A L L I I I (1923–   ) is a professor of English at Boston College and the author of *The Landscape and the Looking Glass: Willa Cather's Search for Value* (1960). In 1958 he was awarded a Houghton-Mifflin—New England Quarterly Fellowship for literary excellence.

The following is a piece of speculative criticism about *The Great Gatsby*. I think I have isolated one corrupt business transaction Gatsby is involved in as a result of his effort to win Daisy. Although the evidence is circumstantial, it fits in with facts already known about the story, helps clear up the mystery of Gatsby's sudden rise to great wealth, and exemplifies the whole theme of the corruption of man's aspiration in America. So my criticism, even though speculative, may heighten the significance of Gatsby's career by identifying the exact nature of some of the "foul dust [that] floated in the wake of his dreams."[1]

I stumbled onto this speculation indirectly as a result of trying to solve the problem of exactly why it is that Gatsby crumples under Tom's verbal attack in the New York hotel suite at the climax of the book in Chapter Seven. Other critics who have touched on this topic don't seem to have discussed this particular point.[2] The passage reads as follows:

"She's not leaving me!" Tom's words suddenly leaned down over Gatsby. "Certainly not for a

[1] F. Scott Fitzgerald, *The Great Gatsby* (New York: Charles Scribner's Sons, 1953), p. 2. All subsequent references are to this edition.

[2] Cf. Henry Dan Piper, *F. Scott Fitzgerald, A Critical Portrait* (1965); Andrew Turnbull, *Scott Fitzgerald* (1962); Marius Bewley, *The Eccentric Design* (1959); Richard Chase, *The American Novel and Its Tradition* (1955); cf. also the essays in *F. Scott Fitzgerald: a Collection of Critical Essays*, ed. Arthur Mizener (1963); *The Great Gatsby: a Study*, ed. Frederick J. Hoffmann (1962); and *F. Scott Fitzgerald: the Man and His Work*, ed. Alfred Kazin (1951).

common swindler who'd have to steal the ring he put on her finger."

"I won't stand this!" cried Daisy. "Oh, please let's get out."

"Who are you, anyhow?" broke out Tom. "You're one of that bunch that hangs around with Meyer Wolfsheim—that much I happen to know. I've made a little investigation into your affairs—and I'll carry it further to-morrow."

"You can suit yourself about that, old sport," said Gatsby steadily.

"I found out what your 'drug-stores' were." He turned to us and spoke rapidly. "He and this Wolfsheim bought up a lot of side-street drug-stores here and in Chicago and sold grain alcohol over the counter. That's one of his little stunts. I picked him for a bootlegger the first time I saw him, and I wasn't far wrong." [247/248]

"What about it?" said Gatsby politely. "I guess your friend Walter Chase wasn't too proud to come in on it."

"And you left him in the lurch, didn't you? You let him go to jail for a month over in New Jersey. God! You ought to hear Walter on the subject of *you*."

"He came to us dead broke. He was very glad to pick up some money, old sport."

"Don't you call me 'old sport'!" cried Tom. Gatsby said nothing. "Walter could have you up on the betting laws too, but Wolfsheim scared him into shutting his mouth."

That unfamiliar yet recognizable look was back again in Gatsby's face.

"That drug-store business was just small change," continued Tom slowly, "but you've got something on now that Walter's afraid to tell me about."

I glanced at Daisy, who was staring terrified between Gatsby and her husband, and at Jordan, who had begun to balance an invisible but absorbing object on the tip of her chin. Then I turned back to Gatsby—and was startled at his expression. He looked—and this is said in all contempt for the babbled slander

*John H. Randall III, "Jay Gatsby's Hidden Source of Wealth," *Modern Fiction Studies*, XIII (Autumn 1967), 247-257. *Modern Fiction Studies*, © 1969 by Purdue Research Foundation, Lafayette, Indiana. Reprinted with the permission of the author and the publisher.

of his garden—as if he had "killed a man." For a moment the set of his face could be described in just that fantastic way. (134-135)

What breaks Gatsby down in the hotel room scene? True, Daisy has already begun turning away from him shortly before, when, thinking he can remake the world nearer to the heart's desire, he asks the impossible of her: that she told her husband that she never loved him; and when Tom invokes memories of Kapiolani and of carrying her down from the Punch Bowl to keep her shoes dry, all the rancor goes out of her. But although Gatsby feels a touch of panic at this ("You don't understand. . . . You're not going to take care of her any more." [134]), he still feels quite sure of himself in his social and business roles. Thus when Tom begins his diatribe Gatsby is still able to answer him "steadily" and "politely," and refer to him by that early twentieth-century British upper-class slang term, "old sport,"[3] probably picked up at Oxford, which he uses, when secure in his social role, as a badge of his assumed status. He isn't a bit worried by Tom's revelation of his bootlegging activities; bootlegging after all was a more or less acceptable business enterprise in the Twenties and did not irretrievably downgrade the entrepreneur [248/249] on the status scale.[4] (Tom probably indicates an awareness of this by uttering this part of

his speech "rapidly.") But when Tom announces that his friend Walter Chase, who had gone in with Gatsby on one illicit liquor deal, could have Gatsby prosecuted under the betting laws if Wolfsheim hadn't scared his mouth shut, an "unfamiliar yet recognizable look" (134) appears on Gatsby's face.[5] Why?

This could be an allusion to Wolfsheim's having "fixed" the World Series of 1919, a transaction which is widely known[6] and in which Gatsby himself is apparently implicated.[7] Or again it might be a reference to a more recent betting law violation—although the chances are greatly against this, since it would have to be something illegal on a really large scale in order for the potential revelation of it to jar Gatsby's composure. But when Tom continues his indictment (speaking "slowly" now, not rapidly) and states that Gatsby is now on to something so big that in comparison with it his drug-store business was just small change and that his friend Walter is afraid to tell him what it is, Gatsby simply goes to pieces. "He looked—and this is said in all contempt for the babbled slander of his garden—as if he had 'killed a man.' " Evidently he is very much afraid of having the company—and particularly Daisy

---

[3] The *OED* Supplement lists "Old Sport, Often used ocularly for a person of any description"; the first two references it cited are from *Punch:* "I shouldn't mind, Old Sport" (1905) and "Toodle'oo, Old Sport" (1907). That there was English precedent for Gatsby's apparently indiscriminate use of the term, to which Tom violently objects, is seen from a 1919 quotation from *Punch:* "The old sport just leaned forward in her seat." Significantly, one of the references cited by *OED* is from Compton MacKenzie: "You're no sport, Maudie. You've got the chance of your life and you're turning it down" (*Sylvia Scarlett*, 1918). Compton MacKenzie was the author of *Youth's Encounter* and *Sinister Street*, which detail the childhood and youth of a talented, imaginative, and passionate boy, following him from home to school to Oxford and then out into London and the life beyond. Fitzgerald was a passionate admirer of these books, which are known to have influenced him in writing *This Side of Paradise:* Michael Fane becomes Amory Blaine, Oxford becomes Princeton, etc. Cf. Henry Dan Piper, *F. Scott Fitzgerald: A Critical Portrait* (New York: Holt, Rinehart and Winston, 1965), pp. 44-46.

[4] Cf. Henry Dan Piper, p. 119. Piper says of Arnold Rothstein, who was probably Fitzgerald's model for Meyer Wolfsheim: "He was also reputed to be engaged in numerous other criminal activities, including the oper-

ation of gambling houses, shops selling stolen gems, brothels, and a lucrative bootlegging business—enterprises which did not affect his social standing."

[5] This look had appeared once before, prior to the party's leaving East Egg for New York. When Tom wants to drive Gatsby's car and Gatsby objects, saying there isn't much gas in it, Tom replies:

"Plenty of gas . . ." He looked at the gauge. "And if it runs out I can stop at a drug-store. You can buy anything at a drug-store nowadays."

A pause followed this apparently pointless remark. Daisy looked at Tom frowning, and an indefinable expression, at once definitely unfamiliar and vaguely recognizable, as if I had only heard it described in words, passed over Gatsby's face. (121)

Tom has already "made a little investigation" into Gatsby's affairs, as he says later in the hotel room scene; in this earlier passage Gatsby probably guesses he has done this, and the uneasy expression that passes over his face probably arises from a fear that, if Tom has found out this much about his business activities, he may find out much more.

[6] "Why isn't he in jail?" "They can't get him, old sport. He's a smart man." (74)

[7] "We were so thick like that in everything"—he held up two bulbous fingers—"always together." I wondered if this partnership had included the World's Series transaction in 1919. (172)

—guess what it is he is involved in: ". . . he began to talk excitedly to Daisy, denying everything, defending his name against accusations that had not been made. But with every word she was drawing further and further into herself . . . and only the dead dream fought on as the afternoon slipped away. . . ." (135)

What was bigger than bootlegging? Here is where a literary detective must make some guesses and do some fancy foot and head [249/250] work. *The Great Gatsby* came out early in April 1925. What was the biggest financial scandal of the American Twenties? The Teapot Dome affair.[8] The first important disclosures of the Senate Committee on Public Lands were made early in 1924;[9] Teapot Dome became the major scandal of the recently deceased Harding Administration and was an issue in the election in the fall of that year as well as in the election of 1928.[10] Almost anyone who as much as picked up a newspaper in 1924 must have known what Teapot Dome was. This is the period during which Fitzgerald was at work on *The Great Gatsby*.[11] I submit that the "deal" so big that Tom's friend was afraid to tell him about it is Teapot Dome.

I can hear someone mutter, "Nonsense! What earthly relevance does Teapot Dome have for *Gatsby?* This is neither scholarship nor criticism, but merely a wild guess!" It is a guess, yes, but I think not a wild one. Scholarship can unearth certain evidence which supports this view,

even though circumstantially, and the results have very precise implications for critical analysis of the novel.

In a letter dated November 20, 1924, Maxwell Perkins of Scribner's congratulated Scott Fitzgerald on *The Great Gatsby.* He said he had only two criticisms to make. One was that the character of Gatsby was somewhat vague:

The other point is also about Gatsby: his career must remain mysterious, of course. But in the end you make it pretty clear that his wealth came through his connection with Wolfsheim. You also suggest this much earlier. *Now almost all readers numerically are going to be puzzled by his having all this wealth and are going to feel entitled to an explanation.* To give a distinct and definite one would be, of course, utterly absurd. It did occur to me, though, that *you might here and there interpolate some phrases, and possibly incidents, little touches of various kinds, that would suggest that he was in some active way mysteriously engaged.* You do have him called on the telephone, but couldn't he be seen once or twice consulting at his parties with people of some sort of mysterious significance, from the political, the gambling, the sporting world, or whatever it may be. . . . *The total lack of explanation through so large a part of the story does seem to me a defect—or not of an explanation, but of the suggestion of an explanation.* [250/251] . . . *What Gatsby did ought never to be definitely imparted, even if it could be.* Whether he was an innocent tool in the hands of somebody else, or to what degree he was this, ought not to be explained. *But if some sort of business activity of his were simply adumbrated, it would lend further probability to that part of the story.* (Italics mine)[12]

Fitzgerald seems to have followed this advice. Writing to Maxwell Perkins circa December 1, 1924, he comments on his friend's criticisms. Part of his comments reads:

(c) Gatby's business affairs I can fix. I get your point about them.
(d) His vagueness I can repair by *making more pointed*—this doesn't sound good but wait and see. It'll make him clear.[13]

[8] For a good brief account of the oil scandals and an excellent account of the public reaction to their disclosure, see Frederick Lewis Allen's *Only Yesterday* (Bantam, 1946), pp. 158-172. See also Marcus E. Ravage's *The Story of Teapot Dome* (N.Y., 1924) for a contemporary account, and for a modern scholarly account see Burl Noggle's *Teapot Dome: Oil and Politics in the 1920's* (Baton Rouge, 1962).
[9] Frederick Lewis Allen, *Only Yesterday* (New York: Bantam Books, 1946), p. 161.
[10] Burl Noggle, *Teapot Dome: Oil and Politics in the 1920's* (Baton Rouge: Louisiana State University Press, 1962), pp. 152ff, 201, 204, 205.
[11] From May 1924 to February 1925. Cf. Henry Dan Piper, "The Untrimmed Christmas Tree: The Religious Background of *The Great Gatsby*" in *The Great Gatsby: a Study*, Frederick J. Hoffman, ed. (New York: Scribner's, 1962), p. 322.

[12] Alfred Kazin, ed., *F. Scott Fitzgerald: The Man and His Work* (New York: Collier Books Edition, 1962), pp. 86-87.
[13] Andrew Turnbull, ed., *The Letters of F. Scott Fitzgerald* (New York: Dell Publishing Company, 1965), p. 170.

And in a letter circa February 18, 1925, he begins:

Dear Max:

After six weeks of uninterrupted work the proof is finished and the last of it goes to you this afternoon. On the whole it's been very successful labor.

(1) I've brought Gatsby to life.

(2) I've accounted for his money.[14]

How did Fitzgerald fix Gatsby's business affairs and account for his money? From where was all his immense wealth supposed to come? One possibility is that he helped Meyer Wolfsheim fix the World Series of 1919. We know Gatsby was associated with Wolfsheim in a business way ever since he got out of the army: Late in the book Wolfsheim tells Nick that Gatsby had come to him "so hard up that he had to keep on wearing his uniform because he couldn't buy some regular clothes" (172).

"Did you start him in business?" . . .

". . . Right off he did some work for a client of mine up to Albany. We were so thick like that in everything"—he held up two bulbous fingers—"always together."

I wondered if this partnership had included the World Series transaction of 1919. (172)

But according to Leo Katcher, Arnold Rothstein, the gambler upon [251/252] whom Meyer Wolfsheim is supposed to have been modeled, made only about $350,000 by allowing the 1919 World Series to be fixed.[15] This is a lot of money, but not enough to account for the tremendous affluence in which Gatsby is supposed to bask. Besides, back in Chapter V, on the afternoon on which Daisy and Gatsby are reunited for the first time since the war, Gatsby, referring to his house—a huge imitation Normandy Hotel de Ville—tells Nick, "It took me just three years to earn the money that bought it" (91). Since Gatsby spent five months at Oxford in 1919,[16] he couldn't possibly

have had the money to buy his mansion before June 1922 (he would probably tell the truth about the cost of such an expensive prestige purchase as this).[17] So involvement in the World Series fix alone would not account for either the magnitude of his wealth or the period of time over which it was supposed to have been made. Neither, in all probability, would his bootlegging operations: "That drugstore business was just small change," Tom says. He must have made the bulk of his fortune some other way.

The conclusion seems to be that Gatsby made the money to buy his mansion by engaging in some activity that was bigger than bootlegging and even bigger than fixing a World Series. It would have to be something in which he was still actively engaged at the time of the novel: Tom says to Gatsby, "You've got something on now that Walter's afraid to tell me about," and Gatsby crumples. The Teapot Dome affair is an operation that would satisfy the conditions Fitz- [252/

---

[14] *Letters*, p. 177.

[15] Leo Katcher, "The Man Who Fixed the Series," in Frederick J. Hoffman, pp. 148-159 (cf. footnote 11). He insisted he won less than $100,000, and convinced a grand jury that he had nothing whatsoever to do with the fix.

[16] *The Great Gatsby*, p. 129.

[17] Apparently Gatsby's mansion resembles, in magnificence if not in style, *The Breakers*, Cornelius Vanderbilt's mansion at Newport, Rhode Island, which was erected in 1893-95 at enormous cost—$3,000,000, according to the American Guide Series (*Rhode Island, a Guide to the Smallest State*, Federal Writer's Project of WPA, [Boston: Houghton Mifflin, 1937], pp. 233-4), and which according to Howard Mumford Jones, "outshone the palaces of the Medici in oppulence" (caption to illustration facing p. 272, Howard Mumford Jones, *O Strange New World* [New York: Viking, 1964]). *The Breakers* measures 250 by 150 feet, has seventy rooms, when fully staffed was manned by forty servants, and contains a library panelled with Circassian walnut decorated in High Renaissance style with a fireplace taken from a sixteenth century French chateau. Gatsby's mansion is noted for its vast size ("That huge place there?" Daisy cries on learning that it is his), its great number of rooms ("His house had never seemed so enormous to me as it did that night when we hunted through the great rooms for cigarettes"), the six or eight servants (but Gatsby is living there alone), and its "Merton College Library" (another touch of Oxford, by the way) where Owl Eyes serves as chorus ("On a chance we tried an important-looking door, and walked into a high Gothic library, panelled with carved English oak, and probably transported complete from some ruin overseas.") My point is that Gatsby's mansion is not some modest little $250,000 home but more likely a three million dollar house like *The Breakers* if it would take even a man of Gatsby's financial ability and drive three years to earn the money to buy it. Moreover, while it took Cornelius Vanderbilt's architect two years to assemble the building materials from all corners of the world and put the house up—an incredibly short space of time—Gatsby bought his mansion ready-made from a deceased brewer's descendent. In more ways than one it is an instant palace.

253] gerald has set up. Is there any direct evidence in the text itself that Fitzgerald intended the reader to think of that scandal in connection with Gatsby?

There is. At two different points in the book there are references—very unobtrusive ones—not to Teapot Dome, but to oil. The first one occurs early in Chapter I, when Nick pays his initial visit to Tom and Daisy, and Tom casually mentions that his house had "belonged to Demaine, the oil man" (8). Thus early in the book a connection is made between the glamorous life on Long Island and that source of wealth that glittered but currently reeked of corruption. The second and more important reference comes in Chapter V. In the passage immediately following the one in which Gatsby tells Nick that it took three years to earn the money to buy his house, Nick asks him how he earns his living and receives, first a rebuff, then a vague reply:

I think he hardly knew what he was saying, for when I asked him what business he was in he answered: "That's my affair," before he realized that it wasn't an appropriate reply.

"Oh, I've been in several things," he corrected himself. "I was in the drug business and then I was in the oil business. But I'm not in either one now." (91)[18]

It looks as if Fitzgerald had taken Maxwell Perkins' hint that he "interpolate some phrases . . . little touches of various kinds . . . the suggestion of an explanation . . ." in part at least by incorporating some of the atmosphere of Teapot Dome. Considering the tremendous significance the house has for Gatsby as a means of first impressing and then winning Daisy, it is highly suggestive that it is associated first with "the drug business," which by the end of the book we know to be a euphemism for bootlegging, and then with

oil. The implication is that Gatsby's oil business is illegitimate too.

The chronology of Gatsby's mysterious business activities also fits that of the Teapot Dome affair. The action of the novel takes place during the summer of 1922; the first crucial transaction in the Harding oil manipulations occurred on April 7, 1922, when Secretary of the Interior Albert B. Fall, secretly and without competitive bidding, leased Naval Oil Reserve No. 3, at Teapot Dome, Wyoming, to Harry F. Sinclair's Mammoth Oil Company[19]—a favor for which he later [253/254] received from Sinclair some $260,000 in Liberty Bonds.[20] Someone like Gatsby would have made every effort to be in on this deal, which was in effect during the summer of 1922 and for long after, and which made its beneficiaries (not the American public at large) fabulously wealthy. The groundwork for Teapot Dome was laid as far back as 1921, less than three months after President Harding took office, when Fall got the President to sign an executive order transferring control of the naval oil reserves from the Department of the Navy to Fall's own Department of the Interior.[21] This too falls well within the three-year period during which Gatsby is supposed to have earned the wealth which he mentions to Nick in Chapter V.

Participation in the Teapot Dome affair could easily have provided Gatsby with the enormous wealth he needed to buy his mansion and impress Daisy. A fair idea of the kind of profits that could be made through oil manipulation can be gained when one considers what occurred even before Secretary of the Interior Fall had leased public lands to private operators at a scandalously low rate—on November 17, 1921, to be exact. On that date a little group of men—including Harry Sinclair—

---

[18] We know that the last sentence is untrue in regard to Gatsby's "drug business"; it is probably also untrue in regard to his "oil business." The more large-scale and illegitimate the enterprise in which he is engaged, the more it would be in his self-interest to lie about his current involvement in it. Gatsby lies at other points in the book whenever he deems it necessary in order to impress Daisy.

[19] Allen, p. 150.
[20] Allen, pp. 160-161.
[21] Allen, p. 160.

met in a room at New York's Hotel Vanderbilt to transact some oil business. Just
previous to this a part of the group—again
including Harry Sinclair—had taken advantage of Canadian law to set up a
dummy corporation, The Continental
Trading Company, Limited. They acted,
not on behalf of the companies they were
associated with, but as private individuals.
At the November 17th meeting Col. E. A.
Humphreys of Humphreys Texas Company and Humphreys Mexia Company
sold 333,333,333 barrels of crude oil
at $1.50 a barrel to Continental Trad-
ing Company, which thereupon turned
around and resold the oil to companies
represented by two of the men present—
once again including Harry Sinclair—at
$1.75 a barrel *on the same day.* This quick
and effortless profit of 25 cents a barrel on
333,333,333 barrels of oil[22] would have
added up to over eight million dollars—
no small sum—had not certain members of
the Senate become suspicious and begun
to investigate. The reason they became
suspicious was that the Continental owners had invested their profit in Liberty
bonds, some of which were used to pay
off the Secretary of the Interior. Although
by this time Continental had gone out of
business and destroyed its books, "the government had the num- **[254/255]** bers of
the bonds, and the secret service agents
already had traced $90,000 of them to
Albert B. Fall" (Noggle, p. 181).[23]

This too may be referred to by Fitzgerald in *The Great Gatsby.* When Nick
Carroway takes over Gatsby's affairs after
the latter is murdered, one of the phone
calls he receives is a long distance call
from Chicago:

"This is Slagle speaking . . ."
. . . "Young Parke's in trouble," he said rapidly. "They picked him up when he handed the
bonds over the counter. They got a circular from

New York giving 'em the numbers just five
minutes before. What d'you know about that,
hey? You never can tell in these hick towns—"
"Hello!" I interrupted breathlessly. "Look here
—this isn't Mr. Gatsby. Mr. Gatsby's dead."
There was a long silence on the other end of
the wire, followed by an exclamation . . . then
a quick squawk as the connection was broken.
(167)

It is true that the bonds mentioned here
may be less celebrated than the famous
Liberty bonds which secret service agents
were tracking down in connection with
Teapot Dome; they may be more ordinary
stolen or counterfeit bonds. But it is also
true that when the novel came out in
1925, the word "bonds" would be in
every one's ears and would suggest mainly
one thing, especially when mentioned in
a book that made subtle but effective use
of that other currently suggestive word,
"oil." The discovery that Fall possessed
Liberty bonds obtained from Continental
Trading Company was made early in
March 1924,[24] and so would not fit the
chronology of *Gatsby,* which occurs during the summer of 1922. But a single departure from strict chronology by an author who is merely trying to convey the
impression of corruption rather than state
its details is no strong argument against
my theory, especially when the chronolo-
gies of Gatsby and the Teapot Dome affair coincide exactly at every other point.
I would guess that Fitzgerald's purpose
was to heighten the suspicion that Gatsby
was involved in Teapot Dome by dropping a hint that would be highly suggestive to the reader of 1925 precisely because the event it referred to had been so
recently disclosed, even though the disclosure itself had actually occurred some
eighteen months after the time of the
action of the novel.

The consequences for literary analysis
of Gatsby's Teapot Dome involvement
are two, both of which have already been
hinted at. The first has to do with Daisy's
snobbery and Gatsby's fear that it **[255/**

---

[22] This profit, incidentally, was never reported by the
gentlemen in question to the directors and stockholders
of the oil companies they were supposed to be representing. Cf. Allen, p. 163.

[23] Cf. Allen, p. 162; Noggle, pp. 180-181.

[24] Cf. Noggle, p. 180.

256] will be turned against him. "He knew that he was in Daisy's house by a colossal accident," Nick says in recounting Gatsby's account of his wartime romance with Daisy: ". . . he had certainly taken her under false pretenses. I don't mean that he had traded on his phantom millions [he correctly judged that he could make them], but he had deliberately given Daisy a sense of security; *he let her believe that he was a person from much the same stratum as herself*—that he was fully able to take care of her" (149. Italics mine).

This last he knows he will never be able to provide unless he can keep her in ignorance of his actual origins and the source of his money; hence the fantastic lies he tells about his background and former life. For that matter, Gatsby is a snob himself, as self-made men frequently are. "I didn't want you to think I was just some nobody," he tells Nick after regaling him with tales of his supposed youth as sole surviving heir of a wealthy family who had lived like a young maharajah in all the capitals of Europe. Later, after Tom has faced him down in the New York hotel suite, he remarks, "He told her those things in a way that frightened her—that made it look as if I was some kind of cheap sharper." Earlier, a girl at one of Gatsby's parties to whom he has sent a two-hundred-and-sixty-five-dollar gown because she had torn her dress on a previous occasion remarks, "There's something funny about a fellow that'll do a thing like that. . . . He doesn't want any trouble with *any*body" (43). The implication is that he doesn't want anyone to start investigating his background, business or social.[25] This helps explain Gatsby's breakdown when Tom tells him

he knows he's on to something extremely big: Nick glances at Daisy and finds her "staring terrified between Gatsby and her husband." For Daisy doesn't care if money is tainted or not as long as nobody mentions that it is tainted. She doesn't give a hoot about where Gatsby's money comes from any more than she gives a hoot about the moral implications of her own running down and abandonment of Myrtle Wilson. What she does care about, and deeply, is that these pecadillos should never become public knowledge. On this point she and Gatsby see eye to eye: they both accept the genteel tradition on its more hypocritical side: do what you must, no matter how dirty it is, but don't let anyone know that you're doing it. [256/257]

The other literary consequence of Gatsby's Teapot Dome involvement is that it shows the end result of the American Dream if it is pushed far enough. It is true that the whole matter of financial corruption and political scandal is probably of considerably more interest to certain kinds of readers, including myself, than it ever was to Fitzgerald. The social criticism which is implicit in so much of his work and for which he is so much admired was probably of secondary importance to the author himself. He was more interested in other things, such as the beauty of the moment and the clock ticking away on the mantle,[26] and in certain highly individual personal beliefs of his, such as that a woman can be the death of you if you care enough for her. But if Teapot Dome probably wasn't very important to Fitzgerald, the American Dream was, and he expresses this through his plot. At the end of the book Gatsby is explicitly equated with the American Dream. Gatsby is the kind of character who, if he wants something badly enough, will do anything in order to get it. Daisy on the other hand is the kind of character who values the immunity that comes with riches com-

---

[25] This remark is made in the scene in which the party guests speculate about Gatsby's past: about whether he had been a German spy during the war or had killed a man. It takes place in the garden of Gatsby's palace and is referred to by Nick during the climactic hotel room scene when he remarks that Gatsby looks "as if he had 'killed a man' "—and this is said in all contempt for the babbled slander of his garden" (135). A garden was a prominent feature of the three million dollar Vanderbilt home at Newport (see footnote 17 on *The Breakers*).

[26] Gale H. Carrithers, Jr., "Fitzgerald's Triumph," in Frederick J. Hoffmann, p. 311.

bined with high social station so much that she will do anything in order to preserve it. Gatsby, in order to win the dream of love, tries to catch her with his house, which resembles the three million dollar Vanderbilt mansion known as *The Breakers,* and to obtain the money for it he takes part in Teapot Dome. This makes Gatsby a robber baron, almost on a level with our folk-hero millionaire-picaros of the Gilded Age: like them he has mulcted the American public and defrauded the Federal Government. The government of the United States, which was originally founded and supported by smugglers like John Hancock and free-booters like John Paul Jones, ends up as itself the victim of free-booters, whom it supports while they prey on it.

I. CRIME AND CORRUPTION

Fitzgerald's Jay Gatz and Young Ben Franklin *

FLOYD C. WATKINS (1920–   ) is a professor of English at Emory University. Among his recent books are *Thomas Wolfe's Characters* (1957) and *Writer to Writer* (1966).

According to many recent critics, one of the features of the works of F. Scott Fitzgerald, especially *The Great Gatsby*, is an awareness of the American historical tradition. Jay Gatsby is not only a representative of the Roaring Twenties in which he lived; he also, according to Lionel Trilling, "comes inevitably to stand for America itself."[1] In an article in the *Pacific Spectator* Charles S. Holmes has shown that Fitzgerald was "concerned with the generic American character, the national 'style,' and the native tradition."[2] According to his biographer, Arthur Mizener, "The substance out of which Fitzgerald constructed his stories . . . was American, perhaps more completely American than that of [249/250] any other writer of his time."[3] John Peale Bishop has seen Gatsby as "the Emersonian man brought to completion and eventually to failure."[4] And this documentation of Fitzgerald and Gatsby as personifications of America and the American dream could be carried to much greater length.

In *The Great Gatsby* Fitzgerald was certainly aware of the American tradition as it was being developed by his contemporaries in the Twenties. Describing the very symbolical ash dumps, Fitzgerald in one sentence alluded to two contemporary works that attempted to place the period in an historical frame of reference: "The only building in sight was a small block of yellow brick sitting on the edge of the waste land, a sort of compact Main Street ministering to it, and contiguous to absolutely nothing."[5] Here the meaning of his description is very much in tone with the works to which he refers, Eliot's *The Waste Land* and Lewis' *Main Street*. The most important linking of the novel to the American past, however, is accomplished at the end of the book, where Fitzgerald speaks of Manhattan as "the old island here that flowered once for Dutch sailors' eyes—a fresh green breast of the new world. Its vanished trees, the trees that had made way for Gatsby's house, had once pandered in whispers to the last and greatest of all human dreams. . . ."[6] The import of this passage lies in the implied comparison of Gatsby's incorruptible dream to the dream of the New World.

There is one other significant connection between *The Great Gatsby* and the American past, and it has been only vaguely noted heretofore. Mr. Holmes has described Gatsby as "devoted . . . to the success maxims of the Ben Franklin tradition."[7] Mr. Charles Weir quotes entirely

---

[1] Lionel Trilling, *The Liberal Imagination* (New York, 1950), 251.
[2] Charles S. Holmes, "Fitzgerald: The American Theme," *Pacific Spectator*, VI, 243 (Spring, 1952).
[3] Arthur Mizener, "F. Scott Fitzgerald: The Poet of Borrowed Time," in Willard Thorp, *The Lives of Eighteen from Princeton* (Princeton, 1946), 333.
[4] John Peale Bishop, "The Missing All," *Virginia Quarterly Review*, XIII, 115 (Winter, 1937).

[5] F. Scott Fitzgerald, *The Great Gatsby* (New York, 1925), 29.
[6] Fitzgerald, *The Great Gatsby*, 217.
[7] *Pacific Spectator*, VI, 248.

*Floyd C. Watkins, "Fitzgerald's Jay Gatz and Young Ben Franklin," *New England Quarterly*, XVII (June 1954), 249-252. Reprinted with the permission of the author and the New England Quarterly.

the schedule that Jay Gatsby as the young Jay Gatz had copied into "a ragged old copy of a book called *Hopalong Cassidy*."[8] Then he exclaims: "What childhood dreams of Franklin or Edison lay behind the scrawl, what lectures on self-improve- [250/251] ment, what tradition that every American boy could make a million dollars or become President!"[9]

The source is not nearly so much Edison as it is Franklin, that early American whom Carlyle called "the Father of all Yankees" and who was to Sinclair Lewis' Babbitt "this solid American citizen." Most of the resolutions of Fitzgerald's hero can be traced either to Franklin's own schedule or to his list of thirteen virtues to which he gives "a week's strict attention" in order to attain moral perfection.[10] Thus by five o'clock in his daily timetable Franklin wrote "Rise," and at six o'clock Gatsby intended to "Rise from bed." The early American intended to "prosecute the present study" before eight o'clock, and the modern American planned to "Study electricity, etc." from 7:15 until 8:15; thus Gatsby did not devote himself to study of the philosophers as Franklin had, but to one of the most practical (and American) aspects of his model's career. Whereas Franklin wrote "Work" by the hours from eight to twelve and from two to six, with an hour out for lunch, young Jay Gatz recorded, "Work . . . 8:30-4:30 P.M." Fitzgerald gave Gatsby one greater virtue than Franklin: he was earlier to bed. Gatsby slept from nine until six; Franklin, from ten to five. Franklin's reputation as inventor might have caused the resolve by the later American to "Study needed inventions" from seven to nine.

Many of the "GENERAL RESOLVES" listed at the bottom of Gatsby's schedule can be traced to Franklin's list of thirteen virtues, and the result of the comparison is

often comic as well as pathetic. Franklin's "Cleanliness" becomes for Gatsby "Bath every other day"; "Industry" is "No wasting time at Shafters or [a name, indecipherable]"; "Frugality" is "Save $5.00 [crossed out] $3.00 per week"; "Temperance" is "No more smoking or chewing"; "Sincerity. Use no hurtful deceit" and "Justice. Wrong none by doing injuries, or omitting the benefits that are your duty" possibly become for Gatsby more specific and less inclusive: "Be better to parents." Perhaps a source for Gatsby's "Read one improving book or magazine per week" may be found in Franklin's scheduled notation to "Read" during his noon hour. From five to six o'clock dur- [251/252] ing the day Gatsby plans to "Practice elocution, poise and how to attain it," but in this resolution he remembered none of the virtue to be found in Franklin's description of "Sincerity": "think innocently and justly, and, if you speak, speak accordingly." In every single parallel Gatsby took Franklin's general virtue and listed in its stead one concrete and very specific resolution which was less demanding than that found in his source. These parallels leave only two activities or resolves that are scheduled by Gatsby and that are not to be found in Franklin: "Dumbbell exercise and wall-scaling," from 6:15 to 6:30 in the morning; and "Baseball and sports," from 4:30 to 5:00 in the afternoon. The earlier American's recreations, "Music or diversion, or conversation," were too inactive and intellectual for his follower.

Such close parallels as these surely indicate that Fitzgerald had Franklin's *Autobiography* either in front of him or in his mind when he wrote the schedule of Jay Gatz. It is my opinion that he closely followed Franklin in order to give concreteness to the historical tradition of Gatsby and to make Gatsby something beyond a mere member of the lost generation: an American who was a personification of the national dream as it had been corrupted.

[8] Fitzgerald, *The Great Gatsby*, 208-209.
[9] Charles Weir, Jr., " 'An Invite with Gilded Edges': A Study of F. Scott Fitzgerald," *Virginia Quarterly Review*, xx, 111 (Winter, 1944).
[10] John Bigelow, editor, *The Autobiography of Benjamin Franklin* (New York, 1909), 189-196.

[Rules for Self-Improvement] *

BENJAMIN FRANKLIN (1706–90) is best remembered for his many-sided genius: newspaper publisher, author, physicist, statesman, and diplomat. Born in Boston and long associated with Philadelphia, he embodied the traditional Puritan virtues of industry, thrift, and the will to succeed. These found expression in *Poor Richard's Almanac*, which he published annually from 1732 to 1757, and in his *Autobiography*, which was not published until long after his death, in 1818.

It was about this time I conceived the bold and arduous project of arriving at moral perfection. I wished to live without committing any fault at any time; I would conquer all that either natural inclination, custom, or company might lead me into. As I knew, or thought I knew, what was right and wrong, I did not see why I might not *always* do the one and avoid the other. But I soon found I had undertaken a task of more difficulty than I had imagined. While my attention was taken up in guarding against one fault, I was often surprised by another; habit took the advantage of intention; inclination was sometimes too strong for reason. I concluded, at length, that the mere speculative conviction that it was our interest to be completely virtuous was not sufficient to prevent our slipping; and that the contrary habits must be broken, and good ones acquired and established, before we can have any dependence on a steady, uniform rectitude of conduct. For this purpose I therefore contrived the following method.

In the various enumerations of the moral virtues I had met with [71/72] in my reading, I found the catalogue more or less numerous, as different writers included more or fewer ideas under the same name. Temperance, for example, was by some confined to eating and drinking, while by others it was extended to mean the moderating every other pleasure, appetite, inclination, or passion, bodily or mental, even to our avarice and ambition. I proposed to myself, for the sake of clearness, to use rather more names, with fewer ideas annexed to each, than a few names with more ideas; and I included under thirteen names of virtues all that at that time occurred to me as necessary or desirable, and annexed to each a short precept, which fully expressed the extent I gave to its meaning.

These names of virtues with their precepts were:

1. TEMPERANCE
Eat not to dullness; drink not to elevation.

2. SILENCE
Speak not but what may benefit others or yourself; avoid trifling conversation.

3. ORDER
Let all your things have their places; let each part of your business have its time.

4. RESOLUTION
Resolve to perform what you ought; perform without fail what you resolve.

5. FRUGALITY
Make no expense but to do good to others or yourself; *i.e.*, waste nothing.

*Benjamin Franklin, Autobiography, ed. by Robert E. Spiller and W. W. Reynolds, Jr., (New York: Houghton Mifflin, 1966), 71-77. Reprinted with the permission of the Houghton Mifflin Co.

6. INDUSTRY

Lose no time; be always employed in something useful; cut off all unnecessary actions.

7. SINCERITY

Use no hurtful deceit; think innocently and justly; and, if you speak, speak accordingly.

8. JUSTICE

Wrong none by doing injuries, or omitting the benefits that are your duty. [72/73]

9. MODERATION

Avoid extremes; forbear resenting injuries so much as you think they deserve.

10. CLEANLINESS

Tolerate no uncleanness in body, clothes, or habitation.

11. TRANQUILLITY

Be not disturbed at trifles, or at accidents common or unavoidable.

12. CHASTITY

Rarely use venery but for health or offspring; never to dullness, weakness, or the injury of your own or another's peace or reputation.

13. HUMILITY

Imitate Jesus and Socrates.

My intention being to acquire the *habitude* of all these virtues, I judged it would be well not to distract my attention by attempting the whole at once, but to fix it on one of them at a time; and, when I should be master of that, then to proceed to another, and so on, till I should have gone through the thirteen; and as the previous acquisition of some might facilitate the acquisition of certain others, I arranged them with that view, as they stand above. *Temperance* first, as it tends to procure that coolness and clearness of head, which is so necessary where constant vigilance was to be kept up, and guard maintained against the unremitting attraction of ancient habits, and the force of perpetual temptations. This being acquired and established, *Silence* would

be more easy; and my desire being to gain knowledge at the same time that I improved in virtue, and considering that in conversation it was obtained rather by the use of the ears than of the tongue, and therefore wishing to break a habit I was getting into of prattling, punning, and joking, which only made me acceptable to trifling company, I gave *Silence* the second place. This and the next, *Order,* I expected would allow me more time for attending to my project and my studies. *Resolution,* once become habitual, would keep me firm in my endeavors to obtain all the subsequent virtues; *Frugality* and *Industry,* by freeing me from my remaining debt, and producing affluence and independence, would make more easy the practice of *Sincerity* and *Justice,* etc., etc. Conceiving then, that, agreeable to the advice of Pythagoras[1] in his Golden Verses, [73/74] daily examination would be necessary, I contrived the following method for conducting that examination.

I made a little book, in which I allotted a page for each of the virtues. I ruled each page with red ink, so as to have seven columns, one for each day of the week, marking each column with a letter for the day.

TEMPERANCE

Eat not to Dulness.
Drink not to Elevation.

	S.	M.	T.	W.	T.	F.	S.
T.							
S.	*	*	*		*		*
O.	*	*	*		*	*	*
R.			*			*	
F.		*			*		
I.			*				
S.							
J.							
M.							
Cl.							
T.							
Ch.							
H.							

[1] Pythagoras: Greek philosopher and mathematician. 582 - c. 500 B.C.

I crossed these columns with thirteen red lines, marking the beginning of each line with the first letter of one of the virtues, on which line, and in its proper column, I might mark, by a little black spot, every fault I found upon examination to have been committed respecting that virtue upon that day.

I determined to give a week's strict attention to each of the virtues successively. Thus, in the first week, my great guard was to avoid even the least offense against *Temperance,* leaving the other virtues to their ordinary chance, only marking every evening the faults of the day. Thus, if in the first week I could keep my first line, marked T, clear of spots, I supposed the habit of that virtue so much strengthened, and its opposite weakened, that I might venture extending my attention to include the next, and for the following week keep both lines clear of spots. Proceeding thus to the last, I could go through a course complete in thirteen weeks, and four courses in a year. And **[74/75]** like him who, having a garden to weed, does not attempt to eradicate all the bad herbs at once, which would exceed his reach and his strength, but works on one of the beds at a time, and, having accomplished the first, proceeds to a second, so I should have, I hoped, the encouraging pleasure of seeing on my pages the progress I made in virtue, by clearing successively my lines of their spots, till in the end, by a number of courses, I should be happy in viewing a clean book, after a thirteen weeks' daily examination.

This my little book had for its motto these lines from Addison's *Cato:*[2]

Here will I hold. If there is a power above us
(And that there is, all nature cries aloud
Through all her works), He must delight in virtue;
And that which he delights in must be happy.

Another from Cicero,[3]

"*O vitæ Philosophia dux! O virtutum indaga-*

trix, expultrixque vitiorum! Unus dies bene, et ex præceptis tuis actus, peccanti immortalitati est anteponendus."

[Oh philosophy, guide of life! Oh searcher out of virtues and expeller of vices! One day lived well and according to thy precepts is to be preferred to an eternity of sin.]

Another from the Proverbs of Solomon, speaking of wisdom or virtue:

"Length of days is in her right hand, and in her left hand riches and honor. Her ways are ways of pleasantness, and all her paths are peace." iii. 16, 17.

And conceiving God to be the fountain of wisdom, I thought it right and necessary to solicit his assistance for obtaining it; to this end I formed the following little prayer, which was prefixed to my tables of examination, for daily use.

O powerful Goodness! bountiful Father! merciful Guide! Increase in me that wisdom which discovers my truest interests. Strengthen my resolutions to perform what that wisdom dictates. Accept my kind offices to thy other children as the only return in my power for thy continual favors to me. **[75/76]**

I used also sometimes a little prayer which I took from Thomson's poems,[4] viz.:

Father of light and life, thou Good Supreme!
O teach me what is good; teach me Thyself!
Save me from folly, vanity, and vice,
From every low pursuit; and fill my soul
With knowledge, conscious peace, and virtue pure;
Sacred, substantial, never-fading bliss!

The precept of *Order* requiring that *every part of my business should have its allotted time,* one page in my little book contained the following scheme of employment for the twenty-four hours of a natural day.

THE MORNING Question. What good shall I do this day?	5	Rise, wash, and address *Powerful Goodness!* Contrive day's business,
	6	and take the resolution of the day; prosecute the present study, and
	7	breakfast.

---

[2] Addison's *Cato:* tragedy by Joseph Addison (1672-1719), English poet, essayist, and dramatist.
[3] Cicero: Marcus Tullius (106-43 B.C.), Roman philosopher, orator, and politician.
[4] Thomson's poems: The quoted lines are from "Winter," in *The Seasons,* by the British poet James Thomson (1700-1748).

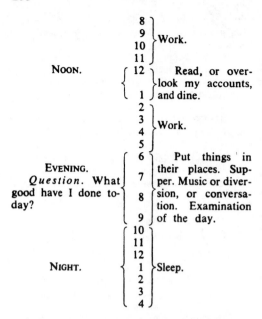

	8	
	9	Work.
	10	
	11	
NOON.	12	Read, or over-
		look my accounts,
	1	and dine.
	2	
	3	Work.
	4	
	5	
EVENING.	6	Put things in their places. Sup-
Question. What good have I done to-day?	7	per. Music or diver-
	8	sion, or conversa- tion. Examination
	9	of the day.
	10	
	11	
	12	
NIGHT.	1	Sleep.
	2	
	3	
	4	

for some time. I was surprised to find myself so much fuller of faults than I had imagined; but I had the satisfaction of seeing them diminish. To avoid the trouble of renewing now and then my little book, which, by scraping out the marks on the paper of old faults to make room for new ones in a new course, became full of holes, I transferred my tables and precepts to the ivory leaves of a memorandum book, on which the lines were drawn with red ink, that made a durable stain, and on those lines I marked my faults with a black lead pencil, which marks I could easily wipe out with a wet sponge. After a while I went through one course only in a year, and afterwards only one in several years, till at length I omitted them entirely, being employed in voyages and business abroad, with a multiplicity of affairs that interfered; but I always carried my little book with me.

I entered upon the execution of this plan for self-examination, [76/77] and continued it with occasional intermissions

The Self-Made Man in America *

IRVIN G. WYLLIE (1920–   ) is a professor of history at the University of Wisconsin and the chancellor of its Parkside campus, Kenosha, Wisconsin. In addition to The Self-Made Man in America (1954) he has also written numerous essays and reviews for historical journals and magazines.

Though it was an American conceit that the self-made man was peculiar to our shores, he had been known in other lands. Since virtually all societies provided some channels for vertical social circulation, men of this type had been common to all. In the older nations of Europe such institutions as the army, the church, the school, and the political party served as agencies for testing, sifting, and distributing individuals within various social strata. Even in associating the self-made man with wealth America enjoyed no special distinction, for in ancient Greece and Rome successful moneymakers often rose into the ruling class, regardless of social origin. And in the Italian city-states and the commercial centers of Western Europe at the close of the Middle Ages moneymaking was one of the most common and omnipotent means of social promotion.[5]

Seventeenth-century England was especially familiar with the economic definition applied to this class of men, for as the English merchant classes rose to power they inspired a substantial literature of justification. Publicists associated with the English business community turned out many pamphlets, sermons, and guidebooks which pointed out the way to wealth. One of these English [10/11] classics was Richard Johnson's Nine Worthies of London (1592), an account of nine apprentices who rose to positions of honor through the exercise of personal virtue. Another of these handbooks, A Treatise of the Vocations (1603), written by William Perkins, a learned Cambridge theologian, was held in special regard by Americans. In the seventeenth century success-minded immigrants sometimes carried Perkins' book with them to the New World, and read it for guidance and inspiration.[6] Of course the great majority who came to America had no room for books, but they doubtless carried in their heads an ample store of self-help homilies, for such maxims were common coin in England.

It is a commonplace of American colonial history that most immigrants came to the New World in the hope of improving their economic status. The agricultural laborer knew that land here was plentiful, and easily acquired, while tradesmen and lay laborers built their hopes around the prospect of the high wages which were a natural consequence of the scarcity of labor. On every side American opportunities damaged class patterns inherited from Europe, and altered old orders of caste and custom. In a land where achievement was more important than titles of nobility there was always the possibility that a nobody could become a man of consequence if he

[5] For a discussion of social promotion under European conditions, consult Pitirim Sorokin, Social Mobility (New York, 1927), pp. 139, 164-183.

[6] Louis B. Wright analyzes English success literature in Middle Class Culture in Elizabethan England (Chapel Hill, 1935), pp. 165-200.

worked hard and kept his eye on the main chance. Ralph Barton Perry put it very well when, speaking of colonial artisans and tradesmen, he observed that "They were neither so unfortunate as to be imbued with a sense of helplessness, nor so privileged as to be satisfied with their present status. They possessed just enough to whet their appetites for more and to feel confident of their power to attain it."[7]

After the starving time had passed and commercial [11/12] towns had sprung up along the Atlantic seaboard, urban dwellers could dream not just of competence but of wealth. Cadwallader Colden, reporting on New York City in 1748, asserted that "The only principle of life propagated among the young people is to get money, and men are only esteemed according to what they are worth—that is, the money they are possessed of."[8] This passion for wealth was one which enjoyed the sanction of religion, especially in New England, where Puritan clergymen assured their congregations that God approved business callings, and rewarded virtue with wealth. Cotton Mather, for example, in *Two Brief Discourses, one Directing a Christian in his General Calling; another Directing him in his Personal Calling* (1701) taught that in addition to serving Christ, which was man's general calling, all men were obliged to succeed in some useful secular employment, in order to win salvation in this life as well as in the next. In *Essays To Do Good* (1710) he argued that Prosperity was the gift of God, and that men of wealth were God's stewards, charged with the responsibility of doing good to their fellows.[9] Such doctrines as these, inherited from seventeenth-century England, occu-

pied a central place in the American success rationale.

It was no accident that the best-known colonial self-made man was Benjamin Franklin, a product of Puritan Boston. At a tender age he read Cotton Mather's *Essays To Do Good,* later crediting them with having had a profound and lifelong influence on his thought and conduct. He also received advice from his father, a humble Puritan candlemaker, who drummed into his head the meaning of the ancient proverb: "Seest thou a man diligent in his business? He shall stand before kings." Forti- [12/13] fied by these principles of self-help Franklin migrated to Philadelphia, the Quaker commercial metropolis, to begin his rise in the printing trade. The story of his upward climb has always enjoyed a prominent place in the folklore of success. Through *Poor Richard's Almanack* (1732-1757) he publicized prosperity maxims which have probably exerted as much practical influence on Americans as the combined teachings of all the formal philosophers. Certainly in the nineteenth century the alleged virtues of the American people closely resembled the virtues of Poor Richard.[10]

During the American Revolution Franklin's energies were diverted into other channels, and it was the third decade of the nineteenth century before his self-help themes were revived by a new generation of success propagandists. In the troubled years after 1763 publicists were too busy framing assertions of political independence, too busy contriving Federalist and Republican polemics, to be diverted to the writing of maxims of trade. And despite the gains made in industry, commerce, and finance between the Revolution and the period of Jackson's rise to power, few prophets arose to call young men to action in these spheres. By 1830, however, the impacts of the Industrial

[7] Ralph Barton Perry, *Puritanism and Democracy* (New York, 1944), p. 298. See also Arthur M. Schlesinger, "What Then Is the American, This New Man?" *American Historical Review,* XLVIII (1943), 227, 237, 239.

[8] Quoted in T. J. Wertenbaker, *The Golden Age of Colonial Culture* (New York, 1942), p. 48.

[9] The best analysis of Cotton Mather's ideas on business success is in Alfred W. Griswold, "Three Puritans on Prosperity," *New England Quarterly,* VII (1934), 475-493.

[10] For Franklin's influence on the nineteenth-century success ideology, see Louis B. Wright, "Franklin's Legacy to the Gilded Age," *Virginia Quarterly Review,* XXII (1946), 268-279.

Revolution could no longer be ignored; in the great cities of the North and East, journalists, clergymen, lawyers and other spokesmen began to lay the foundations for the powerful nineteenth-century cult of the self-made man.

Appropriately Benjamin Franklin became the first object of adoration in this cult, the convenient symbol which linked the success traditions of the two centuries. [13/14] In 1826 Simeon Ide, a Vermont printer, dedicated a new edition of Franklin's *The Way to Wealth* and *Advice to Young Tradesmen* to the mechanics and farmers of New England. He urged every workingman to reflect on his own advantages, and to compare them with the disadvantages that Franklin had encountered, observing that "Perhaps he may, from a comparison, draw the conclusion, that he has greater advantages in his favour, and fewer discouragements to encounter, than had the persevering Franklin. If this be really the case, what other impediment can there be in his way . . . but the want of a resolute determination to merit, by a similar conduct, the good fortune which attended him?"[11] Ide urged any youth who aspired to wealth or station to lean on the counsel and example of Franklin where he might hope to find an almost infallible passport to the ultimatum of his wishes.

At Boston in 1831 a series of Franklin Lectures was begun with the avowed object of inspiring the young men of that city to make the most of their opportunities. Edward Everett inaugurated the series, proclaiming that the story of Franklin's rise could not be told too often. The most successful men in history, he declared, had been men "of humble origin, narrow fortunes, small advantages, and self-taught."[12] Twenty-six years later, when a statue of Franklin was unveiled in Boston, Robert C. Winthrop again used the occasion to arouse the working class from their lethargy:

Behold him, Mechanics and Mechanics' Apprentices, holding out to you an example of diligence, economy and virtue, and personifying the triumphant success which may await those who follow it! Behold him, ye that are humblest and poorest in present condition or in future prospect,—[14/15] lift up your heads and look at the image of a man who rose from nothing, who owed nothing to parentage or patronage, who enjoyed no advantages of early education which are not open,—a hundred fold open,—to yourselves, who performed the most menial services in the business in which his early life was employed but who lived to stand before Kings, and died to leave a name which the world will never forget.[13]

Probably the number of poor boys who were actually inspired to great deeds by the example of Franklin was never large, but at least one, Thomas Mellon, founder of a great banking fortune, has testified to the influence of Franklin on his life. In the year 1828 young Mellon, then fourteen years old, was living on a farm outside the rising industrial city of Pittsburgh. After he had read a battered copy of Franklin's *Autobiography* which he had picked up at a neighbor's house, he found himself aflame with a new ambition. "I had not before imagined," he said, "any other course of life superior to farming, but the reading of Franklin's life led me to question this view. For so poor and friendless a boy to be able to become a merchant or a professional man had before seemed an impossibility; but here was Franklin, poorer than myself, who by industry, thrift and frugality had become learned and wise, and elevated to wealth and fame. The maxims of 'Poor Richard' exactly suited my sentiments. . . . I regard the reading of Franklin's *Autobiography* as the turning point of my life."[14] Abandoning the family farm at Poverty Point young Mellon migrated to

[11] Simeon Ide, ed., *Benjamin Franklin, The Way to Wealth, Advice to Young Tradesmen, and Sketches of His Life and Character* (Windsor, Vt., 1826), p. 39.

[12] Edward Everett, *Orations and Speeches on Various Occasions by Edward Everett* (Boston, 1836), pp. 298-299.

[13] Robert C. Winthrop, *Oration at the Inauguration of the Statue of Benjamin Franklin* (Boston, 1856), p. 25.

[14] Quoted in Harvey O'Connor, *Mellon's Millions* (New York, 1933), p. 4.

Pittsburgh, where he made his way as a lawyer and money lender. Later when he had founded his own bank it was Frank lin's statue that he placed at the front of the building as a symbol of his inspiration, and in the last years of his [15/16] life he bought a thousand copies of Franklin's *Autobiography,* which he distributed to young men who came seeking advice and money.

Important though Franklin was as a symbol and inspiration, the magnificent economic opportunities of nineteenth-century America constituted a far more important inspiration to young men in quest of wealth. The urge to get ahead was especially strong in areas which had been transformed by the Industrial Revolution; it was no accident that three out of every four nineteenth-century millionaires were natives of New England, New York, or Pennsylvania, and that 70 percent won their fortunes in either manufacturing, banking, trade, or transportation.[15] Such activities were concentrated in the cities, in old commercial centers like New York, Philadelphia, and Boston, or in new industrial towns such as Lawrence, Lowell, Rochester, and Pittsburgh, cities which held the key to fortune for the ambitious poor. On the eve of the Civil War it was a backward metropolis indeed that could not boast of its self-made businessmen, and an American who knew nothing of the careers of Amos and Abbott Lawrence, Samuel Appleton, John Jacob Astor, Peter Cooper, Cornelius Vanderbilt, Stephen Girard, or George Peabody was considered hopelessly uninformed.

In and near the great urban centers sensitive observers divined the tendency of the age and gave it their sanction. "How widely spread is the passion for acquisition," exulted William Ellery Channing of Boston, "not for simple means of subsistence, but for wealth! What vast enterprises agitate the community! What a rush into all the departments of trade."[16] As Channing saw it, it was this tendency that explained the progressive vigor of America in the 1840s. Ralph Waldo Emerson agreed. This philos- [16/17] opher who preached self-reliance also pronounced benedictions on those single-minded businessmen who created the wealth that raised man above the subsistence level, blessed him with leisure, and gave him access to the masterworks of the human race. "The pulpit and the press have many commonplaces denouncing the thirst for wealth," said Emerson; "but if men should take these moralists at their word and leave off aiming to be rich, the moralists would rush to rekindle at all hazards this love of power in the people, lest civilization should be undone. . . ."[17] [17/26]

One of the favorite migrations of ambitious country boys was from New England to the urban centers of New York and Pennsylvania. Because of its accessibility New York City was especially attractive to boys from back-country New England. In the years after 1820 they swarmed into the rising metropolis, captured it, and dominated its business life until after the Civil War.[11] "All do not succeed," a contemporary reported, "but some do, and this is quite sufficient to keep the ambition to get a clerkship in New York alive."[12] Joseph A. Scoville, who knew as much as any man about the New York business community at mid-century, thought there was no mystery about the country boy's rise to positions

[15] Sorokin, "American Millionaires and Multi-Millionaires," *Journal of Social Forces,* III (1925), 634, 639. See also C. Wright Mills, "The American Business Elite: a Collective Portrait," *The Tasks of Economic History,* Supplement V (1945), 22.

[16] William Ellery Channing, "The Present Age," in *The Works of William Ellery Channing* (Boston, 1887), p. 165. Channing delivered this address to the Mercantile Library Company of Philadelphia, May 11, 1841.

[17] Ralph Waldo Emerson, *The Conduct of Life* (Boston, 1904), p. 95.

[11] Albion, *Rise of New York Port,* pp. 240-244. Of the distinguished businessmen listed in the *Dictionary of American Biography,* 32 percent were New Englanders, but only 22 percent won their successes in New England. The Middle Atlantic states, contributing 29 percent of the elite, served as the locale in which 39 percent of the leaders achieved distinction. See Mills, "Business Elite," *Tasks of Economic History,* Supplement V (1945), 22.

[12] Joseph A. Scoville, *The Old Merchants of New York City* (3 vols., New York, 1870), I, 56.

of leadership. "He needs but a foothold," said Scoville. "He asks no more . . . wherever this boy strikes, he fastens." According to Scoville New York merchants preferred to hire country boys, on the theory that they worked harder, and were more resolute, obedient, and cheerful than native New Yorkers. Too often city boys objected to menial tasks, complaining that they were intended for better things. Nothing, not even the blackening of the employer's boots, was beneath the dignity of the New Englander.[13] Presumably [26/27] this attitude went far towards explaining his rapid rise.

It would be difficult to say how many farmers' sons thus won fame and fortune but there is little doubt that contemporaries exaggerated their number. In 1883 a Brooklyn clergyman, Wilbur F. Crafts, published the results of his investigations of the lives of five hundred successful Americans representing all lines of endeavor. According to his data 57 percent of the successful men of his day were born in the country, and only 17 percent in the city. "The first conclusion from these facts," said Crafts, "is that a man who wishes to succeed should select a country farm for his birthplace. . . ."[14] Another study, published in 1909, showed that out of 47 railroad presidents who answered questions about their origins, 55.4 percent came from farms or villages.[15] Three more recent surveys, however, point toward the opposite direction. Farm boys accounted for only 24.6 percent of the deceased American millionaires investigated by Sorokin; only 23.8 percent of the elite businessmen whose origins were checked by C. Wright Mills; and only 12 percent of the twentieth-century leaders studied by William Miller.[16] Even so, as a group farmers' sons ranked second

only to the sons of businessmen in the achievement of outstanding success. This and the fact that farm boys started with fewer advantages made them the favorite candidates for heroes in the cult of the self-made man.

The alleged advantages of rural beginnings concerned mostly health and morals. Fresh air and good food kept the country boy in good physical condition, and his daily round of work left him little time for the mischief that distracted his less busy city cousin. Whereas city boys wasted their lives and their substance in [27/28] saloons, gambling dens, and houses of prostitution, country boys supposedly led a Spartan life that prepared them for the hard struggle of the business world. "Our successful men did not feed themselves on boyhood cigarettes and late suppers, with loafing as their only labor, and midnight parties for their regular evening dissipation," a clergyman declared in 1883. "Such city-trained bodies often give out when the strain comes in business, while the sound body and mind and morals of the man from the country hold on and hold out."[17] In 1909 President Louis W. Hill of the Great Northern Railway testified that, despite the personal inconvenience involved, he had chosen to live on a farm rather than in the city in order to give his three boys the best possible start in life. "I believe," said Hill, "there is no end of arguments that living on the farm gives the best chance for a growing boy."[18]

In only one respect, and that a crucial one, did philosophers of success concede that cities offered advantages which rural villages could not match. Opportunities for making money, they agreed, were better in the city. If the farm boy expected to become a millionaire he had to migrate to a metropolis. Even the most insensitive observers seemed to understand that the

[13] Ibid., I, 57, 194-195; II, 101-102.
[14] Wilbur F. Crafts, Successful Men of Today and What They Say of Success (New York, 1883), pp. 16-17.
[15] W. J. Spillman, "The Country Boy," Science, XXX (1909), 406.
[16] Sorokin, "American Millionaires," Journal of Social Forces, III (1925), 635; Mills, "Business Elite," Tasks of Economic History, Supplement V (1945), 32; Miller, "American Historians and the Business Elite," Journal of Economic History, IX (1949), 204.

[17] Crafts, Successful Men, p. 17. See also Thomas L. Haines and L. W. Yaggy, The Royal Path of Life (Chicago, 1879), pp. 234-235; Matthew H. Smith, "The Elements of Business Success," Hunt's Merchants' Magazine, XXXI (1854), 57-58.
[18] Quoted in Spillman, "Country Boy," Science, XXX (1909), 407.

road to fortune must pass through the city. Many self-help handbooks therefore encouraged farm boys to leave home. "A boy at home seldom has a chance," said one blunt adviser. "Nobody believes in him,—least of all his relations."[19] Out of deference to parents most writers tried to be more subtle; instead of telling boys to leave home they advised them indirectly to do so by talking about the importance of setting up in the right location. "No man can expect to become distinguished in any sphere [28/29] unless he has the amplest field for the exercise of his powers," one handbook declared. "A. T.

Stewart located anywhere out of New York City, would not be what he is, and many a clergyman or lawyer, fixed in a small village, would not have reached the eminence which the world freely accords them."[20] It was sad, but true, that if a country boy desired fortune he had to leave home to achieve it. If there was any consolation in this uprooting it was in the conviction that his chance of failure was slight so long as he remained faithful to the virtues that formed his country character.

[19] Matthew H. Smith, *Successful Folks* (Hartford, 1878), p. 204.

[20] H. L. Reade, *Success in Business* (Hartford, 1875), p. 68. See also *The Problem of Success for Young Men and How to Solve It* (New York, 1903), p. 168; Barnum, *Money-Getting*, p. 23.

[The End of the American Dream] *

DAVID F. TRASK (1929–   ) is a professor of history at the State University of New York at Stony Brook. Among his books are *The United States and the Supreme War Council* (1961), *General Tasker Howard Bliss* (1966), and *Victory Without Peace: American Foreign Relations in the Twentieth Century* (1968).

F. Scott Fitzgerald's *The Great Gatsby* is certainly more than an impression of the Jazz Age, more than a novel of manners. Serious critics have by no means settled upon what that "more" might be, but one hypothesis recurs quite regularly. It is the view that Fitzgerald was writing about the superannuation of traditional American belief, the obsolescence of accepted folklore. *The Great Gatsby* is about many things, but it is inescapably a general critique of the "American dream" and also of the "agrarian myth"—a powerful demonstration of their invalidity for Americans of Fitzgerald's generation and after.[1]

The American dream consisted of the belief (sometimes thought of as a promise) that people of talent in this land of opportunity and plenty could reasonably aspire to material success if they adhered to a fairly well-defined set of behavioral rules—rules set forth in a relatively comprehensive form as long ago as the eighteenth century by Benjamin Franklin. In addition, Americans easily assumed that spiritual satisfaction would automatically accompany material success. The dream was to be realized in an agrarian civilization, a way of life presumed better—far better—than the urban alternative. Thomas Jefferson firmly established the myth of the garden—the concept of agrarian virtue and the urban vice—in American minds. During the turbulent era of westward expansion the myth gained increasing stature.[2]

James Gatz of North Dakota had dreamed a special version of the American dream. Fitzgerald tells us that it constituted "a promise that the rock of the world was founded securely on a fairy's wing."[3] When Gatz lay dead, his father told Nick Carraway that "Jimmy was bound to get ahead."[4] As a child, Gatz set about preparing to realize his dream. He early decided that he could contemplate future glory so long as he scheduled his life properly and adhered to a set of general resolves—resolves quite obviously derivative from *Poor Richard.* "No smokeing [sic] or chewing." "Bath every other

[1] This view is frequently reflected in the paperback collection of criticism edited by Arthur Mizener, entitled *F. Scott Fitzgerald: A Collection of Critical Essays* (Englewood Cliffs, N. J.: Prentice-Hall, Inc., 1963). See especially articles by A. E. Dyson and Marius Bewley, pp. 113-141. Mizener is the author of an excellent biography of Fitzgerald, *The Far Side of Paradise* (Boston: Houghton Mifflin Co., 1949).

[2] For a standard study of agrarian attitudes in American life see Henry Nash Smith, *Virgin Land* (New York: Vintage Books, 1957). The idea of the dream as promise is advanced by Herbert Croly in *The Promise of American Life*, originally published in 1909, but now available in paperback. See Capricorn Books Edition, 1964, 1-7.

[3] F. Scott Fitzgerald, *The Great Gatsby* (New York: Charles Scribner's Sons, 1925, reissued in paperback), 100.

[4] *Ibid.*, 175.

*David F. Trask, "A Note on Fitzgerald's *The Great Gatsby*," *University Review* (formerly *University of Kansas City Review*), XXXIII (Spring 1967), 197-202. Reprinted with the permission of the author and the *University Review*, University of Missouri at Kansas City.

day." "Be better to parents."[5] Yes, James Gatz was *bound* to get ahead, bound as securely to his goal as was Captain Ahab to the pursuit of the white whale. *The Great Gatsby* is the chronicle of what happened when James Gatz attempted to realize the [197/198] promise of his dream.

Gatz thought himself different—very different—from the common run of mankind. We learn that his parents were "shiftless and unsuccessful"—and that "his imagination had never really accepted them as his parents at all." He possessed a "Platonic conception of himself. He was a son of God." As a son of God—*God's boy*—he "must be about His Father's business." What was that business? It was "the service of a vast, vulgar, and meretricious beauty."[6] Gatz plainly imagined himself a Christ—one of the anointed—born of earthly parents but actually a son of God. This is what Fitzgerald sought to convey in establishing that "Jay Gatsby of West Egg, Long Island, sprang from his Platonic conception of himself." That conception moved him to seek out goodness and beauty—certainly a prostituted goodness and beauty, but goodness and beauty nevertheless.[7]

When his moment came at seventeen—James Gatz changed his name. The question of the name change has not received the attention it deserves. Some believe that Fitzgerald derived "Gatsby" from the slang term for pistol current during the Jazz Age—gat. Others see in the act of changing names an intimation of "Jewishness" in the hero, a view supported by the frequency of the name "Jay" among the Jews. Jay Gould comes immediately to mind as do Jay Cooke and J. P. Morgan. Also, it is known that the inspiration for the novel came from Fitzgerald's chance encounter with a Jewish bootlegger.

It is, of course, conceivable that Fitz-

gerald had some or even all of these things in mind, and it is also possible that he had still another thought. Could it be, however unlikely, that he was rendering the literal "Jesus, God's boy" in the name of Jay Gatsby? (In ordinary pronunciation, the "t" easily changes to "d" as in "Gad.") This conjecture might appear hopelessly far-fetched, were it not for Fitzgerald's discussion of Gatz's "Platonic conception of himself," and his direct use of the phrase "son of God." In any case, Gatsby began his pursuit of goodness and beauty when he changed his name, and that pursuit ultimately ended in tragedy.

Fitzgerald develops the tragedy of Jay Gatsby as the consequence of his quixotic quest for Daisy Buchanan. Daisy represents that "vast, vulgar, and meretricious beauty" to which Gatsby aspired. When Jay met Daisy, he realized that he had "forever wed his unutterable visions to her perishable breath." He knew that "his mind would never romp again like the mind of God." When he kissed her, "she blossomed for him like a flower and the incarnation was complete."[8] What was the incarnation? In Daisy, Gatsby's meretricious dream was made flesh. He sought ever after to realize his dream in union with her.[9]

The trouble with Gatsby's quest was that Daisy was completely incapable of playing the role assigned to her. She was as shallow as the other hollow people who inhabited Fitzgerald's Long [198/199] Island. She could never become a legitimate actualization of Gatsby's illegitimate dream. Gatsby was himself culpable. He was not truly God's boy perhaps, but he possessed a certain grandeur, an incredible ability to live in terms of his misguided dream. Nick Carraway understood this, telling Gatsby at one point that he was "worth the whole damned crowd put together."[10]

---

[5] *Ibid.*, 174.
[6] This was a truly grandiose self-image—but then a vastly inflated conception of self has usually been characteristic of the American dreamer.
[7] The quotations in this paragraph are in *Ibid.*, 99.

[8] *Ibid.*, 112.
[9] The intensity of the commitment is indicated in Gatsby's memorable statement about Daisy's relationship with Tom Buchanan: "In any case . . . it was just personal." *Ibid.*, 152.
[10] *Ibid.*, 154.

Both Gatsby and Tom Buchanan, Daisy's husband, possessed wealth. Gatsby at least used his wealth to seek out beauty and claim it for himself. Buchanan the lecher lacked any larger goals. In the end, Daisy chooses to remain with Buchanan, and Gatsby is murdered by the deranged husband of Myrtle Wilson, Buchanan's mistress, who had been accidentally run down and killed by Daisy. Buchanan serves as Gatsby's executioner; he allows George Wilson to believe that Gatsby had killed Myrtle.

Gatsby was as alone in death as he had been in life. Of all the hordes who had accepted his largesse when alive, only one—an unnamed "owl-eyed man" who had admired Gatsby's books—appeared at the funeral. He delivered a pathetic epitaph: "The poor son-of-a-bitch."[11]

The tragedy is over; Fitzgerald speculates on its meaning through the narrator, Nick Carraway. Carraway notes that Jay and the others—Nick himself, his sometime girl friend Jordan Baker, Daisy, and Tom—all were from the Middle West. It was not the Middle West of popular imagination, of the lost agrarian past, but rather the cities of the middle border. "That's my Middle West," muses Carraway, "not the wheat or the prairies or the lost Swede towns, but the thrilling returning trains of my youth, and the street lamps and sleigh bells in the frosty dark and the shadows of holly wreaths thrown by lighted windows on the snow." Carraway continues: Gatsby and his friends "were all Westerners, and perhaps we possessed some deficiency in common which made us subtly unadaptable to Eastern life."[12] The East held many attractions, but the expatriate Westerner lived there at his peril. So Carraway went home. He could at least survive, though he might not prosper, in prairie cities.

Why had Gatsby failed? It was because the time for dreaming as Gatsby dreamed had passed. In what must be, in its implications, one of the most moving passages in American literature, Fitzgerald completes his commentary on Jay Gatsby: "His dream must have seemed so close that he could hardly fail to grasp it. He did not know it was already behind him, somewhere back in that vast obscurity behind the city, where the dark fields of the republic rolled on under the night."[13]

The future to which Gatsby aspired is indeed in the past. His dream—the American dream—had been nurtured in the agrarian past that was no more. Fitzgerald's symbolism is never more ingenious than in his depiction of the [199/200] bankruptcy of the old agrarian myth. This task he accomplishes through the most haunting and mysterious of the symbols which appear in the book—the eyes of Dr. T. J. Eckleburg. Here is one of the cruelest caricatures in the American novel. For Dr. T. J. Eckleburg is none other than a devitalized Thomas Jefferson, the preeminent purveyor of the agrarian myth.

What is it that Dr. Eckleburg's eyes survey? It is the valley of democracy turned to ashes—the garden defiled: "This is a valley of ashes—a fantastic farm where ashes grow like wheat into ridges and hills and grotesque gardens; where ashes take the forms of houses and chimneys and rising smoke and, finally, with a transcendent effort, of men who move dimly and already crumbling through the powdery air. Occasionally a line of gray cars crawls along an invisible track, gives out a ghastly creak, and comes to rest, and immediately the ash-gray men swarm up with leaden spades and stir up an impenetrable cloud, which screens their obscure operations from your sight . . . [Dr. Eckleburg's] eyes, dimmed a little

---

[11] *Ibid.*, 176. Professor Robert Narveson of the University of Nebraska has suggested to me that Fitzgerald might well have been noting that Gatsby had fallen victim to William James's "bitch-goddess success." The "epitaph" might well be "The poor son-of-the-bitch-goddess success."

[12] *Ibid.*, 177. Fitzgerald's preoccupation with East versus West is represented in the novel by "West Egg" and "East Egg," the Long Island towns in which Gatsby and the Buchanans lived. Fitzgerald notes that they were dissimilar "in every particular except shape and size." In addition, he notes "the bizarre and not a little sinister contrast between them." *Ibid.*, 5.

[13] *Ibid.*, 182.

by many paintless days under the sun and rain, brood on over the solemn dumping ground."[14] Fitzgerald thus presents a remarkably evocative description of the corruption that had befallen Jefferson's garden.

At the very end of the novel, Fitzgerald betrays his affection for the myth of the garden, despite his awareness that it could no longer serve Americans. His narrator Carraway once again serves as the vehicle for his thoughts: "And as the moon rose higher the inessential houses began to melt away until gradually I became aware of the old island here that flowered once for Dutch sailor's eyes—a fresh, green breast of the new world. Its vanished trees, the trees that had made way for Gatsby's house, had once pandered in whispers to the last and greatest of all human dreams; for a transitory enchanted moment man must have held his breath in the presence of this continent, compelled into an aesthetic contemplation he neither understood nor desired, face to face for the last time in history with something commensurate to his capacity for wonder."[15]

Alas, poor Jay Gatsby! "Gatsby believed in the green light, the orgiastic future that year by year recedes before us. It eluded us then, but that's no matter—tomorrow we will run faster, stretch out our arms further . . . And one fine morning—" Alas, all of us! The novel ends on a desperately somber note: "So we beat on, boats against the current, borne back ceaselessly into the past."[16]

American writers in the Twenties were an entirely new breed—divorced from the literary tradition which had matured between the Civil War and World War I. That tradition culminated in the literary Establishment presided over by William

Dean Howells in the last years before the outbreak of the Great War. Henry F. May has summarized the basic tenets of Howells and his minions in *The End of American Innocence:* Howells "had always [200/201] insisted that real truth and moral goodness were identical, and he had always held that politics and literature were both amenable to moral judgment. He had always believed that American civilization was treading a sure path, whatever the momentary failures, toward moral and material improvement."[17]

What had outmoded Howells? It was the realization, anticipated before the Great War but complete only in the Twenties, that America had been transformed—transformed by the onset of an overwhelming process of industrialization and urbanization which had superannuated traditional American beliefs—beliefs nurtured in the bosom of the agrarian past.

In these circumstances, a revolution in manners and morals was inevitable. World War I augmented rather than inaugurated the trend. Postwar writers undertook a comprehensive critique of traditional faith. Some abhorred the change; others welcomed it. In any case, almost all of the great writers of the Twenties accepted the fact of the intellectual and emotional revolution deriving from the obsolescence of pre-war standards. They launched a comprehensive critique of traditional faiths, and for their efforts they received much public notice and approbation.

What accounts for the success of these literary revolutionists? The answer resides in the fact that America was generally "new" in the Twenties. George Mowry and other recent historians have effectively documented the distinctive "modernity" of America in the wake of World War I—a modernity discernible in

---

[14] *Ibid.*, 23. I am indebted to Mr. Edward A. Cole, a graduate student at the University of Nebraska, for the observation that the ashes in Fitzgerald's grotesque valley came from the city, a symbolic indication that the destruction of the garden was a function of urbanization. A further proof of Fitzgerald's intent is the rhythmic correspondence of "Jefferson" and "Eckleburg."

[15] *Ibid.*, 182.

[16] *Ibid.*

[17] Henry F. May, *The End of American Innocence: A Study of the First Years of Our Own Time* (Chicago: Quadrangle Paperbacks, 1964), 7. Cf. Alfred Kazin, *On Native Grounds* (New York: Doubleday Anchor Books, 1956), 25-32.

the mass culture as well as among the elite.[18] The transitional years had passed; the change from the rural-agricultural past to the urban-industrial future was relatively complete, and readers as well as writers responded to this reality. To be sure, the defenders of the old America ensconced behind crumbling barricades in the Old South and the farther Middle West fought extensive rear-guard actions —fundamentalist assaults on evolution, prohibitionist bans on spiritous liquors, and racist campaigns for the preservation of white Anglo-Saxon Protestant America—but these were last desperate attempts to postpone the inevitable. The most important fact about reaction in the Twenties was that it failed. In each instance "modernity" ultimately triumphed over tradition.

Significant writers in the Twenties were above all dedicated to the imposing task of pointing out the error of living in terms of obsolete values—however useful those values, might have been in the past. This effort is perhaps most obvious in the novels of Ernest Hemingway. In *The Sun Also Rises* Hemingway wastes little time investigating the reasons why Jake Barnes, Lady Brett, Robert Cohn, and other characters in the novel must live differently than before.[19] Hemingway's emphasis is on method—on how to live in the revolutionized context. Scott Fitzgerald dealt with the other side of the coin—the bankruptcy of the old way. Jay Gatsby's dream was patently absurd—however noble, however [**201/202**] "American." Benjamin Franklin and Thomas Jefferson were unsound guides to life in the modernity of the vast eastern Urbana, the East of West Egg, Long Island—and also for life in the new Midwest to which the chastened Carraway returned. The final irony of the novel is that Fitzgerald could discern no beauty in the city to compare with the beauty, however meretricious, inherent in Gatsby's Platonic conception of himself.

---

[18] See the collection edited by George Mowry, *The Twenties: Fords, Flappers & Fanatics* (Englewood Cliffs, N. J.: Prentice-Hall, Inc., 1963), especially pp. 1-2.

[19] Ernest Hemingway, *The Sun Also Rises* (New York: Charles Scribner's Sons, 1926, reissued in paperback).

Suggested Topics for Controlled Research

What happens to us when we are exposed to a work of art? The significance of that experience is measured by the *quality* of our response. Therefore, one of the reasons for writing a critical essay about a work of art is that such an undertaking can help us to organize our thoughts and feelings about the work into a coherent statement and thereby help us to understand more clearly and fully the nature of our response. You will notice that the best essays in this volume succeed not only because they are well organized (and well written) but also because they focus on some specific question or problem that was raised in the author's mind by his reading of *The Great Gatsby.*

The purpose of this section is to suggest some additional questions or topics that you may wish to explore in an essay without having to go beyond the covers of this book for additional reading. Like the essays reprinted in this volume the success or failure of your essay will depend on your ability to select a specific question or problem on which to focus your discussion. Most writing is a matter of rewriting (as we have seen in the case of *The Great Gatsby*); therefore, it is essential that you choose a topic so important to you that you will want to stick with it until you have found the best possible way of writing about it.

Since the first section of readings (Part Two) is concerned primarily with Fitzgerald's life, and since the relationship between an author's life and art is always an interesting subject for study, a word of caution about the use of biographical material in literary criticism is advisable at this point. The creative process is so complex and mysterious, and biographical and other historical data are in most cases so fragmentary and incomplete, that the critic can never hope to "explain" a work satisfactorily by means of such limited evidence. On the other hand, biographical data can often be extremely helpful in illuminating certain aspects of the work, so long as the critic uses it tentatively and sensitively and does not let it get in the way of his most important evidence—the text of the novel itself.

Certainly the biographical material and accompanying critical commentary in Part Two raise many interesting questions about *The Great Gatsby.* How important is "Absolution" to an understanding of *The Great Gatsby?* In his essay "The Untrimmed Christmas Tree," Piper writes at the end ". . . *The Great Gatsby* is a religious work because it has as its source a deeply felt religious emotion." Do you agree? Why? Is the relationship between "Absolution" and *The Great Gatsby* made any clearer by what Kenneth Eble is able to tell us about the various stages in the revision of *The Great Gatsby* manuscript? What evidence do you find in Fitzgerald's letters and Modern Library introduction of his intentions in writing *The Great Gatsby?* What evidence is there of his responsibility as a serious craftsman of fiction? Does he seem to have had a coherent theory (as Conrad did) about the purpose of fiction?

The critical essays included in Part Three represent only a few of the many approaches that critics have used in trying to understand and evaluate *The Great Gatsby.* Each method has its special advantages and limitations. The first three selections were newspaper or magazine book reviews written soon after *The Great Gatsby* was published in 1925. H. L.

Mencken was not only one of the most influential and widely-read literary critics of the time but had been one of Fitzgerald's early admirers. He had, in fact, been the first magazine editor to buy a story from Fitzgerald back in 1919 and had encouraged him in his writing. John Kenny was a younger member of the staff of the recently-established liberal Catholic journal of opinion, *Commonweal*. Gilbert Seldes' review was part of a commentary on new American books that he contributed regularly to *Criterion*, a London literary journal edited by the poet, T. S. Eliot. Which of these reviews do you like best? Why? In what ways, if any, do you think a book review should differ from a critical essay?

Arthur Mizener's essay focuses attention on one of the aspects *of The Great Gatsby* that has continued to intrigue its readers. Who is the most important character—the chief protagonist—in this story, Gatsby or Nick Carraway? Who is most affected by its events? Who sees most deeply into the meaning of these events? With whom does Fitzgerald seem to identify the most? With whom do you identify? Why do you think Fitzgerald discarded the third-person form of narration he had used in "Absolution" and substituted Nick Carraway as the first-person narrator? How would the story have been different if Nick had been left out? Would it have been as successful?

Like many other critics, Malcolm Cowley is fascinated by the artistic role that symbols play in this novel—notably the symbol of money. Americans have the reputation of being "dollar chasers." Yet foreigners who visit the United States are often disconcerted by the fact that Americans seem to treat money so casually. Instead of hoarding it like sensible people, they waste it or blithely give it away. Is it true that Americans do not value money so much for its own sake as for what it represents—as the symbol of freedom and choice? What symbolic role does money play in *The Great Gatsby*? Does money still have this symbolic power in our lives today? What other things besides money have this kind of power? Education? Status? Family history?

What do you think about the justice of Fitzgerald's judgment of the rich? Do you think he is harsher in judging the conduct of people who have inherited their money than he is in judging the conduct of those who had to get theirs the hard way? Should the poor little rich boy who inherited his money and privileges through no fault of his own be held to higher standards of moral behavior than the poor boy who has to make his way up the ladder by climbing over his peers? Is this a characteristically American view? Do Americans attach a metaphysical value to the possession of riches, so that they expect that wealthy people should be "better" than poor people? Is this just?

Every social group or culture creates certain traditional stories or myths that embody those values the culture holds most important. Thus it is not surprising that professional story tellers instinctively make use of these myths—often unconsciously—as a means of organizing their feelings about the nature of their society. John Raleigh's essay on the mythical background of *The Great Gatsby* is representative of a number of similar essays that have been written about this novel. We find Fitzgerald's use of myth also operating in Charles Samuels' discussion of the "greatness" of *The Great Gatsby*. Can you think of other American myths or traditional ideas that underlie the novel? What about the assumption that people raised in the country (or from "the West") are morally superior to those who live in the city (or come from "the East")? What about the idea that innocence is somehow morally superior to the possession of knowledge that can be gained only through the loss of innocence?

When Daisy decides to stick to Tom rather than go with Gatsby do you think she is making the "right" choice? Fitzgerald seems to suggest that Tom's masculine virility—brutal and ruthless though it may be—is psychologically more appealing to Daisy than Gatsby's idealization of her as his dream girl. Does this make sense? Does Gatsby ever really understand Daisy? What about Nick? After he goes home will he be capable of enjoying a more satisfying relationship with a woman than he could with the flawed Jordan? How far has Nick's initiation into the nature of reality carried him?

We know from the evidence of the manuscript that Fitzgerald worked hard to find exactly the right way to tell Gatsby's story. Much of this painstaking labor involved the rearrangement of structural elements into a more compelling rhythmical composition, as well as the search for the exact image—the precise word or cluster of words—to make his intentions clear. The essay by Victor Doyno and the one by Daniel Schneider describe the importance of recurring patterns and images in his art. Doyno emphasizes the importance of thematic parallels—the artful introduction of similar scenes, incidents and situations throughout the novel, much as the composer of a symphony interweaves recurring musical motifs and themes. Schneider calls attention especially to Fitzgerald's use of color images. Other important symbols and images that have attracted critical comment are the glasses of Dr. Eckleberg, houses, motorcars, parties, clothes, geography, and the weather. Are there others? Some critics believe that such "symbol hunting" is self-defeating since it gets in the way of a more balanced understanding of a work of art. In the case of *The Great Gatsby* does such analysis help or hinder your appreciation?

In the final section of readings on the historical and social backgrounds of the Jazz Age, the section on "Crime and Corruption" centers around two historic personalities of the era, Edward Fuller and Arnold Rothstein. Fitzgerald knew both men. Fuller was his Great Neck neighbor, and Fitzgerald had met and talked with Rothstein on at least one occasion. How much of this personal knowledge went into the creation of Gatsby, Wolfsheim, and the background of the novel? How much does this background history help you toward a better understanding of the novel as a work of art?

In *The Great Gatsby* Fitzgerald is also concerned with the moral implications of the power structure that controls a complex urban society like that of New York City. But that was almost fifty years ago. Today the United States is an even more highly organized urban complex than it was in 1925. Is Fitzgerald's assessment of the interrelationships of government, business and organized crime germane to the situation that exists today? Are there present-day analogies in business, government, and the entertainment and sporting worlds to the Teapot Dome scandal, the World Series fix, and the Jazz Age traffic in drugs, vice and other bootleg goods? What do you find that is most dated about this novel—theme, subject matter, moral values, idiom, style?

What do you understand "The American Dream" to be? What did Gatsby understand it to be? What is its relationship to "the green light"? What connection has it with the traditional American faith in the value of "the self-made man"? In the old fairy tale the poor boy from the country defeats the fabulous dragon, rescues the beautiful princess, marries her and becomes a knight of the round table. Or, in some modern versions, he marries the boss's daughter and inherits the family business. To what extent do you think Fitzgerald treats this fable sympathetically in *The Great Gatsby?* To what extent is he ridiculing it? Is his view of it primarily comic or tragic? What vitality has this old fairy tale in our popular culture today? What other myths have we invented to take its place?

Suggested Topics for Library Research

For the reader who wants to go beyond the covers of this book in his quest for research topics, the source that naturally comes to mind first is Scott Fitzgerald's other writings. He was the author of five novels: *This Side of Paradise* (1920), *The Beautiful and Damned* (1922), *The Great Gatsby* (1925), *Tender Is the Night* (1934), and the unfinished, posthumously published *The Last Tycoon* (1941). He also published four volumes of short stories: *Flappers and Philosophers* (1920), *Tales of the Jazz Age* (1922), *All the Sad Young Men* (1926), and *Taps at Reveille* (1935). The best twenty-eight of these stories (with the exception of "The Jelly-bean") have been collected and edited by Malcolm Cowley, *The Stories of F. Scott Fitzgerald* (1951). A selection of previously uncollected stories and sketches, edited by Arthur Mizener, is *Afternoon of an Author* (1957). Altogether, Fitzgerald wrote well over one hundred magazine stories for popular magazines like the *Saturday Evening Post* and the *Ladies' Home Journal,* many of which have never been reprinted. For the location of these, as well as for a complete guide to all his published writings see Henry Dan Piper, "F. Scott Fitzgerald: A Checklist," *Princeton University Library Chronicle,* XII (Summer 1951), 196-208. Fitzgerald also wrote a full-length play, *The Vegetable* (1923). And a selection of his essays, sketches, autobiographical writings, notebooks, and other miscellaneous writings, *The Crack-up* (1945), has been edited by Edmund Wilson.

For readers interested in Fitzgerald's life one of the best introductions is *The Letters of F. Scott Fitzgerald,* edited by Andrew Turnbull (1963). There are two excellent biographies: Arthur Mizener, *The Far Side of Paradise* (1951, rev., 1959); and Andrew Turnbull, *Scott Fitzgerald* (1962). Henry Dan Piper, *F. Scott Fitzgerald: A Critical Portrait* (1965), is primarily the story of Fitzgerald's development as a writer. Other full-length critical studies are James E. Miller, Jr., *The Fictional Technique of F. Scott Fitzgerald* (1957); Sergio Perosa, *The Art of F. Scott Fitzgerald* (1965); Richard D. Lehan, *F. Scott Fitzgerald and the Craft of Fiction* (1966); and Robert Sklar, *F. Scott Fitzgerald: The Last Laocoön* (1967).

Two general collections of critical essays on Fitzgerald's writings are Alfred Kazin, ed., *F. Scott Fitzgerald: The Man and His Work* (1951), and Arthur Mizener, ed., *F. Scott Fitzgerald: A Collection of Critical Essays* (1963). There are also two volumes of essays by various hands dealing directly with *The Great Gatsby;* Frederick Hoffman, ed., *The Great Gatsby: A Study* (1962), and Ernest Lockridge, ed., *Twentieth Century Interpretations of "The Great Gatsby"* (1968). A detailed up-to-date listing of all the criticism that has been written about Fitzgerald will be found in Jackson R. Bryer, *The Critical Reputation of F. Scott Fitzgerald: A Bibliographical Study* (1967). A summary of changing critical attitudes towards *The Great Gatsby* since it was first published in 1925 will be found in the essay by Jackson Bryer and G. Thomas Tanselle, "*The Great Gatsby:* A Study in Literary Reputation," *New Mexico Quarterly,* XXXIII (1964) 409-425.

As we noted at the beginning, one of the most helpful ways of understanding a writer is to get acquainted with more of his work. It is interesting, for instance, to compare *The Great Gatsby* with Fitzgerald's two earlier novels, *This Side of Paradise* and *The Beautiful and Damned* and to ask why *Gatsby* is so superior artistically to these predecessors. What has Fitzgerald achieved in *The Great Gatsby* that is new? Is it a matter of subject? Has he found a better structure? Is it a question of style? It is also interesting to compare *The Great Gatsby* with *The Vegetable,* the play that Fitzgerald wrote in 1923 at the same time that he was working on *The Great Gatsby.* Notice here the similarity of themes, especially the ironic treatment of the American myth of success. But where *The Vegetable* is broad farce, *The Great Gatsby* is more serious and tragic in spirit. Why does *The Vegetable* fail and *The Great Gatsby* succeed?

Other interesting sources for comparison are some of Fitzgerald's short stories, in which we see him exploring themes and points of view that we also find in *The Great Gatsby.* Among the best-known of these stories are "The Jellybean," "May Day," "The Diamond as Big as the Ritz," and "The Rich Boy." The last of these he wrote immediately after finishing *The Great Gatsby.* It was intended to be a more sympathetic treatment of the very rich than *The Great Gatsby;* and a comparison of Tom and Daisy Buchanan with Anson Hunter, the hero of "The Rich Boy" is enlightening for the reader who is trying to understand Fitzgerald's complex attitude toward people of wealth and privilege.

Another revealing approach to *The Great Gatsby* is to compare it with Fitzgerald's later novels, *Tender Is the Night* and *The Last Tycoon.* In *Tender Is the Night* Fitzgerald consciously chose to write a novel very different both in subject matter and in technical form from *Gatsby.* But the two continue to share many affinities. How do they differ and how are they the same? Afterwards, Fitzgerald decided that *Tender Is the Night* had failed in part because it was so different from *The Great Gatsby* in form. Do you agree? In planning *The Last Tycoon,* he therefore went back and studied *The Great Gatsby* and used it as the model for *The Last Tycoon.* Even in its fragmentary, unfinished state, *The Last Tycoon* shows

signs of this dependence on *Gatsby.* Was this a good idea? Which do you prefer, the tighter and more sharply focussed structure of *The Great Gatsby* and *The Last Tycoon,* or the looser more panoramic *Tender Is the Night?* To what extent do you feel that the different form of these novels is determined by different subjects?

Another fruitful way of shedding light on a work of art is to compare it with similar works by other writers. This is especially helpful when you can compare a given work with one that the author admired and even borrowed from. Probably the writer whom Fitzgerald most admired at the time he was writing *The Great Gatsby* was Joseph Conrad. He liked especially those novels and stories of Conrad's which make use of a first-person narrator named Marlow—*Lord Jim, Victory, Heart of Darkness, Youth,* and *Chance.* It is interesting to compare not only the themes of these stories with that of *The Great Gatsby,* but the functions performed artistically by the two first-person narrators, Marlow and Nick Carraway. Fitzgerald was also greatly impressed by the famous preface to *The Nigger of the "Narcissus,"* in which Conrad expressed so eloquently his view of the artist's responsibilities (see Fitzgerald's reference to it in his introduction to the Modern Library edition of *The Great Gatsby* reprinted in this book). Fitzgerald himself never wrote out a comparable statement of his views of the artist's responsibility. But he left many clues in his letters, as well as in his own performances as a writer. From such evidence can you reconstruct his "theory" of the artist's task? How does it compare with that described in Conrad's Preface?

Another novelist whom Fitzgerald greatly admired when he was writing *The Great Gatsby* was Willa Cather. Here, as with Conrad, there is evidence that Fitzgerald was indebted to this author's work in matters of both structure and style. The two novels by Willa Cather that influenced him most were *My Antonia* and *A Lost*

Lady. He also admired Edith Wharton's novel *Ethan Frome,* a short dramatic story told in the first person, and Henry James brilliant short novel, *Daisy Miller,* which —it has been said—was the source for the name of Daisy Buchanan. What interesting points of comparison can you find between *The Great Gatsby* and these other works?

Another great writer whom Fitzgerald admired was James Joyce—especially the early Joyce of *Dubliners* and *The Portrait of the Artist as a Young Man.*

Finally, there is Fitzgerald's favorite poet—Keats. Some critics believe that Fitzgerald's discovery of the poetry of Keats—especially his great odes—was more important than anything else in awakening Fitzgerald to an understanding of the importance of concrete imagery in his fiction. The question of the extent to which one writer has been influenced by another is always a difficult one. Nothing really can be proved. Nonetheless when used sensitively and tentatively, a comparison of two works on the same theme by different writers can often be helpful in high-lighting what is particularly unique or original about these works.

It is also enlightening to compare a novel like *The Great Gatsby* with the novels of other writers who have acknowledged their admiration for it. Fitzgerald did not meet Ernest Hemingway until shortly after he had finished *The Great Gatsby.* But the two young men talked about it a great deal, and Hemingway admired it. And readers have noted certain similarities between *The Great Gatsby* and Hemingway's next major published work (and first novel) *The Sun Also Rises* (1926). What do you think? Other novels by admirers of Fitzgerald's that offer interesting comparisons with *The Great Gatsby* are John O'Hara's *Appointment in Samarra* (1934), Charles Jackson's *The Lost Weekend* (1944) and J. D. Salinger's *The Catcher in the Rye* (1951).

A somewhat different subject for exploration is Fitzgerald's relationship to his times, particularly the 1920's. *The Great Gatsby* was published in 1925, midway in the decade that stretched from the end of World War I to the stock market crash of October, 1929. Fitzgerald's first novel, *This Side of Paradise,* had appeared in 1920 when he was twenty-three and heralded for many readers the beginning of the post-War I revolution of youth. It was an immediate best-seller and caused Fitzgerald to be looked upon as something of a celebrity. Fitzgerald's fame and popularity were heightened with the publication of his first two volumes of short stories, *Flappers and Philosophers* and *Tales of the Jazz Age.* These early magazine stories express a naive, oversimplified faith in success and the importance of wealth. By comparison, *The Great Gatsby* is striking in its expression of a more mature and even tragic view of the popular cultural values it dramatizes. How do you explain the differences between the vision of American life expressed in these commercial magazine stories and that expressed in *The Great Gatsby?*

One of the best introductions to the intellectual and social history of the 1920's is the volume edited by Malcolm and Robert Cowley, *Fitzgerald and the Jazz Age* (1966). We should not overlook, of course, Fitzgerald's other lively comments on the period, such as "Echoes of the Jazz Age," reprinted in the Cowley collection, "Early Success," "How to Live on Nothing a Year," and "How to Live on $36,000 a Year," as well as the evidence of his many Jazz Age short stories and sketches. The best introduction to the social history of the times is still Frederick Lewis Allen's *Only Yesterday* (1931). Other useful histories are George Mowry, *The Twenties: Fords, Flappers and Fanatics* (1963), Lloyd Morris, *Postscript to Yesterday* (1947), and William E. Leuchtenberg, *The Perils of Prosperity,* 1914-1932 (1958). Two good introductions to the literary history of the period are Frederick Hoffman, *The 20's: American Writing in the Post-War Decade* (1949, rev. 1962), and Malcolm Cowley, ed., *After the Genteel Tradition* (1937, rev. 1964). Probably the best contemporary expression of the disillusion and cynicisim with which writers of Fitzgerald's generation faced the post-War I world is to be found in Harold Stearns, ed., *Civilization in the United States* (1922).

How accurate is the picture of widespread political and economic corruption that Fitzgerald portrays in *The Great Gatsby?* For more light on Arnold Rothstein and his associates see Leo Katcher, *The Big Bankroll: The Life and Times of Arnold Rothstein* (1959). Rothstein's far-flung connections with the Mafia and other nationally organized crime rings are described in Hank Messick, *The Silent Syndicate* (1967). For the biography of the lawyer who defended both Rothstein and Edward Fuller, and who was finally indicted for having tried to bribe one of Fuller's jurors, see Gene Fowler, *The Great Mouthpiece; A Life Story of William J. Fallon* (1931). A more general survey of the New York scene is Stanley Walker, *The Night Club Era* (1933). And the connections between the oil industry (in which Gatsby had an interest) and national politics and crime has been described in Burl Noggle, *Teapot Dome: Oil and Politics in the 1920's* (1962). In the light of these readings one might ask what insight *Gatsby* gives us into the relationship between government, business, and organized crime during the 1920's, and whether there is evidence of such a relationship today.

The so-called "American Dream" has been the subject of a number of studies, among them Daniel J. Boorstin, *The Image, or What Happened to the American Dream* (1962), and James J. Clark and R. H. Woodward, eds., *Success in America* (1966). One of the liveliest accounts of Benjamin Franklin's role in the history of the American myth of success is the chapter, "Poor Richard: The Boy Who Made Good," in Dixon Wecter, *The Hero in America* (1941). Related studies are Moses Richin, ed., *The American Gospel of Success: Individualism and Beyond* (1965); Marshall Fishwick, *American He-*roes: *Myth and Reality* (1954); Richard Weiss, *The American Myth of Success, From Horatio Alger to Norman Vincent Peale* (1969); and Kenneth Lynn, *The Dream of Success* (1955), which analyzes the fiction of such earlier American novelists as Jack London, Frank Norris and Theodore Dreiser. An especially lively and up-to-date collection of readings on the meaning of success in present-day America will be found in Audrey J. Roth, ed., *Success: A Search for Values* (1969).

All of the above readings turn around the same fundamental questions. What is "The American Dream"? What is its connection with the ideas of individual success and self-fulfillment? How do we define success—in materialistic or idealistic terms? How do we reconcile the pursuit of material success with the principles for which America was founded—the ideals of the American Revolution and The Declaration of Independence. Who are our popular national heroes, and what common values and principles about the American experience do their careers embody? Here it is often helpful to turn to other writers who have been preoccupied with these questions. Henry James's *The American* and *Daisy Miller* are two earlier novels that search for answers in a foreign setting. Among Fitzgerald's contemporaries, Willa Cather's *My Antonia* (1918), Theodore Dreiser's *An American Tragedy* (1925), and Hart Crane's *The Bridge* (1930) are three notable explorations of the meaning of the American Dream. During the Depression of the 1930's John Steinbeck examined its meaning under different conditions in *The Grapes of Wrath* (1939) and John Dos Passos in his trilogy, *U.S.A.* (1930-36). And Fitzgerald himself returned to it again in *The Last Tycoon* (1941). What disparities, if any, do you find between the vision of America expressed in popular mass media today—the magazines, television, motion pictures—and the views you have found in *The Great Gatsby* or the novels of these other Americans?

GUIDE TO RESEARCH

Guide to Research

THE IDEA OF RESEARCH

Research is the organized, disciplined search for truth; the aim of all research is to discover the truth about something. That thing may be a historical object like the Stonehenge monuments or a historical event like the Hungarian Revolt or the Battle of Waterloo. It may be a work of literature like Shakespeare's *Julius Cæsar* or Miller's *Death of a Salesman*. It may be a recurring event like the motions of the planets or the circulation of the blood. It may be an experimentally repeatable phenomenon like behavior of rats in a maze or perception apparently unaccounted for by the five senses. Or it may be a political problem like the decision to use the atomic bomb in World War II. Archeology, history, political science, literary criticism and scholarship, astronomy, physiology, and psychology—these are some of the many divisions of research. Indeed, all the sciences—physical, biological, and social—and all other scholarly disciplines share this organized, disciplined search for truth.

The search for truth has often been confused with such aims as confirming prejudice, instilling patriotism, and praising friends and blaming enemies. The attempt to prove the preconceived conclusion *that* one college is superior to another, for example, is not research (though the attempt to discover *whether* one college is so superior is). Research is hostile to prejudice.

General Methods of Research. The best general method of research is first-hand observation. But this method is not always possible and, when it is possible, not always practical.

The best method to begin discovering the truth about something is to observe that thing and the circumstances surrounding it. To discover the truth about *Julius Cæsar* or *Death of a Salesman*, get the play and read it, or go to the theatre and watch a performance. To discover the truth about the planets, observe them through your telescope. To discover the truth about the intelligence of rats, build a maze and run some rats through it.

This first-hand observation is not always possible, however. To discover the truth about the Battle of Waterloo, you can't observe the battle. The best that you or anyone else can do is to observe other persons' observations, the recorded observations of eye-witnesses: diaries, letters, and memoirs, for instance, of soldiers and generals who were in the battle. With more recent historical events—for example, the Hungarian Revolt—you are better off. You can watch films and listen to tape recordings. You may be able to interview people who were there. But these observations are still second-hand; and, on the whole, history can be observed only at second-hand. The sole exception is history that you have been part of. You may have fought in the Hungarian Revolt—though, if you did, you may be prejudiced.

Even when first-hand observation is possible, it is not always practical. You may have a copy of or tickets to *Julius Cæsar* or *Death of a Salesman* but not know enough about the principles of dramatic criticism to interpret the play unaided. You may have a telescope but not know how to use it or, if you do, not know what to make of what you observe through it. You may have some rats but not know how to build a maze or, if you do, not know enough about animal psychology to run your rats through it properly. The best that *you* can do under these circumstances is to supplement whatever first-hand observations you can make with observations of the first-hand observations of other people better-trained or better-equipped than you. Read *Julius Cæsar* or *Death of a Salesman* and also critics' interpretations of the play. Observe the planets, if you can, and read treatises on astronomy. Do what you can with your rats, and read reports of experiments with rats. After all, no one can master the special methods and come by the special equipment of all scholarly disciplines. Indeed, few people can do this with more than one discipline, and then not before they're thirty. But all people who want a liberal education should try to discover as much of the truth about as many scholarly disciplines as their abilities and their circumstances permit. Indeed, the achievement of this is what is meant by "a liberal education."

Primary and Secondary Sources. As the foregoing account of the general methods of research suggests, there is, ultimately, only one source of the truth about something—the thing, the event, or the phenomenon itself: the Stonehenge monuments, the Hungarian Revolt, or the Battle of Waterloo; the text of *Julius Cæsar* or *Death of a Salesman;* Robert Oppenheimer's testimony on the use of the atomic bomb against Japan; the motions of the planets or the circulation of blood; extrasensory perceptions or rats running in a maze. Such a source is a *primary* source. And, in historical research, where the thing itself (the Hungarian Revolt or the Battle of Waterloo) cannot be observed at first hand, a report of an eyewitness or a film or a tape recording is also counted as a *primary* source. But any other second-hand source (an interpretation of *Julius Cæsar* or *Death of a Salesman,* a treatise on astronomy, a report of an experiment with rats) is a *secondary* source.

A primary source is, of course, better. But, if a primary source is unavailable to you (if it is a book, perhaps your school library does not have it) or if you are not trained or equipped to use it (you don't know how to run rats through a maze or you have no telescope), then a secondary source must do. In any case, except for the most mature scientists and scholars, a good

secondary source is useful and often indispensable.

It is worth noticing that being primary or being secondary is not an intrinsic characteristic of the source itself. It is, rather, a relationship that either exists or does not exist between a given source and a given topic of research. Consequently, a given source may be primary in relation to one given topic but secondary in relation to another. Two examples may serve to make this important point clear. Edward Gibbon's *The Decline and Fall of the Roman Empire* (1776-1788) is a secondary source in relation to the topic of the Roman Empire but a primary source in relation to that of eighteenth-century English prose style or that of eighteenth-century historiography. Samuel Taylor Coleridge's *Lectures on Shakespeare* (1811-1812) is a secondary source in relation to the topic of Shakespeare's plays but a primary source in relation to that of nineteenth-century principles of dramatic criticism or that of Shakespeare's reputation.

It is worth noticing also that a given source may be primary or secondary in relationship to more than one topic. James Joyce's novel *A Portrait of the Artist as a Young Man* is a primary source in relation not only to the topic of the structure of *A Portrait of the Artist as a Young Man* (and dozens of other topics on the novel itself) but also to the topic of use of the stream-of-consciousness technique in twentieth-century fiction.

THE RESEARCH PAPER

A research paper is a paper giving the results of research, the methods by which they were reached, and the sources, primary or secondary, which were used. A research paper attempts to tell the truth about a topic, and also tells how and where this truth was discovered. As we have seen, the sources of a research paper may be either written sources (literary texts and historical documents, for example) or sources of other kinds (experiments, for example). Since a research paper written in school is almost always based upon written (printed) sources, we shall here discuss only that kind. A research paper based upon written sources may be either a library-research paper or a controlled-research paper. A library-research paper is a research paper for which your search for sources is limited to those sources contained in the libraries available to you; a controlled-research paper, to those sources contained in one anthology —to those contained in this volume, for example. Here we shall emphasize the latter kind.

Finding Your Topic. The first step in writing a research paper based upon written sources, whether a library-research or a controlled-research paper, is finding a topic. We say "finding a topic" rather than "choosing a topic" because the process is more like finding a job than choosing a sandwich from a menu. Unless your instructor assigns you a topic, which he may do, you must look for one; and the one you find may not be just what you want but the best one that you can find. But, if you look long and carefully, you may find a topic that so well suits your interests, your capacities, and the time and the space at your disposal that your paper will almost surely be a success.

Finding a topic is the most important single step in writing a research paper, and the things that you should have in mind when looking for a topic are (1) your interests, (2) your capacities, and (3) the time and the space at your disposal. If you are interested in a topic, if you know something about the special methods of research that the topic requires, and if your topic is narrow enough to require no more time than you have for research and no greater development than you can give it in a paper of the length assigned you, then the paper that results will probably be satisfactory. For example, the topic of figures of speech in *Julius Cæsar* may interest you greatly. But, if it does, you must ask yourself whether you know enough about figures of speech to do research on them

and, if you do, whether this topic is narrow enough. Even the topic of metaphors in the play would be too broad for most papers; metaphors in Brutus' soliloquies might be about right. In any case, before you take a topic for a paper, you should do some reading on that topic; otherwise, you won't know whether it is interesting, within your ability to handle, and within the scope of your assigned paper.

Once you think that you've found a topic, take great care in phrasing it. The best phrasing is a question or a series of closely related questions. Better than "The character of Brutus" is "To what extent is Brutus motivated by self-interest and to what extent by the public interest?" The latter is not only more narrow and more precise; it provides you with a criterion of relevance in selecting your sources. At the end of this volume, you will find a list of suggested topics, intended to call your attention to topics that might not occur to you. But these topics are suggestive rather than definitive or precise.

Finding Your Sources. Finding sources for a library-research paper and finding ones for a controlled-research paper, though different in several respects, are alike in certain others. Finding sources in the library requires knowledge of how to use the card catalogue, periodical indexes, special bibliographies, reserve shelves, and encyclopedias. Finding sources in this volume or a similar one does not. But, in either case, you must have a clear idea of what you are looking for; and you must be prepared to put up with a high ratio of looking to finding. In other words, you must have not only criteria of relevance but also a willingness to do a good deal of skimming and a good deal more of careful reading, some of it fruitless.

The basic criterion of relevance you provide by careful phrasing of your topic, a problem discussed in the preceding section. The other criteria you provide by making a preliminary or tentative outline —perhaps in the form of subtopics, perhaps in the form of questions. Such an outline is not to be used for your paper. The outline for your paper will probably be quite different and, in any event, cannot be made until after you find your sources and take your notes. This preliminary outline guides your research and, as we shall see, provides you with the subtopic headings necessary for your note-cards (see "Taking Your Notes," page xiii).

Making Your Working Bibliography. Once you have found a promising source ("promising" because, though it seems to be relevant, it may turn out not to be) you want to make some record of it so that, once you have completed your search for sources, you can turn back to it, read it, and, if it turns out to be relevant, take notes on it. This record of promising sources is your *working* bibliography. It is so called for two reasons: first, because you work with it as you proceed with your research and the writing of your paper, adding promising sources to it and discarding irrelevant ones; and, second, because this designation distinguishes it from your final bibliography, which appears at the very end of your research paper and contains only sources actually used in the paper. For a controlled-research paper, your working bibliography may be nothing more elaborate than a series of check marks in the table of contents of your research anthology or a list of page numbers. For a library-research paper, however, you need something quite different.

A working bibliography for a library-research paper is a collection of three-by-five cards each representing a promising source and each containing full information about that source. Once you have completed your research, written your paper, and discarded all promising but (as they turned out) irrelevant sources, this bibliography is identical with your final bibliography. Having a separate card for each source enables you to add and to discard sources easily and to sort and arrange them easily in any order you please. Eventually, when this bibliography becomes identical with your final bibliography, you will arrange sources alphabetically by au-

thors' last names. Having full information about each source on its card enables you to turn back to it easily—to locate it in the library without first looking it up again. You find this information in the card catalogue, periodical indexes, or other bibliographical aids; or, when browsing through the shelves or the stacks of the library and coming upon a promising source, you find it in or on the source itself—for example, on the spine and the title page of a book.

If the source is a *book*, you should put the following information on the three-by-five working-bibliography card:

(1) the library call number,
(2) the author's (or authors') full name (or names), last name first for the first author,
(3) the title of the book,
(4) the name of the city of publication,
(5) the name of the publisher (*not* the printer), and
(6) the year of publication (often found on the other side of the title page).

See the example of such a card on the opposite page (note the punctuation carefully).

If the source is a *periodical article*, you should put the following information on the three-by-five working-bibliography card:

(1) the author's (or authors') full name (or names),
(2) the title of the article,
(3) the name of the periodical,
(4) the volume number,
(5) the week, the month, or the season of publication, together with the year, and
(6) the page numbers covered by the article.

See the example of such a card on the opposite page (note the punctuation carefully).

These two forms take care of the two standard cases. For special cases—such things as books with editors or translators as well as authors, books published in several editions or in several volumes, and daily newspapers—see any good handbook of composition.

860.3
J23

Jones, John A., and William C.
Brown. <u>A History of
Serbia</u>. New York: The
Rowland Press, Inc., 1934.

WORKING-BIBLIOGRAPHY CARD FOR A BOOK

Smith, Harold B. "Fishing
in Serbian Waters." <u>Journal
of Balkan Sports</u>, VII
(May 1936), 26-32.

WORKING-BIBLIOGRAPHY CARD FOR A PERIODICAL ARTICLE

Taking Your Notes. Once you have found sources, entered them in your working bibliography, read them, and found them relevant, taking notes requires your exactly following a standard procedure if your notes are going to be useful to you when you come to write your paper. An extra five minutes given to taking a note correctly can save you a half hour in writing your paper. Here is the standard procedure:

(1) Take all notes on four-by-six cards. Never use notebooks, loose sheets of paper, or backs of old envelopes.

(2) Limit each note to information on a single subtopic of your preliminary outline *and* from a single source. It follows from this that you may have many cards on the same subtopic and many cards from the same source but that you may never have one card on more than one subtopic or from more than one source.

(3) On each card, in addition to the note itself, put

  (a) the appropriate subtopic heading in the upper left-hand corner,

  (b) the name of the source (usually the author's last name will do) in the upper right-hand corner, and

  (c) the page number (or numbers) of that part (or those parts) of the source that you have used in taking your note. If you have used more than one page, indicate your page numbers in such a way that, when you come to write your paper, you can tell what page each part of the note comes from, for you may not use the whole note.

(If you follow these first three rules, you will be able, when you come to outline and to organize your paper, to sort your notes in any way you please—by subtopic, for example—and to arrange them in any order you please. Such flexibility is impossible if you take your notes in a notebook. If you follow the third rule, you will also be able to document your paper— write footnotes, for example—without again referring to the sources themselves.)

(4) In taking the note itself, paraphrase or quote your source or do both; but do only one at a time, and use quotation very sparingly.

Paraphrase and quotation require special care. Anything between paraphrase and quotation is not acceptable to good writers: you either paraphrase or quote, but do nothing in between. To paraphrase a source (or part of a source) is to reproduce it in words and word orders substantially different from the original. When you paraphrase well, you keep the sense of the original but change the language,

retaining some key words, of course, but otherwise using your own words and your own sentence patterns. To quote a source (or part of a source) is to reproduce it exactly. When you quote well, you keep both the sense and the language of the original, retaining its punctuation, its capitalization, its type face (roman or italic), and its spelling (indeed, even its misspelling).

Omissions and additions require special care. If, when quoting, you wish to omit some of the original, you may do so only if the omission does not change the sense of the original (never leave out a "not," for example!) *and* if it is indicated by ellipses (three spaced periods: ". . ."). If you wish to add something to the original, you may do so only if the addition does not change the sense of the original (never add a "not"!) *and* it is indicated by square brackets. The most usual additions are explanations ("They [i.e., the people of Paris] were alarmed") and disclaimers of errors in the original, indicated by the Latin *"sic,"* meaning "thus" ("Colombis [*sic*] discovered America in 1592 [*sic*]"). You must, of course, carry these ellipses and square brackets from your note-cards to your paper. And, if you type your paper, brackets may be a problem, for most typewriter keyboards do not include them. If your keyboard does not, you may do one of two things—either use the slash ("/") and underlining ("__" and "——") in such a way as to produce a bracket ("⊏" and "⊐") or draw brackets in with a pen. In any event, don't substitute parentheses for brackets.

In your paper, quotations no longer than three or four lines are to be enclosed within a set of quotation marks and run into your text; longer ones are to be set off from the text, without quotation marks, by indention from the left-hand margin and, especially in typewritten copy, by single-spacing. But never use either of these devices unless the language is exactly that of the original.

Your usual treatment of a source should be paraphrase; use quotation only if the

Fly - fishing   Smith

Smith says that fly-fishing is a method of fishing used chiefly by wealthy Serbians and foreign tourists, that the flies used are generally imported from Scotland, and that "Serbian trout are so snobbish that they won't glance [27/28] at a domestic fly."

[Query: How reliable is the information in this rather facetious article ?]

NOTE-CARD

language of the original is striking (strikingly good or strikingly bad), if it is the very topic of your research (as in a paper on Shakespeare's style), or if it is so complex (as it might be in a legal document) that you don't want to risk paraphrasing it.

Let us look at the sample note-card above. The topic of research is methods of fishing in Serbia; the subtopic that the note deals with is fly-fishing in Serbia; the source is Harold B. Smith's article "Fishing in Serbian Waters," from the *Journal of Balkan Sports* (see the second of the two working-bibliography cards on page xiii).

Note the subtopic heading ("Fly-fishing") in the upper left-hand corner; the name of the source, abbreviated to the author's last name ("Smith"), in the upper right-hand corner; the page numbers ("[27/28]"), indicating that everything, both paraphrase and quotation, up

through the word "glance" is from page 27 and that everything after that word is from page 28; the sparing and appropriate use of quotation; and the bracketed query, to remind the note-taker that he must use this source with caution.

Writing Your Paper. Many of the problems of writing a research paper based upon written sources—organization, the outline, the thesis paragraph, topic sentences, transitions, and the like—are problems of expository writing generally. Here we shall discuss only those problems peculiar to such a paper. Two of these problems —paraphrase and quotation—we discussed in the preceding section. Two others remain: reaching conclusions and avoiding the scissors-and-paste organization.

When you come to make the outline for your paper and to write your paper, you will have before you three things: (1) your *preliminary* outline, containing ordered subtopics of your topic; (2) your working bibliography; and (3) your note-cards. These are the *immediate* results of your research; they are not the *final* results. They are only the raw material out of which you must fashion your paper. At best, they are an intermediate stage between finding your topic and making your final outline. The preliminary outline will not do for the final outline. The working bibliography will almost certainly require further pruning. And the note-cards will require sorting, evaluation, organization, pruning, and exercise of logic and common sense. All this needs to be done, preferably before you make your final outline and begin to write your paper, though almost inevitably some of it will remain to bedevil you while you are writing it. To put the matter in another way, you are, with these things before you, a Sherlock Holmes who has gathered all his clues but who has reached no conclusions from them, who has not come to the end of his search for truth. You must discard irrelevant clues, ones that have no bearing on the questions that you want answered. You must arbitrate the claims of conflicting or contradictory clues. You must decide which one of several probable conclusions is the most probable.

Once you have reached your conclusions, you must organize your paper and set forth this organization in your final outline. Organization and the outline are, of course, problems common to all expository writing. But a problem peculiar to the research paper is avoiding the scissors-and-paste organization—avoiding a paper that looks as though you had cut paraphrases and quotations out of your note-cards, pasted them in columns on paper, and connected them only with such phrases as "Jones says" and "On the other hand, Brown says." Such an organization is the result of a failure to reach conclusions (with the consequence that there is nothing but "Jones says" to put in between paraphrases and quotations); or it is a failure to see the necessity of giving the conclusions reached *and* the reasoning by

which they were reached (with the consequence that, though there is something to put between paraphrases and quotations, nothing is put there, and the reader is left to write the paper for himself).

Documenting Your Paper. To document your paper is to give the source of each paraphrase and quotation that it contains, so that your reader can, if he wishes to, check each of your sources and judge for himself what use you have made of it. To give the source is usually to give (1) either the information that you have about that source in your working bibliography (except that the name of the publisher of a book is usually not given) or the information that accompanies each source in a research anthology *and* (2) the information about page numbers that you have in your notes. This information you may give either formally or informally, as your instructor decides.

Formal documentation is given in footnotes. For a full discussion of footnotes, see any good handbook (one cheap and widely accepted one is *The MLA Style Sheet*). The form of footnotes is similar to, but not identical with, the form of bibliographical entries. With these three sample footnotes, compare the two sample working-bibliography cards on page xiii:

[1] John A. Jones and William C. Brown, *A History of Serbia* (New York, 1934), p. 211.
[2] Harold B. Smith, "Fishing in Serbian Waters," *Journal of Balkan Sports*, VII (May 1936), 27.
[3] Smith, pp. 27-28.

Informal documentation is given in the text of the paper, usually parenthetically, as in this example:

Fly-fishing in Serbia is chiefly a sport of wealthy Serbians and foreign tourists (Harold B. Smith, "Fishing in Serbian Waters," *Journal of Balkan Sports*, VII [May 1936], 27), though in some mountain districts it is popular among the peasants (John A. Jones and William C. Brown, *A History of Serbia* [New York, 1934], p. 211). The flies used are generally imported from Scotland; indeed, Smith facetiously adds, "Serbian trout are so snobbish that they won't glance at a domestic fly" (pp. 27-28).

As this example suggests, however, informal documentation can be an annoying distraction. It probably works out best in papers that use only a few sources. In such papers, there are few occasions for long first-references to sources: for example, "(Harold B. Smith, "Fishing in Serbian Waters," *Journal of Balkan Sports,* VII [May, 1936], 27)." But there are many occasions for short succeeding-references: for example, "(Smith, pp. 27-28)" or "(pp. 27-28)." Occasionally, informal documentation may be profitably combined with formal, as in a paper about Shakespeare's *Julius Cæsar.* In such a paper, references to the play might well be given informally —for example, "(III.ii.2-7)"—but references to critics formally.

How many footnotes (or parenthetical documentations) do you need in your paper? The answer is, of course, that you need as many footnotes as you have paraphrases or quotations of sources, unless you group several paraphrases or quotations *from the same page or consecutive pages of a given source* in such a way that one footnote will do for all. One way to do this grouping—almost the only way— is to introduce the group with such a sentence as "Smith's views on fly-fishing are quite different from Brown's" and to conclude it with the raised numeral referring to the footnote. Your reader will understand that everything between the introductory sentence and the numeral comes from the page or the successive pages of the source indicated in the footnote.

Making Your Final Bibliography. Your paper concludes with your final bibliography, which is simply a list of all the sources—and only those sources—that you actually paraphrase or quote in your paper. In other words, every source that you give in a footnote (or a parenthetical documentation) you include in your final bibliography; and you include no other sources (inclusion of others results in what is unfavorably known as "a padded bibliography"). The form for entries in your final bibliography is identical with that for ones in your working bibliography, given above. You should list these sources alphabetically by authors' last names or, if a source is anonymous, by the first word of its title, but not by "a," "an," or "the." For example:

BIBLIOGRAPHY

Jones, John A., and William C. Brown. *A History of Serbia.* New York: The Rowland Press, Inc., 1934.
"Serbian Pastimes." *Sports Gazette,* XCI (October 26, 1952), 18-19, 38, 40-42.
Smith, Harold B. "Fishing in Serbian Waters," *Journal of Balkan Sports,* VII (May 1936), 26-32.

MARTIN STEINMANN, JR.